*From the painting by Benjamin West*

Penn's Treaty with the Indians

V. F. CALVERTON

# The Awakening of America

THE JOHN DAY COMPANY
NEW YORK

*Designed by Robert Josephy*

MANUFACTURED IN THE UNITED STATES OF AMERICA

*To Elsie Sise*

# PREFACE

WHAT this book tries to do is to reread American history in different terms—in terms of the ruled instead of the rulers, the underdogs instead of the top dogs. It aims to give voice to the oppressed, to the anonymous and inarticulate millions.

In general the approach can be described as Marxian; but it is not that of the orthodox Marxian who resorts to the dialectic triad for proof of his case. The author is a Marxian only to the extent that he believes that Marx did more to illuminate the historical processes than any other thinker of the modern age, and that no one who aims to write history intelligently today can escape the influence of his work. Marx was to history and economics what Lyell was to geology, Darwin to biology, Freud to psychology; but that does not mean that Marx is to be worshiped any more than Lyell, Darwin, or Freud, or that his conclusions are to be viewed as any less open to correction or revision. The attempt to make Marx infallible has resulted in making Marxism into a myth instead of a science. In fact, it was not without reason that Marx himself declared: "Thank God, I'm not a Marxian."

Viewed in that light, with the qualifications indicated, this book can be called the first extended Marxian history of America. Its only predecessors have been James Oneal's pioneer volume *Workers in American History* and A. M. Simons' *Social Forces in American History*, both of which helped clear the ground for a new interpretation and revaluation of American history. The works of Louis M. Hacker and Curtis P. Nettels have been most significant in extending and deepening the research of Oneal and Simons and giving greater significance to such revaluation.

*The Awakening of America*, of which this is the first volume, is more of a social than an economic history. Although its primary object is to interpret the lives of the American people in terms of their divers and dissident economic interests, it aims to trace the evolution of those interests in political and social form. Its concern is with the populace rather than with kings, proprietors, governors; and it tries to deal with American history from that angle.

The result is that this volume constitutes in large part a history of those early colonial revolts, those incipient class struggles, that embodied the early outcroppings of the rebellious spirit and prepared the way for the Revolutionary War and the establishment of what today is known as the American democratic tradition. I have also dealt in considerable detail with those early religious groups which came to America to found co-operative communist colonies; with their social outlook they represent an aspect of American life which stands out in sharp contrast to the individualistic outlook, usually the only one stressed. In order to concentrate attention upon these aspects of American colonial life, I have purposely avoided discussion of the French and Spanish colonies, and even of the Atlantic Island colonies of the English, consideration of which will be included in the succeeding volume, dealing with the development of the country from the middle of the eighteenth century to the Civil War.

This volume ends at approximately 1750, although in many cases it includes the consideration of events and tendencies which extend beyond that date. The chapter on the frontier, however, embraces an even later period.

I have worked over the materials of this book for the last five years, collecting evidence, facts, and tangential data; as far and as often as possible I have gone back to the original sources for my material. I am indebted to a number of libraries and librarians for their assistance in this research—in particular, to the New York Public Library, the Enoch Pratt Library in Baltimore, the Congressional Library, and the British Museum; also to various friends and associates: Ethel Cohen, Harold Rotholz, and Miriam Mann, who have helped me to check and recheck various materials, to type and retype the manuscript, and to help in putting it into final shape. I am also deeply indebted to Harry Elmer Barnes, George Counts, Ernest Sutherland Bates, Carl Becker, Louis M. Hacker, and Allan

Nevins, who read the book in manuscript form and made many excellent and fruitful suggestions, from all of which the study has incalculably benefited.

V. F. Calverton

*New York City*
*May* 15, 1939

# CONTENTS

## BOOK I



## BOOK II

BOOK III



BOOK IV



EPILOGUE

# BOOK I

## CHAPTER I

# India: The Magic Land

MAN has always hungered and searched for new lands, new sources of wealth, new dreams of utopia. His visions of utopia have seldom been the same in form, but they have always been the same in essence. In various lands and climes he has struggled against environments that were indubitably hostile, but which somehow he survived. More than that, he has almost always added something to those environments, improving them by improving himself, increasing his own ingenuity.

Man's main quest naturally has been for food, shelter, and sex; but his interest in them has been conditioned by his economic assets. In the way of food, the poorer classes have accepted what they got without undue protest, provided they could eke out enough to live on; when they didn't, revolutions began. The richer classes have never been willing to accept what they got if they thought they could get something better. The result has been that the richer classes, in pursuit of something better, something rarer, something more exciting and more precious, have helped to change the face of the world. They were not concerned with the world, to be sure, but with themselves; but, being concerned with themselves, they also had to be concerned with the world.

The tastes of men vary with the prevailing economy. They are content with simple things until they have become acquainted with the subtler; after that, simple things will not suffice. This is true of food, shelter, clothes, ornaments, and all that curious and fascinating variety of physical decorations and appurtenances—cosmetics, perfumes, ointments, and whatnot—which have lent charm and wonder to the human body and personality. More money and more energy have been invested in the acquisition of such things than in all the wars and conquests of the ages. Without question, a goodly proportion of the conflicts recorded in history have been immediately connected with, or at least closely related to, precisely those things; and, in the final accounting of the whys and wherefores of nations, they play a more conspicuous part than is usually realized.

All people would live better if they could; but in the world as we have known it the many have never possessed that opportunity; only in a new social world in which economic classes vanish would they possess it. To date it has been the few who, because they possessed that opportunity, have done the most to improve the conditions and circumstances of their lives. It was the wealthy classes some centuries ago that encouraged geographers to plot new maps, dreamers to envision new climes, explorers to go around the world, and navigators to hazard uncharted seas—all in hopes of discovering happier connections with the countries which were the dreamlands of the era.

Those countries were India, Cathay, and Cipangu.

They were the magic lands of those days because they housed all those things, elements, substances, mixtures, compounds, patterns, designs, which were necessary to the better way of life of that time.

The poor knew about those things only from hearsay, gossip, rumor. The things meant little to the poor because the poor could not purchase them even if they wanted them. In their wretched state there were multitudes of things that they wanted more. Of what avail for a simple hoyden to possess sweet perfumes, fine tapestries, embroidered garments, when she lived in a windowless hovel or mud-smirched hut and had barely enough to eat?

Only the rich, who lived in stately houses and castles, who had more than enough to eat and drink and wear, could concern themselves with such luxuries. For when people become rich, necessities become unimportant and luxuries important. What happens under such circumstances is that luxuries become necessities.

### INDIA, CATHAY, AND CIPANGU

India was the land of endless marvels; the land apostrophized by travelers, adventurers, soldiers, tradesmen; the land in which miracles were a commonplace, and dreams of fair things, sheathed in jewels, were as real as flesh, as tangible as earth. It was richer than Blake's "land of dreams," richer than poetic vision or philosophic aspiration. It was a land of fantasy, of strange portents and promises, of fabulous resources, a land like no other land in the world at that time—a land apart, a land lit with magic and wonder.

To discover a shorter sea route to India, to Cathay, and to Cipangu,* consequently, was imperative. The new world, which to-day we know as America, was not of interest to the wealthy classes in Europe at that time. Columbus would never have been sent across strange seas in quest of a continent about which nothing was known; he was sent, aided, subsidized, because he set out to find the lands of gold and spicery. When he found a new world, no one was more surprised than he. For a considerable time he insisted upon believing that America was India, and called the inhabitants Indians, a name which clings to them to this day. More than that, for years, even on his third voyage, Columbus believed that South America was the mainland of Asia; and it was over a generation before the European world realized that he had discovered not India but a new continent. Other explorers suffered from the same illusion. When John Cabot set forth in 1496 and landed in Labrador, he believed he had discovered another part of Asia. The West Indies derived their name from the same source.

In earlier days there had been land routes to India which were as intricate as they were extensive, weaving their way through strange countries, across mischievous frontiers, into climes and regions with hostile mountains and with an obdurate and implacable desert to span before their point of destination was reached. Protracted and uncertain though the expeditions were, they did bring back to the aristocrats and merchants of European lands those things for which they craved. When Constantinople was captured by the Turks in 1453, the route through it was interrupted; and it became increasingly difficult to secure the products and treasures of the golden land of the Maharajahs. Professor Lybyer has proved with abundant evidence that the conquest of Constantinople did not close the main Levantine trade routes; the fact remains, however, that none of those trade routes, even when they were most flourishing, ever promised such rich rewards as a speculative sea route.

To discover a short sea route to India was to acquire a means of

* Cipangu (also spelled Chipangu and Cipango) was, as Marco Polo points out, the original name for Japan. The only authority to claim otherwise is Mr. George Collingridge, who maintains that it is Java and not Japan. His contention, however, has been rejected by all other authorities. Marco Polo called Japan "Zepang," the land of gold and silver.

despoiling the land. The land routes had been agencies of commerce, buying and selling media, but nothing more. India with all its tremendous and incalculable sources of wealth still remained intact; a short sea route to it promised far greater gains. Vessels like those of Columbus, equipped not only to explore and discover, but also to plunder, promised far greater things. They could do more than deal with the natives—they could kill and rob them and bring back to Europe the wealth they acquired. They could secure, without having to bargain for them, the riches of the East for which Europe yearned.

Columbus failed to sell his idea, or dream, to Genoa, because Genoa had aims which conflicted with those in which he was interested. Genoa was an important city in the Levantine land route, and stood to lose vastly by the discovery of a short sea route to India. If Columbus succeeded in finding a direct sea route to the magic land, it meant disaster for Genoa, because then it would no longer be a center of the richest commerce of the day. But it did not threaten disaster for Spain.

Although no one knew it at the time, what Columbus's discovery meant was a transference of power from the Mediterranean to the Atlantic nations. For centuries the Mediterranean nations had represented the center of commerce, and the Atlantic nations were subsidiaries. Columbus's discovery in time made it possible for the Atlantic route to triumph over the Mediterranean—which triumph has remained unchanged until today. Perhaps tomorrow, as some historians suspect, it may shift to the Pacific. The sea routes to the East at that time had proved disastrously precarious. Shorter and safer routes were needed, and those who needed them, the wealthy classes, didn't care whether they were routes by land or sea. When the land routes were less accessible or less secure, the wealthy were willing to trust to the sea. They would trust to anything which promised them what they wanted, and that meant the things of the East, of India and Cathay, which would make it possible for them to live in the style they desired.

India, we must remember, had been discovered by sea by the Norsemen, who had early voyaged into most of the remote and obscure parts of the world. India was only one of their numerous discoveries. Norsemen were the first to discover America as well as the first to discover India.

Columbus set forth, therefore, not to discover just a sea route to India, Cathay, and Cipangu. The purpose of his voyage was twofold: to find a shorter route to the magic lands, and then to rob and plunder them.

It was the hope of Ferdinand and Isabella that Columbus would bring back cargoes of gold, jewels, spices, perfumes, fine clothes and tapestries, and other rare stuffs. Their interest was in these things and not in his theory of the shape of the world, nor in his navigational genius.

## II

### THE FABULOUS WEALTH OF INDIA

India in the fourteenth and fifteenth centuries possessed a culture superior to that of Europe. It was richer in the things that man then prized, was economically more advanced, technologically more progressive, and altogether more civilized. The Europeans, however, were not interested in its civilization or its culture. Their interest was in its products and possessions. First of all there was gold, which made the land seem like the paradise of Midas. When Mahmud made his attack upon the Hindus at the dawn of the eleventh century, a booty fell into his hands which "amounted to 700,000 golden dinars, besides large quantities of vessels of gold and silver, and of unworked gold and silver and jewels. With this plunder he returned to Chazni and exhibited it, piled on carpets in the courtyard of his palace, to the wondering eyes of his subjects."[1] Later, in 1310, Malik Naib was able to make off with an even larger loot which included "312 elephants, 20,000 horses, 2,750 pounds gold, equal in value to 100,000,000 tongas and chest of jewels."[2]

The reports and records of many travelers who ventured into India in those centuries abound in descriptions of the fabulous wealth of the country. Ludovico Di Varthema, who peregrinated through various parts of India in the early years of the sixteenth century, tells about "a mountain where they dig out diamonds," and also of other

[1] All source references will be found at the end of the book, grouped according to chapters.

mountains from which carnelians and chalcedonies were extracted; he also describes the rubies he found "two miles from the seashore," and the "great quantity of garnets, sapphires, jacinths and topazes." [3] Friar Jordanus declared, "In this India be many islands . . . wherein are many of the world's wonders . . . there is one called Silem, where are found the most precious stones in the whole world, and in the greatest quantity and number, and of all kinds. Between that island and the main are taken pearls or marguerites in such quantity as to be quite wonderful. So indeed that there are sometimes more than 8,000 boats or vessels, for three months continuously [engaged in this fishery]." [4]

Although the reports of these travelers suffered from the characteristic exaggerations of such folk, there can be no doubt that India possessed of the precious metals as much as, if not more than, any other known country in the world of that day.

We should not make a common mistake at this point and conclude that the people of India shared in this mountainous wealth. They fared as poorly as the populace in other parts of the world. It was the small class at the top, the aristocracy and the merchant group, which profited from such possessions. The nobles "were wont to be carried on their silver beds, preceded by some twenty chargers caparisoned in gold, and followed by three hundred men on horseback and five hundred on foot, and by horn-men, ten torch-bearers, and ten musicians." [5]

But it was not simply for silver and gold and the other precious metals that the men of the West hazarded their lives in quest of the East. The precious metals, once known to Rome, and used for a considerable time during the days of the Empire, were a great allure, but other possessions of India were scarcely less attractive.

### FOOD: THE ETERNAL QUEST

Food has always been man's greatest concern. In primeval days he spent the larger part of his life acquiring it; and in later days, after he had acquired enough of it, he became concerned with improving it. Again it was the wealthy classes who became interested in that art. They were eager to do two things: to improve the taste of food and to discover methods of preserving it. India possessed the answer to both of those needs. The spices of India made it possible not only to make food more edible and delectable, but also to preserve it from putrefaction. Meat, in particular, when it was spiced acquired a quality which it had never possessed before; it could be prepared so that it would keep for days and flavored in ways which lent it a taste almost magical. Without the spices of India, meat tasted very much like eggs without salt—flat, insipid. But spiced meat became a gustatory joy, and all those who had tasted it could no longer do without it. And not only meat was so enriched, but also cakes and puddings which, livened with ginger, became exciting foods.

All such condiments and flavors, ranging from spices to subtle fruits, from pepper to sugar and honey, are so common today, so inexpensive, that they are shared by the poor as well as the rich; in the fourteenth, fifteenth and sixteenth centuries, however, they were so rare and expensive that only the rich could afford them, and in order to get them they were willing to sacrifice the lives of mariners, travelers, tradesmen, adventurers—anyone or anything that would insure their arrival. The poor knew nothing of them. "The rich have wines, spices, and fine bread," shouted John Ball, the communist cleric, "when we [the poor] have only rye and the refuse of straw."

Pepper was almost as valuable as the precious metals. Only the wealthy possessed it. In fact, its possession was a proof of wealth, of class or caste, of social distinction. There were times when in Egypt it was used as a medium of exchange.[6] In some nations pepper was accepted in payment for rents. In other places pepper was equivalent to its weight in silver. When Alaric sacked Rome, he insisted upon two thousand pounds of pepper, as well as two thousand pounds of silver, as part of his tribute. Cinnamon, too, was very precious. Garlands of cinnamon were displayed by Roman emperors at dedicatory exercises, and in honor of his wife Nero burnt more cinnamon than was imported into Rome in one year:[7] there was no greater, no finer tribute that could be paid to a royal personality. When foreign kings came to Rome they were greeted on streets fragrant with cloves and purified by precious spices.[8] In Europe a pound of cloves was worth seven sheep, and a pound of ginger was worth one sheep: here is a fairly good indication of how valuable such spices were considered in those days.

The desire for pepper and other spices, for use as meat preservatives as well as condiments, inspired a vast part of the commerce with India in that day. Portugal was able to maintain its dominant commercial position mainly because it was more successful than any other country in cornering the pepper market of India. The first conflict of the Portuguese with the Moslems resulted from a struggle over pepper.[9] The first East India Company organized in England was more concerned with pepper than gold. "The merchants of London, in the year of our Lord 1600," one of the East India narrators records, "joined together and made a stock of seventy-two thousand pounds, to be employed in ships and merchandises, for the discovery of a trade in the East India, to bring into the realm spices and other commodities." [10]

England's interest in the Far East, India as well as Cathay and Cipangu, was not only in its spices, jewels, and metals but also in its inspiring possibility as a new economic market. England was manufacturing more woolen goods than its populace could purchase or the continental market absorb; it needed new markets to which it could sell its surplus. The Far East, possessing so much that Westerners desired, was the ideal market.[11]

### SUGAR AS A MEDICINE AND A DELICACY

In addition to spices there was sugar, that ineluctably exquisite delicacy, which was not only exciting as an ingredient but invaluable as a preservative. With it many foods that had been scarcely edible before became dramatically delicious, and many other foods which had spoiled in a few days were now preserved for weeks. Sugar was so scarce in Europe that pirates often captured and sacked vessels in search of it; often they sought it more than anything else. In many parts of Europe sugar was regarded so highly as a stimulant that doctors prescribed it. Among some European peoples it was used as a drug. Among all European peoples it was valued as more precious than fine foods, rich garments, or exquisite fragrances.

"They have trees which produce fruit continually . . . they sow and reap at all seasons," John Montecorvino wrote in the fourteenth century, and added that they possess "trees that produce sugar and others that produce honey and others that produce a liquor that has a smack of wine." [12]

### COCONUT, CINNAMON, AND PEPPER

Marco Polo, who was concerned with the fascinating India as well as China, comments on the fact that in the kingdom of Melibar he discovered "a great quantity of pepper, and ginger, and cinnamon and turbit and nuts," and that in Coilum ginger also abounded.[13] Ludovico Di Varthema describes the "eight or nine kinds of small spices" which he found in the country, and also expatiates upon the other rare possessions: "the rare pepper trees . . . ginger . . . the tree (best in all the world) which is called Tenga" (obviously the coconut tree). He then goes on to record the virtues of the coconut tree in terms of its useful properties. It furnishes, he says, "wood to burn, nuts to eat, ropes for maritime navigation, thin stuffs which when they are dyed appear to be made of silk; charcoal in the greatest perfection; wine, water, oil, and sugar: and with its leaves which fall, that is, when a branch falls, they cover the houses."[14]

Varthema reveals what was at stake by his remark that "we arrived at a city called Cacaolon . . . many merchants arrived . . . because a great deal of pepper grows in this country, and in perfection." He goes on in great detail to describe the kind of pepper, and the different kinds of peppers, which were plentiful in the land. He speaks of the "long pepper," called Molaga, which "weighs very little . . . is not so biting as that of ours . . . [and which is carried out every year] by eighteen to twenty ships." He also comments upon the "elephants, horses, sheep, cows and buffaloes, leopards and peacocks" which exist in prodigious numbers in the country. Dozens of travelers and explorers likewise describe the abundance of the pepper and ginger and cinnamon which were as cheap in India at that time as salt is in our country today.

Duarte Barbosa relates in graphic detail the wondrous materials and products which he found in India in the early part of the sixteenth century. "Bengal," he avowed, "was the richest country in the world for cotton, ginger, sugar, grain and flesh of every kind."[15] India supplied the East with most of its best products. Among its numerous customers were Persia, Tartary, Africa, Syria, Turkey, and other surrounding lands. Khambayat alone, Barbosa stated, was visited by "three hundred ships a year."

It is no wonder, then, that European countries—Spain, Portugal,

England, France—were eager to discover the shortest route to India, and then to conquer and despoil it for their own ends. They wanted the things and stuffs that glittered and glowed, that enriched and embellished, and gave brighter character to the dull, drab Europe of that day. The East, Cathay as well as India, was radiant, lit with color and charm; Europe lacked that iridescent splendor.

### CLOTHES: THE UNENDING DREAM

But people also wear clothes, and if they have the money to purchase them, as did the upper classes in Europe at the time, they want to wear the best they can obtain. European clothes at that time suffered from lack of diversity, lack of color. Colors were solid, not blended and varied, and the garments worn were unhappily monotonous. The vegetable dyes, of which in those days indigo was the most exciting, could not be procured in European lands. They could be purchased only from India and Cathay, which was the name by which China was known to medieval Europe.

Indigo was one of the chief products of India. It was invaluable as a dye that could be used to secure a fascinating composite of blues, which could lend to materials those enchanting variations of color necessary to decorative design. Hindustan was noted for the dyeing industries which thrived in its cities.[16] "The land was rich in indigo," Ashraf writes, "and the people were fond of bright colors. . . . Thus the dyeing industry and calico-painting went hand in hand with the manufacture of cloth."[17] In addition, India was the land where the best silks and cotton goods, the best tapestries and pottery work, were to be procured. Varthema declared that there was a greater abundance of cotton to be found in Banghella than in any other country in the world. "Fifty ships are laden every year in this place," he stated, "with cotton and silk stuffs," which were despatched to various parts of the world: Persia, Arabia, Turkey, Ethiopia. He also describes "the immense quantity of silk produced in this country," as does Barbosa, who comments on "the very rich cloths of cotton and silk and gold" which he saw in that country. The Hon. Mountstuart Elphinstone avers that "of the Indian manufactures, the most remarkable is that of cotton cloth, the beauty and delicacy of which was so long admired, and which in fineness of texture has never been approached in any other country."[18] He writes, too, about their silk manufactures, which he considers excellent, and of the gold and silver brocade work they did, and of their dyes, which were never "equalled in Europe."

Niccolò dei Conti, who traveled through India in the early part of the fifteenth century, is not less enthusiastic about the city of Maazaria, which he depicted as "filled with gold, silver, and precious stones." He also writes of the "most sumptuous buildings, elegant habitations and handsome furniture" of the land, and avows that they "lead a more refined life (than the Europeans), removed from all barbarity and coarseness. The men are extremely humane, and the merchants very rich, so much so that some will carry on their business in forty of their own ships, each of which is valued at fifty thousand gold pieces."[19] Cambay was filled with better artisans and more manufactures than Flanders. The silks of Cambay, the carpets, cushions and beddings, were the best in the world of that period. The truth of the matter was that Cambay was "the port of the whole Indian Sea," a manufacturing center for "every sort of goods: as Talach [gowns half-cotton and half-silk], damask, Khan [satin], Hiota [blankets], and there they prepare the blue stone of color."[20]

### THE BACKWARDNESS OF THE OCCIDENTAL WORLD IN THE FIFTEENTH CENTURY

It is a common delusion to think of the Indians, Chinese, and Japanese in the fifteenth and sixteenth centuries as backward peoples. That delusion is born of the characteristic European and American belief that the world has always revolved about the Occidentals. Nothing could be farther from the truth. The role of the Occidentals in terms of world influence has been far from what is usually concluded. At times the Occidentals have been important in world affairs, but not often! The Greeks, the greatest of all the Occidental peoples, never exercised vast geographic influence; their dominion never extended far beyond two seas. Even with Alexander, their ancient Napoleon, they were never able to Hellenize the barbarians for long. The Romans were the only Occidental people who managed to dominate a large part of the world for a long time, and after the Romans —nothing. Between the fall of the Roman Empire and the rise of the Italian city states, with Venice and Florence at their head, world history should dedicate itself to the study of the peoples of India, of Africa, of China, not to the peoples of the West. Progress in those days occurred with them, not with us. It was only after the modern commercial and industrial revolutions that the West managed to dominate and dictate to the world.

### THE RICHES OF CATHAY AND CIPANGU

Cathay and Cipangu were scarcely less rich than India in economic possessions and resources—the gold mines of Japan were among the great wonders of the period, and explorers and adventurers continually dreamed of plundering them—but the Chinese and Japanese peoples were less hospitable than the Indians to foreigners. Merchants found little trouble in trading with the Indians; they found it difficult to have commerce with Chinese or Japanese. The latter erected impregnable and almost topless walls of economic and geographic defense beyond which it was supremely difficult to penetrate. A number of Westerners, particularly Dutchmen, did succeed in getting beyond those walls, but their number was not great.

Nevertheless, many explorers were more concerned with Cathay and Cipangu than India, and some nations viewed them as greater prizes. Cabot in particular headed in the direction which he believed was direct for Cipangu, but landed, as we have already pointed out, in Labrador. The stories about Cathay and Cipangu were exciting and alluring enough to intrigue any adventurer. Marco Polo declared that in Cipangu "the quantity of gold . . . was endless." [21] There were stories that gold was so abundant in Cipangu that dog collars were made from it. Sulphur was also produced in abundance in the land.[22] Similar information about Cathayan riches percolated into Europe. "Their country (Cathay) is very rich in corn, in wine, gold, silver, silk," wrote John of Plano Carpini in 1246, "and in every kind of produce that tends to the support of mankind." [23] Cathayans were reputed to be first-rate craftsmen in the manual arts, and their silk was ofttimes declared to be even better than that of India.

### RELIGIOUS TOLERANCE IN INDIA

Indian civilization profited from its contacts with the West but did not allow the West to undermine its culture. Not until several centuries later did it succumb to Western power. Even then it was its body and not its soul that was subjugated. During Elizabeth's time, when European nations were lacerated with religious conflicts, Akbar, the great Indian ruler, held court and insisted that the peoples of all religions should speak their message before him and none should have preference. He would hear them all and tolerate them all. Tolerance of religious differences existed in India centuries before it ever arrived in the Western world. And Akbar was not an erudite man; he was not even able to write. But he was bred in a culture which was far more advanced and enlightened than that of the West in that age.

India was the magic land, then, not only because it was so incredibly rich in resources and techniques, but also because it was culturally progressive. It suffered from false ideas, dangerous superstitions, and unhappy customs and practices; but no more so than the West. Its religious sacrifices, which enlightened Indians condemned, were scarcely worse than the witchcraft executions in Europe and New England. Their punishments were no more horrifying than the eye-gouging, finger- and ear-chopping practices of the West, to which must be added all the tortures of the wheel, the strappado, and that appalling variety of subtler methods and techniques devised to augment agony.*

* As an indication of Indian humanity, which has been construed by many Westerners as a proof of its backwardness, there stands out its singular attitude toward animals. Christian theology has reserved no place for animals at all; it has relegated them to the sub-infernal regions of extinction. The Indians, on the other hand, have revered life so much that they never failed to include the animals within the life category. Their reverence has been for life as a whole and not for man in particular. They have always believed that in the eternal scheme of things, whatever its origin, nature, or destiny, all life, the entire life force, animal as well as human, is included. Christian theology has never achieved such comprehensiveness. Owing largely to the reprehensively narrow-minded concept of the soul promulgated by the Catholic Church, animals have been refused entrance into the paradise of the future. They have been discarded, flung into the dark abysses of oblivion. The Indians, on the contrary, for reasons economic as well as spiritual, have viewed the animals in a gentler and nobler way.

Some of the consequences of that philosophy have been unfortunate. One is that the Indians have never been able to compete with the Europeans in music. The Hindus cannot use stringed instruments, because the strings are made from catgut, and the cats are sacred animals in their eyes.

To use the body of any animal is considered sacrilegious by a devout Indian. More than that, the Mohammedans, who at various times have dominated India, have regarded the human body as so sacred that they have refused, because of religious conviction, to allow it to be used in art. The result has been a severe limitation in the art field. Vines, leaves, trees, landscapes of infinite varieties, skies, seas, mountains, all the impressive exteriors of the world have constituted the basis of their art, but men, women, animals are absent from it.

### INDUSTRIAL PROGRESS IN INDIA

The industries of India, far more advanced than those of the West, were the product of clever brains, fine abilities, creative genius. To begin with, they constructed in those early centuries, when Occidental navigation was still in an undeveloped stage, ships of "a thousand and a thousand and two hundred *bahares* burden," which were built "without any nails," as Barbosa points out, "but the whole of the sheathing was sewn with thread." These ships sailed for the Red Sea, Judah, Mecca, and their products were transported by smaller vessels to Cairo, Alexandria, and Venice. The trade carried on in the ancient seaports of India, which lent increasing inspiration to the native industries, resulted in an accumulation of wealth unparalleled in any other land. It was from India that Solomon got his "ivory, apes and peacocks," which were carried to him in the rich cargoes of the ships from Tarshish.[24]

In Hindustan the manufacture of textiles was the leading industry, and the goods produced, which included divers cloths, cotton, and silks, were internationally admired and craved. In addition, thirteenth-, fourteenth-, and fifteenth-century Hindustan had metalwork, stonework, sugar, indigo, and paper industries. In other parts of India, woodwork, pottery, and leather industries flourished. Besides, there were the agricultural industries, derived from the products and by-products of coconuts, oil, and various food substances.[25] Dyeing, to be sure, was the leading industry in many parts of India, and in a number of centers gold thread work and different forms of embroidery were developed to a high point of perfection. Many centuries before cotton machinery was invented in Europe, Indian "gins were separating fiber from seed, Hindu wheels were spinning lint into yarn, and frail Hindu looms weaving their yarns into textiles." [26]

Lead and mercury mines, combined with a few iron mines, constituted another industry of importance. The manufacture of glass by methods which were the most ingenious of the time was one of the best developed industries. Many travelers commented on the excellent quality of the iron manufactured, and concerning the chemical industries there is not a single word of disapprobation that can be discovered. They were superior to all the European chemical industries of the era. Porcelain, too, as in Cathay, was a conspicuous product.

Hindustan's ivory was sought after by all the nations. Out of it were made bracelets, rings, dice, bedsteads, beads, and a score of other things which enchanted the eyes of Europe. Great skill was shown in many different industries, especially in work on precious stones.

This India was not a magic land to the Indians. The majority of the Indians lived in a state of poverty no less squalid or unhappy than that in which European commoners suffered. The irony was that Indian artisans, who lived lowlier than animals, were at work upon those things which the aristocrats and merchants of Europe were willing to pay for out of the best of their spoils and gains. India was a magic land only for the rajahs and maharajahs and merchant princes who could profit from the talents and skills of the populace, and for those Europeans who could afford to buy what the populace produced.

In Akbar's time, canal works were projected which were unrivaled in the rest of the world. Akbar insisted that they be more than utilitarian, so on both sides of the Juma Canal trees were planted in order to make it a paradise of travel with "the sweet flavor of the fruits [reaching] the mouth of everyone." [27] He had built numerous dams across treacherous rivers, constructed many reservoirs and bridges. In addition, he had established over a score of colleges. Roads were constructed, water-supply systems developed, and a police force organized to free the country from robbers and bandits. In many cities there were tall houses and large buildings constructed of stone and mortar; they were graced with windows, roofed with tiles, and embellished with jewels. There were streets carved with the precision of an artist, and roads scarcely inferior to those of ancient Rome.

At that time, in the sixteenth century, England had no canals, no central water supply, little police protection, and no streets or roads comparable to those that existed in India. England was so inferior to India that all comparison becomes pathetic. Its roads were cattle-tracks; its houses were crude, clumsy structures; and even its castles were without the grace and charm of Indian architecture. Its postal system was hopelessly inefficient. Its whole way of life was that of an undeveloped, backward people, inferior in practically every respect to the life of the mature, progressive peoples who inhabited India. Even when compared with Spain, Portugal, or any of the prosperous Italian cities, England lacked color and challenge. Henry VII had backed Cabot, and Henry VIII had become interested in Cathay, but the country as a whole in the early sixteenth century was unvital and unprogressive.

Under Alauddin, at the beginning of the fourteenth century in India, banditry and brigandage were eliminated, and limited patronage was provided for the learned and pious. The populace even then attained a higher standard of living than in Europe.[28] Alauddin was determined to regulate prices so that merchants could not profit unduly from them and thereby exploit the populace. Merchants were penalized and imprisoned if they withheld a single "maund" of grain from a customer, and were treated not less severely if they attempted to raise the price in violation of government decree.

Even before Alauddin, Ibn Batuta, the famous Moorish traveler, told about the marvelous postal system which had been built up in India, of how efficient and expeditious it was in the fourteenth century when he visited the land.[29] Other writers, like Abd-er-Razzak, described the flower decorations, the inlay work, the jeweled mosaics which were conspicuous in India in the fifteenth century, finding their culmination in the famous Taj Mahal, which has never been surpassed in design or magnificence.

All this work could never have been undertaken had it not been that the sovereigns of India were more eager to invest the money of the kingdom for such purposes rather than for armaments, in which direction the major moneys of European and American nations are being expended today. The Indian rulers of those centuries preferred putting their surplus funds into economic and social projects, which they realized were a most ingenious way of preserving and solidifying their power. As late as the eighteenth century, Indian manufactures and industries were equal to those of Europe.[30] From ancient days, when Indian fabrics, tapestries, gems, carpets, enamels, and mosaics adorned the private and public buildings of Rome, down to the beginning of the Industrial Revolution, the world looked to India for its most arresting and exciting wares. India not only was the land of rich resources, but was also the place where those resources could be manufactured and transformed into works of art.*

* Like Egypt, India was a gift of geography. Its vast plains, watered by the Ganges, were prodigiously fertile. Its soil was a paradise of productivity. It needed little cultivation to fructify.[31] Consequently, India had a headstart upon other countries, and was able in early centuries to turn its talents in other directions, toward the beautification and perfection of

## III

Italians, Portuguese, and English set out in quest of India, Cathay, and Cipangu because those lands possessed the elements, substances, and compounds which Europe lacked and craved. They represented the economic Meccas of the time. It was India, however, which meant more than Cathay or Cipangu. India was not only the magic land; it was the magic word. People talked of India as men in later days talked of Utopia and envisioned the City of the Sun. India was on the tongue of thousands in every European land. There was not a country which did not have navigators who claimed they knew the way to the golden kingdom, the land of wonder and dream.

India had been discovered long before; the task, therefore, was not to discover it, but to find the shortest and safest route to it.

Columbus set out to discover this magic land.

By accident he discovered America. If he had not discovered America, one of a dozen other navigators of the period would have done so. There were a multitude of men obsessed with the belief that the world was round; Columbus had no monopoly on the idea. Columbus, however, was the one who succeeded in profiting most from it. He sold it to Ferdinand and Isabella, and, as a result, succeeded in discovering not India but America.

What he aimed for was the Far East, but what he found was a new world, a world unknown to the horizons of geographers or the dreams of utopians. That America, which was India in the eyes of Columbus, was to prove a greater India in time. It was to outlast and surpass the fairest and finest dreams of India entertained by the Europeans of the period. Fifteenth- and sixteenth-century India was more progressive than Europe, but seventeenth-, eighteenth-, and nineteenth-century India was out-paced by Europe, and it was not long after the Industrial Revolution gained momentum and modern imperialism became an international force that India fell victim to European power and became a vassal colony of England. Ever since it has been little more than an exploited possession, its resources robbed, its labors cheated, and the wings of its aspirations clipped by its mercenary master.

its products, and it had the resources, glittering and glamorous, to which it could devote its advancing genius.

The intransigent spirit of the land, however, has managed to survive, and in the protests and revolts led by Gandhi, Nehru, and Bose, there can be little doubt that the time is not far off when it will free itself from the British yoke, and achieve that independence without which it cannot progress. Then it may be a powerful India, industrialized, equipped to meet the West on equal terms, possessing the materials, machines, and weapons, the lack of which resulted in its subjugation; then it may take its place again among the great nations of the earth. It is still ahead of the West in its spiritual philosophy; its religious literature, with its Mahabharata and Upanishads, is equal if not superior to that of the ancient Jews and Christians; its ethical doctrines are loftier and more inspiring than those of any other nation.

It was the search for India, the magic land, that gave birth to the American dream. Before the battle for religious freedom began, before the imperialistic expansion of Europe became a fresh and challenging reality, India was the haunting chimera of the centuries. Many set out for it, but few reached it. Columbus was only one of many who failed to reach it—but he reached a greater India, a new world, which was to become the India of the future.

## CHAPTER II

# The Main Streams of European and American Culture

ALTHOUGH it was India that inspired the discovery of America, it was nothing of India that the Europeans brought to the new world. What they brought stemmed from different sources. The Englishmen, for instance, who finally conquered all the continent north of Mexico, brought with them an economic philosophy embracing those individualistic values that finally became the basis of American life. In addition, they carried with them a spiritual philosophy that embodied the roots of far more ancient cultures.

Those roots were twofold: Jewish and Greek.* The Pilgrims, Puritans, Quakers, Anabaptists, Familists, Labadists, Mennonites, and Scotch Presbyterians were far more Jewish than Greek in derivation. There was more of Palestine than of Athens living in the hearts and minds of the men who settled this country; they were far more concerned with Moses and Isaiah than with Plato and Aristotle. They belonged to the Judaic-Christian stream of our culture. The Greeks, with their rationalistic, hedonistic view of life, were anathema to them. These Englishmen were moralistic, not hedonistic, and believed, like the ancient Jews from whom they acquired their vision of good and evil, that all the Sodoms and Gomorrahs of the world would be destroyed by the righteous and just Jehovah. Their influence has continued down till today, and is to be found active still in those inhibitions, prohibitions, and asceticisms which are commonly associated with the word puritanism.

* This should not be confused with the racial theory popular in the nineteenth century, developed by Ludwig Borne and advocated by Heinrich Heine and others; neither does it have anything to do with Matthew Arnold's theory about the difference between Hebraism and Hellenism. The attempt to explain the genius of either the Jews or the Greeks in racial terms is patently absurd and futile. Scarcely less preposterous was Heine's attempt to classify all men as either Jews or Greeks. The point of this chapter is simply to show how Western culture has been derived from the Jewish and Greek traditions, both of which have been profoundly modified by the changing circumstances of different economic and social epochs.

There can be no doubt that in the Western world the most popular as well as the most influential book of the last fifteen hundred years has been the Bible. In later years Rousseau's *Social Contract*, and still later Marx's *Capital*, have competed with it in influence, but have never equaled it in power. The Bible through the years has remained *the* book in Occidental lands. Its words have proved the source of goodness and wisdom, as well as of wickedness and ignorance. It has illuminated the minds of men, imbued them at times with new ethical aspirations, motivated revolt and reaction, instigated wars and inspired peace, dictated the hopes and dreams of countless millions. For centuries men thought in no other terms than those of religion, which in Europe meant in terms of the Bible. The Bible was the sacred book. It was the inspiration, the touchstone, the shibboleth of the era. Reactionaries and radicals, clergymen and laymen, scientists, and charlatans, dullards and dreamers, all exploited it as the final source of authority. It constituted the spiritual breath of Western man.

In our time, when so many other criteria have interpolated themselves, it is difficult to realize what a complete and unbreakable hold the Bible had over the minds of men in those centuries. It had a monopoly upon all wisdom. Even though most men couldn't read it, they knew it, were fed upon it by their teachers, preachers, and priests. And it was not only the Lord of Hosts and the Son of Man that they knew, but also Moses, Isaiah, Daniel, Joseph, Ruth. These were intimates in their lives. They talked about them as if they had known them always and would go on knowing them even after death.

In the main the Europeans derived their whole concept of good and evil, right and wrong, from this same Biblical source. Although they called themselves Christians, they were really more Jewish than Christian, more Old-Testamentish than New-Testamentish in their beliefs and practices. It was the Ten Commandments, not the Sermon on the Mount, which they respected and tried to follow. They gave lip-service to the Sermon on the Mount, but knew better than to attempt to practice it. To turn the right cheek after the left one had been slapped, as Jesus had urged, might be good practice for a saint, but few people were saints, and saints did not have to earn their living by hard bargaining or arduous toil. The Ten Commandments, on the other hand, were more adaptable to their way of life. They could follow them with impunity. At times, it was true, deviations were necessary, but if such deviations were sheathed in the aura of respectability, they could be condoned. To kill a human being was an undoubted sin, but to kill an Indian was different, because an Indian was not a human being; and besides, it was very likely necessary to kill the more obstinate and recalcitrant Indians in order to convert the gentler to the gospel of Christ.

It is most interesting that Jesus played a relatively inconspicuous role among the Protestant sects which made their way to the new world. Their interest was far more in Jehovah, who guided Moses with a pillar of fire, extracted Jonah from the belly of the whale, and saved Daniel in the lions' den, than in the simple man of the cross who preached a communist doctrine which threatened to undermine the extant state. They believed in the Jehovah who righted wrongs, extirpated evils, demanded an eye for an eye and a tooth for a tooth, and was constantly on the side of the good and the just. The Jews have been condemned all too often for believing that they were and are "the chosen people" (incidentally, a dozen other peoples have believed the same thing), but it was the Protestant sects who took over that idea and translated it into practical doctrine. The religious groups which founded New England, Pilgrims as well as Puritans, and many of the other sects that followed, believed they were *the chosen people,* and that they continue to believe it even today is evidenced in their various societies, organizations, lodges, clubs, fraternities, and whatnot.

### THE JEWS AS THE FIRST PURITANS

In other words, what the Puritans emphasized in their religious philosophy was not Jesus' desire to forgive but Jehovah's determination to punish. They were more willing to condemn than to condone, more eager to imprison men than to reform them. Their puritanism, like that of the Jews, was built upon an edifice of denial and repression. Their whole legislation was based upon the Jewish code; their view of the Sabbath was a direct outgrowth of the Jewish attitude. Moses had declared that anyone who defiled the Sabbath day "shall surely be put to death" (*Numbers* 15:35),* and though the Puritans eliminated the death threat, they succeeded in making the Sabbath day little short of a living death. They forbade every possible form of joy and amusement on that day. Children were taught not to smile or play; they had to listen to long readings from the Bible and Foxe's *Book of Martyrs*, and were lectured upon the awful fate awaiting them if they violated the sanctity of the day. Though the Puritan Sunday differed from the Jewish Sabbath in many respects, the spirit in which both people regarded it was unmistakably similar. Just as the Jews could not, and even until today the orthodox Jews still cannot, work, cook, beautify themselves, or resort to any diversions or amusements on their Sabbath, so the Puritans frowned upon the same things on their Sabbath.

The early Christians had revolted against this morbid concept. The apostle Mark had declared that "the Sabbath was made for man and not man for the Sabbath." The Christian church had changed the Sabbath day from Saturday to Sunday, "the day of the Sun," and it was exalted as a day of joy and not of gloom. But the puritanic sects, which included French Huguenots and German Lutherans as well as English Dissenters, found the Judaic outlook preferable to the primitive Christian view. The economic struggle which they had to wage against their aristocratic adversaries, resembling as it did something of the incessant struggle which the Jews had to carry on against their numerous invaders—Egyptian, Babylonian, Assyrian—naturally inclined them to adopt a harsh rather than a gentle ethic.

Their god was, as Jehovah himself had declared, exacting, demanding, severe. Even during the Great Awakening, after the acerbities and asceticisms of the early years had passed, Jonathan Edwards, the greatest of all the New England hierophants, could still thunder and fulminate against sinners in words that scorched with every syllable. His description of what happened in hell, in which sinners sizzled like banana fritters in an eternal pan of fire, was

* One instance in which that threat was executed is unforgettably vivid. A man who had gathered sticks on the Sabbath was summoned before Moses and Aaron and the whole congregation:

"And the Lord said unto Moses, The man shall be surely put to death: All the congregation shall stone him with stones without the camp.

"And all the congregation brought him without the camp and stoned him with stones, and he died, as the Lord commanded Moses." [1]

typical of the punitive psychology that dominated the Protestant sects in Europe and America.

It was such a psychology that the leaders of the Protestant groups which founded New England carried with them as intellectual baggage—all except those Protestants who derived from the Established Church of England, which at that time was more Catholic than Protestant in spirit. It was a psychology absorbed from the Jews, from the Bible, from the Old Testament, but adapted to the new form of economic life which was emerging in many parts of Europe. No psychology could have better fitted the needs and demands of the early entrepreneurs of capitalist enterprise than that which lived in the words of the old Jewish prophets.

New-Testament doctrine demanded saints but forgave sinners; Old-Testament gospel revealed less concern for saints but refused to forgive sinners. The Old Testament was founded upon the pre-feudal economics of the ancient world; the New Testament was based upon the equalitarian economics of a revolutionary prophet who made heaven his goal. In later years, after that prophet was crucified and the possibility of his advent became less and less immediate, his doctrines, in the hands of his more consecrated followers, acquired a new formulation. They resolved themselves into various forms of Christian communism which during the Middle Ages stormed at the citadels and gates of many cities and fortresses. The majority of his followers adapted his doctrines to the more exigent necessities of everyday life and very soon, as the churchmen of those eras discovered, it was possible to make Christ into what in our day is known as an up-to-date Christian. It was not long before Jesus' followers reconciled themselves to that reality. The minority, however, continued to revolt, and it is with that minority that this volume is mainly concerned.

The Jews, to be sure, were not the only ancient people to develop a high moral code, but it was their moral code, and not that of the Hindus, Chinese, or Egyptians, that was adopted by the people of the West. The Jews brought with them from the small, narrow, perilous strip of land that was their home a rigor of discipline, a firmness of conviction, and a concept of conscience which gave to their morality severity as well as strength, and a driving power of irresistible intensity. Owing no doubt to the misfortune of their geography, which rendered their land immediately subject to invasion by surrounding nations, and owing to the smallness of their numbers, which made them practically defenseless before their multitudinous foes, they were driven in upon themselves and forced to invent a God and to excogitate a morality advantageous to their destiny.

The result was Jehovah (Jahweh), a strong, formidable god who could be fierce as thunder, but whose eyes were ever watchful of his children, and who never failed to punish the sinful and reward the sinless. Their god was one of which they stood in awe; he would have no other gods before him, would tolerate no competition with lesser deities, and refused to countenance any images made of him. He was the great patriarch, before whom the whole Jewish nation bowed. He was a father who was more stern than tender, but everlastingly just. He discouraged the lighter aspects of life, the frivolities and trivialities to which many other peoples were addicted, and encouraged the graver and more serious applications of the heart and the soul.

The Jews, consequently, became a great moral and spiritual people. They became the first Puritans in the ancient world. It was natural, therefore, that later *puritans*—I am using the word in this connection to describe those people and groups who believed in goodness instead of pleasure, in a moral instead of a hedonistic ethics—turned to Jewish scripture for inspiration.

### THE GREEK INFLUENCE

The Greek influence was less direct, less immediate, less intimate. It contributed little to our moral outlook. We turn to the Greeks for something which is beyond morality, beyond good and evil.

The Greeks were the first people in the world to introduce the method of rational inquiry. They were concerned not with morality but with the science of ethics. Their test of goodness was not in terms of heavenly commandments or decrees but in terms of individual and social results. One of their most challenging philosophers, Epicurus, founded his whole system of ethics upon a purely hedonistic basis: an act was good if it gave more pleasure than pain. Aristippus went farther and exalted bodily pleasures above mental, denouncing the latter as largely fictitious.

Even Plato, a far more profound thinker than Epicurus, and far removed from the latter in philosophic attitude, wrote boldly and beautifully in defense of homosexuality, declaring that it was finer and nobler than heterosexuality. Plato did not prefer homosexuality, however, because it was more pleasant, but because it was more beautiful. Like many other Greeks, he exalted the aesthetic into a moral credo. An act, a gesture, was good to the degree to which it was exquisite. The ethical and the exquisite were thus inalienably allied. They became part of a developmental principle which represented not a lack of ethical values but a higher form of ethics.

Greek ethics was based upon the theory of "the good life." It was free from the *Verboten* psychology of the Jews because it believed that "the good life" could be achieved better by reason than by repression. Reason was the Greeks' guide. What was reasonable was good; what was unreasonable was evil. "The good life," therefore, was a striving after the rational, which meant that it was anthropomorphic instead of theological in approach.

### DIFFERENCE BETWEEN ZEUS AND JEHOVAH

A great part of this difference between the Jew's and the Greek's idea of morality can be traced to the antithetical nature of their religions and their concepts of the supreme deity. Jehovah was remote, invisible, and implacable; Zeus, on the contrary, was a genial and personal creation, not only visiting the earth from time to time but impregnating women who caught his fancy with illegitimate but god-inspired children. Most of the Greek gods found the earth a thoroughly jolly place, and the Greeks felt themselves constantly on intimate terms with them. Naturally, with such gods for their models, they did not develop that profound sense of sin and morbid magnification of conscience which Judaism, and later Christianity, evolved and perpetuated. There were, to be sure, exceptions, of which the Orphic and Dionysiac religions with their profound influence on Greek drama were the most conspicuous. In addition, there were the Eleusinian mysteries with their purification motif, and later the Gnostics with their purgational complex; but their role was minor.

The Greek gods were as much products of the geographic and economic conditions of Greece as Jehovah was a product of Palestine. Advantageously situated on an elusive peninsula, and barricaded by well-nigh impassable mountains, the Greeks were protected so adequately from invasion that it was possible for them to invent more human and less exacting deities and to cultivate an interest in the arts and the sciences surpassing that of any other people of their time. They even developed a sense of humor which was sharp, subtle, and ofttimes devastatingly uproarious—a virtue which the Jews in those days lacked. More than that, at a time when the Indians were unable to progress in music because their worship of the cat prevented their using catgut for stringed instruments, and when the Jews made little progress in the plastic arts because their Jehovah forbade the creation of anything in his image or the image of any other gods, or any other things which might become idols in the eyes of the people—at that time Greek musicians were playing upon stringed instruments, and their sculptors and painters, notably Phidias and Praxiteles, were dedicating their plastic genius to the glory of the Greek gods. The fact that their gods did not condemn or discourage such arts accounts in large part for the early artistic supremacy of the Greeks.

Such genial gods would not have sufficed for the Jews, who were constantly in fear of invasion, and so much of whose bitter history has been written with the tears of slavery and exile. The fact of the matter is that after the Greeks lost their geographic security, discovered that they were helpless before invasion, and were converted into a conquered people, the light went out of their genius. The Jews, on the other hand, better equipped spiritually to survive in a ubiquitously hostile world, have remained one of the great peoples of the earth.

But it is not with the Jews of today or the Greeks of today that we are concerned here. We are interested in the Jews who provided the inspiration for American puritanism and the Greeks who supplied the background for modern philosophy and science.

### INTELLECTUAL CURIOSITY OF THE GREEKS

The Greeks of the days of Aristotle, Plato, Empedocles, Democritus, Euripides, Sophocles, Aeschylus, Phidias, Praxiteles, provided the second main stream of Western culture. Those Greeks were the founders of what is commonly known as the pagan aspect of our culture. They were interested in inquiring into the ways of life, the ways of understanding it and the ways of improving it. From the early philosophers, Thales, Anaximenes, and Anaximander, who were concerned with discovering the original element from which all things emerged and became animate, to Plato and Aristotle, who involved themselves with the problems of nature, ethics, politics, evolution, the Greeks manifested an attitude toward life which was indubitably scientific. Aristotle's theory of evolution, with all its inadequacies and lacunae, was a harbinger of the concept of evolution which found its culmination in Darwin. Many of the lucubrations of the pre-Aristotelian philosophers lacked what today would be called the scientific approach, but there was in them the same candid, fearless inquiry into origins and ends which ultimately led to the evolution of the scientific method. With Democritus and his theory of the atom we approach closer to the spirit of contemporary science. Although the Greeks did not possess the modern equipment necessary to check and recheck their theories, they were relatively free from the religious pressures which in other countries then discouraged and thwarted such investigations, and they were free from such political pressures as, in Germany, Italy, and Soviet Russia today, have proved such tragic impediments to scientific progress.

It is of such stuff that the Greek influence upon Western culture was made. It did not descend upon the European world as directly as did Jewish culture through the medium of the Bible. Without it, however, the Western world today might be as unscientific and as unprogressive as China, India, or Africa.*

It was the Bible, finding its fulcrum in Jesus and the Virgin Mary, that in the main determined the prevailing attitudes and actions of men. Greek thought was swallowed up by a Sahara of ignorance, and it was not until centuries later, at the time of the Revival of Learning and the Renaissance, that what was Greek was excavated from

* Greek drama—a thing unknown to the ancient world except by imitation—Greek sculpture and painting, and above all, Greek philosophy and science, were taken over by the Romans after Greece was subjugated, but what the progeny of Romulus and Remus made of them was little more than extremely blurred carbon copies of the originals.

In the immediate centuries after the fall of Rome in 476 A.D., most of what was Greek was lost. Certain of the Church Fathers strove to keep alive what they deemed was good in the Greek tradition, and many centuries later leaders like Aquinas were even willing to go so far as to accept Aristotle as an authority on matters which were not religious. Through men like Philo and Plotinus another aspect, a more mystical and subjective aspect, of Greek culture persisted. Nevertheless, Greek thought was never a forceful factor in conditioning the spirit of the Middle Ages.

the sands in which it had been buried.* That cultural excavation combined with the leading mechanical inventions of the time—the printing press and the compass—helped to create the Italian Renaissance, which spread to England a century later and made a new country of it.

The most significant outgrowth of that newness was the new England which was founded in the new world.

### THE GREEKS FOUND MODERN SCIENCE

Although Greek thought was introduced into Europe in the twelfth century, it was not until the fifteenth, at the time of the Italian Renaissance, that it became a dominant influence. From that time on it became a main stream. It was Greek philosophy and science, plus all the ingenious and illuminating additions made by the Arabians, that encouraged the early discoveries of Copernicus and Kep-

* During the Middle Ages, the Arabians were the main people to keep alive various forms of Greek lore, in particular the logic of Aristotle, and make possible that infiltration into Europe of Greek culture as well as their own, which combination in the twelfth century was to create the Medieval Renaissance. Maimonides, the famous Jewish philosopher, in his classic *Treatise on Logic,* contributed vastly in the same century toward the reinstatement of Aristotelian logic in the Western world. The medievalist Gerard of Cremona translated into Latin seventy-one books from the Arabian, among which were the works of Aristotle, Euclid, Archimedes, Galen, and Hippocrates, thus doing more than anyone else in his time to introduce scientific knowledge into twelfth-century Europe.

Feudalism had discouraged learning because it had little need for it. The Crusaders who fought their way through the Levant and battled down the Saracens were not concerned with the intellectual riches of the East, but only with its economic riches. They were interested in the precious wares and metals of the Mohammedans, but not in their science and philosophy. With but rare exceptions the Crusaders, products of the rural decadence which feudalism represented, were cultural barbarians, more concerned with wars than with wisdom, whereas the Mohammedans carried on where the Greeks and Romans left off and possessed the most striking culture of the period. Set Richard the Lion-Hearted beside Saladin the Saracen, and the contrast is complete.

The Medieval Renaissance, or the Twelfth-Century Renaissance, as it is often called, was the mother of the Italian Renaissance. The Arabians, who housed the treasures of Greek knowledge when the medieval West had abandoned them, were most conspicuous in this earlier Renaissance. Their culture far surpassed that of Europe during the Middle Ages. They were advanced in almost every field of science: medicine, mathematics, astronomy, astrology, alchemy. The importance of their contributions to Western culture can be seen in the multitudinous words which we have adopted from them, all revealing the extent and profundity of their learning: algebra, zero, cipher, zenith, nadir, chemistry, alcohol, alembic, etc. The fact that today we still use Arabic numerals is sufficient testimony to their mathematical precocity.

The route by which Greek literature, philosophy, and science reached the West was often as follows: "from Greek into Syriac or Hebrew, thence into Arabian and thence into Latin, often with Spanish as an intermediary, but it was much traveled and led at last to the Latin West." [2]

ler, and inspired Galileo, Torricelli, and their followers with a new conception of the universe.

Since that time the scientific, rationalistic approach of the Greeks has become an indestructible part of Western culture, and all the long struggles between religion and science, the supernatural and natural, the divine and the rational, have been outgrowths of Greek influence. The economic changes which resulted from the decay of feudalism and the rise of commercialism prepared the way during the Renaissance for the success of the scientific approach. Science became necessary to the new economic world which was in the process of birth. Leonardo da Vinci with his experimental ideas—in science as well as in art—became a challenging and symbolic figure of the new epoch. He set out to re-examine the universe, and it was not long before he revised most of the prevailing conceptions which men entertained about air, water, and other materials, substances, and stuffs of the world.

Science and economics became handmaidens in the same process. The commercial revolution encouraged and advanced science, and science in turn encouraged and advanced the commercial revolution. In ancient days science was included in the field of natural philosophy; it was a theoretical rather than a practical pursuit. In the modern world, which was born with the Renaissance, science changed character and became a technique, a method, which men put to use in the everyday activities of their lives. To do that, however, it had to evolve a philosophy of its own which in our time is known as the philosophy of science.

Before long that new philosophy put a quietus upon old philosophies—and especially upon religion. In our time science has become the new deity. Men swear by it, bow before it, dedicate their lives to it. Science may be, as C. E. Ayres once described it, "a false Messiah," but without it the world we live in today would have been impracticable and impossible, and as remote as the visions of the hoary-faced, glacial-eyed philosophers of the past with their conception of a perfect world. By its rigorous discipline, its scrupulous procedure, and its reverence for fact, it has given man that power over his environment which has made possible the world in which we live today.

### THE CLASS INFLUENCE

The legacy which the Jews and the Greeks bequeathed to Europe and thence to America was in the form of ideas, morals, beliefs, aspirations. There was no transference of tools, machinery, weapons, techniques, or methods. Europe did not conquer the Jews or the Greeks: the Jews and the Greeks conquered Europe. The conquest, to be sure, was psychological, not physical.

What the Jews and the Greeks contributed to Europe was its spiritual and intellectual bloodstream, but like all bloodstreams this was conditioned by outside forces and factors. The contribution was dynamic, not static. The Bible, deriving in its original form from the Jews, was not just a book, not just a code, not just a gospel, not just a revelation. It was something men used to fit their needs, to justify their ends. It could be used by all men at all times for divers purposes. The uses to which the Bible was put during the centuries depended upon the people using it.

The Bible with its ethical urgencies, and Greek thought with its scientific emphases,* became malleable stuff in the hands of those dictating the destiny of the centuries. At one time Jehovah was more important than Jesus, and later Jesus became more important than Jehovah. The same is true, in a different way, in regard to science. Attitudes toward both religion and science have always been determined by the conditions, needs, and interests of society, or rather of the class which controls society. Behind it all, to be certain, is the mode of production which gives to society its economic skeleton.

The classes in power used scientific as well as religious technique to abet their own ends. With the compass they sent their emissaries out into the undiscovered corners of the universe to bring back spoils from weird, fantastic lands; with the printing press they made all those who could read aware of what before had been the secret

* Science in the hands of the Greeks was a glorious adventure into the philosophy of things, materials, space, time, and all those admixtures and compounds of opposites, and that infinite variety of immeasurables, which they tried to reduce to measurement. Unfortunately it never got beyond the close-coddled environs of philosophy. The explanation is simple. The Greeks didn't need science except as a cerebral exercise. Plato's dreams of utopia, where philosophers would be kings and kings philosophers, Aristotle's theory of the state and the evolution of life, Archimedes' conclusions about space and motion, Democritus' conception of the atom, constitute the dream-stuff of a great people. But little more! They could not be put to practical use in the society of their time, because such use did not then exist.

possessions of priests and wise men; with gunpowder they remade the world, destroyed feudalism, broke down castles and fortresses, bridged moats, created cities, conquered strange and outlandish peoples in remote and resistant countries, and gave form to a civilization in which the earth soon became an international marketplace.

The discovery of America was part of that world change. In this struggle for markets, for pepper, for all variety of spices, for the precious metals, for ointments, for cloths, for jewels, for embellishments and adornments of every kind, for things which made life charming and delectable for the rich, all nations participated. The battle which ensued was not one of peoples, or even of nations, but of rulers, of kings, of nobles and their economic retinue. The rest of the populace, in England, France, Italy, Spain, Portugal, revealed small interest in such adventures and explorations; they had little to gain from them. But the rulers had much to gain from them. They needed them to make their life interesting, exciting, various.

So Europe was born ideologically out of Jewish and Greek loins, but what happened to it after its birth depended upon the character and challenges of time, place, and circumstance. Its moral and intellectual heredity was definite, but the ways in which that heredity manifested itself depended upon the plasticities and potencies of the extant environment. America was a spiritual as well as a geographical extension of Europe. The people who settled in the new world transported the traditions that they had learned in the old. But the new world before long began to reveal significant *newnesses,* and those old traditions underwent profound changes as the drive of a different *milieu* impacted upon them. The social spirit of the Middle Ages was replaced by the individualistic spirit of the modern age. The moralistic, puritanic spirit of the Jews became an indissoluble part of the psychology of the Protestant groups which settled upon these shores.

What we know as Puritanism * derives from the Jews and not from the Greeks. It is an ancient, not a modern outgrowth; it is not an invention of Protestantism, but a vestige of Judaism which found a disciplined morality an important means of survival. Protestants allied themselves with the Judaic tradition because it was one which

* In a later chapter I shall show that the official Puritans were far less puritanic than non-Puritan groups, whose *Puritanism,* so-called, was most deplorably severe and ruthless.

could best abet an upward-struggling, hard-harassed people. Like the Jews they had to fight off their oppressors; enemies rose up against them on every side. They possessed no isolated peninsula like the Greeks; they had to depend upon themselves, not upon the magnanimities of nature, in order to maintain their integrity. The Jews, as we have seen, found alien nations threatening them upon every horizon; the Protestant sects found the state, dominated by the aristocracy, opposing them upon every front—religious, political, economic. The life of both depended upon their genius to endure and persist.

### THE CATHOLIC OUTLOOK

The Catholics in Italy, at the time of the Renaissance, imbibed more of the Greek spirit than did the Protestants. Although they opposed science and fought it from every quarter, forced Galileo to recant and burned Giordano Bruno at the stake, they adopted some of the Greek attitude toward morality. To this day the Catholics are gentler in their judgment of sin than the Protestants; they are more willing to forgive than the Protestants, and they utilize their confessional mainly as an instrument of psychological condonement and expiation. The unforgivable and unpardonable sins of the Protestants are all forgivable and pardonable with the Catholics, who, despite their anti-progressive intellectual outlook, view human nature and individual frailty with something of the generosity and tolerance of the Greeks. In that respect the Catholics are more closely identified with the early Christian spirit than with the Judaic. Their attitude toward the Sabbath is strikingly illustrative of their outlook. Unlike the Jews and puritanic Protestants who made the Sabbath into a day of mortification, the Catholics refused to rob the day of its earlier pleasures and privileges. Even now the Catholic attitude toward the Sabbath has not changed. It is the Protestant groups—the Baptists, Presbyterians, Methodists, Congregationalists—who insist upon the perpetuation of Blue Sundays, clamor for the closing of cinema houses, ball parks, and dance halls, whereas the Catholics view such diversions as salutary rather than sinful. The Prohibition fiasco illuminates another aspect of the same religious contradiction. The Protestants, continuing the puritan tradition, fought for the Prohibition Amendment, determined still to purify the populace by repression and suppression; the Catholics, believing in a more elastic ethic, fought against it.

Only in the moral sense, however, were the Catholics superior to the Protestants, encumbered though the latter were with their puritanic prejudices. In every other field Protestantism, child as it was of the modern world, excelled. Protestantism, by virtue of its individualistic character, made it possible for the mind to attempt investigations, question theories, challenge conclusions, none of which efforts Catholicism would tolerate. It was not that Protestantism was so progressive in intellectual outlook, but that the nature of the religion itself admitted of progressive possibilities. Protestant countries have been invariably superior to Catholic countries in economic, political, and scientific development. Despite the handicap of their Judaic-puritanic morality, the Protestants have given the individual the chance of creating a new world. The Catholics, on the other hand, despite their freedom from the severities of that morality, have conspired to bind him within an old world.

## THE AMERICAN SCIENTIFIC OUTLOOK

The Greeks were more interested in the theory of science than in its practice. We, on the other hand, have become the most scientific country in the world, and yet the one least interested in the theory of science.

Cotton Mather might interest himself in the furbelows and fringes of science, but he knew nothing of the scientific spirit. He belonged to the tradition of the Jewish prophets, Isaiah, Jeremiah, Hosea, and not to that of the Greek thinkers: Plato, Aristotle, Democritus. No country has been so barren of scientific originality or theoretical insight, and yet at the same time so productive of inventive genius, engineering efficiency, and mechanical skill as America. Americans are a practical and not a theoretical people. They like to press buttons, shift gears, release brakes, whirr dynamos, and observe and utilize what the instruments do, but they are little interested in the why and wherefore of what they do. They are content with an Edison and feel no need for an Einstein. Still intellectual frontiersmen, Americans are more concerned with doing than with thinking, and with thinking mainly in terms of doing.

The reason is not difficult to discern. The nature of the country demanded a practical approach; it encouraged doers rather than thinkers, moralists rather than dreamers. Like the Palestinians of old who were faced by hostile nations, the early Americans were confronted with an inimical environment, and to preserve themselves they had to direct their energies almost exclusively in economically constructive channels. Jehovah was as much of a practical necessity to them as he was to the Jews. He was the life line of their spiritual empire. Without him, without the Bible which was his word, they would have been lost in chaos.

Although men may need bread more than anything else, they do not live by bread alone. The Englishmen who came to America were mainly lower middle-class Protestants, and the Bible was their moral guide. The lower middle class in European countries adopted and cultivated similar religious and moral attitudes. In this country, however, those attitudes became accentuated and intensified by the new environment, and in time they came to dominate almost an entire continent.

In Europe the lower middle class constituted a minor part of the populace; in America, a major part. In Europe lower middle-class influences were tempered by those of the upper middle class and the aristocracy. In America there was no aristocracy of consequence, and the upper middle class carried on the lower middle-class tradition. Lower middle-class ideas, therefore, embodied the crux of American economic, political, and moral philosophy.

There was in that philosophy all the flame and fury of the Jewish prophets from whom it derived its spiritual challenge. It cannot be understood except in terms of that Biblical background. Even later, when Greek influences began to penetrate the land through French sources, it was the puritanic attitudes of the lower middle class which finally triumphed. On the frontier, the Methodists and the Baptists who became the leading denominations of the country perpetuated the puritanic tradition throughout the nineteenth century, and in the twentieth century it was their anti-scientific attitudes—they were no more anti-scientific in this regard, however, than the Catholics—which provoked the battle over the teaching of biological evolution in Southern colleges.

Even today the battle is not over, although economic and intellectual changes in the country have driven many of the puritanic old guard into retreat. But our concern in this volume is with this old guard in the seventeenth century, for it was the new guard of that time.

## CHAPTER III

# Reaction and Revolt in England

*The common song is that we must obey our kings, be they good or bad, for God hath so commanded . . . but it is not less than blasphemy to say God commanded kings to be obeyed when they commanded impiety.*

—JOHN KNOX

IN THE dark winter of 1584, when the Englishmen, dispatched by the buccaneer aristocrat Sir Walter Raleigh, settled on Roanoke Island, the English empire was begun. There had been settlements before, but they had proved ephemeral. Although the Roanoke colony, made up of murderers, pickpockets, adventurers, landless farmers, jobless workmen, and also one of the first great scientific artists, White, soon disappeared and the colonists were swallowed up in war and famine, the name of the colony did not die. It was remembered as the first English colony which succeeded in settling Englishmen on foreign soil, even though the settlement proved to be disappointingly and discouragingly short-lived.*

The wild awakening of the adventurous impulse which surged over the Western world in the fifteenth and sixteenth centuries found delayed and reluctant repercussions in England. While other countries, most notably Spain, had begun to build up world empires, England had stood on the sidelines, watching, waiting, and debating. At the end of the sixteenth century, she still remained a country without colonies, a nation without external aids and resources. She had whipped the Spanish Armada in 1588, her lithe, agile British vessels driving the Spanish ships, cumbersome as marine dinosaurs, into swift and ignominious retreat; but out of it all she had gained nothing but glory and profit. The profit had been derived mainly from the piracies of her unscrupulous and unconscionable sea captains, daredevils beside whom a Captain Kidd [1] looked like a namby-pamby

* In recent years, Paul Green, the well-known American playwright and novelist, has dramatized in amazingly effective form, at Nags Head, North Carolina, the life of a still earlier colony, concerning which, however, we have only a fragmentary record.

seaman in Gilbert and Sullivan guise. Without John Hawkins and Francis Drake, whom Elizabeth made a knight after he had robbed a Spanish treasure ship of all its wealth, there would have been no English navy and no English commerce of dimensional significance.

But it was not the defeat of the Spanish Armada, however much it inspired William Shakespeare and other English dramatists, which made England into an empire. It was the colonization of America that achieved that end.

As we shall see, it was America that made England, not England that made America.

Without the defeat of the Armada and the final annihilation of the Spanish fleet in the Battle of Seville, however, the colonization of America might have proved too difficult for Englishmen to undertake. After these defeats of Spain, Englishmen found the seas unmolested. They had rid them of their greatest menace.*

## II

England, to be sure, lagged far behind Germany and Italy in commerce. The Hanseatic League had given Germany an early commercial superiority over its northern neighbors, and this had continued until Charles the Bold shattered its cities with his newfangled armaments and explosives. As late as Shakespearean days English commerce was infinitesimal compared with that of Venice. Enriched by the profits which it had accumulated from the last Crusade and from its traffic with the Greeks and Egyptians, Venice became the commercial center of Europe when London was a rough, crude, dirty city, unglittering and ungolden. Venetians circumnavigated the European and Asiatic worlds when Englishmen were mere bunglers in the new world of commerce. Venetian outposts and industries dotted the entire Levant, in Tripoli and Tyre and in the far-flung Trebizonde on the Black Sea. Venice made the seas into the avenues of prosperous transactions; the English, ignorant of the economic subtlety and finesse of the Venetians, relied more upon piracy than upon bargaining for their profits.

Many years passed before the gaiety and glitter of Venice were

* The Dutch and other colonizing nations gained also from the eclipse of Spain's naval supremacy.[2]

to find a parallel in England. The defeat of the Spanish Armada, whose ships were modeled upon the old Venetian Armada, marked the turning point in British economy. From that time on piracy was succeeded by commerce, and England became in the modern world what Lübeck and Venice had been in the post-medieval age.

Paradoxical though it may seem, the fundamental force which made it possible for England, after such a slow start in the theater of international politics, to become the greatest empire in the world, was internal rather than external. In England in the sixteenth century a new nation was being born within the womb of the old. While Frenchmen, Germans, Spaniards, and Portuguese were still bound within the walls of a feudal economy, Englishmen were breaking down those walls, which were already beginning to crumble like dry clay in their hands. Their eyes were fixed upon the vistas of a new civilization, founded not upon the magnitudes of land but upon the mischievous intricacies and extensities of commerce. Like the Venetians, the English were learning that the rewards of commerce were greater and more lasting than those of piracy.

Contrary to their later history, the English were slow to develop the colonial compulsion. Before Elizabeth's death they organized numerous trading companies: the English Levant Company, the Muscovy Company, the East India Company, which later was to prove the greatest and the most profitable of all, but they did little to convert this commercial activity into colonial enterprise.

What made England different from the Continent, and what also had a great deal to do with the fact that America became different from Europe, was that in France, Germany, Spain, Portugal, commercial enterprises were subsidized in the main by kings and nobles, whereas in England they were backed chiefly by the upward-struggling middle class. On the Continent, in the countries above noted, the middle class was either still in the embryo, unborn as a dominant economic force, or decadent as such; however active it was in the pursuit of its interests, it was hampered and harassed by the power and influence of the aristocracy. In England, on the contrary, the aristocracy lost that power in the middle of the seventeenth century. English merchants proved too canny, too enterprising, too audacious, to allow the aristocracy to block their progress. They were concerned with the fresh possibilities which were opening up on the commercial horizons of many seas, and they gathered together the moneys they made and invested them in ships, goods, and whatnot, all in a hungry endeavor to multiply their means beyond the ordinary limits established by domestic enterprise.

While the aristocracy in the main was content to hug its land and preserve its properties intact within their enclosed geographies—there were, of course, exceptions among the more adventurous aristocrats: Gilbert, Raleigh, Warwick, Sandys, etc.—the middle class went out in search of different possessions, different properties, which had to be won by new techniques and new tactics. Vessels flaunting flags, pennants, and piratical insignia, carrying wares across seas which few Englishmen ever saw or ever hoped to see, became the new forms of property, which were to create new worlds and make over the English and European world in the image of this new middle class.

Barter, by which people had lived for centuries, was insufficient for men and women who no longer lived by domestic economies. Money, that translatable metal which all peoples, humble men on the obscure shores of the Levant and haughty aristocrats in the unnavigable inlets of the Muscovy empire, had come to respect and revere, became the new token of contact and communication. Long before, the Venetians had learned the utility of money and had come to value what we today call "cash transactions," but it was not until a later date, the arrival of which was considerably accelerated by the British, that money became an internationally accepted medium of exchange.

This change from a barter to a money economy was necessary for the success of this new social class, which could not have survived within the limitations of a static economy. The elasticities of monetary exchange made possible those financial adventures which were prerequisite to commercial expansion on an international scale. As money accumulated in the hands of the growing middle class, that class's power increased. Soon its dominance was felt throughout the nation.

By the time the seventeenth century rolled around, the middle class had begun to forge out an entirely new way of life. Out of its economic conflicts with the aristocracy developed those religious, moral, and intellectual conflicts the resolution of which formed the basis of modern civilization. Englishmen in the middle and lower ranks of society had developed an outlook by which they had come to live, and which they transported with them, along with their baggage, their wives, and their children, to the new world to which they emigrated.

### WHY ENGLAND BECAME THE GREAT COLONIZER

This outlook upon life which the middle class, or what today is better known as the bourgeois class, foisted upon the world, made England the greatest colonizing nation of Europe. The Venetian middle class, like the Hanseatic German middle class, had arisen long before the English, and through the years had become far wealthier. Venice was known as the Golden City, and ornament of attire and familial display had to be restricted by the authorities in order to save the city from that premature decay which spells the death of urban opulence and splendor. But Venice never learned the art of colonization; with all her commercial skill, she preferred profits to possessions. England learned the opposite, which was the key to her dominance—that possessions were better than profits, because in the end they paid the biggest profits of all.

While other countries had planted colonies long before England, it was England that planted the longest-lived colonies, which in time were to constitute part of the most powerful empire in the modern world. A little island smaller in size than most of the American colonies, and hardly larger than Portugal, was to send its sons across the earth's surface, scattering them in islands, peninsulas, and continents, in arctic zones as well as equatorial, exterminating red-skinned peoples on the far-flung coasts of America, subjugating brown-skinned peoples in the treacherous interiors of Asia, and driving dusky-skinned Bushmen into the arid lowlands of Australia.

This history reads like fiction—this story of how a small nation conquered so vast a part of a large world.

The fact that England was separate from the Continent and could not be attacked except by water saved the English people from the necessity of keeping a large standing army, and made it possible for them to throw their main strength upon the sea. This fact, too, leading as it did to the encouragement of commerce, helped hasten the development of the English middle class and endow it with powers and privileges greater than those possessed by Continental middle classes of the time.

That superiority, manifesting itself in its whole way of life, religious, moral, and political, gave England the great advantage over her Continental rivals and paved the way for her unequaled success as a colonizing nation. In England it was not a decadent aristocracy which became interested in colonization, but a rising, energetic middle class, which became so strong in the seventeenth century that it was able to challenge the power of royalty, and when that challenge was defied, to execute the king. The decapitation of Charles I in 1649 marked the turning point in the struggle between the English aristocracy and the bourgeoisie; from that time on England became the most modern nation in the world, which meant, in terms of the times, the most middle-class nation in the world.

### EMANCIPATION FROM FEUDALISM

While France remained predominantly feudal up to the time of the French Revolution, and Germany for generations after, England disencumbered itself rapidly of its feudal appendages in church and state, in thought and action, and soon became the haven of progressivism in all its most multifarious and exciting forms. That progressivism was not confined to any one field, but was extended to all fields; it permeated the whole social structure, from its economic roots to its intellectual conceptions.

Among the Germans during the days of the Hanseatic League, and among the Italians when Venice and Florence were at the acme of their power, the middle class achieved phenomenal success. Individualism grew among the merchants who prospered, and the art of the time changed from heroic, social forms to intimate, familial, individual ones. But Venice never developed the middle-class individualist philosophy of England in the seventeenth and eighteenth centuries. Too much of the Middle Ages, too much of the dark spirit of feudalism, hung over the life of Venice to make it possible for its inhabitants to free themselves from the influence of the past. Venice might murder enemies for fortune, sell its religion for gain, dispatch its commercial emissaries across sea and ocean to expand its enterprise, but it never learned to send out its own people to colonize the places it conquered. Its individualism was centripetal, not centrifugal. It was pampered within but not distributed without.

The nature of English middle-class philosophy was different. It was not only developed but also disseminated. It became not an urban, not a national, but an international reality.

### ENGLAND: THE INTELLECTUAL MECCA

That philosophy, born of the exigencies of the new economic era, made Voltaire declare, in the eighteenth century, that England was the most advanced country in the world, and made intellectuals all over the European continent view England as the intellectual and spiritual Mecca of the time. It was this individualist philosophy that was carried from England to the United States and gave form to the American conception of life. American conditions gave a new turn to that conception, endowed it with new emphases, new tangents, new peripheries, and infused it with fresh vigor and force. But the conception itself was born in England, not in America, and it is to England that we must turn to trace its early evolution.

Although the conception itself sprang out of the social changes resulting from the decay of feudal economics and the rise of capitalism, its first dynamic cultural expression was to be found not in economics but in religion, in which, in those times, all the major beliefs of society were housed. In the early religious revolts of the Lollards and later of the Diggers, the Levellers, the Ranters, the Independents, the Separatists, and finally the Puritans, that individualist philosophy was groping for birth, struggling to sever its umbilical cord and to find a language of its own by which it could voice its inarticulate strivings and aspirations. In time that language came, and with it came a new religious life, which in those days meant a new way of life.

That difference in way of life manifested itself in the minds of men as well as in their occupations. Not only were men able to find livelihoods from sources other than the land; they became able, as villages grew into towns and towns into cities, and as opportunities for craftsmen, shopkeepers, and merchants increased, to think of themselves as individuals instead of appendages of a manor, pawns of a manufacturer, or servants of a master.

### THE GROWTH OF INDIVIDUALITY

As new economic opportunities made it more and more possible for individuals to depend upon themselves instead of upon the aristocracy for their livelihoods, they began to think of themselves as entities in their own right, autonomous beings, each housing within himself a definite and indivisible part of the mystery of creation. The more they came to believe in themselves, the more they came to believe that each one of them was different from everyone else, each one responsible within himself for what he was or wasn't. This sense of individual responsibility, growing like a new tissue within the texture of their personalities, changed them in time into new beings, charging them with desires and drives, appetencies and aspirations, which revolutionized their behavior. The world outside was changing, but not changing as rapidly as they were changing *inside*—inside themselves, psychically.

The modern age of which these Englishmen were the precursors was unconfined by race, nation, or continent. In time it was to conquer continents.

It was of such stuff that these Englishmen who first settled the coast land of America were made. They were different from the swarthy-skinned Spaniards with their irresponsible adventurism, their swashbuckling pretense and bravado, who long before had settled in the more obviously habitable sections of the new hemisphere. They were different also, as time was to show, from the brunette Frenchmen, who with their mental as well as metal crucifixes were to root themselves in the more northern sections of the continent. They were different not because of blood—French blood in its Norman ebullience had mixed promiscuously since 1066 with Anglo-Saxon blood, and Spanish blood had spread itself over half of Europe—but because of culture.

### SPREAD OF THE MERCHANT'S PSYCHOLOGY

Earlier than any other power, because of its insular isolation, England, like Syracuse many centuries before, encouraged the merchant's psychology and developed a populace quickened to the challenges of a merchant's way of life. Petty, obscure shopkeepers in the remote sections of the country; frugal, hard-struggling manufacturers of domestic materials; masters, journeymen, and apprentices, broken now from their medieval routine, striving for a personal market, built their entire lives about their wares, materials, and techniques. They no longer depended upon society for their survival, but upon themselves and their personal, individual possessions. Possessions *became* the man. In earlier centuries only the few, the aristocracy, had possessions. But now possession became the inspiration of the age, and out of it sprang the class of small possessors, the middle class, who in the future as plutocrats were to supplant the aristocrats of the past. To possess became the challenge of the hour. Men went to America to possess—or to possess more.

It was this revolution in social relations which effected the great revolution in human psychology out of which the modern world was born. It was in the English womb that this psychology first stirred, and it was from English loins that modernity first sprang, full-born, vital to the fingertips.

More than a century before in Italy, and a little later in France, at the time of the Renaissance, modernity had made its presence felt. But it was a modernity confined largely to the intelligentsia; the masses knew little of it. It was the modernity of science, of Copernicus, Galileo, Torricelli, Bruno, and the modernity of invention in the form of gunpowder, the compass, the printing press, which gave life to the Italian Renaissance.

Two centuries earlier a more important Renaissance had occurred in Spain, where the fertilizing concepts of the Moors, reaching their apex in the mathematical and philosophical genius of Averroës and Avicenna, had given birth to the scientific methodology which was to prevail in the modern world.[3]

But both of these Renaissances were conceptual rather than cultural. Only much later, after cultural changes of a progressive variety, did these concepts become rooted in *the minds of men.*

It was in England that those cultural changes first occurred, just as in England at the beginning of the Industrial Revolution the scientific concepts originated in Spain and Italy were first put into practice. In other words, England was the first country able to take advantage of these modern concepts, because it was the first country to rid itself of the decaying vestiges of feudalism. On the Continent lonely intellectuals, strange scions of Cagliostro, weird-eyed chemists, devotees still of the tradition of Paracelsus, struggled in their sunless attics and improvised laboratories to convert lead into gold and to discover the elixir of life. In England men were busy with more immediate matters. English intellectuals and scientists became less concerned with mystic essences than with practical substances, and this more pragmatic approach made them the founders of modern industrial civilization.

While the majority of Europeans continued to live mentally under the flag of feudalism, accepting as inevitable their economic and social status in the hierarchical structure, Englishmen began to erect the scaffolding of a new structure of their own creation. It was this new structure, preparing the way as it did for the industrial structure of the modern age, which converted modernity from a concept into a way of life.

## III

### THE BIBLE AS THE TOUCHSTONE

It was about the Bible that the struggle between the old and the new was to revolve. Feudalism had stood for solidity of religious concept; the new age stood for the opposite. In the Middle Ages unity of outlook prevailed; in the new age diversity supplanted it. In the former period there was one Church; in the latter there were many churches.

Behind and beneath this change, charging it constantly with new voltage, was the economic challenge of the new way of life. Hard-working English cobblers, shopowners in their own right, simple weavers, struggling night and day in little establishments of their own, and energetic tradesmen of all varieties, came to believe in themselves as they saw their economic independence grow, and to believe in their right to worship as they pleased in accordance with their own individual consciences and compulsions. As England became more and more successful as a commercial nation, this class of small tradesmen multiplied in both numbers and influence. Their insistence upon their own rights, in religious as well as economic matters, both of which in those days were inextricably allied, inspired the first significant religious revolt against the dominance of Roman Catholicism. Long before Huss, Huter, Luther, Muenzer, Labadie, Calvin, and Zwingli, these humble English tradesfolk, disciples mainly of Wyclif and known familiarly throughout the nation as "Lollard heretics," had inaugurated a movement which was to change the face of the Western world.

Those people believed in the right to read the Bible themselves and interpret it according to their own lights, regardless of the opinions of church, clergy, or king. They resented the authoritarian dominance of the Roman Catholic Church and later of the state Church of England, both of which in those days endowed the priesthood with that right but denied it to the laity. The Lollards believed in neither church nor priests; where they met did not matter. After a while the places in which they met began to be designated as "meetinghouses," "chapels," and sometimes as "tabernacles." But the names were unimportant. All that was important was what went on in their minds and hearts and souls.

### WYCLIF'S CONTRIBUTION

John Wyclif, of sturdy Saxon stock, whose iconoclastic concepts had in 1377 stirred Gregory XI to denounce him in a papal bull, and whose translation of the Bible into English had rendered Christian doctrine readable to the English populace, was the center and crux of this revolt.* Wyclif's attack on the Eucharist and the challenge he flung at the papal bureaucracy—the challenge was dramatized in St. Paul's Cathedral, where, defended by the armed cohorts of John of Gaunt, he defied the archbishop and succeeded in quashing the trial—were but the uncertain and undefined beginnings of what was soon to prove the first and most fundamental revolt in the religious sphere. Luther and Calvin were to appeal to the more latitudinarian princes and more successful merchants for their backing. Wyclif, by necessity more than by choice—for he was a landowner and not a plebeian—was to turn to the lower classes for his support. His translation of the Bible into the vulgate, the language of the people, so that all who could spell could read, was almost as revolutionary in its day as Prometheus' discovery of fire had been in the antediluvian world.

Wyclif brought to these humble people, manual workers as well as ambitious tradesmen, something as inspiring as knowledge in its most pristine, its most fundamental, form. He brought them the book which they had believed in for centuries, but which none of them had ever read. He brought them "the thing in itself," and they seized upon it with all the avidity of neophytes who suddenly

* It is very possible that Wyclif's disciples may have translated, or helped him translate, the Old Testament.

believe they have discovered the *sine qua non* of existence. It all seemed so simple. Heretofore only the hierophants had possessed that knowledge. They had kept it packed in close-written pages, sheltered it within the mysterious syllables of a foreign language, and dispersed it amid the parade and pomp of ecclesiastical theatricality, as if it were some magic thing over which they and no one else had control.

By making the Bible a book for all men, Wyclif robbed that magic of its charm and disabused the populace of its belief in the superiority of the clergy over the laity.

Illiterate people were inspired to become literate just to be able to read God's word, which had now been translated into their tongue. Smutty-faced blacksmiths who found it easier to swing a hammer than sign their names, wandering tinkers who understood the language of the birds better than the speech of the aristocracy, keen-eyed shopkeepers who could count only with their fingers, began to study the alphabet as children do today, letter by letter, in order to read for themselves what God had written. The Bible became their guide and salvation. Like Bunyan, they read into it all the rich, unsubdued imagery of their simple, untutored souls. They found in it what poets find in nature when it pushes its way to the surface in spring, rich with all the colors of creation. They discovered in it the spiritual wherewithal of existence. Having found it, their search was finished. They had found God.

### GOD AND THE INDIVIDUAL

And God for them was what substance is to the philosopher, matter to the chemist, and motion to the physicist. It was the ultimate, the lowest common denominator, of things living and things dead. They no longer needed priests or preachers to tell them what God was, or a meeting place in which God was to be discovered.

They needed only themselves now—nothing more. The psalms and the hymns they sang were not the Gregorian chants, mellowed with historicity, which had enclosed religion in a seductive mask of sound, but the simple words of simple men, who despised organs, robes, incense, and sang from their hearts humbly, wholeheartedly, ecstatically, forgetful of all else but themselves and their personal alliance with God. They were like a newborn race. The past meant nothing to them; tradition was without significance in their eyes; ritual, however exquisite and compelling, was abhorrent and taboo. They wanted no past, no tradition, no ritual. They wanted only what they knew, what they could create themselves, out of themselves, out of the spiritual candor of their own souls. They wanted nothing that had been created before by anyone. All they needed was the Bible, which was created out of time and space, and which had been misused and misinterpreted by the Catholics through the centuries.

The Quakers, who later were to develop out of this same tradition, carried this tendency to its ultimate limit in refusing to have any preachers whatsoever. Everyone in the Quaker congregation became a preacher! In each man the spirit of the Lord dwelt, and in each, as inspiration struck him, divine wisdom was given different and fresh birth.

Behind all this, to be sure, as in all historical developments, were forces determining the new mind-set and cultural compulsive of the era. It was not only the middle class, with its new psychology evolving out of its new economics, that conditioned the change, but also the political fact represented by the presence of the Normans. The Normans had come to England in 1066, conquered the island and made it over, as far as they could, in the Norman image. Their conquest had been politically but not culturally complete. The English ruling class had been conquered, but not the English commoners. Harold had been destroyed, but not the things Harold had stood for and not the people who had lived under him.

### TWO WORLDS IN ONE

After the Norman Conquest, the English were divided into two cultural worlds: the world of the Norman aristocrats, who brought with them the Gallic traditions of their ancestors, and the world of English commoners, who carried on the simple traditions of their forebears. English nobles began to imitate the habits and manners of the French conquerors, but the English common people, prosperous as well as impoverished, held themselves apart and stubbornly refused to adopt the French way of life. The result was, in the crucible of the centuries, that the Normans were amalgamated into the English pattern instead of the English into the Norman.

Before that amalgamation took place, however, England was split wide open with cultural strife, the nature of which in time was to have a great deal to do with the early history of the American colonies. The English populace not only did not allow itself to be assimilated, physically or culturally, by the French invaders; but, what was of even greater significance, it developed a hatred for everything associated with them. Undoubtedly that hatred was to a considerable extent a class hatred, at least on the part of the rising middle class, which hated the aristocracy for economic as well as religious reasons. Yet it was also more than that. It was in addition a cultural hatred—what might even be called a national hatred—which assumed a class form.

The group which earliest expressed that hatred was the Lollards, who had the deepest-rooted opposition to the whole Norman aristocratic tradition. Without doubt part of the inevitable hatred of the conquered toward the conquerors was written into the Lollard attitude. But it would be inaccurate to say that such antagonism was sufficient to explain the whole ideological hostility which developed in later years.

What really was at work, underlying national antipathy, were class factors, economic conflicts which resolved themselves in psychological forms. In those days, as I pointed out before, psychology found its focus in religion, which was the political camera of the time. Consequently it was in religion that the Lollards concentrated their revolt against the French conquerors and later against those Englishmen who, in the eyes of the Lollards, took over the French conception of life.

## THE LOLLARD INFLUENCE

It is very doubtful whether the early Lollards knew what they were about in their religious deliberations and lucubrations, but this much they did know: that they hated the religion of the Normans, with their priests and pope, their churches and cathedrals, and were willing to fight them to the death. They not only hated the sight of the Normans with their French countenances and French dress and their French women attired to evoke the worst impulses in men; they hated still more the way the Normans lived, the entertainments they staged, the parties they held, the games they played, the immoralities they condoned, the loose words they spoke. They hated with almost equal intensity the English aristocrats who pursued the same practices on their own manors and imitated, with a servility intolerable to the average Englishman, French gestures and graces.

The Lollard attitude, however, like all attitudes sprang out of the social context which dictated it. Tendencies congeal into attitudes by virtue of the social context which gives them psychological form. The Lollards in the main were poor, lower-class folk who had to resort to all the extremes of care and caution, of painfully circumspect living, of canny frugality and uncanny thriftiness, in order to eke out a livelihood in the difficult economic environment of their time. Their lives centered around the home, about which everything of importance revolved. In the home the mother as well as the father worked, as also did the children as soon as they were able to contribute their mite, all in a concentrated and consecrated endeavor to "keep the wolf from the door" and, at the same time, to "save for a rainy day." Their life was hard, impecunious, exigent, and they were inured to all that it meant; they were willing to endure it so long as they knew that they would be rewarded for their sacrifice.

### WORK AS A MANIA

But, living as they did, they naturally came to hate and despise those who lived without such sacrifice and fortitude. They came to hate the aristocrats because the latter lived upon the fat of the land without having to work it, and they despised the "groundlings" because they lived upon the aristocrats and liked it. They despised, too, all those who, like the mummers, ballad singers, fiddlers, wandering handymen, and rootless craftsmen, were not occupied with steady work. In short, these simple, homespun, middle-class folk lived to work, and they scorned anybody and everybody who merely worked to live. Even more, if that were possible, they scorned the aristocrats who never worked at all. Work, for these hard-struggling people, became a sacred thing, a mission in itself. They endowed it with a halo, exalted it into an ideal. Work became the means by which they disciplined themselves, tested their character, proved their mettle. Work in their eyes was hallowed by God; idleness was the invention of the devil. Righteousness with them was more than an ethical concept; it was an economic concept also. No man could be righteous who did not work; no man could be good who spent his time in useless endeavors.

And they worked hard and long, but not without reward. They believed in working for themselves, but they considered themselves even in those pre-Calvinist days, God's ambassadors. "Work and pray" was their motto, and later when that motto was woven into a hymn, the people stood up and sang it—sang it with all the unconstrained and undisciplined ardor of their souls. The words they sang, or more often shouted, were not just words—which is all they have become in modern Protestant churches—but part of the spiritual flesh and blood of their lives. They not only believed them; they lived them.

And they lived them, without realizing it, because those words served them well. They were necessary to the new form of life which was hatching in the villages, towns, and cities of England at the time, where work had assumed a different cast. In earlier days, when feudal economy was still intact and dominated the life of the island, work was scorned rather than esteemed. Work then benefited no one but the landowners: the lords, the barons, the king. It was only now that feudalism was breaking down, and new ways of living were growing up, that work became worth-while for the lower classes. Work now meant something valuable to those who worked. It became a form of protection, a guarantee of independence, to the individual. It was no longer a burden but a joy, and proverbs and apothegms, mottoes, and prayers, invented with egregious prodigality, endowed it with sacred significance. To work was to be good; not to work was to be evil—for work now was a holy function. It was God's way of testing men, testing their devotion, their allegiance to a Christian way of life. To those who worked all things would come; to those who did not work nothing would come, nothing could come.

In time this devotion to work became a mania. Year after year those who worked discovered that their work counted. They found that the harder they worked, the more secure, the more independent, the more powerful they became. Work made it possible for them to stand on their own feet instead of on those of their superiors.

They could stand alone now, purchase their own food, pay their own rents, eke out their own living. They needed no support from others, aristocrats or priests. They could support themselves, economically as well as spiritually.

And so it was with these humble folk who discovered in the new world beckoning to them outside the windows of their houses, and ofttimes within their own houses, something they had never known before but now would never surrender, something which gave to life a meaning which it had never possessed in the past, and which they were determined to cling to at all cost and at no matter what sacrifice. They were determined to be themselves, to stand by themselves, and to brook no interference from those higher up or those lower down in the social scale.

As the years passed, and this protestant movement acquired momentum, its followers became the hunted men of the era. They would meet in out-of-the-way barns, unfrequented cellars, woodland hideouts—any place where they could worship as they pleased, unmolested by the minions of clergy or state. John Ball, the English Thomas Münzer, whose voice roared across the countryside like that of the lion of Judah, was executed; but the movement went on. Nothing could stop it.

In time it assumed nation-wide proportions, and what for many years had been known as the "Lollard heresy" became the credo of the populace. Lollardism lost its heretical aspects when its doctrines became absorbed by the larger part of the nation. During the reign of Henry VIII, the Lollard opposition to ecclesiastical property found realization in the English Reformation, when the king disendowed the clergy of its landed possessions and made these part of the civil state.

Inspired by Wyclif, who had advocated the confiscation of the wealth of the clergy [4]—confiscation for the aristocracy, it is true, rather than for the commonwealth—the Lollards had long fought against the clerical bureaucracy and its predatory propensities. They loathed the bishops who lived luxuriously on the combined contributions of their impoverished parishioners, and who refused unless compensated to bestir their unprepossessing and unwieldy bodies to bury, to marry, or to baptize those parishioners. Class hostility was written into the Lollards' condemnation of a clergy which would do the bidding of the rich, in heaven as well as upon the earth, because they could pay for it, but would not do that for the poor because they could not pay for it.

## HENRY VIII'S REFORMATION

By the time Henry VIII took up the challenge, the clergy had succeeded in absorbing one-half of the substance of the realm.[5] Simon Fish's anticlerical booklet, *The Very Beggars' Supplication Against Popery,* exercised the effect it did because the ground of revolt against popery had been prepared by these humble people, these honest, hard-working Lollards, who for centuries had denounced the clergy for the very vices which Fish used as a springboard for his violent and venomous attack upon the Church.

Henry's Reformation, better known as the English Reformation, was achieved with such unprecedented and unexpected expedition because the country was behind him at the time. The middle classes were hostile to the power and privilege which the Church had usurped, and the feudal aristocracy was eager to seize the lands of the Church in order to enrich itself without a struggle. The fourth estate was indifferent to whatever occurred.

Henry was the Constantine of his day. Like Constantine in Rome over a thousand years before, Henry took advantage of the "psychological situation." The Lollard groups had prepared the ground for the anti-Church attitude which prevailed throughout most of England, just as the Christians in Rome had developed an antagonism toward the Roman religion, which had prevailed throughout most of the Empire. The Christians, like the Lollards, had risen from the ranks, and were far more radical in their philosophy than Constantine could tolerate. Constantine's gesture, which has become a familiar one in many countries since that time, was simple and effective. He removed the radicalism from Christianity in 321 A. D. by making the Christian religion the religion of the Roman state. Henry VIII, though he was faced by a different situation, used something of the same technique. Aware of the widespread anti-Church attitude which existed in England at the time, an attitude bred in the main by the Lollard opposition, he took advantage of it by hitching it on to his own program. When he decided upon his anti-papal policy, he knew that he would have most of the country behind him. But, like Constantine, he never meant to give voice to the demands of the people whose revolt he was turning to his own purposes. His aim was to eliminate the Church, seize its lands, and then, like Constantine, forget the rest of the demands of those who had advocated that procedure.

And that was exactly what he did. He achieved his Reformation, denounced the Lutheran Reformation, and declared that his Reformation was waged in the cause of *freedom*. Anglo-Catholicism was the result.

But things did not work out with Henry the way they did with Constantine, who took over the Christian religion lock, stock, and barrel. The English middle class was not fooled so easily as the Roman Christians had been, and before long, pursuing its different economic objectives, the English middle class continued its revolt. The more successful, the Puritans, fought for a purified church, while the less successful—namely the Dissenters, descendants of the Lollards—battled for a new church, a free church, an autochthonous church.

American life and culture can be understood only in terms of that struggle. Out of that struggle, with this birthright, came the Englishmen who were to found, settle, and give significance to a country which they had never seen, and out of which they were to make something which their forefathers had never known—which no one had ever known: an amalgam of contradictions, paradoxes, and impossibles which was to constitute something new on the face of the earth.

# CHAPTER IV

## Puritans and Dissenters

It is to the Puritans and Dissenters, then, that we must turn to understand the kind of people who came to America. For it was the Puritans and Dissenters who constituted the bulk of the middle class of which the *new world* was soon to be compounded. Both were products of the same change in economic and spiritual life that was beginning to sweep over the face of Europe, but which in England had already become part of the psychological texture of British personality.

A familiar error has been to identify the Puritans with the Dissenters. This has done much to distort and confuse prevailing interpretations of American history. The Puritans and the Dissenters came from different groups, different sections of society, and they carried with them the attributes of those differences of social strata and psychological outlook.

The Puritans in the main were members of the upper middle class, of the wealthier commercial groups, and their relations were closer to the aristocracy than to the lower middle class. They hobnobbed with dukes and earls and lords; they lent money to kings; they were involved in the high finance of the nation. Their ideas about economics, ethics, and religion were different from those of the ruling aristocracy, it is true, but they were not so different that association and co-operation were impossible. They ofttimes affected to loathe, but in their hearts envied, the interests and tastes of the aristocracy. They were the *parvenus,* the *arrivists,* of their day, and they combined in their psychological make-up all the traits of that type of personality. The Puritan leaders were successful men; they had saved their money, invested it, and profited by it. They were middle-class in their psychology, but middle-class aristocrats; they were as contemptuous of the Lollards, who represented the humble, unsuccessful, lower middle class, as contemporary plutocrats are of aspiring parvenus. They wanted economic advantages that would assist their transactions; they wanted freedom from political molestation, which crippled and threatened to ruin their enterprises; they wanted that religious freedom which their fathers had taught them and which they had learned from bitter experience was necessary to their way of life.

These freedoms in time became challenges, fetishes, symbols. It was not freedom that the Puritans believed in, but *these* freedoms. They were willing to fight for these freedoms, as in time they did, because without them they could not survive and prosper; but that did not mean that they believed in freedom for others. On the contrary, as their experience in America was soon to reveal, they were opposed to such freedom and were willing to suppress it whenever it menaced their interests. In combatting freedom as a principle they were as inexorable as the aristocrats. The aristocrats sought to squelch the Puritans because the latter believed in freedoms which jeopardized the power of the landed interests; the Puritans, in the Civil War, which culminated with the decapitation of Charles I in 1649, squelched the Dissenter elements because the latter believed in freedom as a principle.

### INDIVIDUALISM AS A PHILOSOPHY

The only thing the Puritans and the Dissenters agreed upon as a principle, a theory, a philosophy, was individualism. They were both opposed to feudal economics, with its state-controlled, centrally restricted, totalitarian organization of society. They both demanded a looser, less monolithic social structure. They both insisted upon the *right of the individual* to deal freely in the open market, without curbs and circumscriptions on the part of the state. They both wanted a state that would not interfere with their economic maneuvers and stratagems. In short, they both believed, however embryonically and inarticulately, in the *laissez-faire* philosophy which was not to achieve definite and declarative formulation until 1776 in Adam Smith's *Wealth of Nations*.

They were both opposed to the open-field system of production in which all farmers, as a unit, decided on the crops they were going to raise and, before a new product was tried, had to decide, as a unit again, whether they wanted it or not. They considered that procedure a violation of the right of the individual to take advantage of his own privileges and prerogatives. The result was disaster. In thirty years, for instance, less than six patents were granted for inventions and improvements in agricultural implements. The farmer was helpless. Feudalism killed off all incentive toward *individualistic* production. The farmer had no security of tenure upon the land; the individual farmer was a pawn in the hands of the country gentry. The moment that the farmer improved his land or bettered his equipment, the country gentry drove him from the soil and took possession of it in order to reap the reward of the farmer's labor. So pronounced did this tendency become that a rhyming jingle sprang up about it:

> He that havocs may sit,
> He that improves must flit.

What was equally discouraging was the fact that the farmer did not have an incentive to produce even if the country gentry did not drive him from his soil. There were not enough markets in which he could dispose of his surplus.

The Dissenter groups, which sprang from the soil as well as from the lower middle class, felt this limitation more severely than the Puritans, whose followers among the agrarians were relatively negligible. The earnings of the English farmer in the seventeenth century, according to the Gregory King and Davenant reports, were four shillings a week, without food; and from September to March, the dull season, they were reduced to three shillings sixpence. This wage was fixed by the justices of quarter sessions and was as rigid as a legal mandate.

The Puritans, to be sure, were not nearly so concerned about agricultural difficulties as they were about commercial ones. The Dissenters were concerned about both, because it was from both that their followers were derived. The Puritans, however, were more concerned about the wages of mechanics, from whom a considerable proportion of their profit had to be obtained. The average pay of the mechanic in the manufacturing industries was one shilling a day, often less. The mechanics were not united, and they had no paper or periodical, and no politician, to defend their cause. Their protest and hatred of their lot were congealed in rhymes and ballads. The following is illustrative of the sentiment which prevailed among them:

> We will make them work for sixpence a day
> Though a shilling they deserve if they had their just pay;
> If at all they murmur and say 'tis too small,
> We bid them choose whether they'll work at all,
> And thus do we gain all our wealth and estate,
> By many poor men that work early and late;
> Then hey! for the clothing trade. It goes on brave,
> We scorn for to toyl and moyl, nor yet to slave.
> Our workmen work hard, but we live at ease;
> We go when we will and come when we please.

The absence of unions, however, and the lack of any sense of solidarity on the part of toilers, made the industrial aspect of the economic problem simple for employers.

It was the political side that was more exigent. What threatened the middle classes at that time was not so much the protests of the workers as the constrictions and circumscriptions of the state. The state, a landed body of aristocratic origin, was opposed to the newfangled concepts and practices of the new groups, middle-class in outlook and tendency, which challenged its supremacy. Those groups challenged the feudal state not in one field but in all. Consequently they had to be opposed, fought, and suppressed.

### STRUGGLE BETWEEN THE MIDDLE CLASS AND THE ARISTOCRACY

It was not religion, but economics, that drove the English feudal state into battle with the middle class. The state limitations on commerce, industry, and finance, with the fixed prices that were incurred, caused the conflict to become violent. The feudal aristocracy cared far less about how the middle class worshiped than about its opposition to the acts of the realm. Its attacks upon the religious practices of the Puritans and Dissenters sprang not so much out of hostility to the concepts at stake, as out of fear of the social chaos that might result from their economic opposition. If the middle class had been content to remain in its place, to obey the commands of the king and contribute a large share of its profits to the kingdom, the aristocracy would have desisted gladly from persecuting it because of its religious deviations and heresies. But the middle class had no other choice but that of opposition. If it had succumbed to royal demands, surrendered to the tyranny of the feudal state, it could not have survived. It would have died, and all that has come out of middle-class insurgency and dominance, the new commercial, industrial, and scientific world, with its miracles of invention and discovery, would have remained little more than the fantastic reveries of amiable-minded philosophers and prophets.

The Puritans led in this struggle because they were the group most immediately affected by the conflict at stake. Being wealthier than the Dissenters, they had interests, enterprises, and investments which were directly subject to imposition by the Crown. The Dissenters, representing the poorer groups, had little more than their souls to protect. The Puritans, on the other hand, were able to utilize moneys and forces that were beyond the reach of the Dissenters, and in the Civil War that resulted, they were able to fit out an army, purchase supplies, and conquer the kingdom. To do so, however, they had to have an army to fight for them, and that army under the circumstances was inevitably made up, in large part, of Dissenters, who constituted the uncompromising and radical contingent of the antigovernment forces.

## DISSENTERS AS RADICALS

When the king was captured, it was the Dissenter elements who demanded his head and the Puritans who fought to save it. If it had not been for the insistence of the radical Dissenter groups, Charles I would never have been executed, and there would never have been a Cromwellian Commonwealth. The Puritans were not hostile to the king on principle; they were not even hostile to the Established Church on principle; they were willing enough to abide the king provided he would disembarrass and disenslave them from the burdens of taxation which the realm had imposed, and they were willing enough to tolerate the Established Church provided it was *purified* of its papal remnants and vestiges. It was the Dissenter groups who would abide no such compromise and whose demands had to be met if a Puritan triumph was to endure. It was to placate those elements that the Puritans finally agreed to behead the king, and it was also to satisfy those groups that the Puritans finally hazarded the Commonwealth. The Puritans, it must not be forgotten, had everything to lose if the Commonwealth failed; the Dissenters had nothing to lose but their skins, and since they believed more firmly and fanatically than the Puritans in the joys of immortality, their skins concerned them less than their souls.

The Puritans, as has been indicated, were far closer to the aristocratic class in their leanings and predilections than to the Dissenters, but in the battle that broke out in the 1640's they had to ally themselves with the Dissenters in order to triumph. But it should not be thought that the Puritans had allies only among the lower middle-class groups. They were too close to the aristocracy not to have allies there also. Many aristocrats, recognizing the sign on the door, joined up with the Puritan forces, just as many Roman senators, everlastingly quick to take advantage of expediency, joined up with the Christians before Constantine made Christianity into the state religion. Needless to say, no English aristocrats allied themselves with the Dissenters. The Dissenters were radicals, visionary *sansculottes*, who demanded, with a violence indubitably Biblical, a new way of life, a new religion, a new economics, and who were willing to storm the gates of every city, town, and hamlet in order to achieve them.

### PURITANS AS COMPROMISERS

The Puritans shared no such feeling, knew no such intensities. They felt no such need for them. They knew what they wanted and saw no reason to become so excited and melodramatic in their gestures and convictions. They believed the Established Church could be *purified;* they believed the kingdom could be transformed by curbing the power of the king; they believed a new England could be created if only enough Englishmen would assist them in their struggle for it. In short, they were the evolutionary radicals of their day (the Social Democrats of the nineteenth and twentieth centuries), and were forced into a revolutionary struggle because the king would not have it otherwise. The Dissenters wanted the *revolution;* the Puritans did not. The king made the *revolution* inevitable.

When the Civil War flared up, the Puritans led it, and the Dissenters, constituting the rank and file, fought it. Among the Puritans at that time were not only the wealthy middle-class elements but also members of the aristocracy who believed in the Puritan cause. The Earl of Essex, for instance, was first commander-in-chief of the army of Parliament.[1] Pym, the Puritan leader, rallied over thirty peers to his support.[2] In the meanwhile, many other nobles had shifted their activities from landed to commercial enterprise, and felt themselves more closely allied to the economic propositions of the Puritans than to those of the king and his cohorts.

The Puritans, then, as is abundantly clear, were not just a middle-class group dedicated to the destruction of aristocratic supporters and followers who constituted an important part of their strength. They absorbed by immediate contact and spiritual osmosis a considerable part of the aristocratic attitude toward life. Cromwell, for example, was a great lover of music, and after he became Lord Protector of the Commonwealth he was accustomed to entertain foreign ambassadors with all the more fascinating devices of that art.[3] It was Cromwell also who insisted upon the nation's retaining possession of the cartoons of Raphael and the "Triumph of Caesar" by Montegna, which Charles II later attempted to sell to the King of France.[4] Colonel Hutchinson, another Puritan of conspicuous note, was a patron of art and learning, with an intense zest for living which was remote from the ascetic. A skilled musician himself, he maintained an animated interest in painting and literature as well as music. Like Cromwell, he was fond of hunting and all the various attractions of the sportsman's life.[5] Many other Puritans had similar interests and concerns.

What all this means is that the Puritans were not the ascetic, narrow-minded, spiritually myopic, pleasure-hating fanatics that legend has made of them. Instead they were a reasonably moderate, conciliatory people who believed in certain ideals but were not too prone to fight for them. They did not loathe music, painting, and literature, or any other art. While they were determined to exclude those forms of art from their churches which tended to strengthen Catholic superstition, they were not fanatically bent, by principle, upon destroying art.

Cotton Mather, who was one of the leading American Puritans, advised the reading and writing of poetry, and even worked out his own theory of prose style. Other Puritans displayed similar interests. Many of the Puritans were close enough to the nobility in wealth and intellectual interests not to share those antagonisms and antipathies to things aristocratic which dominated the psychology of the Dissenters.

### ORIGIN OF THE DISSENTER PHILOSOPHY

The Dissenters, on the other hand, represented a different social species. They possessed few of the economic and social advantages of the Puritans. They were, in a word, a poorer tribe, a poorer class. They were not serfs, menials, or groundlings, but they were little shopowners, little tradesmen, little entrepreneurs. *Little* was the word which best described them. The Puritans, on the whole, were *bigger*, more successful, more prosperous. The Dissenters differed from the Puritans because their interests in life differed. The Puritans had wealth to protect, property to preserve. They had reason to compromise with the ruling class; the Dissenters had not. The Puritans owned vessels and were involved in the network of commerce. The Dissenters were involved in nothing except the immediate demands and concerns of their lives. Transoceanic commerce meant nothing to them, for they had no ships and no interest in countries beyond the horizon; they were interested in the everyday things of life, their little shops, their specific jobs, the places they lived in and bought their food from, the meetinghouses and tabernacles they attended, the people they talked to on the highways and byways, the animals they fed and housed. They were a simple people, democratic not from philosophical conviction or political creed but from experience, from association, from necessity. Life itself had taught them the wisdom and value of democracy. They needed no teachers to convince them of what was so obvious, any more than a baby needs a physician to lead it to its mother's breasts. They were *demos*, the English *demos*, and *demos* wants its power respected, defended, and asserted, whether it is in Greece, Rome, or England. The Puritans were not *demos;* they were comfortable citizens, men of moderate station, who were on the "up-and-up," and who were as much opposed to *demos* as the aristocracy, although they were willing enough to use *demos* to fight the aristocracy in order to win power for themselves—and this is precisely what they did in the revolution of the 1640's, which finally ended in their triumph.

The Dissenters were a sect, or rather an aggregation of sects. The Puritans were not a sect, for they believed in clinging to the Established Church, not in separating from it, and for that reason succeeded in preserving a form of religious continuity uncharacteristic of the Dissenting groups.

As sects the Dissenters necessarily fought for independence and freedom. They did not extend that freedom within their own group, but were perfectly willing to allow freedom to those outside their group. In other words, Brownists refused to allow individual Brownists to dissent from the Brownist creed, but they had no objections to Quakers or Anabaptists worshiping freely in accordance with their own creeds. All sects revealed the same tendency: they believed in freedom outside their group but not inside it.

The Puritans, part of the established religion, seeking only to change it, were opposed to freedom for other groups, and when they founded their colony in Massachusetts they immediately denied liberty to all Dissenters. The Pilgrims, on the other hand, who were the first of the Dissenting groups to arrive, granted that liberty, which is now the cornerstone of American psychology.

### THE BASIS OF AMERICAN TRADITION

These Dissenters, not the Puritans, were the founders of the American democratic tradition. They gave reality to what in England had been but a hope, a dream. They transplanted in the new country the tradition which has since become the most significant part of its heritage. Fighting for preservation for themselves, as separate groups and sects, they unconsciously abetted the fight for freedom which has become part of the American tradition, avowed by Franklin D. Roosevelt today as well as by Thomas Jefferson a century earlier.

That fight was not native to America. It began in the old country and was transported to the new along with everything else—tools, possessions, techniques, wives, animals. It had been born in the early Lollard protest and revolt, nurtured through the years by secret societies in dark and oblique places, by multitudes of poor tradesmen, mechanics, wayfarers—all seeking a glimpse of the Lord. What happened in America to the Dissenters, who were the children of the Lollards, is familiar today. They came, they saw, they conquered.

Eventually they made America over in their own image. The Puritans lost; the Dissenters triumphed.

Many have tried to show that it was America itself, its vast trackless wilderness, which made the country the most individualistic in the world, and that the only reason for the flourishing of the sects there was the geographic generosities of the frontier.* It is true that America developed over two hundred religious denominations, more than any other country in the world, but they were products of European conflict rather than American. However much America modified them, they were of European derivation; America gave them new challenge but not new character. Their character had been crystallized centuries ago in the old country.

The independence of the Dissenters, then, was of ancient tradition tempered by a new environment, out of which emerged a new concept of life and a new civilization.

### THE NORMAN INFLUENCE

For centuries the native English, known familiarly in those days as Saxons, fought the Normans. Ever since the Conquest of William the First in 1066, the Normans had dominated and plundered the country. The Normans, who scorned the indigenous population, were

* John M. Mecklin in his most interesting volume *The Story of American Dissent* contends that the frontier was the main developmental force in the history of American religion. Following the Turner thesis, he dismisses Thomas Cuming Hall's conclusions by remarking that the latter's work has "but one reference to the frontier" (p. 9). He fails to see, as Mr. Hall points out with superb clarity and cogency, that it was European religious influences that made the Dissenters so adaptable to the American environment. The frontier unquestionably conditioned and changed those influences, but their origin, it must be emphasized, was European and not American. Mecklin's conclusions are deplorably unconvincing in that regard. If savages or barbarians, by some miraculous mischance, had landed upon American soil, they would never have made of it what the Europeans did who settled here. The English, Dissenters in the main, were embodiments of centuries of culture, and they foisted that culture upon the new land, which they speedily made into their own. In practically all cases, that is a familiar phenomenon. The main thing to bear in mind, however, is that the final amalgam was a product of both European and American environment. The frontier of America conditioned but could not change the essential philosophy of those who settled upon it. Important as the frontier was, it was a conditioned and not an absolute thing. People did not venture into the frontier as savages or aliens, lacking culture and heritage; they ventured as Europeans, equipped with a culture which was part of their marrows. Unusual and individualistic as American religion ultimately proved to be, its singularity was as much European as American. Without the European background it never could have matured. The American environment changed but did not control, determine, or command its development. That development was locked within its intellectual womb and achieved birth through the circumstances of the new environment.

the elite, the aristocratic group, to whom gallantry was a criterion; they lived, however, with such lavishness and prodigality, ate and cooked in such incredible and incalculable styles, so blithely slept with women who were not their legal spouses, and made such a clamor across the land, that the native Englishmen of lower stock viewed them not as superiors, but as heathen, barbarians, philistines, who merited annihilation. The legendary figure of Robin Hood was the British hero: he slew the rich Normans and defended the poor Anglo-Saxons.

Part of this hatred undoubtedly was due to the sheer fact of foreignness: the Normans were French, not English. They spoke a language which the common people didn't, couldn't understand. They lived in ways which the poor Lollards despised. The latter didn't believe in wealth; they had none of their own and believed that all people who had it were wicked. Wealth and wickedness were, in their eyes, synonymous. The Normans danced, dressed gaudily, read books, bought pictures, worshiped idols. The impoverished Lollards, members of a lower economic class, hated such habits.

From the time of Harold's defeat and the bloodshed that followed, the conflict had been one of unabated and unmitigated bitterness. Many Robin Hoods sprang up and perished before the Norman and Saxon elements became reconciled and resolved into a unity.

The Lollards, out of their economic as well as psychological hostility to the ruling class, developed a religion, an ethic, a philosophy of life which centuries later made them desert the land of their birth —the places, the villages, the roads, the shops, the huts they knew— and wander across miles of sea, first to Holland and later to the new world, all because they believed that God had said that it should be so.

God has always served myriad purposes and ends in the history of man, and the role He performed in the lives of the Lollards was in no sense unique. If it had not been for the concept of God, it is doubtful whether men could ever have attempted or achieved the things they have done. By making God responsible for what they do, or don't do, or undo, men have succeeded in saving themselves from being aware of most of the crimes of which they have been guilty. God has been always a convenient shock-absorber for just such purposes, and the race has never been loath to employ him accordingly.

## PILGRIMS AS THE FIRST OF AMERICAN DISSENTERS

There can be no doubt that the Dissenters, scions of the Lollards, and known more familiarly in early American history as Pilgrims, would never have dared to desert their native land for Holland and, not long after, for America had it not been for their belief in God and their conviction that God was with them, part of them, guiding them, defending them. Economic conflict, with its repercussive class differences, was unquestionably at the root of it all. But it was not economic conflict which moved their minds and hearts and souls; economic conflicts seldom do that. It was an idea, or a multiplex of ideas, derivative from the economic conflict at stake, which stirred and aroused and inspired them to action—the strangest, most fantastic, and most venturesome action of their lives. In retrospect, historians can account for such phenomena as the product of economic change, and state that the men who hazarded the wilds of an uncertain and perilous sea were doing so because of the ineluctable pressures of the economic environment, but the fact still remains that in their minds most of these Englishmen were doing it because of an idea, a religious idea, an *idée fixe,* which electrified their lives.

## CONFLICT OF IDEAS AND FORCES

If one is interested only in the conflict of economic systems, the decay of feudal economics and the rise of commercial and industrial capitalism, the idea—be it religious or otherwise—becomes secondary in the causative process. If one is interested in people, however, and after all it is people who make history, one must be concerned with the ideas, wherever or however derived, that make them what they are. Economic systems may condition ideas, but it is ideas that condition people, and to understand people one must understand not only what is happening to their civilization but also what is happening to them.

In recent years history has been concerned mainly with what happens outside, not inside, men. Neither can be understood without the other. It is just as fallacious to substitute things, systems, forces for feelings, emotions, and convictions as it is to do the opposite. Both react to and interact with the others, and to understand the people of any epoch it is necessary to appreciate the psychological as well as the sociological motivations that determine their conduct.

The current notion, for instance, that the Englishmen who settled America in the early seventeenth century did so for economic and not religious reasons is typical of that fallacy. There can be no doubt that the vast majority of Englishmen who came to these shores were men of relatively unexalted economic station, and that they entertained hopes of living better in the new world than in the old. But the real reason they came was more psychological than economic, more religious than materialistic. It was their economic status in the old country, to be sure, which determined in large part the nature of the religion they adopted, but they adopted it not because they believed it was economically advantageous, or had any relationship to their economic status, but because they believed it was right. It is only in more recent times that we have been able to recognize the relationship between economic status and religious affiliation. In the minds of those hardy Englishmen of the seventeenth century the suggestion that they had become Dissenters because they were poor would have constituted a grievous and uncondonable insult. They were men of high integrity, men who believed that being right was more important than being rich.

Being right has always been, all too ironically, the monopoly of the poor. Their prophets in every country have taught them that righteousness is the highest virtue, that honesty is the best policy and purity the noblest ideal. The rich have always succeeded in making might into right, and consequently have achieved their ends by the greatest economy of effort. In other words, the poor have provided the ideals and the rich have thrived upon them.

The Dissenters who first came to America not only believed in a religion of uncompromising idealism but wanted to live by it, and it was they who first tried to establish on this soil a true democracy of body and spirit.

## CHAPTER V

# The True Natives

*The wild Indians became troublesome at a very early period . . . [and] it was found convenient to take possession of their country without recompense, rob them of their wives and children, kill them in every cowardly and barbarous manner that could be devised, and when that was impracticable, drive them as far as possible out of the way. Such treatment was not consistent with their rude ideas of justice, wholly unacquainted with our enlightened institutions. They could not understand why they should be murdered, robbed, and hunted down in this way, without any other pretense or provocation than the color of their skin, and the habits of life to which they had always been accustomed. . . . The idea, strange as it may appear, never occurred to them that they were suffering for the great cause of civilization, which in the natural course of things must exterminate the Indians.*

—J. ROSS BROWNE (*Harper's Magazine*, August 1861)

*Why not Christianize and civilize the white man?*

—WALTER COLBERT, Chickasaw Indian

THE people whom the European foreigners met when they landed upon this soil became known as Indians. The so-called Indians, however, never thought of themselves as Indians and resented the appellation. The real Indians, who lived in India, would never have recognized the American aborigines upon whom was foisted their name.

The Indians whom the Spanish colonists met in Mexico and in Central and South America were immeasurably superior in cultural achievement to those the English found in North America. The Indians in the North had built no pyramids, developed no subtlety of language, invented no calendar, cultivated no science of the skies or the earth. They were a simple people with simple mores, who had learned to live in simple ways, unambitious of power and uninspiring of mind. They were in the main a naïve, trustful folk who wanted to live their lives as they had in the past, and who were moved by few of the impulses which are the prods of progress. They had found the American environment adequate for their needs and, in their plain way, had built a primitive civilization which in some respects was more progressive than that of most of the white men who invaded their shores.

### INDEPENDENCE AND AUTHORITY OF INDIAN WOMEN

On the whole, their communities were more democratic in economic and political organization than those of the Europeans. Their women possessed a higher and more independent status than the women of England, France, or Spain. In a number of tribes the squaws had more power than the men and practically governed the community. Among the Iroquois and other tribes the women chose the chiefs. Although they walked behind their husbands, it was not because of a sense of inferiority, as has usually been concluded, but because the husbands were supposed to clear the ground for them, see that the earth was good, and fight off any enemies that might be ambushed in the territory. "Marriage among my people," declared an Indian, "was like traveling in a canoe. The man sat in front and paddled the canoe. The woman sat in the stern, *but she steered*" [italics mine].[1] "For mankind they say a woman was made first," declared Thomas Hariot, condensing a custom into a sentence.[2]

Among the Iroquois, property inhered in the name of the squaws as definitely and inclusively as it did in the names of primitive women in all matriarchal societies. While the women shared with men the labors of society, toiling often from sunup to sundown, they never surrendered their economic or political rights and never accepted a position of inferiority or servitude. In marriage the Iroquois squaw was far more free than the women in nineteenth-century England. She had a perfect right to her own freedom, and could leave her husband at her own desire and pleasure. She was subject to no masculine coercion. The address with which the American authorities were greeted when they signed their alliance with the Iroquois was typical of the feminine dominance prevalent within the Indian group: "Brothers! Our ancestors considered it a great offense to reject the counsels of their women, particularly of the Female Governesses. They were esteemed the mistresses of the soil. Who, said our forefathers, brings us into being? Who cultivates our lands, kindles our fires, and boils our pots, but the women? Our women, Brother, say that they are apprehensive their uncles have lost the power of hunting, but take this opportunity of thanking you for preventing the fall down the precipice to which their uncles have brought them. They entreat that the veneration of our ancestors in favor of the women be not disregarded, and that they may not be despised: the Great Spirit made them. The Female Governesses beg leave to speak with the freedom allowed to women and agreeable to the spirit of our ancestors. They entreat the Great Chief to put forth his strength and to preserve them in peace. For they are the life of the nation." [3] *

In marriage the Iroquois husband acquired marriage rights over his wife only by her own consent, on the advice and consent of the elder women of her own ohwachira." [5] An even more striking evidence of the matriarchal character of the Iroquois tribe is that a woman's life "was regarded as of double value to that of a man." [6] When a man was killed by another man, the punishment was 20 strings of wampum, 10 strings for the dead person and 10 strings for the life of the killer. But when a woman was killed by a man, "the legal tender was fixed as 30 strings of wampum, 20 for the woman's life and 10 for the killer." In the event that a woman killed another woman, the penalty was 40 strings of wampum. All Iroquois culture was dominated by this feminine or matriarchal influence. "The creation of our kind," one of the Iroquois rituals declares, "has indeed endowed the person of our mother [symbol for woman] with high honor and also with the full measure of mind and reason. Give heed, therefore, to her words of admonition and advice."

The highest official in the Iroquois community was the woman trustee chief.[7] † She maintained such authority by virtue of the fact that "the country, the land, the fields with their harvest and fruits,

* Margaret Mead and others, it is true, have stressed the inferior role that women have played in aboriginal American culture, but their vision has lacked the sociological acuteness and philosophical comprehensiveness of other authorities.[4]

† "The principal function of the maternal family," Dr. Goldenweiser writes, "was in connection with the election and succession of chiefs." When a chief died, he notes, "the matron of the maternal family to which the chief had belonged, determined his successor . . . in all cases a member of the same maternal family. . . ." The matron thereafter continued to survey and supervise the behavior of the chief. "It will thus be seen," Dr. Goldenweiser further observes, "of what transcendent importance the women were in the Iroquois body politic. Although the office of hereditary chief was denied them, this office was largely in their control." [8] In several cases women were actually made honorary chiefs of the tribe.

belonged to her." The order of succession was found in her blood;[9] her children belonged to her. She never hesitated, as Rev. A. Wright observed, "to 'knock off the horn,' as it was technically called, from the head of a chief and send him back to the ranks of the warriors." She presided at the contracting of marriages affecting her ohwachira and in the crisis of events the decision on questions of war and peace fell to her arbitrament; her plans and wishes molded the policy and inspired the decision of councils."[10] Among other Indian tribes, too, this form of feminine dominance prevailed. "They were content to be ruled by women," John Esten Cooke declared, "which quite overturns the general theory that Indian women were despised subordinates. When Smith was captured, he was waited upon by the 'Queen of Appomattock'; there was a 'Queen of the Paspaheghs,' and the old historian Beverley, speaking of the tribes about the year 1700, tells us Pungoteague was governed by 'a Queen,' that Nanduye was the seat of 'the Empress,' and that this Empress had the shore tribes 'under tribute.' To this add the singular statement made by Powhatan, that his kingdom would descend to his brothers, and afterwards to his sisters, though he had sons living."[11]

Not all Indian tribes, it should be noted, were matriarchal, and the purpose of this chapter is not to defend the thesis, advocated by many and in particular by Morgan,* that all Indian life was originally matrilineal. There were patriarchal as well as matriarchal tribes: the Abnaki, Ottawa, Potawatomi, Chippewa, Menominee, Sauk, Fox, Miami, Shawnee, Omaha, Winnebago, Iowa.[12] Among the Cheyenne it would seem that the patriarchal mores also existed.[13] The Micmacs were also patriarchal. "When Indian make bargain, squaw never speakum," Silas Rand observed, describing the domestic relationships of the tribe.[14] It has also been affirmed that among the Indians north of Mexico descent is "counted prevailingly in the male line."[15] † On the whole, however, even among the patriarchal tribes—

* Bernhard J. Stern in his book *Lewis Henry Morgan, Social Evolutionist,* clarifies Morgan's position. Without denying the validity of Morgan's specific analysis, he shows that though Morgan may have erred in making his generalization so complete, he was unquestionably correct in his conclusions about the particular tribes that he studied. Briefly, he is opposed to Morgan's generalization but not to his specific studies. In that respect, Goldenweiser is in agreement with Stern.

† Mr. Hodge deals with a number of other tribes, showing that many of them were patrilineal as well as matrilineal. His study is very important in that connection.

and this is what I am trying to stress—the attitude toward women was far more advanced than it was in European countries of the same century.

Wherever woman is economically independent she is a relatively free creature, and wherever she is economically dependent she is a slave, no matter what she may be called. When women are economically dependent, morality is defined by men. In ancient and modern civilizations, with the exception of a few intervals in the Roman and medieval worlds, the history of morality has been the history of male supremacy. Women have been ground beneath this juggernaut of masculine morality. Indian squaws were not, because they were economically independent.

In the European world of the sixteenth century woman was viewed as an inferior creature, unendowed with any of the rights which would have made her a being in her own right, independent, unenslaved.

Women in the days of the English king Ethelred were pieces of property to be bought or sold at the caprice of husband, father, or guardian. If a man seduced the wife of another man, Ethelred required nothing more than that the guilty party pay the husband trespassed against a fine and provide him with another wife. The exact wording of the law is most interesting and curious: "If a freeman have been familiar with a freeman's wife, let him pay for it with his wergild and provide another wife with his own money and bring her home to the other." That is, the seduction of a wife was far more serious as a violation of property than of person. The sexual violation was a matter of microscopical consequence. It could be paid for easily, and the provision of another wife was only an additional buttress to the property factor involved.

No Indian squaw would have submitted to such an indignity.

### THE SIMPLICITY OF INDIAN LIFE

What makes the American Indians so interesting and challenging is the fact that their attitude toward women, as toward democracy and many other fundamental things, was so superior to that of the whites who came over and conquered the land. The squaws realized that sex had nothing to do with essentials of heroism or romance, but that economic fact, economic relationship, economic *rapport,* were the decisive factors involved.* What was important was that women worked as well as men, had rights like those of men, and refused to surrender those rights under any conditions or for any fictions, however tender or poetic.[17]

"The women not only provided bark and stakes, the materials of their houses and cabins," Hutchinson informs us, "but were the housewrights who built them, and as often as the family moved for the sake of fishing or hunting, the women took down the houses and carried them on their backs. They planted, hoed, and gathered the corn and provided barns (holes in the ground cieled with the rind of trees) for the reception of it. Not to mention their employment in providing shellfish and other fish for the family, bearing burdens of wood and water, dressing their food, etc." [18] All of which explains why the Indian women had rights equal to those of the Indian men.[19] † Hutchinson then goes on to describe the absence of laws among the Indians, which fact is a good reflection on why the colonists found prisons an early necessity: "We hear of no laws. Where they had no idea of property, but few laws were necessary." ‡

It is interesting today to revisualize the Indians, not as the Hollywood films have done, but as they really were: to see them as an independent people, to see their women as independent as their men, to see them living with the earth as their table, believing in the present and unconcerned with the future; to see them eating without regard for hours or day but as food-supply conditioned, keeping fasts when their edibles were gone,¶ gorging themselves when their food was abundant, lacking salt and bread, having water as their only drink

* "They [Indians] used but little ceremony in the business of marriage," Samuel Hopkins wrote, "'tis their law that the children and all the household stuff belong to the woman; and indeed everything else but the gun, for that is the man's livelihood. *The man, according to their custom, has no right to the children or any other person whatever*" [16] [italics mine].

† Mr. Sears declares that the Indian woman "was not only at least as good a farmer as the average early English settler, but was happy in her work."

‡ The Quaker Thomas Chalkley tells us in his *Journal* about how highly the Indian women were exalted in the tribes he visited. "I asked our interpreter," he writes, "why they suffered or permitted the women to speak in their councils. His answer was that some women are wiser than men. Our interpreter told me that they had not done anything for many years without the counsel of an ancient, grave woman, who, I observed, spoke much in their council; for I was permitted to be present at it; ... *he told me she was an empress* [italics mine]. ... She looked upon our coming to be more than natural, because we did not come to buy, or sell, or get gain, but came in love and respect to them." [20]

¶ In Neal's *History of New England* (1700, p. 26) an interesting commentary on the "mañana" psychology of the Indian is to be discovered.

and tobacco as their lone stimulant; to see them with nothing but a skin or a mat for a bed, and without a stool or chair, but only the ground for a resting place. They were a weird, quaint people, with ways and habits which were strange and paradoxical, but not a bad people, not a fierce people, at least not nearly so bad or fierce as the white men who beat and whipped and slew them.

### THE INDIAN'S HOSTILITY TO SERVITUDE

It has been a well-recognized fact for centuries that neither Indian women nor Indian men would subject themselves to a state of servitude. White men were willing enough to become slaves, servants, and menials of divers varieties. Negroes, snatched from Africa, often accepted their conditions of servitude without serious protest; the Indians, however, would never resign themselves to such an existence.* When they hired themselves out as servants, they did so with the utmost reluctance and upon many occasions robbed and sometimes even killed their masters. It did not take the whites very long to realize that the Indians were impossible as servants or in any other menial capacity. The whites were always willing to trade three Indians for two Negroes. The following item, which appeared in the *Boston News-Letter* in October 1707, is typical of many other items regarding Indian servants:

> Run away from her master Baker. A tall, Lusty Carolina Indian woman named Kezia Wampum, having long, straight Black Hair tyed up with red Hair Lace, very much marked in the hands and face. Had on a strip'd red blue & white Homespun Jacket & a Red one. A Black & White Silk Crape Petticoat, a White Shift, as Also a blue one with her, and a mixt Blue and White Linsey Woolsey Apron.

It is interesting to observe that a "reward of four pounds is offered for this barbaric creature." [24] Very soon, as Roger Williams was one of

* Some of the Indian tribes made slaves of whites as well as their own people. Indian slavery sprang mainly out of wars, in which the captured were reduced to servitude. The Florida Indians, for instance, kept a band of captured Cuban Indians as their slaves.[21] Indians did not regard their slaves as social inferiors. Frequently slaves would be adopted by the tribe; others would be allowed to marry into the tribe, and "Bartram found that among the southern Indians the slaves were dressed better than their owners." [22] Even in Pennsylvania, "Indian slaves were brought from other colonies," and William Markham, Penn's deputy, owned one.[23] In New Jersey there were more Indian slaves than in either Pennsylvania or Maryland, but never was the number large. The majority of the Indians just would not submit to slavery.

the first to admit, the New Englanders discovered that it was better to employ their own white people as servants or to buy Negroes, who cost "from twenty to forty Pistoles," rather than to attempt to domesticate the Indians. At length, when many Indians had left their owners, dressed in the "fine apparel of their masters," even wearing beribboned flaxen wigs, the New Englanders called a halt to the practice of employing the red men in domestic capacities.

In Rhode Island a law was passed in 1715 forbidding the introduction of Indian slaves because of their conspiratorial tempers. Throughout most of the South an Indian slave was worth less than one-half the price of a Negro slave.[25]

The Indians were not a difficult people to deal with, to associate with, or even to be friends with. All their early relations with English settlers were of a most felicitous variety. Conflicts developed later, after the Indians had been sold the firewater of the settlers and had been taken advantage of in so many crude and exasperating ways. "Their drink," Josselyn wrote, describing how the Indians were poisoned by the white man's alcohol, "they fetch from the spring and were not acquainted with other until the French and English traded with them cursed liquor called Rum, Rum-bullion or Kill Devil. . . . It hath killed many of them. . . . Thus instead of bringing of them to the knowledge of Christianitie we have taught them to commit the beastly and crying sins of our Nation for a little Profit." [26] John Lederer went so far as to advise all settlers to feed liquor to the Indians as a form of commercial strategy. "Sometimes you may with brandy or strong liquor dispose them to an humour of giving you ten times the value of your commodity," he wrote, and never failed to practice what he preached.

### THE INDIAN'S CO-OPERATIVE WAY OF LIFE

George Catlin, who lived for years among the Indians, painting portraits of them and vivifying their habits in words of intimate description, stated that few peoples were more "kind and honorable." [27] Catlin's observations of Indian life stand out in direct contradiction to the false ideas about it which have been cultivated and distorted by so many of our historians and fictionists. Catlin elaborates upon the social-mindedness of all the tribes he visited. Their political philosophy was social rather than individualistic. They were "entirely severed and free from influences of wealth, which is seldom amassed by any persons in Indian communities." [28] He adds a striking observation to the effect that many Indians in high places of the community "for the sake of popularity, render themselves the poorest, and most meanly dressed and equipped of any in the tribe." Wissler also stresses the fact that "the social structure upon which they [most of the Indian tribes] rested was communistic." [29] James Adair makes a similar observation when he notes that a "community of goods... prevailed among them...they would share with those of their own tribe, the last part of their provisions, even to a single ear of corn." [30]

"Communism, to a degree, was practiced in these early Iroquois communities," Goldenweiser points out, "the excess supplies of more favored families being frequently divided among the needy members of the village." [31] Morgan showed also in *Ancient Society* that among the aborigines "the principle of communism in living was practiced." [32] The absence of prisons among the tribes stands out in sharp contrast to the prisons built by the settlers. Punishments were meted out by the nearest kin with great expedition and effectiveness.

Contrary to the general conception of the Indian which has practically become part of American legend, he was more gentle than fierce, more kind than cruel, more loyal than treacherous. He came far closer to Rousseau's conception of the "noble savage" than most people believe. In a sermon preached at Plymouth in 1620, the Rev. Mr. Cushman declared that "the Indians are said to be the most cruel and treacherous people in all those parts, even like lions, but to us they have been like lambs, so kind, so submissive and trusty, as a man may truly say, many Christians are not so kind and sincere." [33] Practically everyone who ever lived with the Indian corroborates that conclusion. "All history proves them to have been found friendly and hospitable, on the first approach of white people to their villages in all parts of the American Continent," writes George Catlin, and adds that "what I have seen (which I offer as proof, rather than what I have read), I am willing and proud to add, for the ages who are only to read of these people, my testimony to that which was given by the immortal Columbus, who wrote back to his Royal Master and Mistress, from his first position on the new Continent: 'I swear to your Majesties that there is not a better people in the world than these; more affectionate, affable, or mild. They love their neighbors as themselves, and they always speak smilingly.' "

Nevertheless the same Columbus was the first person to turn upon the Indians, enslave them, and transport "forty thousand of these innocent aborigines [from the Bahamas] . . . to a wretched death in the mines of Cuba." [34]

It was not the Indians but the Europeans who were the betrayers, the disrupters, the destroyers of the friendship which had sprung up between the two peoples. Much has been written about the fact that Columbus was "the man who was ambitious to become the first slave driver of the New World," [35] but Columbus was but a beginner in the art. Those who followed him perfected it. When they found that the Indians did not make good enough slaves, they turned to the Negroes, and horrible as Columbus's record was as a slave driver, it was no less horrible than that of the Puritan New Englanders who carried the Negro slaves to our shores. As Alice Morse Earle writes, "The Massachusetts Puritan . . . did not hesitate to sell Indian captives as slaves to the West Indies. In 1703 it was made legal to transport and sell in the Barbados all Indian male captives under ten, and Indian women captives. Perhaps these transactions quickly blunted whatever early feeling may have existed against Negro slavery, for soon the African slave-trade flourished in New England as in Virginia, Newport being the New England centre of the Guinea Trade." [36]

### THE WHITE BETRAYAL

The Indians turned against the white man only after the white man turned against them. The white man talked of peace, believed in a religion whose leader was the Prince of Peace, but over his shoulder he carried a gun and in his hand he flashed a sword. It was difficult for minds as simple and generous as those of the Indians to understand such a contradiction. They were more like children than savages in the ordinary connotation of that word, and they had not yet learned to distrust "Greeks bearing gifts." The irony of it all is that the phrase "Indian giver" applied not to the red man but to the white man. The Indians would have lived in harmony with the whites had the latter played fair with them, trafficked with them without double dealing, maintained pacts and treaties, and had not violated the friendship which had been originally established. "They are really better to us than we are to them," wrote Lawson, describing his own experiences. "They always give us victuals at their quarters, and take care we are armed against hunger and thirst. We do not do so by them... [but] daily cheat them in everything we sell, and esteem it a gift of Christianity not to sell them so cheap as we do the Christians, as we call ourselves." [37] No one has ever disputed the fact that the Indians were the best friends and the worst enemies one could have. The whites made the Indians their enemies instead of their friends. The Indian King Haglar, in a speech delivered as late as 1754, strove to show the white men that it was they themselves, not the Indians, who caused so many of the conflicts between the two peoples. At the signing of the treaty on Thursday, the 29th of August of that year, he challenged the white men with these words:

King-Brother here is One thing You Yourselves are to Blame very much in That is You Rot Your grain in Tubs, out of which you take and make Strong Spirits You sell it to our young men and give it them, many times; they get very Drunk with it this is the Very Cause that they oftentimes Commit those Crimes that is offensive to You and us and all thro' Effect of that Drink it is also very bad for our people, for it Rots their guts and Causes our men to get very sick and many of our people has lately Died by the Effects of that strong Drink, and I heartily wish You would do something to prevent Your People from Dareing to Sell or give them any of that Strong Drink, upon any Consideration whatever for that will be a great means of our being free from being accused of those Crimes that is Committed by our young men and will prevent many of the abuses that is done by them thro' the Effects of that Strong Drink....

I desire a stop may be put to the selling strong liquors by the White people especially near the Indian Nation. If the White people make strong drink let them sell it to one another or drink it in their own Families.

...Should any of my people do any mischief to the White people I have no strong prisons like you to confine them for it, Our only way is to put them under ground and all these men [pointing to his Warriors] will be ready to do that for those who shall deserve it.[38]

### RELIGIOSITY OF THE INDIANS

The whites taught the Indians, who were a most religious and moral people,[39] that religion could be most irreligious in practice. The reverence of the Indians for the Great Spirit was unsullied by the cant and hypocrisy exhibited by the Europeans in their relationship to their Christian gods. Indians could not understand how one could believe in a God who taught the very principles which one violated. In their minds such gods—and the white men, with their God the Father, God the Son, and God the Holy Ghost, were polytheists, not monotheists—were scarcely gods at all. Why should one worship such *beings* when one paid no attention to what the *Being* said or desired? The Indians themselves lived in constant awe of their Great Spirit; they would rather die than violate his command. "Morality and virtue," Catlin declared, "the civilized world need not undertake to teach them." The Indians knew more of religion in the true sense of the word, knew more of morality in the higher sense of the word, than the whites who came over here and described them as "savages." Thomas Chalkley, the Quaker, described how happily the Indians and Quakers always fared, because the latter respected the Indians, refused to take economic advantage of them, and would not take up arms against them.[40]

The Indians learned of deceit, treachery, and murder from their Christian invaders. Accustomed to deal honestly with people, they learned the advantage of dishonesty, but lacking experience in the art were never able to succeed in it.

### A FATAL INDIAN VENTURE

One of the most tragic illustrations of their inability to compete with the European adventurers is told by Lawson. Admiring the English more than the settlers, whom they considered "no better than Cheats," they decided to traffic with the former instead of the latter, and contrived a scheme whereby they hoped they might get to England and make a better deal there than they could with the colonists. They held a consultation, devised a program, got the whole tribe to work on the project, built a new and impressive fleet of large canoes suitable for their voyage, and, when everyone was ready, set sail for England. They left behind only the old people and the children, who were to keep the land fertile while they were gone. They were sure they would return in triumph, bringing with them wealth from a different and unknown land, and that thereafter they would all live better than ever before. England, they believed, was just across the horizon, a voyage of hours, not days and weeks. Their knowledge of the sea was limited by their experience with American rivers; the ocean to them was a mirage, something that lived in the eyes of God—their Great Spirit.

Their journey proved pathetically short-lived. One-third of their group was lost in a storm; another third was captured by an English ship and sold into slavery; the remaining third got back to the coast, half-drowned, bedraggled and tattered, a desperate and defeated lot. After that their faith in England was no greater than in the English colonists. They had learned their lesson and lost their faith.[41]

### INDIAN CRUELTY

Indian savageries, in the main, were inspired by the tactics, strategies, and chicaneries of the whites. As the word is usually construed, it was the whites who were the *savages,* not the Indians.

How the Indians felt about such matters is well-evidenced by the comments and questions of a Sioux chief in upper Missouri:

He told me he had often heard that white people hung their criminals by the neck and choked them to death like dogs and those their own people; to which I answered, "yes." He then told me he had learned that they shut each other up in prisons, where they keep them a great part of their lives because they can't pay money. I replied in the affirmative to this, which occasioned great surprise and excessive laughter, even amongst the women. He told me that he had been to our Fort at Council Bluffs, where we had a great many warriors and braves, and he saw three of them taken out on the prairies and tied to a post and whipped almost to death, and he had been told that they submit to all this to get a little money, "yes." He said he had been told that when all the white people were born, their white medicine men had to stand by and look on what in the Indian country the women would not allow . . . they would be ashamed . . . that he had been along the Frontier, and a good deal amongst the white people, and he had seen them whip their children . . . a thing that is very cruel . . . he had heard also from several white medicine men that the Great Spirit of the white people was the child of a white woman, and that he was at last put to death by the white people. This seemed to be a thing that he had not been able to comprehend, and he concluded by saying, "The Indians' Great Spirit got no mother . . . the Indians no kill him, he never die." [42]

## THE MORAL BASIS OF INDIAN CRUELTY

A great deal has been written describing the cruelties of the Indians, the unspeakable and uncondonable tortures they inflicted upon their captives; and few have denied the extremities of punishment to which the Indians so often subjected their enemies. What is important in this connection is that these agonies were never inflicted upon their own tribe or their own people, but upon the people who attacked them and whom they viewed as aliens and enemies. The Indians were always kind to those whom they considered their friends, but equally unkind and merciless to those who, they were convinced, were their enemies. Catlin himself admits that the Indians have often been "in the habit of inflicting the most abhorring tortures" upon their enemies, but he also stresses the fact that those "cruelties are practiced but upon the few whose lives are acquired to atone for those who have been similarly dealt with by their enemies." [43] In short, Indian cruelty was more a matter of atonement than sadism.* After such atonement was achieved, "the remainder [of the group] are adopted into the tribe by marrying the widows whose husbands have fallen in battle, in which capacity they are received and respected like others of the tribe, and enjoy equal rights and immunities."

Mrs. Jemison, a white woman who was captured as a girl by the Indians and spent the rest of her life with them, has provided us with an admirably impartial and objective account of their life. After having lived with them four years, she confessed that she practically lost all desire to go back to her white folks, so happy did she find her life with the red men. Years afterward she was offered an opportunity to return to her people, but refused because she felt more at home with the Indians. She also realized that her white friends and relatives would never accept her Indian children as their equals.[45]

* Luzerne Ray declares that "lex talionis" was the only Indian law. "An injury was never forgiven until expiation had been made; on the other hand, a benefit never forgotten until repaid in the kind." [44]

She minces no words in her descriptions of the cruelties the Indians practiced upon their enemies. This description alone is evidence of the fact that she held back nothing in her account of the extremes of torture to which the natives resorted in their punishments of their enemies:

At the trading house we found a party of Shawnee Indians, who had taken a young white man prisoner, and had just begun to torture him. . . . They at first made him stand up, while they slowly pared his ears and split them into strings; they then made a number of slight incisions in his face, and then bound him upon the ground, rolled him in the dirt, and rubbed it in his wounds; some of them at the same time whipping him with small rods. The poor fellow cried for mercy and yelled most piteously.[46]

In another place she describes how "they made a small opening in the abdomen" of a victim, "took out an intestine, which they tied to a sapling, and then unbound him from the tree, and drove him round it till he had drawn out the whole of his intestines. He was then beheaded, his head was stuck upon a pole, and his body left on the ground unburied." [47]

Unspeakable though those tortures were,* they were no worse than those practiced by white men upon their own kind in the old world. One has but to turn to the Romans of ancient days who found a vicious joy in giving Christians to the lions, or to the mediaevalists

* Joseph Jouvency, a priest of the Society of Jesus, writes:

"In battle they strive especially to capture their enemies alive. Those who have been captured and led off to their villages are first stripped of their clothing; then they savagely tear off their nails one by one with their teeth; then they bind them to stakes and beat them as long as they please. Finally they kindle a fire about them, and roast the miserable creatures with slow heat. . . .

"Thus they treat their enemies; but at home they cultivate peace and carefully avoid quarrels, except those which the fury of drunkenness has aroused. . . . They know nothing of anger. . . . These people seek a reputation for liberality and generosity. . . . From the same desire for harmony comes their ready assent to whatever one teaches them. . . .

"The nature of our Savages is in itself generous and not malicious. They have a rather happy disposition, and a fair capacity for judging and valuing material and common things, deducing their reasons with great nicety.

"The little offenses and quarrels are easily adjusted by the Sagamores and common friends. And in truth they are hardly ever offended long. . . . We have never seen anything except always great respect and love among them; which was a great grief to us when we turned our eyes upon our own shortcomings. For to see an assembly of French people without reproaches, slights, envy, and quarrels with each other, is as difficult as to see the sea without waves. . . ." [48]

who burnt people over hot coals, or to the Inquisitors of later days, to be confronted with tortures no less horrible in either subtlety or extremity. Torquemada, and all the lesser Torquemadas that followed, not only matched the Indians but surpassed them in their ingenuity in torture.* They invented the stretching-machine, the strappado, the burning crown, the white-hot pincers, and a countless variety of other techniques of the rack and wheel by which men could be tortured to death so slowly and deviously that the hair went gray in the process and the face turned green and the body became pulseless and purple.

"Notwithstanding all that has been said against the Indians, in consequence of their cruelties to their enemies, cruelties that I have witnessed and had abundant proof of," Mary Jemison wrote, "it is a fact that they are naturally kind, tender and peaceable towards their friends, and strictly honest, and that those cruelties have been practiced only upon their enemies, according to their idea of justice."[50] Practically everyone who has ever lived with the Indians attests that fact. One thing the red men could never understand was the white man's cruelty to his own people.

### WHY THE INDIANS FOUGHT

There can be no doubt that the quarrels with the Indians, and the Indian wars which ensued, were not the product of the natives but of the invaders. The words of Dr. Elias Boudinot describe, with admirable succinctness, what happened:

> It is a matter of fact, proved by most historical accounts, that the Indians, at our first acquaintance with them, generally manifested themselves kind, hospitable, and generous to Europeans, so long as they were treated with justice and humanity. But when they were, from a thirst for gain, overreached on many occasions, their friends and relations treacherously entrapped and carried away to be sold for slaves, themselves injuriously oppressed, deceived and driven from their lawful and native possessions, what ought to have been expected but inveterate enmity, hereditary animosity and a spirit of perpetual revenge? To whom should be attributed the evil passions, cruel practices and vicious habits to which

* Unlike the Europeans, whose witch-burnings still smoulder down the highways and byways of history, *the Iroquois never burnt a woman at the stake.*[49] This is but another evidence of the superiority of the Indians' attitude toward woman.

they are now changed, but to those who first set them the example, laid the foundation and then furnished the continual means for propagating and supporting the evil? [51]

The complaints of the Indians themselves, which echo down the avenues of history like the wails of a mourner, are even more challenging:

"It was we," say the Lenape Mohicans, and their kindred tribes, "who so kindly received them [the whites] on their first arrival into our country. We took them by the hand and bid them welcome to sit down by our side, and live with us as brothers; but how did they requite our kindness? They at first asked only for a little land on which to raise bread for themselves and their families, and pasture for their cattle, which we freely gave them. They soon wanted more, which we also gave them. They saw the game in the woods, which the Great Spirit had given us for our subsistence, and they wanted that, too. They penetrated into the woods in quest of game; they discovered spots of land which pleased them; that land they also wanted, and because we were loath to part with it, as we saw they already had more than they had need of, they took it from us by force, and drove us to a great distance from our ancient homes.

"When the Yengeese [an Indian corruption of the word 'English'] arrived at Machtitschwanne, they looked about everywhere for good spots of land, and when they found one, they immediately and without ceremony possessed themselves of it; we were astonished, but still we let them go on, not thinking it worth while to contend for a little land. But when at last they came to our favorite spots, those which lay most convenient to our fisheries, then bloody wars ensued; we would have been contented that the white people and we should have lived quietly beside each other; but these white men encroached so fast upon us that we saw at once we should lose all if we did not resist them. The wars that we carried on against each other were long and cruel. We were enraged when we saw the white people put our friends and relatives, whom they had taken prisoners, on board of their ships, and carry them off to sea, whether to drown or sell them as slaves, in the country from which they came, we knew not, but certain it is that none of them have ever returned or even been heard of. At last they got possession of the whole of the country which the Great Spirit had given us." [52]

The strategies and chicaneries employed by the white men to get the land away from the Indians are too familiar to repeat. What is most amazing is that the white men after resorting to them were surprised when the Indians objected and fought for the restoration of that of which they had been robbed. The most popular procedure was to get the Indian drunk and then purchase his land or wares for a pittance. Jasper Danckaerts, in his seventeenth-century *Journal*, describes this technique in striking detail:

> The people in this city, who are almost all traders in small articles, whenever they see an Indian enter the house who they know has any money, they immediately set about getting hold of him, giving him rum to drink, whereby he is soon caught and becomes half a fool. If he should then buy anything, he is doubly cheated in the wares and in the price. He is then urged to buy more drink, which they now make half water, and if he cannot drink it, they drink it themselves. They do not rest until they have cajoled him out of all his money, or most of it; and if that cannot be done in one day, they keep him, and let him lodge and sleep there, but in some out of the way place, down on the ground, guarding their merchandise and other property in the meantime, and always managing it so that the poor creature does not go away before he has given them all they want. And these miserable Christians are so much the more eager in this respect, because no money circulates among themselves, and they pay each other in wares, in which they are constantly cheating and defrauding each other. Although it is forbidden to sell the drink to the Indians, yet everyone does it, and so much the more earnestly, and with so much greater and burning avarice, that it is done in secret. To this extent and further, reaches the damnable and insatiable covetousness of most of those who here call themselves Christians.[58]

## LAWS AGAINST LIQUOR DISTRIBUTION TO INDIANS

Not all white men engaged in such practices. Among the New Englanders there was a strong opposition to such treatment of the Indians, and laws were passed forbidding the colonists to sell the Indians alcohol and also to steal their lands by underhanded deals. As early as 1633 a law was passed by the General Court of Massachusetts, declaring: "That what lands any of the Indians in this jurisdiction have possessed and improved, by subduing the same, they have just right unto, according to that in Genesis I, 28, and Chapter 9-I, and Psalms 115, 116." [54] It is interesting that the New Englanders resorted to Biblical authority instead of legal statutes. In another court order, it was stated that: "For the further encouragement of the hopeful works amongst them for the civilizing and helping them forward to Christianity, if any of the Indians shall be brought to civility, and shall come among the English to inhabit, in any of their plantations, and shall there live civilly and orderly, that such Indians shall have allotments amongst the English, according to the custom of the English in like case." [55] In the same order, it was further stated: "That no person whatsoever shall henceforth buy land of any Indian, without license first had and obtained of the General Court; and if any offend herein, such land so bought shall be forfeited to the country." [56]

In other colonies similar laws were passed from time to time. In Connecticut, Maryland, and South Carolina there was the threat of heavy penalties on any settlers who purchased land while the Indians were under the influence of liquor or who, in doing so, made "unfair representations" or bargains.

But these proved to be nothing more than salves to the white man's conscience, for upon every possible occasion he violated the laws and defied their execution. In short, despite the laws and statutes passed, the white man never respected the right of the Indians to the land upon which they had lived for centuries. Whenever opportunity presented itself, most white men were willing and eager to swindle, steal from, or murder the red men in order to get what they wanted. An excellent indication of that spirit is to be found in the words of the Virginian who stated:

> Because the way of conquering them is much more easie then of ciuilizing them by faire meanes, for they are a rude, barbarous, and naked people, scattered in small companies, which are helps to Victorie, but hindrances to Ciuilitie: Besides that, a conquest may be of many, and at once; but ciuility is in particular, and slow, the effect of long time, and great industry. Moreover, victorie of them may bee gained many waies; by force, by surprize, by famine in burning their Boats, and Canoes, and Houses by breaking their fishing weares, by assailing them in their huntings, whereby they get the greatest part of their sustenance

in Winter, by pursuing and chasing them with our horses, and blood-Hounds to draw after them, and Mastiues to teare them, which take this naked, tanned, deformed Savages for no other than wild beasts, and are so fierce and fell vpon them, that they feare them worse than their old Deuill which they worship, supposing them to be a new and worse kinde of deuils then their owne.

Let them have a perpetual warre without peace or truce; . . . we cannot but advise not only the sparing but the preservation of the younger people of both Sexes, whose bodies may by labor and service become profitable. . . .

To maintaine continually certaine bands of men of able bodies and inured to the Countrie, of stout minds and active hands, that may, from time to time, in several bodies pursue and follow them, surprising them in their habitations, interrupting them in theire hunting, burning theire Townes, demolishing theire Temples, destroyinge their Canoes, plucking upp theire weares, carrying away theire corne, and depriving them of whatsoever may yeeld them succor or relief.[57]

Even some of the higher-minded settlers felt that in bringing Christianity to the American shores and disseminating it among the savages they were contributing something for which land was less than adequate compensation. Much of the instruction in Christian doctrine given the Indians stressed the importance of spiritual and immaterial values—a thing that the Indians soon found difficult to harmonize with Christian practice, which was just the opposite. The Indians had never made an issue of land or property; they had always been true primitive Christians in that respect. Christianity had nothing to teach them there. It was the Christians who were concerned with landed rights, who signed pacts, treaties, and bargains, and who insisted that the English king, as a Christian sovereign, had the prior right to the possession of the country.

### THE ROLE OF ROGER WILLIAMS

Only Roger Williams had the courage to assert that the Indians had, to the lands upon which they lived, a title superior to that of the English king. But Roger Williams's voice was but one among a multitude. He was a lone Isaiah crying out in the wilderness. Williams, the most searching thinker produced by early New England, was the first to take up the cause of the Indians. In the charters of the New England companies it was explicitly stated that one of the main reasons for settling in the new world was to convert the Indians to Christianity, but once the settlers landed they found it more convenient to rob them than to proselytize them. Williams was the only one who adhered to the original ideal. A man of lofty vision, who strove to reconcile dream with reality, and to infuse the simplest things with abiding significance, he refused to believe, as the rest of the English did, that "a dead Injun is the best Injun." He knew that what was wrong with the Indians was what the white men had done to them. He was the first of the foreigners to learn the Indian tongues, the first to be able to converse with Indians in their various dialects and bring Christian doctrine to them phrased in the patterns of their own language. He defended their rights to their land, attacked the colonists for believing that they had a superior right to it, and, adopting an attitude toward the Indian which later was to be exalted by Rousseau, penned the following poem:

Boast not, proud English, of thy birth and blood,
  Thy brother Indian is by birth as good.

The courteous pagan shall condemn
  Uncourteous Englishmen;
Who live like foxes, bears and wolves,
  Or lion in his den.

Let none sing blessings to their souls,
  For that they courteous are.
The wild barbarians with no more
  Than nature go so far.

### THE NOBLE SAVAGE

Underlying the philosophy of that poem was not only Roger Williams's attitude toward the Indian and the white man, but also an attitude which soon was to capture the imagination of the entire European world, even though it made little headway in the American. That attitude, born of the upheaval in economic life occasioned by the decay of feudalism and the rise of commercialism, expressed the revolt begun in Europe against things artificial and conventional in favor of those genuine and natural. Roger Williams gave early voice to it in religious form. The feudal world had been static. At its heyday, it was fixed as a star, tight as a drum. About it and within it clustered all the rituals of state, the conventions of class, the fixities of concept and custom, the regulations of enterprise and organization, the orderlinesses and artificialities of taste characteristic of its structure. The commercial world, soon to be known as the capitalist world, developed out of its own propulsive energies and directions an opposition to those tendencies. It wanted not rituals, conventions, fixities, regulations, but freedom—freedom from them all. Freedom and naturalness became the demands of the new era, the shibboleths of the new day which had just begun to dawn. Although it was freedom in economics (*laissez faire*) which they needed most, freedom from the feudal restrictions which retarded and harassed their enterprise, they soon learned to want more than that.

European philosophers who had never seen primitives except in pictures began to worship them because they represented that freedom which was the antithesis of the feudal world they knew. The primitive, or the savage, as he was better known in those days, became *noble*, exalted, sublime, in comparison with the so-called civilized European whom the intellectuals had come to despise for his artificial manners, affected gestures, pompous bearing, and bepowdered and bedizened attire. The intellectuals believed that the savage was good, happy, joyous; that he lived close to nature, which is how all human beings should live, and did not try to circumvent her designs with property laws, fences, walls, artifices, and stratagems. The Indian was a symbol of the goodness of nature, an extension of her most intimate heritage. Wise men should become like him: they should emulate his ways, aspire toward his freedoms. To be sure, they did not know that actually, slave as he was to his tabus, the primitive was less free than they. But their concept of freedom meant freedom from a controlling state, a dominant aristocracy, and the economic handicaps and encumbrances imposed upon them by state and aristocracy.

In Europe, as the years passed, the savage became more sacrosanct than ever. In time he became an idol to be worshiped. Rousseau apostrophized him in his famous essay "The Noble Savage." Locke, in considering the "state of nature," made him the closest approach to the ideal. Even Americans like Freneau exalted him in verbiage of the same tradition:

> Nor think this mighty land of old contained
> The plundering wretch, or man of bloody mind.
> The gen'rous soul inspired the honest blame
> 'Till East winds did here Columbus blow.

In the drama a number of playwrights dedicated themselves to Indian themes. Major Robert Rogers, as early as 1766, wrote an Indian play, *Ponteach*, or "The Savages of America," which was followed by Barker's *Indian Princess* in 1808 and then by John A. Stone's *Metamora*, or "The Last of the Wampanoags," in 1829, George Washington Parke Custis's *Pocahontas*, or "The Settlers of Virginia," in 1830, and Mrs. Charlotte Barnes Conner's *Forest Princess* in 1848. Later, James Fenimore Cooper in his *Leather-Stocking Tales*, Henry Wadsworth Longfellow in his *Hiawatha* epic, and Chateaubriand in *Atala*, endowed the Indian with the virtues and valor of an American Siegfried. Of course, the Indians these writers depicted were no more real than those in the American movies of yesterday; such writers were concerned with the Indian not as something real but as something ideal. Longfellow's Hiawatha and Minnehaha behaved in their affection for each other not like young Indians but like Victorian adolescents who had just escaped from a stuffy and overdraped drawing room. Youths among the Indians were accustomed to reasonably free relations and "trial marriages." They never associated the word "virgin," for example, with the feminine sex at all. But the Indian youths described by the American poet were as romantic and incredible as Romeo and Juliet. Romeo and Juliet, however, belonged to a tradition which was romantic; Hiawatha and Minnehaha did not. The Indians were realistic, not romantic. They believed in tenderness, devotion, loyalty, but not in romance. But the European and American romanticists would not have it that way: they had to create the Indian in the image of their ideal.

Much has been written about Indian music, which was conspicuously undeveloped, the flute being the only melodic instrument. Nevertheless, by use of the voice and the drum the Indians achieved certain musical effects that were most impressive. They delighted in songs and, as Frances Densmore shows, often they would "pay the value of one or two ponies for a song." Their songs, however, usually were not love songs—love songs developed only among those tribes living near pioneer towns or cities or those which were corrupted by the missionaries—but ceremonial songs for evoking rain, warding off evil spirits, or avoiding disaster. Some of these ceremonial songs are extraordinarily effective. "Love songs are dangerous," declared a Papago interpreter to Frances Densmore. "If a man gets to singing them we send for a medicine man to treat him and make him stop." [58]

Indian songs were poetic, but they were the poetry of the prairies and the forest, of the curved bowl of the sky, or the sunken back of the sea, and not of the importunities and ecstasies of love.

### THESE HEATHEN DOGGES

Roger Williams was realistic in his attitude toward the natives. He believed the Indians were as good as the white men and had every right to be as proud of their blood; he believed they were "wise in natural things beyond the white man; he was convinced that they were less wanton than the Europeans and so modest as to "shame our English." He found them "remarkably free and courteous," and most "sensible to kindness." "I could never hear of murders, robbers, etc., so frequent as in parts of Europe amongst the English and French." [59] Yet at the same time he recognized their vices, especially when under the influence of liquor. The Indians regarded him as their best friend and called him the "good man" and the "Quencher of our Fires."

Part of the original program of all the colonists had been to settle in America in order to convert the savages to Christianity. What happened is well condensed in Mark Twain's witticism describing the behavior of the Puritans after they landed in the new world: "First they fell upon their knees, and then upon the aborigines."

"There was a time when our forefathers owned this great island," declared the Senecan, Red Jacket. "Their seats extended from the rising to the setting sun. The Great Spirit had made it for the use of the Indians. All this he had done for his red children, because he loved them.... But an evil day came upon us. Your forefathers crossed the great water, and landed on this island. Their numbers were small. They found friends, not enemies. . . . We gave them corn and meat; they gave us poison in return.

"You have got our country, but are not satisfied; you want to force your religion upon us. . . .

"If there is but one religion, why do you white people differ so much about it?"[60]

Long into the nineteenth century the same practice continued. Honest, friendly Indians, eager to live at peace with their neighbors, were attacked and massacred mercilessly by white settlers greedy for land. In that remarkable biography of *Old Jules* by Mari Sandoz, we hear the old man denouncing one of the latest massacres in his own simple, effective words:

"The news of the shocking annihilation of Big Foot's band at Wounded Knee: men, women, and children mowed down by Hotchkiss guns while they with their pitifully inadequate arms asked for the peace they had not broken. . . . A blot on the American flag."[61]

Roger Williams himself tells us how often he heard both the English and Dutch say, "These Heathen Dogges, better kill a thousand of them than we Christians should be indangered or troubled with them; better that they were all cut off, and then we shall be no more troubled with them; they have spilt our Christian blood, the best way to make riddance of them is to cut them all off and so make way for Christians."

And they did. They oppressed the Massachusetts and Mohegan tribes, exterminated the Pequots in 1637 and the Wampanoags and Narragansetts in 1676. It is scarcely any wonder that the Puritans achieved little success in converting the natives to Christianity. When the Massachusetts Bay minister Mayhew solicited Ninigret, the sachem of the Nyantic tribe, for permission to preach to them, the Indian retorted, "Go make your English good Christians first." Ninigret had learned from Roger Williams what being a good Christian meant.

Nevertheless, all Williams's preaching from 1631 to 1683 resulted in the organization of no Indian congregations or churches, because Williams, being a Seeker, was opposed to such organizations. Like the early Lollards and most of the Dissenters, the Seekers believed in individual conversion and not in mass gatherings and ecclesiastical structures. They were sceptical of all organizational and ritualistic forms, which they believed were barriers to true religion. Williams lived with the Indians, shared intimately their way of life, participated in their joys and sorrows, and ventured far into the remote wilderness to seek out the more obscure tribes to tell them of the message of Christ. No sacrifice was too great in this cause. Without question Williams was one of the few *real* Christians who settled on the North American continent in the seventeenth century.

## SIGNIFICANCE OF THE INDIAN STRUGGLE

The Indians were not, of course, angels or relatives of any other heavenly host. There were bad Indians as well as good Indians, dishonest as well as honest, cruel or well as gentle, and it would be an error to idealize them. Their tribes had fought among themselves before the white men landed upon these shores. But within each tribe fights rarely occurred. Their attitude toward the white men, as has been amply demonstrated, was generous, kindly, and considerate. After the white men began to rob them of their land, drive them away from the soil they had possessed for centuries, they fought back with every weapon and strategy at their command. The conflict, continuing through the years, evoked the worst traits of both races. Upon occasions no doubt the Indians made unjustified attacks upon the whites, perpetrated atrocities of unforgivable extremity, and even individually were guilty of most vicious and violent crimes. Horrible as all this was, it must be remembered that it was the whites who drove them to these extremes. When the whites treated them with consistent friendliness, as did Roger Williams, William Penn, and the early Quakers, the Indians were more than friendly and did everything in their power to further and perpetuate that friendship. If the other colonists had been as considerate, had treated the Indians with equal respect, most of the Indian wars could have been avoided. The tragic paradox is that if there had been no Indian wars, there might have been little colonial expansion and no United States of America.

The red men were fighting for their homes; the white men were fighting to take them away. Under such circumstances the Indians merit more generous consideration than most historians have accorded them. They may have fought often in evil ways, but they were always fighting for a good cause. No cause in the history of the human race is nobler than that of fighting to preserve one's home, the land of one's birth. Whatever the Indians did in trying to defend their homeland was far more justifiable than what the white men did in trying to wrest it from them.

### THE LAST OF THE MOHICANS

Now that the Indians have been practically exterminated—in 1925 they held only 39,976,452 acres, by grace of the United States Government—the Americans have come to idolize them. Instead of believing, as they did for two centuries, that "a dead Injun is the best Injun," people boast of their Indian origin. A recent Vice-President continually referred to his Indian descent. Lodges, hotels, universities, are named after them; poets write paeans about their valor and courage; genealogists search through Indian records to establish the aboriginal heritage of their clients.* Indians no longer being rivals or a menace to whites, the latter now make a museum piece of them. Even publicists like Heywood Broun can defend their cause with impunity: "I know a girl who would be tongue-tied if it were not possible for her to say every once and so often, 'Let's give that back to the Indians.' She thinks it's an epigram. But it would be an even more uproarious joke if the Indians increase so much in the next few generations that it will be quite unnecessary to give back anything to them. They might just step out and take it."

Newspapers are replete with humorous stories about old Indians who are curiosity relics. In one paper we read about the Indian, John Stink, who, "a rosary in one hand and a cigar in the other, was laid to rest . . . in a mausoleum"; in another we are confronted with "genial braves [showing up] wearing store clothes, equipped with $1.50 watches and other appurtenances of civilization."[63]

All this is a far cry from the parlous days when Tecumseh, the great Indian warrior and prophet, attempted to organize the Indian Federation and drive out the inferior whites into the "stinking Lake,"

* White men and women are even being "adopted" and made members of Indian tribes, through the "blood-brother" test.[62]

the Atlantic.[64] * Ironically, today Nazi influences have encouraged the last, remaining Indians, now secluded on reservations,† to adopt an Aryan philosophy. Chief E. A. Towner, Spirit of Red Cloud, as he is better known, has declared that not Americanism but Indianism will ultimately triumph on this continent. He maintains that the whole American form of government is an outgrowth of Indian polity, and adds, with telling force, that "the program of Hitler in Germany today is American Indian in outline."[66] The German-American Bund Fascist organizations support his arguments and are devoting their energies to encouraging the Indian to "battle against Jewish Communism."

Fortunately Chief Towner does not represent the majority of the red men whom the white man has permitted to survive in the land. The majority are still pro-American and anti-Nazi. They have every reason, however, historical as well as immediate, to be anti-American and *pro*-anything else—including pro-Nazi. They have been robbed of their continent and today are a lonely, defeated people. If we are to save them from Nazi influences, we owe them more than a new deal: a fair deal from which they can profit infinitely more than they have from the deal we have given them in the past.

* In that regard, James Adair claimed that the Shawnees, who were largely conjured out of the brain of Tecumseh, were of Jewish descent—descendants of the Lost Tribes. It is also interesting to observe that T. E. Lawrence and Doughty made much of the similarities between the ancient Arabs of Jewish descent and the American Indians.[65] Tecumseh knew nothing of such comparisons, but he knew enough to endow his Shawnees with the virtues and powers of an independent people.

† Indian reservations are a final salve for the American conscience. After having shot down most of the Indians and rendered them impotent as an opposing force, we now provide them with all the variegated protections of a menagerie.

## CHAPTER VI

# The First Foreigners

*A great parte of libertie is a well-governed belly.*

—William Bradford.

The first foreigners to settle in North America, as we have seen, were Englishmen of Dissenter extraction,* commonly known in our history as Pilgrims because of their pilgrimage from England to Holland and thence from Holland to America. They went first to Holland, where, despite the magnanimity and tolerance of the Dutch, they found it difficult to live as they wished and to realize their ideals in terms of their own culture. After all, they were Englishmen and not Dutchmen, and they wanted their children to speak English instead of Dutch. It was not patriotism in the modern sense of the word that motivated their decision to leave Holland for America; they had no profound respect for the English king and were not moved by the sight of the British flag. Their religious beliefs, democratic as the elements, were unconfined by national boundary or conception. Their interests were international, not national; their belief was in the race, in all humanity, even though their knowledge of peoples beyond their own shores was painfully limited. Gentle as the Dutch were, they still remained strangers. They were pleasant strangers, generous strangers, but strangers just the same.

The Pilgrims had not left England because they were no longer in love with the English land or the English houses, villages, and towns they knew. They loved England, English things and English speech, as all people tend to love the countries in which they are born and the people and speech they know. The people they loathed

* Actually, of course, the Spaniards were the first foreigners, and among the English the Virginians settled earlier than the New Englanders. The Pilgrims, however, were "the first foreigners" to establish a colony whose spirit gave character to the future history of the continent.

were those who ruled and tyrannized over them, and refused to allow them to live and worship as they wished. There is nothing singular in such an attitude. The greatest happiness and the greatest misery of the human race can be traced to it. People like what they are familiar with—places, friends, customs, traditions, language—and they are uncomfortable and unhappy with, if not inimical toward, the things they do not know. It is because of that fact that kings and queens, politicians and demagogues, have been able to cultivate the devotion to place, the affection for the familiar, and the affinity of language and tradition, into the mad extremities of modern nationalism.

### THE PLYMOUTH PILGRIMAGE

William Bradford, one of the oldest members of the Pilgrim group, described in his *History of the Plymouth Plantation* just what the members of his group had to endure in England before they fled to Holland as a refuge:

For some were taken and clapt up in prison, others had their houses besett and watcht night and day, and hardly escaped their hands; and the most faine to flie and leave their howses and habitations, and the means of their livelihood. Yet these and many other sharper things which affterward befell them were no other than they looked for, and therefore were the better prepared to bear them by the assistance of Gods grace and spirite. [1]

It was only after such sufferings and persecution, as he states, that they decided to go to Holland:

Yet seeing themselves thus molested, and that ther was no hope of their continuance ther, by a joynte consente they resolved to goe into the Low-Countries, wher they heard was freedome of Religion for all men; as also how sundrie from London and other parts of the land had been exiled and persecuted for the same cause, and were gone thither, and lived at Amsterdam and in other places of the land. So affter they had continued togeither aboute a year, and kept their meetings every Saboth in one place or other, exercising the worship of God amongst themselves, notwithstanding all the dilligence and malice of their adversaries, they seeing they could no longer continue in that condition, they resolved to get over into Holland as they could; which was in the year 1607 and 1608.[2]

The Pilgrims had made their hegira to Holland, then, because they wanted a place in which they could be themselves, with themselves, unmolested by those who were not like themselves. They would have preferred staying in England if that had been possible; it was only because it became impossible that they fled.

Their first attempt to flee had been rendered abortive by the perfidy of their sea captain, and the result was that the group was dispersed and a number of them were imprisoned. Not much later a second escape was attempted and succeeded, and shortly thereafter most of the group had settled safely within the tolerant religious atmosphere of the thriving city of Amsterdam. A year later they moved to Leyden, where they established a permanent residence—permanent until ten years later, when they determined to migrate to the new world.

Bradford's own words, descriptive of precisely why the group decided to leave Holland for America, are most illuminating:

They saw that though the people generally bore all these difficulties very cheerfully, and with a resolute courage, being in the best and strength of their years, yet old age began to steale on many of them, (and their great and continuall labours, with other crosses and sorrows, hastened it before the time) so as it was not only probably thought, but apparently seen, that within a few years more they would be in danger to scatter by necessities pressing them or sinke under their burdens, or both. And therefore according to the devine proverb, that a wise man seeth the plague when it cometh, and hideth him selfe, Pr. 22., 3., so they like skillfull and beaten soldiers were fearfull either to be intrapped or surrounded by their enimies, so as they should neither be able to fight nor flie; and therefore thought it better to dislodge betimes to some place of better advantage and less danger, if any such could be found. Thirdly, as necessitie was a taskmaster over them, so they were forced to be such, not only to their servants, but in a sorte, to their dearest children; the which as it did not a little wound the tender harts of many a loving father and mother, so it produced likewise sad and sorrowful effects. For many of their children that were of best dispositions and gracious inclinations, haveing lernde to bear part of their parents burden, were often times so oppressed with their hevie labours, that though their minds were free and willing, yet their bodies bowed under the weight of the same, and became decreped in their early youth; the vigor of nature being consumed in the very budd as it were. But that which was more lamentable, and of all sorrowes most heavie to be borne, was that many of their children, by these occasions, and the great licentiousness of youth in that countrie, and the manifold temptations of the place, were drawne away by evil examples into extravagante and dangerous courses, getting the raines off their neks, and departing from their parents. Some became souldiers, others tooke upon them farr viages by sea, and others some worse courses, tending to dissolutne and the danger of their soules, to the greefe of their parents and dishonour of God. So that they saw their posteritie would be in danger to degenerate and be corrupted.

Lastly, (and which was not least) a great hope and inward zeall they had of laying some good foundation, or at least to make some way thereunto, for the propagating and advancing the gospell of the kingdom of Christ in those remote parts of the world; yea, though they should be but even as stepping-stones unto others for the performing of so great a work.

These, and some other like reasons, moved them to undertake this resolution of their removall; the which they afterward prosecuted with so great difficulties, as by the sequell will appeare.[3]

They believed that in the new world they could have everything they had in Holland, plus much more.* There they would not have to traffic with Dutchmen or with any other kind of men, except savages, who were not men in the ordinary sense of the word. There they could raise their children as they pleased, to speak their own tongue, behave in their own manner, follow their own traditions,[4] and though faced by land and skies more alien than those of Hol-

* Henry Mortyn Dexter, *The England and Holland of the Pilgrims,* p. 508, wherein a letter is quoted from Mr. Motley, written in 1871 at the Hague, while he was studying Dutch history. A selection from the letter follows:

"I cannot doubt that the motive for members of Robinson's company to become citizens was for business purposes. Leyden, from earliest times, was famous for its cloth manufacture.... And there... and in many other towns it was provided as far back as the twelfth century that no man should deal in cloth that was not a member of the guild. To be a member of the guild, the right of citizenship was an essential requisite. The same rule would apply to the many other trades and manufactures there flourishing in the Netherland Republic."

land, they were certain that, God being with them, they could make them familiar in time.

### THE TWIN GODS: RELIGION AND ECONOMICS

It would be absurd to maintain that the Pilgrims were unmoved by economic considerations. Like all peoples of that time, they were affected by the shift from feudal to capitalist economics. They were unaware, to be certain, that their new religious ideology was conditioned by the economic change at stake. When they found that conditions in Holland were not so happy as they had anticipated, they were convinced that their religious concepts were jeopardized. They said to themselves that they could not find there the religious freedom which they desired.

To understand a group or nation it is important not only to see in retrospect, as we all do, the sociological drives governing their behavior, but also the psychological illusions which they believed in and lived by. It is easy to say, centuries later, when we have the advantage of time on our side, that the changes in national or international behavior have been economically determined. There is no argument about the truth of that conclusion, but what is more important is to understand the actions of the people at the time, to learn what they thought when they made their decisions.

History is not just a matter of retrospective conclusion. If it were, it would be simple—too simple. What makes many historians so ridiculous is that they believe it *is* simple—and this makes *them* simple. History, if the word has any meaning at all, is not only an attempt to understand what the past is in terms of today, but also what it was in terms of its own day.

It is more important to realize that the Pilgrims emigrated to America for religious reasons than it is to assert that they did so only for economic reasons. At the present time we can see how economic considerations governed a large part of their religious decisions, but if we had lived at that time we should have seen little of economics in their thoughts. If we want to understand the Pilgrims, we must try to understand them in terms of what they themselves felt and knew, and not in terms of what we ourselves today know about them.

These Pilgrims were human beings, like everyone of their day, living within the scaffolding of their time, no more guilty and no more innocent than the rest of the people who converted the seaboard into a continent. They carried with them the brickload of the past, the toils and struggles of untold millions who had given life, however infinitesimally, obscurely, or obliquely, to their race. Their failures were an inevitable by-product of circumstance; they were the failures of the age.

### MAYFLOWER DEMOCRACY

Among the Pilgrims who made their way to America in the *Mayflower* there was a closer bond of brotherhood than among most of the other groups of settlers that followed. Among them prevailed a democracy of sentiment which was conspicuously absent, for instance, from the Puritan group which settled at Massachusetts Bay shortly afterward. Among the Pilgrim group were some men of substance, to be sure, but those men did not believe in depriving the men without substance of their democratic rights and privileges. When the Mayflower pact was signed, it was signed by *everyone* on the vessel, by the sailors and servants as well as by those in command. Not only in God's eyes, but in the eyes of the Pilgrims themselves, all men were equal, because each one housed within himself an indestructible part of God.

It should not be thought, however, that the Pilgrims were as revolutionary in the economic sphere as religious sects like the Levellers, Diggers, Millenarians, Seekers, Ranters, and Quakers that developed in England and terrified everyone but the poor. The Pilgrims, closer to the Brownists than any other group—although many among them denied the Brownian association and heritage—were an in-between sect. They were revolutionary only in the sense that, unlike most of the Puritans, they advocated the complete separation of church and state and defended the right of all people to have a democratic share in the determination and organization of government. Beyond that they did not go. When they got to America, they practiced a temporary communism because of the exigencies of the environment, but not because they were pledged to communism as an economic doctrine. The Levellers, Diggers, Quakers, and other groups who had connection with continental Anabaptism were, on the other hand, definitely communistic, in an apostolic sense, in their outlook upon life.

When the Pilgrims arrived on November 11, 1620, faced with the gray, bleak landscape of what threatened to be a hostile country, they had no choice but to dedicate their efforts to the supreme necessity of survival. Their reconnoitering expeditions, including a conflict with the Indians and sundry series of mishaps, culminating in the final settlement in Plymouth, prepared them for the even greater hardships that were to follow. The death of the governor of the colony, John Carver, who was succeeded by William Bradford, was insignificant compared with the developments that ensued. The cordial relations which Carver had established with the neighboring Indian tribes were cultivated into friendship by Bradford, who nurtured the colony from sickness to health. It was not long before the Pilgrims, beset as they had been by plague and famine, developed warm friendship with the Indians, especially with Samoset, an English-speaking native, and later with Massasoit, an Indian chief, and with their aid managed to establish a permanent colony. The Indians taught them how to raise corn and other foods in the obdurate New England soil; without such instruction the Plymouth colony could not have survived.

## THE SEVEN-YEAR PLAN

The concept that prevailed among these adventurous Pilgrims—the most adventurous the world had, or has, ever known—was "common stock." The Pilgrims talked, thought, and acted in terms of the "common stock." In the *Conditions*, as Bradford described them, which were accepted by the colony, provisions were made for everyone, the lowliest as well as the highest, regardless of sex or ancestry. Seven years was agreed upon as the convenient period when inventory was to be taken. At the end of seven years "the capitall and profits, viz., the houses, lands, goods and chatles, be equally divided betwixte the adventurers, and planters; which done, every man shall be free from other of them of any debt or detrimente concerning this adventure." The agreement went on further to state that "all such persons as are of this collonie are to have their meate, drink, apparel, and all provissions out of the *common stock* and goods of the said collonie." [Italics mine.] [5]

That this Seven-Year Plan did not work out was not the fault of the Pilgrim founders, who labored with unstinting energy to put it into effect. Convinced from the beginning that they would have to accustom themselves to the "grimme and grislie face of poverty," they set themselves to the stern task of eking a living out of an ungenerous and unyielding soil. The original scheme of common or collective tillage was soon discarded, and the system of family enterprise was substituted in its place. But the concept of democratic government did not die. It lived in the community, palpitated there like a dynamic thing; it was something that the community not only believed in but lived by.

## MARRIAGE WITHOUT BENEFIT OF CLERGY

The Pilgrims not only were convinced that the church should be separated from the state, but believed that even in such a sacred matter as marriage the clergy should not interfere, but should relegate the whole matter to the civil state. The first marriage in the Plymouth settlement was memorable. Edward Winslow, a widower, was wed to Susanna White, a widow, by a magistrate and not by a cleric, because as Bradford wrote it "was thought most requisite to be performed by the magistrate, as being a civil thing, upon which many questions aboute inheritances doe depende, with other things most proper to their cognizans, and most consonante to the scripture (Ruth 4) and no wher found in the gospell to be layed on the ministers as a part of their office." [6] In fact, among the Plymouth settlers, who were Separatists, Brownists, the church was unimportant, almost irrelevant. A number of preachers were even penalized for performing the marriage ceremony in a religious manner.

Undoubtedly the lower-class character of the community determined its ethics. The very poverty of the inhabitants had a great deal to do with their outlook upon marriage and, what was more important, their views upon society—the right to inheritance, the right to vote, and all such privileges as in time were to be the *sine qua non* of the American way of life.

Many among the Pilgrims, to be sure, were far from ideal in their actions. Bradford describes in voluminous detail how a great many members of the colony swerved from its moral principles. In 1623, when illness struck like a lightning bolt upon the inhabitants of Plymouth, many of the settlers "sould away their cloathes and bed coverings; others (so base were they), became servants to the Indeans and would cutt them wood and fetch them water for a capfull of corne; others fell to plaine stealing, both night and day from the Indeans of which they greevously complained." [7]

### RELATIONSHIP BETWEEN PILGRIMS AND INDIANS

The relationship between the Pilgrims and the Indians was most happy. From the day when Samoset introduced himself in his own pigeon English until many years later, the Pilgrims and the Indians achieved an accord which was close to ideal. The Indians not only helped the settlers in giving them instructions as to how to cultivate the land, "how to set their corne, wher to take fish," and "to procure other commodities, but also signed a pact with them which lasted for many years. The pact, which included many provisions, explicitly stated that if any group should "unjustly warr" against the other, the other should "aide" the group attacked.[8] So determined were the Pilgrims to maintain their friendship with the Indians that when various members of their colony continued to steal from the natives, "they were faine to hange one of their men whom they could not reclaime from stealing to give the Indeans contente." [9]

It is important to remember, at this point, that the Pilgrims who settled at Plymouth had originally planned to settle in Virginia. Only a navigational error swept them from the warm, inviting shores of Virginia to the cold, perilous ones of New England.[10] The people who settled in Virginia, as is obvious, were not very different from those who settled in Plymouth. If the Pilgrims had landed in Virginia instead of New England, they would not have found themselves very much out of place in the cultural atmosphere. But the accident that sent the Pilgrims to the New England coast proved advantageous in terms of the years. In New England the climate and soil, vexatious and ungiving as Noah's wife, egged the inhabitants on to more and more effort in order to survive. New England, in short, despite its discomforts and difficulties, was an inspiration and not a desperation—for which the Pilgrims and all North America could be thankful.

Originally the Pilgrims had sent Robert Cushman and John Carver to London for no purpose other than to negotiate with the Virginia Company, which was controlled by churchmen, for territory in which to settle in the *new world.* If the Pilgrims had landed in the vicinity of the Jamestown colony, the whole history of America might have been different. The difference would not have resulted from the fact that the Pilgrims were so unlike the Virginians, but from the fact that the Pilgrims would have been unable to be themselves in Virginia. They would have had to compromise with the Virginians, and compromise almost inevitably means dissolution of original principle. In New England they were able, for a time at least, to work out their own way of life. The major argument between the Pilgrims and the Virginians had revolved about the Established Church and the acceptance of its doctrines. The Pilgrims could not and would not accept the dictatorship of the Church of England.

The Pilgrims believed in man as an individual, abstracted from everything else, supreme within himself. All the Dissenter groups believed this. They were Dissenters of the Lollard strain; they were seventeenth-century Lollards who had acquired spiritual trousers and shirts and learned to knot their ties. They did not believe as the medievalists had believed, and as modern Communism is prone to believe, that man as an individual is nothing except as he is allied to a group, is part of a mass, is a microcosm within a macrocosm. They believed that man as an individual is an unqualified entity, a reality deserving of the consideration of everyone, including the Lord.

Although the Virginia colony had been founded, according to its charter, to spread Christianity among the Indians, and its leaders had early insisted that its members be upright men of God, it was not very long before it became inhabited by men governed by commercial instead of religious motivations. Money soon played an unconscionable role in the career of the colony: it stood out like a signal, a flag, a banner before which everyone genuflected. But the Pilgrims, deprived and disciplined by the environment, continued to be more concerned with religion and less with the magics of exchange. The exigencies of the environment forced them in the beginning to be more interested in survival than in success. The result was that the Pilgrims succeeded better than any other group in adhering to their original religious ideals, and in working out a way of life which came closest to realizing the dream of democracy and freedom that had been born in the womb of Lollardism.

### THE FAILURE OF COMMUNISM AMONG THE PILGRIMS

It should not be concluded, however, that the Pilgrims lived in perfect harmony and that everyone was equal in a utopian sense of the word. The Pilgrims were not utopians. They had no illusions about equality except in a religious and political sense. They believed in giving everyone a right to vote, but that right did not alter their economic station. Bradford confesses that "much was stolen both by night and by day before it became scarce eatable, and much more afterward. And though many were well whipt (when they were taken) for a few ears of corne, yet hunger made others (whom conscience did not restraine) to venture." [11] At length they found that their communal way of living could not be pursued any further, and they "assigned to every family a parcell of land, according to the proportion of their number for that end, only for present use (*but made no devission for inheritance*), and ranged all boys and youth under some familie." [12] This procedure, Bradford goes on to say, "had very good success; for it made all hands very industrious, so as much more corne was planted than other waise.... The women now wente willingly into the field, and took their little ones with them to set corne, which before would aledg weakness, and inabilitie." [13]

Bradford insists that the temporary communism practiced in Plymouth did not work; that only when the land was restored to private families and individuals did anything resembling economic prosperity return. In the light of his experience with his own followers, he became convinced that the "comone wealth" idea as advocated by Plato and many other ancient utopians was impracticable and futile. Bradford unhesitatingly condemned all those who maintained "that the taking away of propertie and bringing in the community into a common wealth would make them happy and flourishing." He criticized such people severely because they thought "they were wiser than God."

It is informing to follow Bradford's argument in more detail. "The communitie," in its communal phase, "was found to breed much confusion and discontent," he insisted, "and retarded much imployment that would have been to their benefit and comforte. For the yong-men were most able and fitte for labour and service did repine that they should spend their time and strength to worke for other mens wives and children without any recompence. The strong, or man of parts, had no more in devission of victails and cloaths than he that was weake and not able to doe a quarter the other could; this was thought injuestice. The aged and graver men to be ranked and equalised in labours and victails, cloaths, etc., with the meaner and younger sorte, thought it some indignite and disrespect unto them. And for mens wives to be commanded to doe service for other men, as dresing their meate, washing their cloaths, etc., they deemd it a kind of slaverie, neither could many husbands well brooke it. Upon the poynte all being to have alike, and all to doe alike, they thought themselves in the like condition, and one as good as another; and so, if it did not cut of those relations that God hath set amongst men, yet it did at least much diminish and take of the mutuall respects that should be preserved amongst them. And would have bene worse if they had been men of another condition. Let none object this is men's corruption, and nothing to the course it selfe. I answer, seeing all men have this corruption in them, God in his wisdome saw another course fiter for them."

## THE INELUCTABLE SERPENT

It is revealing to record Bradford's allusion to "men's corruption." What he is talking about, of course, is man's individualistic, anti-co-operative tendencies, which he believes are biologically and psychologically ineradicable. It is the characteristic Christian belief, derived from the Garden of Eden story, that man is born evil and has to redeem himself in order to become good. What it all goes back to is the problem of human nature. Is it essentially good or evil? Is the evil which lives in man a product of his own nature or is it a result of the evils of the environment which instigate wicked impulses in him? Bradford believed that the evil, or the "corruption," which lives in man was planted there by God. He was convinced that those who contended, as many did in those days and many more have contended since, that all man had to do to be good was to destroy the evil relationships in society, were futile romancers and fools. It is not surprising, therefore, that from the beginning Bradford had no illusions about the possibilities of a communal settlement in Plymouth. It was simply the agreement established between the Pilgrims and their capitalist backers that necessitated their seven-year communal plan. To describe the failure of the Pilgrims to organize a successful communistic colony as an evidence of the failure of communism in practice is unfair and inaccurate. The Pilgrims were not a communally minded group, and they resorted to a co-operative economy only because of their agreement with their financial sponsors and because of the necessities of the environment.

Under the new economic setup the Plymouth Colony achieved rapid success. "The Lord prospered their trading," as Bradford declared, and before long many people in the colony began to acquire the increasing forms of wealth. The effects of this prosperity were not altogether felicitous. As Bradford himself admits, "this benefit turned to their hurte, and this accession of strength to their weakness." What resulted was that the co-operative spirit of the colony was splintered into so many different parts, with acquisitive tendencies eliminating the communal. "No man thought he could live," Bradford pointed out, describing the new attitude which had developed, "except he had catle and a great deal of ground to keep them; all striving to increase their stocks. By which means they were scattered all over the bay, quickly, and the towne in which they lived compactly till now was left very thin, and in a short time allmost desolate, and if this had been all it had been less, though too much; but the church must also be divided and those who had lived so long together." Since the landed property assigned to each family in Plymouth constituted a small lot in the village, it is obvious that considerable economic progress was achieved under the new regime.

The colony eventually was dispersed by the simple necessities of economic and geographic division. In their struggle for a livelihood, the colonists soon scattered to more and more remote parts of the land, so that, to quote Bradford again, "those that lived on their lots on the other side of the bay (called Duxberie) . . . could not long bring their wives and children to the publick worship and church meetings . . . and sued to dismiss and become a body of themselves; and so they were dismissed (about this time) though very unwillingly."

In time this centrifugal tendency became so disruptive that it was necessary, as Bradford said, "to give out some good farms to spetiall persons that would promise to live at Plimoth, and likely to be helpful to the church or commonewelth, and so tye the lands to Plimoth as farmes for the same." But even this did not work. After a while these people also moved away to more fertile territories, and Bradford in despondency confessed that this meant "the ruine of New England, at least of the churches of God ther, and will provock the Lord's displeasure against them."

### THE FIRST PRISON

As a practical corroboration of Goldsmith's words that when "wealth accumulates, men decay," the Plymouth group became less co-operative and more competitive, less social and more individualistic, as soon as prosperity crowned their efforts. In England and Holland they had been a hard-working, struggling sect, unacquainted with economic success; in the new country they were able to add to their "propertie" and acquire comforts if not luxuries which they had never possessed before. As soon as they found that their cows and calves and goats and kids were selling at high rates, they found it necessary, as a means of protecting their property, to erect a prison in which to house the have-nots who attempted to steal from the haves. Bradford puts it precisely when he states that "with the first fruits of which [their new prosperity] they builte a house for a prison—built in Sumer Street where the brook called Prison Brook crosses the street." [14]

In the old country prisons were viewed by the religious rebels as places where they were incarcerated by the state, which in their eyes was an instrument of Antichrist. Many of the members of the Pilgrim group as well as other Dissenters had been clapped into the prisons from time to time. They hated prisons on principle. They had never dreamed of using them against members of their own group, followers of the same faith. But prosperity, with the economic divisions which it inevitably brings in its wake, created the necessity. With the Pilgrims as with all other peoples, when some grow rich, more grow poor, and still more grow wicked. Bradford, like most people of his time, was prone to explain what occurred as a product of "Satane." Although he was convinced that man's "corrupte nature" was a result of God's will, he feared the dreadful possibility that "Satane" was more powerful in "these heathen lands" than back in the Christian lands of Europe.[15] He railed mainly against moral sins—fornication, adultery, buggery, sodomy, and that ilk—although written beneath the lines was his conviction that the "original sin" of woman in the Garden of Eden was really what caused most of the sins with which the colony was afflicted.

### THE PURITAN VIEW OF WOMAN

Bradford and most of the people of the time believed, in fact, that *woman* was the root of evil, the temptation which vitiated man's better impulses and led him into disasters. Woman, not man, was the *bête noire*. But not only the Pilgrims entertained such ideas; everyone else did. In London, in 1632, a volume was published which expressed the same philosophy: it said in no equivocal fashion that "the reason why women have no control in Parliament, why they make no laws, consent to none, abrogate none, is their *original sin.*" [Italics mine.] [16]

New England records are full of references to women which disclose that attitude. In the *Boston News-Letter*, for example, one can discover innumerable allusions to women suggestive of their susceptibility to Satanic influences. Very often it is in the tone of the account rather than in specific details that the attitude is to be detected. The case of Elizabeth Whetlie is illustrative:

> On Wednesday morning the 17th instant, died Elizabeth Whetlie, Single Woman, for want of help, being big with Child, who would not own that she was with child, was afterwards opened and found to be so.[17]

But it was not only immoral women who suffered from such penalties. Woman as a species was subject to them—more subject than men. After all, women still had to pay the price for having made man iniquitous. It was woman, not man, whom Satan beguiled. Susanna Griffin, for instance, was a good woman, but Satan was too much for her, as we discover:

> Salisbury, Aug. 10. On the 3rd instant Susanna Griffin, of this Town, was found dead in a small Pond of Water about a Foot and a half deep, into which 'tis judged (through the Violence of Satan's Temptation) having first twisted her Neckcloth very hard about her Neck she cast

herself and was drown'd or suffocated. She was esteemed to be a Person of a Pious and Sober Conversation; And we hope the Inserting of such an awful Providence here may not be offensive but rather a warning to all others to watch against the Wiles of our Grand Adversary.[18]

Woman was viewed not only as a more evil creature than man but also as definitely inferior in economic, social, and psychological status. It was a despotic, patriarchal ethic which the New Englanders transported from the old to the new country. While the origin of that ethic, in terms of historical development, was economic, its derivation and defense were Biblical. It should not be thought, however, that its source was Judaic. In that regard all ancient patriarchal peoples were similar. Woman's position was economically inferior and politically unexalted. To be precise, the Jews treated their women better than the Greeks, and if they had no Aspasias or Sapphos, they had Esthers and Ruths.

Among the Puritan theocrats, with whom we shall deal in the next chapter, that attitude toward woman was even more conspicuous than it was among the Pilgrims. Women were excellent in their place, but their place was far from elevated. They could be made love to by proxy, as John Alden did for Miles Standish; they could be commanded by their parents not to "let . . . your fancy overrule your necessity"; in fact, they could be made to do anything which the males in the community decided was right. And what was right, and what was best, was for a woman to bear children and bear them bountifully. One colonist left a heritage of 108 children, grandchildren, and great-grandchildren. Mather himself described the marital industry of one of his own contemporaries as follows:

He was twice married. By his first wife, the vertuous daughter of parents therein resembled by her, he had six children. But his next wife was a young gentlewoman whom he chose from under the guardianship and with the countenance of Edward Hopkins, Esq., the excellent governor of Connecticut. . . . By the daughter of that Mr. Launce, who is yet living among us, Mr. Sherman had no less than twenty children added unto the number of six which he had before. . . . One woman [in New England] had had not less than twenty-two children; whereof she buried fourteen sons and six daughters.

> Another woman has had no less than twenty-three children by one husband; whereof nineteen lived unto men's and women's estate. A third was mother to seven and twenty children: And she that was mother to Sir William Phips, the late governor of New England, had no less than twenty-five children beside him; she had one and twenty sons and five daughters. Now unto the catalog of such "fruitful vines by the sides of the house" is this gentlewoman Mrs. Sherman to be enumerated. Behold thus was our Sherman, that eminent leader of the Lord, blessed of Him.

It is not true, however, that women, because of the Biblical idea, were deprived of all rights. In Plymouth, even when creditors seized the lands of a deceased husband, a part of the value was preserved for the wife and children. In 1636 it was made impossible for a husband to sell land without the consent of the wife. On the other hand, women could be punished by their husbands with impunity provided physical violence was not employed. If a man struck his wife, he was liable to a fine of ten pounds or corporal punishment. A woman who treated her husband in a similar manner was subject to the same penalty; and since the wife in those days didn't have any money with which to pay such a fine, she was at the mercy of her husband, who, if he refused to pay the fine, could have her publicly whipped. In the case of divorce, female adultery was always a sufficient cause, but "male adultery after some debate and consultation with the elders, was judged not sufficient." In the case of bastardy, the man had only to appear before the parish church and admit his guilt, whereas the woman involved was often subjected to a public lashing. "In 1649," James Oneal states, "a woman was given fourteen lashes, while the father of her child was sentenced to build a bridge across a creek."[19] Often, Oneal also points out, when "masters were fined for this offense, the violated mothers were required to repay their masters by an extension of their terms of servitude."[20]

In brief, women found themselves as handicapped by law and custom in the new world as they had been in the old. The Pilgrims were eager to free themselves from the domination of the Established Church, but they were not interested in freeing women from the domination of men.

## THE MORTON INTERLUDE

The ethics of the Pilgrims were just as ascetic as those of the Puritans. They hated Thomas Morton's Merrymount settlement, which he founded in 1626, as much as the Puritans did, and they were just as eager to see it destroyed. Like all lower middle-class groups from every land—Holland, Germany, France, England—the Pilgrims exalted denial into a virtue and made of joy a vice. When Thomas Morton, the American Dionysian, encouraged his followers to desire moral as well as political liberty, the Pilgrims as well as the Puritans denounced him and wanted to see him and his group annihilated. Morton represented everything they loathed. He was a vestigial aristocrat, who lent emotional and spiritual charm and color to the drab American landscape. He could not tolerate the repressive psychology of the Pilgrims and Puritans and was determined that in Merrymount everyone would be free to enjoy himself in all the ways that man had invented. Morton embodied more of the "Merry England" psychology of the aristocrats than any other Englishman who settled in America in the seventeenth century.[21]

He was destroyed because he could not be endured.

The Pilgrims and Puritans came to America with religion in their hearts and money in their pockets; Morton came with little religion and still less money. He was an adventurer who was truly adventurous, a spiritual wayfarer, a moral vagabond.

Although a student of law in his youth, when he grew up he became as lawless as a buccaneer and was quick to recognize the promise of the new world. When he set out for America, shrouded in his vast cloak, which took the breeze like the wings of a large bird, he was determined to make America into the kind of country he loved. The England he had known had already become drab and drear, sullied with priests and preachers and men of the street who were shot through with the mad pieties and sanctities of the day. He fell in love with America with explosive spontaneity. His words are suggestive of his outlook:

> The more I looked, the more I liked it. And when I had more seriously considered of the bewty of the place, with all her faire indowments, I did not thinke that in all the knowne world it could be paralel'd, for

so many goodly groves of trees, dainty, fine, round, rising hillucks, delicate, faire, large plaines, sweet cristall fountaines, and cleare running streams that twine in fine meanders through the meads, making so sweete a murmuring noise to hear as lull the senses with delight asleepe, so pleasantly do they glide upon the pebble stones. . . .

Morton represented exactly the reverse of what the Puritans and Pilgrims stood for; his psychology was aristocratic and not middle-class. He preferred the aristocratic way of life; he typified everything the middle class condemned. He was swashbucklerish in manner, Rabelaisian in speech, violent in action. He made Merrymount the most exciting, romantic, and joyful settlement in New England. All this Elizabethan exuberance of spirit annoyed and exasperated the serious, staid men of Plymouth and Massachusetts Bay, and when he added to the festive delights of the place the ancient Maypole dance, it was the straw that broke the camel's back. Morton believed in holidays—the more the merrier—and in gaiety, abandon. He wanted to perpetuate the countryside joys and jollities of old England; he wanted men to be drunk with merriment, vocal with Bacchanalian glee. He was called all things by many men. All Dissenters loathed him.

Morton's own words about the Maypole festivity are most revealing:

The setting up of this Maypole was a lamentable spectacle to the precise Separatists that lived at New Plimmoth. They termed it an Idoll; yea, they called it a Calfe of Horeb, and stood at defiance with the place, naming it Mount Dragon; threatening to make it a woefull mount and not a merry mount.[22]

Morton's "schoole of athisme," as Bradford described it, inspired by the fiery waters of the Bacchanalian spring, threatened to undermine the religiosity of the other settlements. Morton's Maypole, eighty feet high, soon became a legend. It represented something which alarmed the Puritan and Pilgrim countryside. Morton had to be destroyed.

Morton was not an idealist, not a crusader. He could be as shrewd as any Yankee trader, and in fact in his dealings with the Indians, with whom he became such fast friends, he never failed to profit.

The Pilgrims and Puritans were jealous of his Indian friendships and feared that he might use these to annihilate them.* [23] But what they were most concerned about was the beaver trade, in which Morton had been more successful than they. Miles Standish, the unimaginative captain who, according to legend, knew better how to kill than to love, was instructed to murder and disperse the Mortonites. He did. And New England thereafter became a bleaker, barer place.

The attack upon Merrymount and the arrest and deportation of Morton marked the final triumph of middle-class psychology in New England. After that all trace of gaiety disappeared. There were only two classes in those days who knew how to be merry: the aristocrats who could afford it and the peasants who could afford nothing else. The middle class could not afford it and therefore condemned it as evil.

"The Separatists," as Morton wisely observed, "envying the prosperity and hope of the plantation at Ma-re-mount" [24] and envying too the profits he was making from the beaver trade, were determined to monopolize the territory for themselves. It was not by chance that Miles Standish threatened to shoot Morton as the latter got into his boat after his followers had been scattered. Morton was anathema to "King Winthrop," as he called the Massachusetts Bay leader, as well as to Bradford. It was not only the Maypole festivities to which the Pilgrims and Puritans objected but also Morton's familiar associations with the Indians and his affairs with the "lasses in beaver coats." Morton was accused of selling arms as well as liquor to the Indians. He denied both accusations, and there is reason to believe that, though he did treat the Indians hospitably with alcohol, he did not sell them rifles or guns. As Morton averred, it was the Pilgrims and Puritans themselves who perpetrated that mischief.

At all events, Morton was different. He did not typify the middle-class psychology of the rest of New England; he represented a feudal remnant, a backwash of aristocratic tradition. The destruction of his settlement meant the destruction of a whole way of life.

A haphazard personality, the spirit of an adventurer compounded

* Morton called his place Ma-re-mount. It was the Pilgrims and Puritans who derogatorily captioned it as Merrymount. Ma-re-mount simply meant "a hill by the sea."

with the philosophy of a "heathen," he lent more color to the American scene than any other individual of his time. Fond of the Indians, he came to know them far more intimately than did any of the inhabitants of Salem or Plymouth. The most interesting part of his book *New English Canaan* is the part dealing with Indian life and customs. His claim that "the Massachusetts Indian [was] more full of humanity than the Christians," a sympathy which he extended to the point of selling the Indians firearms later allegedly used against the Puritans—was enough to stamp him immediately as a desperate enemy of the theocracy. His ridicule of the religionists of that day belonged to a tradition that did not survive his own disappearance from New England; it was snuffed out by its enemies before it had a chance to flame. The assault upon his Maypole festivities put a swift end to this one aspect of New England life which for a brief moment had escaped middle-class tyranny. Certainly these verses of Morton's, culled from the *New English Canaan* and associated with the Maypole rites, echoed a tradition that was foreign to that of Michael Wigglesworth and Anne Bradstreet:

Drink and be merry, merry, merry, boys,
Let all your delight be in Hymen's joys,
Jo to Hymen now the day is come,
About the merry May-pole take a Roome.

Make green garlons, bring bottles out;
And fill sweet Nectar freely about,
Uncover thy head, and feare no harme,
For hers good liquor to keep it warme.
Then drinke and be merry, and
Jo to Hymen, etc.

Nectar is a thing assign'd,
By the Deities owne minde,
To cure the hart opprest with griefe,
And of good liquors is the cheife.

## CHAPTER VII

# The Theocrats

*I think that in no country in the civilised world is less attention paid to philosophy than in the United States.*

—ALEXIS DE TOCQUEVILLE

THE Puritan group that settled in Salem and the vicinity, and later became known as the Massachusetts Bay Colony, was exactly what its name implied—a group that wanted to *purify* the Established Church of England, but did not want to separate from it. The Pilgrims, on the other hand, were Separatists, whose main objective was to separate from the Established Church of England, to separate from all churches but their own, to separate in order to be themselves, freed from the papalisms and ritualisms superimposed by the organized ecclesiastical bodies of their day.[1] The conflict between the Pilgrims and Puritans was fundamental, irreconcilable.

It was both economic and religious. The Pilgrims representing the poorer and more intransigent group were naturally in favor of independence from the ruling class whose religion was embodied in the Established Church of England; the Puritans representing a more successful and wealthier group were inevitably closer to the ruling class and did not want to destroy their connection with it, religious or otherwise, so long as their interests could be preserved. In fact, the Puritans contended that the state should be authoritative in religion, whereas the Pilgrims believed in the separation of the powers of church and state.[2]

Unlike the Pilgrims, who had everyone on the boat sign the Mayflower pact, the Puritans, Calvinist in politics as well as theology, established their community upon a class basis from the start. Places in their meetinghouses were assigned according to economic station, the rich sitting in pews different from those of the poor, and church and state being united into a theocracy. The democratic spirit of the Pilgrims was anathema to the Puritans. "Democracy," John Cotton wrote in 1638, "I do not conceive that ever God did ordain as a fit government either for church or commonwealth. If the people be governor, who shall be governed? As for monarchy and aristocracy, they are both of them clearly approved and directed in scripture, yet so as referreth the sovereignty to himself and setteth up theocracy in both, as the best form of government in the commonwealth as in church." [3] In general, the Puritans had little sympathy for the commoners. John Winthrop, for example, declared that "the best part of a community is always the least, and of that best part the wiser is always the lesser." [4]

Winthrop's whole attitude, as evinced in his *Journal* as well as in his conduct as a governor, was that of an absolute sovereign and never that of a representative of the people. As a matter of fact, the entire government of the Massachusetts Bay Colony in the beginning was a government dictated by those at the top, not by those below. The church was dominant, and those who governed the colony were responsible to the church for their actions.

### PURITAN AUTHORITARIANISM

The antidemocratic spirit of the Massachusetts Bay Colony found vital expression in its hostility to religious liberty. It is important to remember that in the charter drawn up by the Puritan colony no promise was made of guaranteeing religious freedom to the inhabitants. The Puritans entertained no concept of freedom in their tradition; they believed in authority, not freedom. The state in their eyes was supreme, not the individual. The Pilgrims, on the other hand, like all the Dissenters, believed that man derived his knowledge of God through and within himself and not by means of church or clergy. The church with the Pilgrims was incidental; with the Puritans it was fundamental. The latter were opposed to unauthorized interpretations of the Bible; the clergy was the only group empowered with the right to give an authorized interpretation of it. Consequently any group or individual in the Massachusetts Bay Colony who hazarded an interpretation of the Bible or of religion which differed from that of the clergy was considered guilty of a most grievous and heinous offense.

It was that philosophy which underlay the theocratic government established by the Puritans. Divine wisdom was vested in the clergy and, since church and state according to their lights were inseparable, the ministers became the rightful rulers of the colony. The result was a community in which the laymen had to goose-step in rhythm with the commands of the clergy, whose dictatorship forbade criticism or challenge. What the people could and couldn't do was determined not by law but by religion, for in a theocratic state law is but a subordinate aspect of religion. Civil law had little meaning in the community; religious law, derived from Biblical contexts, was far more important and decisive. The hierophants were judges as well as spiritual guides and leaders, and in their hands rested the powers of punishment and exile, which they invariably exercised in defense of their own interests. They could exile a Roger Williams from the colony as easily and expeditiously as they could put a blasphemer or fornicator in the stocks or subject him to a public lashing.

Fortunately, early conditions forced the leaders of the colony to give freedom to their *indentured* servants, and, after considerable debate and conflict, a more representative and more democratic form of government was instituted in the colony. Nevertheless, the dominance of the clergy did not disappear for several generations, and life under its aegis was far from pleasant and joyous.

## THE PSYCHOLOGY OF TERROR

To begin with, the religious psychology of the Puritans was grounded in fear and terror. They believed that every child was born in sin and would die in sin unless he underwent the experience of conversion and regeneration. The clergy insisted that the conversion and regeneration should not be private, but public. In Lechford's *Plaine-Dealing: Or Newes from New England* (published in 1642) the five steps in the procedure are outlined in minute and graphic detail. Many of the people viewed the ordeal with such horror that they preferred "to goe without Communion, than undergoe such publique confessions and tryals." [5] Needless to say, the ministers did everything in their power to convince their congregations that "the wages of sin is death," denouncing sinners in violent and sulphurous diction, and painting pictures of hell beside which Dante's Inferno seemed a mild and gentle place.

These diatribes by the New England Jeremiahs and Isaiahs of the time thundered in meetinghouse after meetinghouse, up and down the length and breadth of the settlement. Even children could not escape the detonations. Sunday after Sunday children were forced to accompany their parents to the torture chambers of the church and listen to the stories of hail and brimstone, of typhoon and hurricane, of plague and pestilence, which awaited sinners in the bottomless recesses of hell. Although the children, fortunately, could not understand most of what they heard, they understood enough, no doubt, to be intimidated and terrified, so that they spent the rest of their lives in a continuous agony of fear.

In the schoolbooks that children studied the same spirit was manifest. In the *New England Primer*, for example, which sufficed as a schoolroom text for many generations, terrifying pictures of martyrs being burned at the stake were conspicuous, followed by poems and object lessons of a most forbidding and depressing variety. Michael Wigglesworth's *Day of Doom*, a poem depicting the flaming hell in which sinners were consumed, was also used extensively in the New England schools. Another widely read book at that time was James Janeway's *Token for Children*, in which the following passage, culled from the second preface, is typical of the spirit of the book as a whole:

> Did you ever go to your father and mother, master and mistress, and beg of them to pity you, and pray for you, and to teach you what you shall do to be saved? Do you dare to run up and down upon the Lord's Day? Or do you keep in to read your book? They which lie must go to their father the devil, into everlasting burning; they which never pray, God will pour out his wrath upon them; and when they beg and pray in hell fire, God will not forgive them, but there must lye forever. Are you willing to go to hell to be burnt with the devil and his angels? Would you be in the same condition as naughty children? O, hell is a terrible place, that's worse a thousand times than whipping.*

In other words, everything and anything conducive to fear was popular pabulum in those days, and the dosage given to children was even more severe than that administered to adults. Children were

* Quoted from Fleming, *op. cit.*, p. 85, which gives an excellent description of the condition of children under the Puritan regime.

viewed not as children but as miniature adults; as sinners, they were as subject to God's punishment as adults, and were given no extenuating treatment because of their age. After all, they were unregenerate, afflicted with the depravity of the race, and until they became regenerate they were agents of evil. Even in legal terms a boy became a man at sixteen; but if he was converted before he became sixteen, he was forced to give in public as detailed an account of his conversion as any adult of thirty or forty. The Puritans, it must not be forgotten, were much more interested in hell than heaven, and found infinitely more satisfaction in punishing the erring than in rewarding the virtuous.

### OBSESSION WITH SIN

Few communities have been so rigid and ruthless in the treatment of their inhabitants as the Massachusetts Bay Colony. Sins were countless. They were the great bugaboo, the great obsession of the day. There were few things one could do, no matter how inconsequential, that did not carry some suggestion or implication of sin within them. Sabbath-breaking, for example, was viewed as one of the gravest sins. "Of the manifold sins which then I was guilty of," Nathaniel Mather confessed, "none so sticks upon me as that being very young, I was whittling on the sabbath-day; and for fear of being seen, I did it behind the door. A great reproach of God. A specimen of that atheism that I brought into the world with me."[6] Men were lashed for neglecting to attend church and lovers were tried for "sitting-together" on the Sabbath day; others were fined and still others put in the stocks for working on Sunday, taking a journey, or whipping a servant.

Commenting on whipping as a punishment, Edward Ward, a widely traveled cynic, who wrote with his tongue in his cheek, tells in his *Trip to New England,* which he published in 1699, that "Whipping is a punishment so practicable in this Country upon every slight Offence that at a town upon the Sound called New Haven, the people do confess that all the Inhabitants of that Place above the age of Fourteen have been Whipped for some Misdemeanour or other (except two) the Minister and the Justice."

"The laws of the country against prophaneness and immorality are strictly put in execution insomuch that there is as great an appearance of Sobriety and Virtue in New England as in any place in the World," wrote Neal, in his *History of New England;* "there are no games nor plays, Swearing, Drunkenness, and all sorts of Debauchery are out of Fashion." [7] Extreme as such words may seem, they are by no means unconsonant with the general tenor of New England life in the seventeenth century.

In short, every gesture, every suggestion, every action that deviated from the Puritan norm, merited condemnation of the most severe and excruciating variety. Ward, tongue in cheek still, even describes how the severity of the laws led to all manner of violations. "If you kiss in Publick," he writes, "tho' offered as a Curteous Salutation, if any information is given to the Select Members, both shall be whipped and fined. But the good humor'd Lasses, to make you Amends, will kiss the kinder in the Corner." In another place, Ward describes the experience of a captain who kissed his wife in the street:

> The Captain of a Ship who had been on a long Voyage happen'd to meet his Wife and kist her in the Street, for which he was fin'd Ten Shillings. What a happiness, thought I, do we enjoy in old England that can not only kiss our own Wives but other men's too, without the danger of such a penalty.[8]

Ward gives many other illustrations of how severely the Puritans treated people who violated their moral code. "Another Inhabitant of the Town was fined Ten Shillings for kissing his own wife in his Garden," Ward writes, "and, obstinately refusing to pay the money, endured twenty lashes at the Gun." [9] As a result of this austere moral code, which in part was a compensation for their economic immoralities, the Puritans cultivated a form of life that made pain a joy and joy a pain. Ward, his tongue even deeper in his cheek, to be sure, makes still sharper stabs into their economic skin:

> It is a Proverb with those that know that Whosoever believes a New England Saint shall be sure to be cheated; and he that knows how to deal with their traders may deal with the Devil and fear no Craft." [10]

### BUYING CHEAP AND SELLING DEAR

What we have in the case of the Puritans is an excellent illustration of the contradiction which developed in Protestant ethics as a result of the rise of capitalist economics. The exigencies of the economic struggle drove men to lie, to cheat, to steal, to enslave, and even to murder, all in an attempt to "buy cheap and sell dear," which practice became the necessary means of survival and success in this new era. That necessity had arisen in the old world and continued in the new. It was not a new tendency, to be sure, but an old one which acquired new aspects. Men had lied, cheated, stolen, enslaved, and murdered for untold centuries, but they had done it bluntly, boldly, without concern for conscience or conviction; now they did it subtly, deceptively, hypocritically, convincing themselves that what they did was a righteous necessity, something blessed by the Lord. If they robbed the Indians of their lands, which were but temporal possessions, they saved their souls, which were eternal ones.

It was not long before the Puritans found themselves double-crossing the Indians, swindling them out of their lands, capturing them and shipping them off to the Barbados as slaves, and exterminating them as far as possible—as they did the Pequots and Narragansetts in swift, fierce wars, the horror of which the Indians never forgot or forgave. More profitable than Indian slave traffic, however, was Negro slave traffic, in which the Puritans soon became superlatively adept. The New Englanders justified this traffic by assuring themselves that what they were doing was for the benefit of the slaves, since it brought them within the reaches of "the gospel dispensation" and would save their souls from the eternal punishment of hell. At the same time that the Puritans were guilty of these larger immoralities, they insisted all the more strongly upon the practice of the smaller moralities, meting out ever more and more severe punishments for violations of the Sabbath, theft of an ear of corn, inebriety, profanity, blasphemy, obscenity. Therein lies the great contradiction in morality that capitalist economics introduced and that Protestantism has never been able to solve—and that continues like a social cancer down until today.

### PUNISHMENT FOR SIN, NOT CRIME

Winthrop informs us that the servant Philip Ratlif "was censured to be whipped, lose his ears, and be banished from the plantation" because he mouthed "most foul scandalous invectives against our churches and government,"[11] but Winthrop does not relate any instances in which Puritan captains or merchants were reprimanded, lashed, mutilated, or exiled for selling Indians or Negroes into slavery. He records the "many laws made against tobacco and immodest fashions and costly apparel, &c." [12] and even describes how the court became so alarmed at the costly apparel being worn that it "sent for the elders of the churches and conferred with them about it . . . but little was done about it for diverse of the elders' wives &c. were in some measure partners in this general disorder." [13] In fact, nothing of an irreligious or obscene nature escaped their everlastingly vigilant attention. Indeed, it can be said without exaggeration that the theocrats were far more proficient in ferreting out sin than crime. It was this tendency that undoubtedly led to the development of the mentality which succumbed to the witchcraft craze not many decades later. In time the moralists got to the point where they could detect sin by telepathic technique. After that, no one was safe in the community save those in the high places. It is interesting to note in that connection that few of the better-standing and wealthier members of the community were ever found guilty of immorality or criminality. It was the poorer classes who were mainly susceptible to those evils. The fact that a man was poor or of low station, or lived at all irregularly, was sufficient to make him suspect in the eyes of the church fathers and magistrates, and when their suspicions became aggravated by gossip or behavior of the slightest obliquity they stopped at nothing to imprison the guilty or innocent.

Winthrop tells of the case of a "loose fellow" who was executed for having impregnated a sow. Winthrop's words describing the case are indicative of their persecutory psychology: "At New Haven there was a sow which among other things in a litter had one without hair and some other resemblances and it had also one eye blemished just like one eye of a loose fellow in the town which occasioned him to be suspected and being examined before the magistrates he confessed the fact . . . [and] they put him to death." [14]

Unlike Bradford, who was a gentler and wiser man, and whom American historians have never given his just due, Winthrop seemed to rejoice in these punishments and at times to gloat over the victims with almost pathologic satisfaction. It was not only that he wanted to see justice done, but like most of the other Puritan leaders he got a morbid and perverted pleasure out of seeing it done. His sense of righteousness, in short, like that of the Cottons and Mathers, was born of a "better-than-thou" psychology which derived its strength from the weaknesses and sins of his inferiors. In punishing his inferiors he confirmed his own superiority. In other words, the psychology of these Puritans was not that of good Samaritans, but that of haughty, untender, and unbending theocrats.

### TREATMENT OF LABOR

When it came to the matter of employment of labor, the New England Puritans were neither gentle nor generous. Winthrop himself relates in his *Journal* how a scarcity of workmen had raised wages to such an excessive rate that "a carpenter would have three shillings the day, a laborer two shillings and six pence." [15] Like most other entrepreneurs, Winthrop complained that the love of idleness and the affinity for tobacco and "strong waters" were the curse of the working class. In order to rectify the situation, Winthrop and his colleagues had the court issue an order reducing wages and fixing prices at a lower level—ostensibly for the sake of the improvement of the community. It was such tactics and their continuation throughout the century that led Ward to describe the New Englanders in the following way:

> The inhabitants seem very Religious, showing many outward and visible Signs of an inward and spiritual Grace, but though they wear in their Faces the Innocence of Doves, you will find them in their Dealings as Subtile as Serpents. Interest is their Faith, Money their God and large Possessions the only Heaven they covet.

No doubt Ward was a little unfair in his description, but there was enough truth in his indictment to make it unerasable.

The contradiction between the religiosity of the theocratic community and the irreligiosity of its economic life was too obvious to escape attack. In England these Puritan leaders had been forced to play fifth or sixth fiddle to the aristocratic regime. In the new country they played first fiddle. It was that difference which caused the major part of the contradiction. The Puritans were more, not less, religious in America, but the nature of life in the new country evoked their worst instincts. They found themselves invested with power, and power corrupts the best of men and communities. Their treatment of laborers, as we have seen, was far from fair or decently motivated, and their attitude toward servants was far from magnanimous. Winthrop's *Journal* abounds in allusions to servant rebellions. Although it was necessary to free several hundred of the indentured servants when the settlers first arrived, the servants employed later were seldom treated like free men; in general they were sharply reprimanded, whipped, and imprisoned when found unsatisfactory. When servants were insufficient, the Puritans bound out criminals in various capacities. If servants misbehaved, it was a simple matter to have their tenure of service extended.

### TREATMENT OF SERVANTS

Winthrop in his *Journal* relates the following case, in which the very nature of the description betrays the general feeling toward servants that prevailed: "Two men servants to one Moodye, of Roxbury, returning in a boat from the windmill, struck upon the oyster bank. They went out to gather oysters, and floated away, and they were both drowned, although they might have waded out on either side; but it was an evident judgment of God upon them, for they were wicked persons. One of them a little before being reproved for his lewdness and put in mind of hell, answered that if hell were ten times hotter, he had rather be there than he would serve his master, etc. The occasion was because he had bound himself for divers years, and saw that, if he had been at liberty, he might have had greater wages, though otherwise his master used him very well." [16]

Out of Mr. Randolph's papers we find other illustrations of the same class attitude. In Mr. Randolph's struggle against a recalcitrant faction, he writes to the Earl of —— on June 14, 1682, that "as for the persons joyn'd and concerned in the Faction here, I know but one man who was not himself a servant or a servant's son." [17] In an even earlier letter, Randolph makes a similar allusion to an individual servant whose name he does not specify, declaring that "he is one of the Faction, a man of mean extraction, coming over a poor servant." [18] On October 27, 1686, in a letter to the Archbishop of —— he complains of the fact that of the Seven Persons called Commissioners or Trustees, the chief is Mr. Dudley, the President, "a man of a base *servile* and anti-Monarchical Principle."

Servants naturally had more to revolt against than free men, and certainly more than rich men, and one is not to be surprised that they did revolt at times. What is more interesting, however, from a democratic perspective, is the attitude toward such revolts which obtained among the New England plutocrats. There was no difference here from the attitude which prevailed in the Southern colonies toward the Negro slaves who were bound for life.

In another place Winthrop tells us about "a man servant in Boston, having stolen from his master and being threatened to be brought before the Magistrates, went and hanged himself." [19]

Fixed wages and prices made it easy for the employers to be certain of their profits regardless of economic impediment or crisis.

Although indentured servitude was a strong support for the ruling class, the policy of fixing wages was an even stabler support of its power. This policy assured a reasonably definite income from investment, and for those back in the old country who had hazarded their savings in colonial ventures, as well as for those in the new world who possessed economic resources they wished to see increased, it was a guarantee of stability, if not always of success. After all, America was not settled in the main by free men but by men bound to other men, to capitalists in England who invested their fortunes in colonial projects and to men of substance, however slight, who themselves came to the country to settle and derive from it whatever they could. The poor were theirs to exploit, to return to them the moneys they had invested, and to give to those moneys the quality of enduring and increasing value. The poor were not co-fellows, not colleagues, but inferiors, low fellows, who had come to make it possible that the more substantial men might realize their rightful economic heritage. These wealthier men treated the poor men as such: in economics, religion, education, and before the law. Many of the servants had their initials and the date when they were purchased branded on their arms or other parts of their anatomy. Illegitimate boys were bound out until they were thirty years old; orphan children, until they were twenty years of age.

No extreme of punishment or degree of servitude was considered too severe in suppressing insubordination on the part of the lower classes. Servants, for example, were forced to dress in common clothes, in jackets, "breeches of serge, linen shirts, worsted stockings and beaver hats" [20] to distinguish them from the upper classes. The food they were given would scarcely have satisfied a Chinese coolie. What was even worse was that indentured servants could actually be sold like bond slaves to different bidders, and thus be separated at times from their wives and children. Attempts to escape were punished by nailing the ears of the culprit to a post and later chopping them off; sometimes branding was resorted to as a punitive measure. Punishments for theft, which naturally meant punishments of the lower classes, since (in those days at least) the upper classes had little need to steal, were not less vicious. There was also the inevitable debtor's prison, into which men were plunged when they failed to meet their debts, most of which resulted from conditions, circumstances, and stratagems over which they had little if any control. The description of such imprisonments is one of the most horrifying records in the history of the Western world.* Such imprisonments were no worse, to be sure, than those practiced in the old world at the time, but that was little consolation for those who suffered from their tortures.

Even children did not escape the extremes. In Boston impoverished persons were forced to lease out their children as indentured servants. A workhouse, as James Oneal describes, was constructed to imprison children who wasted their time on the streets. Often such children, as in Connecticut, were forced to become slaves of masters until they became of age. In short, child labor can be traced back to our Puritan ancestors, who used it and justified it as a religious procedure. They believed—and expressed that belief in voluminous sermons and addresses and decrees—that the children of the land benefited from such treatment. It protected them from the wiles of the Devil and fortified them with strength to face the multiplying hardships of life.

## LIMITATIONS OF SUFFRAGE

In consonance with such policies, the franchise was limited to people who had enough wealth to entitle them to some standing or station

* McMaster has given the most detailed and graphic descriptions of the appalling fates of multitudes of men and women who suffered and died in these prisons. His picture of the Newgate Prison in Connecticut, "which surpassed in horrors the Black Hole of Calcutta . . . an old worked-out copper mine in the hills near Granby . . . (where in little pens of wood from thirty to one hundred culprits were immured, their feet made fast to iron bars, and their necks chained to beams in the roof)" is unforgettable for its hideousness and horror.

in the community. Only landowners and those with an income tantamount to forty pounds a year could vote. In every state along the Atlantic seaboard similar circumscriptions of the franchise were introduced, and they prevailed until long after the Revolutionary War. As late as 1842, Thomas Dorr was arrested and imprisoned for no other reason than that he led a movement in Rhode Island which was dedicated to the proposition that all men should have the right to vote, regardless of economic or property qualifications. In other words, he made the mistake of believing that democracy should be put into practice. His movement naturally received the backing of the populace, and in order to quell it once and for all, Dorr was given a life sentence and his followers were dispersed by force of arms. Three years later Dorr was freed by the succeeding governor, and the court records were reversed in his favor.

### CULTURAL SUPERIORITY OF THE PURITANS

With all their faults, it must not be forgotten that the Puritans also had their virtues. They were less democratic than the Pilgrims, but more cultured; they were less tolerant, but more capable. They came from a higher economic class and carried over with them the culture as well as the riches they had acquired. As was pointed out in the previous chapter, the Puritans were not the art-hating, culture-loathing people that most American historians and critics have contended.

One of their initial efforts was the founding of Harvard College, an institution which, despite all its limitations of program and perspective, did not compare unfavorably with many of the English and European colleges of the time. Although theology was its chief emphasis, as it was likewise in similar institutions in the old world, it also gave courses in Hebrew, Greek, and Latin. Its beginnings were simple, uninspiring, unimpressive. Jasper Danckaerts, in his *Journal*, gives a most depressing picture of the college in its early years:

> We reached Cambridge about eight o'clock. It is not a large village, and the houses stand very much apart. The college building is the most conspicuous among them. We went to it, expecting to see something unusual, as it is the only college, or would-be academy of the Protestants in all America. In approaching the house we neither heard nor saw

anything mentionable; but going to the other side of the building, we heard noise enough in an upper room to lead my comrade to say, "I believe they are engaged in disputation." We entered and went up stairs, when a person met us, and requested us to walk in, which we did. We found there eight or ten young fellows, sitting around smoking tobacco, with the smoke of which the room was so full we could hardly see; and the whole house smelt so strong of it that when I was going up stairs I said, "It certainly must be also a tavern." We excused ourselves, that we could speak English only a little, but understood Dutch or French well, which they did not. However, we spoke as well as we could. We inquired how many professors there were, and they replied not one, that there was not enough money to support one. We asked how many students there were. They said at first thirty, and then came down to twenty; I afterwards understood there are probably not ten. They knew hardly a word of Latin, not one of them, so that my comrade could not converse with them. They took us to the library where there was nothing particular. We looked over it a little. They presented us with a glass of wine. This is all we ascertained there. The minister of the place goes there morning and evening to make prayer, and has charge over them; besides him, the students are under tutors or masters. Our visit was soon over, and we left them to go and look at the land about there.[21]

Nevertheless, out of these humble, discouraging beginnings emerged a college and eventually a university which was to become one of the great cultural centers of the land.

Libraries and bookstores increased in Boston. The best books published in England were imported, and before long bookstores became so popular that booksellers had to purchase books in increasing bulk to satisfy the multiplying demand. Between 1679 and 1685 John Usher, the bookseller, bought five hundred and sixty-seven pounds of books from England and elsewhere.[22] Other booksellers did almost as much business. Some individuals, like Cotton Mather, owned several thousand books. Many individuals brought over their private libraries, which in many cases were by no means inconsiderable.

Nothing like this developed in Plymouth or in any other settlement, for nowhere else in the country at that time were so many college graduates gathered, men from both Cambridge and Oxford, whose training and life had made books an inspiration and ideas, albeit theological, a constant challenge. In judging men of that time, it must not be forgotten that theology was the avenue through which their minds functioned, and theological knowledge constituted the main form of knowledge extant. Politics in those days was born in the womb of theology.

It was out of this environment that the first American newspaper was born: *The Present State of New English Affairs*, published by Samuel Green in Boston in the fall of 1689.[23] A year later R. Pierce printed for Benjamin Harris in Boston a publication called *Public Occurrences*.[24] These papers were crude, improvised affairs, but it was out of the seed which they sowed that the modern newspaper was born.

It was Puritanism, unhappily tied up with the past—the remnants of feudalism, the severities of a bygone philosophy which conceived of democracy as a crime and theological totalitarianism as a virtue—that possessed more of a cultural tradition than any other movement on this continent. It was—and still is—Puritanism which has been more misjudged in that respect than any other movement of modern times.

Contrary to the usual picture of the Puritans, they did not dislike drama or poetry; as a matter of fact, they liked both and manifested their likes in dynamic form. Cotton Mather, for example, was very interested not only in poetry but in various forms of scansion; he worked out a whole theory of poetic technique. Puritan intellectuals, wrought up as they were—and as all seventeenth-century intellectuals were—by theological controversies, one more infinitesimal and microscopical than another, continued to be interested in the cultural developments of their day. They did not shut their eyes to what was being done in the theater in London, or to the poetry of various scribes, or to music, or to any other art. The picture painted by most writers to the effect that the Puritans lacked interest in cultural things is egregiously distorted.

That the Puritans had scruples about not staging dances in the sacred rooms of their tabernacles or meeting places, as modern churches put on strawberry festivals and oyster parties, is not difficult to understand. After all, there is or should be, as Ecclesiastes (or Solomon) said, a place for all things, a place to dine and to die, a place to worship and to dance. It is not necessary to use the place in which one worships as a place to make merry and get drunk (and many of the Puritans did drink as well as smoke, laws to the contrary notwithstanding) any more than it is necessary to use the place in which one sleeps as the place in which one delivers orations or makes one's living. If one understands that, it is easy to understand Samuel Sewall's letter to the Honorable Isaac Addington, in connection with the staging of a play in the Council-Chamber of the Colony:

There is a Rumour, as if some designed to have a Play acted in the Council-Chamber next Monday; which much surprises me: And as much as in me lies, I do forbid it. The Romans were very fond of their Plays; but I never heard they were so far set upon them as to turn their Senat-House into a Play-House. Our Town-House was built at great Cost & Charge, for the sake of very serious & important Business; the Three Chambers above & the Exchange below; Business of the Province, County & Town. Let it not be abused with Dances or other Scenical divertisements. It cannot be an Honor to the Queen to have the Laws of Honesty & Sobriety broken in upon. Ovid himself offers invincible Arguments against publick Plays:

Ut tamen hoc fatear; Ludi quoque semina praebent Nequitia: Let not Christian Boston goe beyond Heathen Rome in the practice of shamefull Vanities.

This is the Voice of your most humble & obedient
Servant,
Samuel Sewall.

Sewall's letter does not condemn plays as such; the Puritans were not unaccustomed to plays or ignorant of their value. They felt, as Sewall's letter evinces, that they should be staged in playhouses and not in the Council-Chamber—nor in churches as they are today. In England, for instance, the Puritans produced plays of their own, *Lusty Juventus* being one of the most memorable. They were, it is true, moral plays, but not many decades earlier, when the Miracle, Morality, and Interlude plays were the vogue, plays had been moral too. The Puritans were really carrying on the medieval, not the Protestant, tradition. They were close enough in their cultural as well as their political alliances not to divorce themselves completely from the aristocratic tradition as the Pilgrims and all the rest of the Dissenters had done.

### THE VICTORY OF PILGRIM OVER PURITAN PHILOSOPHY

Ultimately, the Puritans lost out in their struggle to dominate Massachusetts and the rest of New England. Williams and Hooker were the first to resist their dictation and move elsewhere, to found the colonies of Rhode Island and Connecticut. But more important to the Puritans than this desertion, resulting in the actual exile of Roger Williams, was the influence of the country itself, its remoteness from the old world, its separateness from everything they had ever known, its influence upon their minds and convictions. It left them hanging in mid-air, remembering where they had hung before but unable to find the rope to which they had hung.

In the beginning the Puritans had believed in the Established Church of England and had resisted all those groups, of which the Pilgrims were but a single example, who had insisted upon separation from it. They were Puritans, not Separatists. John White, who had been one of their first and best sponsors in the old country, had insisted that they never succumb to the Separatist heresy.* When Higginson, the well-known nonconformist minister, had set out for the new country, he declared, as Cotton Mather has informed us, that "We will not say as the Separatists [the Pilgrims and similar groups] were wont to say at their leaving of England, 'Farewell, Babylon! Farewell, Rome! But we will say, *'Farewell, dear England! Farewell, the Church of God in England,* and all the Christian friends there! We do not go to New England as Separatists from the Church of England; though we cannot but separate [which meant to purify; hence Puritan] from the corruptions in it." [25] John White even got the leaders of the Winthrop group to sign the tract: "Humble Request of His Majestie's loyall Subjects, the Governour and the Company late gone for New-England: To the rest of their Brethren, *in and of the Church of England*" [italics mine], and at Yarmouth, as they were about to sail, Winthrop and Saltonstall, Johnson and Dudley, called the Church of England their "dear Mother" and begged that they be "received in her bosom, and sucked in from her breasts." [26]

The nature of the new country undermined their best resolves.

* Later, even John White rallied to Presbyterianism and openly fought the Established Church, refusing to read the *Book of Sports* from his pulpit in 1633, and thus endangering himself as a nonconformist divine.

Higginson, who began as a nonconformist Established Church minister, soon turned into a Separatist in America, and became one with the Pilgrims in their ecclesiastical polity. He did this not out of decision of mind but from decision of environment. What he found in the new world which he encountered was that the influence of the Established Church was negligible; that the only people who had any influence were those who believed in a church of their own, separated from all other churches, and freed from the domination of the Church of England. He soon realized that there was little hope of trying to perpetuate Church of England doctrines upon New England soil. It did not take him very long after that to accept the Congregational doctrines of the Pilgrim Separatists. He became convinced that the Pilgrim way was the way of the Lord. Undoubtedly Samuel Fuller, the physician, played a decisive role in the proselytizing process.[27]

The Puritans believed in the Established Church but, like Higginson, they discovered the inapplicability of its credo upon American soil. They early saw the necessity of organizing a church of their own, dominated by their own hierarchy. By that act they became Separatists in fact if not in name. They forsook their mother church, the Church of England, for a church which had no name except their own, which meant a church without tradition, without sanctity, without a past. The task of making a church of their own was no simple one. Yet, faced by this new environment, they had little choice in the matter. It had to be an *independent* church—unless they were to wait for each mail, sometimes months apart, for orders as to what to do.

In short, the new world was divinely carved for independence, separatism, the very things which the Puritans had resented and fought in England. It was the Pilgrim Dissenter philosophy and not that of the Puritans which was geographically and economically designed for survival in the new hemisphere.

It was not many decades before the Puritans realized, as Winthrop himself confessed, that the semifeudal, aristocratic government of the Puritans was impossible in the new world. The change, however, from the Puritan theory of government, which was aristocratic, into the Pilgrim theory, which was democratic, was not swift. No other alternative being possible, the Puritans accepted the fact that some form of democracy was inevitable. The nature of the country demanded it. It was necessity of circumstance, then, not altruism of impulse, which determined the change in the policy of the Massachusetts Bay Colony.

### BEGINNINGS OF REPRESENTATIVE GOVERNMENT

Winthrop tells us, in words simple as a seam, how representative government was born in the Massachusetts Bay Colony. It resulted not from democratic desire on the part of the theocrats, or what was then the government, but from pressure on the part of the populace. After all, in Plymouth the people had been given the right to vote and had maintained the privilege; in the Bay Colony no such privilege had been granted. It was the top dogs, the ruling group, who under pressure granted the privilege. The privilege came from the top, not from below. As long as possible the Puritans confined their concept of representative government to the members of their church organization; even when they extended it beyond that pale, they introduced property qualifications which excluded a large per cent of the populace from the right to vote. In addition, they excluded all slaves and every non-citizen. Universal suffrage was anathema in their eyes.

If the Puritans had had their way, there would have been nothing resembling representative government in their colony. They wanted a semifeudal state, with governmental authority vested in the clergy and magistrates, and it was that kind of state that they inaugurated. It was the environment that was against them. The environment bred democracy as naturally as the sun does heat, and all attempts on the parts of various groups to combat it proved inevitably futile. The theocrats who in the beginning had tried to restrict the voting privilege soon discovered that this was impossible. In time the "freemen deputed two of each town to meet and consider of such matters as there were to take order in at the general court." The necessities becoming so great, and the populace by this time having grown so large, it was decided, Winthrop relates, that "they must choose others [representatives] for that purpose."

Thus representative government was born in the Massachusetts Bay Colony. It was out of that grant that democracy evolved in the province. It was not democracy in the complete sense of the word, to be sure; only propertied freemen had the right to elect representatives in the governing body; propertyless freemen, indentured servants, menials, and other subordinates, were denied the privilege. They had no right to vote; years passed before they obtained it.

Thus in time even the theocracy, established in the beginning upon what seemed such a solid foundation, crumbled gradually and gave way to the separatist, democratic philosophy of the Pilgrims, who had transported it first to Holland before they brought it to this land. Even in England Puritanism, with its Calvinistic heritage and pseudo-aristocratic emphases, had been a foreign influence. The English commoners would have none of it. They were simple Dissenters, of a score of varieties, who loathed such foreign doctrines with their aristocratic religiosity. In America, Puritanism found itself doubly foreign and doubly impracticable.

### TRIUMPH OF THE DISSENTERS

Consequently it was not the philosophy of Puritanism which dominated this country, but the philosophy of the Pilgrims, of the lower middle class—the cobblers, tinkers, butchers, bakers, and candlestick-makers—who aspired to be, and in many cases became, the farm owners, the storekeepers, the land speculators, the rum and slave traders, of the next decade. Had the Puritans won out in the struggle between the two philosophies of life involved, the history of this country would have been very different. The Puritans were as much money-grubbers as the Pilgrims and perpetrated as many economic crimes as their rival landsmen; but they were a more cultured group and, despite their fanatical religiosity, would have encouraged a more cultured outlook upon life.

In other words, contrary to the usual contention, it was not Puritanism that developed the anti-cultural, anti-esthetic, utilitarian philosophy upon which this country was bred, but the defeat of Puritanism. It was the success of the Dissenters, which meant the success of Congregationalism, that gave birth to the anti-cultural, anti-esthetic outlook upon life which was to predominate in this country for centuries and which is by no means dead today—as was eloquently attested by Alfred E. Smith's remark in 1928, when he was candidate for the Presidency, that he didn't have to read books—the Bible was book enough for him.

The Puritan movement was relatively short-lived. It was really more a political than a religious force. Calvin was a high churchman who believed in the superiority of the church over the state; both institutions, he was convinced, descended from God, but in the ultimate analysis the church was supreme. Servetus could be imprisoned, tortured, burned, by the state, but only after the church had condemned him first and turned him over to the authorities of the state. Calvin hated the low churchmen, the Dissenters, and denounced them, especially the Baptists, as enemies of religion and righteousness.

It was that theocratic conception which the Puritans carried with them to Salem and which they put into practice in the Massachusetts Bay Colony. It was not an individualistic, democratic philosophy but a postfeudal, aristocratic one, which possessed enough of the economic attributes of capitalism to make it palatable to the upper middle classes of the day. Calvin believed not only in the supremacy of the church, but also in that of the ecclesiastics; it was through the latter that the voice of God could be heard. Theocracy was God's government, and therefore the best government for man.

The Pilgrims and other Dissenting sects sprang from a different tradition: that of the individualistic, democratic Lollards. They resented theocratic governments, opposed the Puritans and their principles. They believed in the supremacy of the individual and his right to worship as he pleased. It was this Dissenter philosophy which triumphed in Europe as well as America. The Puritan philosophy died. Contrary to the customary conclusion in the matter, Puritanism, which was English Calvinism, lost influence whenever and wherever capitalism triumphed.* The democracy of the Dissenters was victorious.

The Pilgrims were truly Protestants—protestants against the re-

* The tendency of Weber, Troeltsch, and others to say that Calvinism is part of modern capitalism is founded upon an entirely false basis. Mecklin has contended the same thing, in terms of America, in his recent volume. The opposite is the case. Calvinism is incompatible with capitalism. Calvinism is aristocratic; believes in divisions of classes, economically as well as religiously; is supported by upper, not lower, middle-class groups; and falls into desuetude as a dominant force wherever capitalism succeeds. For detailed proof of this fact, the reader should turn to Thomas Cuming Hall's *Religious Background of American Culture*. It is the revolt against Calvinism, which Weber and his followers never recognized, that constitutes the best support of capitalism. That revolt is led by the Dissenters.

V. L. Parrington falls into Weber's fallacy in other respects. He often looks to France for the explanation of influences which are unmistakably English, born of the Dissenting tradition, and having new characteristics acquired in the American environment.

ligion and manner of life of the upper classes with their organized and stratified concept of existence. The Established Church of England is not Protestant and, to this day in England, resents the appellation. The Dissenters believed in the right of the individual to interpret religion as he wished, individualistically, and were contemptuous of ecclesiastical authority. Followers of Wyclif and the Lollard tradition could not abide such authority. It was strange, violational. They did not believe in ecclesiastics or in a church, especially not in an Established Church. They believed in nothing but significance of creed, autonomy of sect, independence of conviction.

This was revolutionary doctrine in those days, and the authors of that revolutionary tradition were not Puritans but Dissenters.

### POLITICAL VICTORY DELAYED

Although it was the democratic religious philosophy of the Dissenters which vanquished that of the Puritans, their political philosophy was not victorious for two centuries. Plymouth triumphed religiously but not politically. It was not until the nineteenth century that political democracy achieved reality in America. For almost two centuries the propertied groups maintained control over the vote. Suffrage was limited by them to those of their own kind. The simple democracy of the Dissenters expressed itself in the insurrections and revolts that occurred in most of the colonies. It was not until after the Revolutionary War, in the regimes of Jefferson and Jackson, that the political democracy of the Dissenters, of Plymouth, finally triumphed. Plymouth absorbed Salem religiously, but Salem absorbed Plymouth politically, and it took almost two centuries before the Plymouth philosophy could conquer in the political domain.

### THE MUSE IN CHAINS

Anne Bradstreet, Michael Wigglesworth, and the lesser New England versifiers were all concerned with one thing: the sad, sedate gloom which God had issued forth in remote Galilee and which the New Englanders were determined to extend into the new land they had settled. Their poets, their prose writers, their preachers, snatching words like evil things that had to be purified, wrote of the cavernous recesses wherein men were tortured for sin, torn limb from limb, burnt from pore to viscera, wrenched into fragments, in the infernal territories contrived for those unholy in the eyes of God. Jonathan Edwards's violent depiction of the agonies undergone by sinners sizzling in the environs of hell was no more horrifying than Michael Wigglesworth's conception of their fate in his poem *The Day of Doom*, which was sophomorically Miltonic in execution. They were children of the same philosophy.

There was about all New England literature that same terror-ridden quality which made it read like something sprung from a dark Stygian source. There was nothing of song in it. It lacked the deep sadness and significance, the ringing challenge, of Judaic prophecy; it was violent without being vigorous, fiery without being luminous. It was the literature of a people who did not need literature in order to survive. Literature to them was a department of religion.

In the South there was even less need for literature—scarcely any at all. The aristocratic element that came over during the Cromwellian period brought with them a limited interest in books and plays, and in the parlors of their homes there were upon occasions various literary and thespian diversions. After the Restoration of Charles II in 1660, most of that element returned to England, and though Berkeley and his clique continued some of those practices, they never displayed enough interest in them to cultivate them as an art. George Sandys, an intellectual itinerant, did translate Ovid's *Metamorphoses* during his sojourn in Virginia, but he did it for the English and not for the American public. Little else of significance was published for a number of generations. The New England Puritans, with all their limitations and defects, were far more cultured and far more concerned with the preservation of what culture they knew than were the Virginians. Neither section approved of plays; in seventeenth-century New England they just didn't exist. In Virginia they were suppressed. In 1665 in Accomac County a play called *Ye Bare and Ye Cub* was closed down, and the three people who had staged it were jailed. Middle-class Virginia, like middle-class New England, considered actors "the scum and dregs of the earth." [28]

The tragic part of it is that this attitude continued to prevail for a long time afterward. Poets, dramatists, painters, sculptors found themselves no less lonely in Virginia than in Massachusetts. All artists in early colonial times found creation desperately difficult and lamentably unrewarding in every respect. Even as late as 1832,

Richard Henry Wilde, who had written what Byron described as "the finest poem of the century," declared that it was impossible for a Southern poet to survive in a Southern environment.[29] He even went so far as to refuse to admit his authorship of the poem lest the fact prejudice his friends and neighbors against him. Even Edgar Allan Poe bewailed the status of the poet in the South at a time when the South was at its literary heyday and was a paradise of cultural progress compared with what it was in the seventeenth century.

There can be no argument but that the best literary contributions of New England were not those of its poets but those of its diarists, commentators, and historians. Bradford, Winthrop, the Mathers, Williams, Hooker were not great stylists, but their words possessed literary quality, and ofttimes glimmered and sometimes glowed with poetic eloquence. They were the best to which the period gave birth. They were not inferior to the English ecclesiastics of their day, who strutted when they wrote and said pontifically what they could better have said simply. American theologians, middle-class in their attitudes and convictions, carried on the bourgeois tradition of the old country but gave to it something of the freshness of the new. At least, they endowed it with new issues, new anticipations, new challenges, which were intrinsic to the new world of which they were a part.

## THE WITCHCRAFT MANIA

Characteristic of the temper of the time, the Puritans carried over with them to the new world the witchcraft delusion which had so harassed the old. The belief in the existence of witches was an old and common obsession. As Parce Lida has pointed out, countless women in divers capacities were killed or burned at the stake as witches during the Middle Ages. The Puritans, with their witchcraft mania, invented nothing new; they simply perpetuated the ancient tradition.

Witchcraft was not confined to New England. There were witch trials in Virginia and other Southern states as well as in the Puritan colonies. New England was merely the center, the matrix, of the witchcraft craze; it executed many unfortunate and impoverished creatures, young as well as old, full-cheeked as well as toothless. But they were few in comparison with those executed in Europe. It is easy to exaggerate the Salem tragedy; actually, the witchcraft episode in New England was a microscopic occurrence when compared with the far vaster executions in Germany, France, Spain, and England. People then, lacking the scientific wisdom of today, were prone to blame anyone or anything for the evils that overcame them, and to use a witch as a scapegoat was a most effective recourse.

In those days it was not uncommon for people in a passion of anger to denounce women—and at times also men—as witches. Witch trials in many parts of Europe, including England, were spectacles, theatric episodes in which old people, with the ancientry of the ages in their eyes, were burned to appease the unrest of the populace. Ofttimes aged people, their brains fractured with fear, denounced themselves, shouted into the mischievous crevices of the night the very words which condemned them to the stake. Back in the contused days when the Black Death swept across the land, from the sun-streaked valleys of southern Italy to the far-flung mountains of Norway, out of obscure places—in hovels, backlands, quaint retreats—old, helpless people, weird of face, were seized upon as witches, harassed by mobs, and made into the sad sacrifices of an ignorant age. It was no commoner in Salem than elsewhere. Three thousand miles of geographic disparity were not enough to change the characters and beliefs of men. No people has a monopoly on stupidity or ignorance. It is a universal vice—and Americans could no more escape it than anyone else.

Although today we know that the visitations experienced by the children who cried "Witch, witch!" were by-products of delusion, the people who heard them believed them, felt them, were electrified by them. They hated witches and were always glad to see them exterminated. It was as easy in those days to arouse people against witches as today it is to stir them up against communists. Witches were the common fear of the populace, of everyone; the whole Western world feared them. They were the *bêtes noires* of the age.

Oddly enough, the Salem madness was more the product of hysteria than of ignorance. The preachers were responsive to the hysteria but were not the creators of it. It cannot be denied, however, that they found it to their advantage and perpetuated it once it had begun. Increase Mather, it must be said, despite convictions to the contrary, was not involved in it.[30] He was in Europe when the madness was at its apogee, and when he returned to America he wrote the volume *Cases of Conscience Concerning Witchcraft*, in which he attacked "spectral evidence" and denounced witchcraft as an anachronistic notion, to be condemned and not extolled. But the majority of his colleages succumbed to the madness.

In Salem Village people did not go mad, as the cinema has tried to show; * they simply continued in the new world the same attitudes and prejudices which their fathers had learned in the old. They believed that witches could change the course of things, exercise and exorcise curses, create calamities, cause death. This belief was not confined to the ignorant; it was shared also by the intellectuals of the day. The leading preachers, physicians, judges, and writers believed in witchcraft. It was an accepted, undisputed phenomenon. Sir Thomas Browne, Boyle, Cranmer, More, never doubted for a moment that witchcraft existed and influenced the affairs of men.[31] It was natural, therefore, that the American settlers should believe the same thing.

A century before the witchcraft craze came to Salem in 1692, there had been a not dissimilar outbreak in Aberdeen, Scotland. Twenty-three women and one man were burned at the stake, one woman was tortured to death, another hanged herself, and four others though acquitted were branded and exiled from the territory.[32] In this instance, as in that of Salem, witchcraft was used as a scapegoat device. Since people lacked the scientific knowledge of disease that we possess today, it was not unnatural for them to blame illness upon individuals instead of upon germs, bacteria, and microbes. Satan was more meaningful in their eyes than science. When evil struck, it was much more convincing to explain it as a product of Satan's work than that of nature. Nature was good, because it was God's handiwork; whatever was evil in it was the result of luciferian contrivance. The very conception of bugs and bacteria would have impressed the people then as worse than witchery.

The story of Tituba and the children, which provided the background of the Salem tragedy, was unusual in detail but not in tendency. In all witch holocausts some victim had to be found; if it was not a Tituba it was someone else, the darker and stranger the better. Witches flourished in twilight and tenebrous places. The people who believed in them were certain that they were real, identifiable as cur-

* Cf. *The Witch of Salem*, a terrifically distorted picture of this madness.

few ringers, chemists, and the weird men and women scowling and scurrying along the streets after nightfall. They were as natural and inevitable as sunfall or clammy dew on old soil.

As early as 1645 in Springfield a handful of persons were accused of being witches but were finally acquitted after a long, agonizing trial. In 1647 a man was hanged in Hartford. There were eleven more witchcraft cases between 1647 and 1692. In the latter year, when the witchcraft tragedy reached its climax, executions increased. Nevertheless, the total number of people killed for witchcraft in the New England colonies in the seventeenth century did not exceed twenty-eight.[33] In England, on the other hand, the number of executions was far more impressive. In Massachusetts no one was executed for witchcraft after 1693, whereas in England executions occurred for almost a decade afterward.

The story of how the children created the witchcraft craze in Salem is too familiar now to bear repetition; besides, it is, for our purposes at least, unimportant. We are interested in the social conditions which made it possible for the craze to take hold and accomplish the mischief it did. Massachusetts at the time was suffering from a series of misfortunes which threatened to upset the equilibrium of the colony. Tragedy had followed tragedy; the people were jittery from fears of the future as well as terrors of the present. The political struggle alone had been bitter enough to wreck the nerves of the populace. In the background, yet not far removed, were the Indians and the dark adumbrations of an Indian war.

The witch persecutions were a relief, a dramatic escape, from the sufferings and fears that had magnified in the province. In America as well as in England the hunt after witches had been resorted to time after time because it kept the population concerned with something remote from their actual ills. Today the witch hunt is directed against Jews. In the seventeenth century it was directed against old men and women, hunch-backed, crooked-legged, grotesque-fingered creatures, who were harassed, imprisoned, and burned.

Witchcraft, then, was not only a superstition; it was also a technique. It still is, in different form, a technique exploited by contemporary statesmen and demagogues as a means of social and political camouflage. The Massachusetts theocrats resorted to it not only because they believed in it but also because they knew it was an effective way to throttle popular protest and strengthen their own power.

## CHAPTER VIII

# New Colonial Experiments: The Rhode Island and Connecticut Defections

*Having bought Truth deare, we must not sell it cheape, not the least graine of it for the whole world.*

—ROGER WILLIAMS

*The foundation of authority is laid in the free consent of the people.*

—THOMAS HOOKER

IT WAS a characteristic practice in the seventeenth century for those unable to endure the tyranny and persecution of the Massachusetts Bay sect to flee to Plymouth. Roger Williams was neither the first nor the last to adopt that retreat. Like many others, Francis Higginson, in the early thirties, had left Salem and gone to Plymouth for precisely the same reason. Later, after Roger Williams had become disgusted with Plymouth too, many who were unable to abide the persecutions of the Massachusetts theocracy went direct to Rhode Island, where Williams had founded what was the embryo of a new colony. Most conspicuous among such refugees from the Bay group were William Coddington, John Clarke, Samuel Gorton, Anne Hutchinson, and William Harris, without whose aid Roger Williams's venture in colonial organization might have proved abortive.

But more important than the individuals who founded the colony, more important even than Roger Williams himself, was the idea underlying its foundation. The Puritans were monolithic in their theocratic and political conceptions; the Pilgrims, hostile to the Established Church, Separatists in their religious philosophy, more democratic in political principle, were opposed to such monolithicism; but the Rhode Islanders, dominated by a philosophy voiced originally by Roger Williams, which soon became common to all who found in the new colony a true sanctuary, went further than either of those groups. What the Rhode Islanders believed in, which means what Roger Williams, Anne Hutchinson, and their immediate followers avowed, was more than Separatism, more than independency—more than anything that had been declared upon these shores before. What they believed in was what the early Lollards had believed in; namely, the consecrated significance of the individual. They were convinced that all men were equal in the eyes of God.

The Pilgrims, far more advanced in that respect than the Puritans, nevertheless concluded that *separation* from the Church of England would prove sufficient for their needs. The Rhode Islanders founded the colony of Rhode Island because they believed the Pilgrims were wrong, believed that *Separatism* in itself was inadequate. They wanted more than a divorce from the Established Church; they wanted even more than the right to worship freely, which the Pilgrims had granted: they wanted the individual himself, separately, alone, to be able to worship freely, without regard for group, denomination, or creed. It was on that basis, that original, singular, challenging basis, that the colony of Rhode Island was conceived.

Roger Williams himself, when he made his hegira to the Pilgrim settlement, discovered that superior though Plymouth was to Salem, it would not allow the privileges necessary for the individual freedom implied in his belief and doctrine.

### ROGER WILLIAMS: REVOLUTIONARY

The privileges Roger Williams desired and advocated for his followers were revolutionary in those days. He was opposed not only to the theocratic and paternalistic principles of the Massachusetts group, but also to their economic and legal concepts. Basic to those concepts was the attitude toward the land, toward the Indians who occupied the land and had lived upon it for centuries. Williams stood out alone, like a vast monadnock, in his contention *that the land belonged to the Indians and not to the white men, and especially not to the King of England, who had never seen it and never would see it. No other Englishman had ever dared take that stand.* It was a stand which necessitated courage of the highest order—in which Williams was not lacking. Rousseau, Voltaire, D'Holbach, Helvetius, and many other revolutionary Frenchmen adopted it a century or more later, but it is to Roger Williams that they were all indebted, however unconsciously, for having espoused it in the early seventeenth century when doing so was far more singular and far more hazardous.

Williams's contention was that the land belonged to the people who lived on it; that it had been given to them by God; and that no one had the right to take it away from them. Few people, even in our own day, realize the full import of that declaration. Roger Williams was, in that sense at least, a Karl Marx of his period. The Indians had lived upon the land, had worked it, cultivated it; therefore it belonged to them. Such was Williams's argument. He viewed the king as an outsider, an alien, entitled to no claims whatsoever to the American lands. The land, in Williams's eyes, could be secured from the Indians only by right of purchase—but by honest purchase, not by swindle, which had become all too familiar in his time. He stood alone in his defense of Indian rights in this respect. In fact, so alone did he stand that it was on this basis that he was accused of treason and forced to flee from the Massachusetts Bay Colony, take up refuge with the Indians and, finally, to found the colony of Rhode Island.

### THOMAS HOOKER'S HEGIRA

Roger Williams, to be sure, was not the only person who could not abide the Massachusetts Bay theocrats. Thomas Hooker, although a less daring and compelling personality than Williams, shared most of the latter's feelings of hostility to the theocrats; and, believing in a society in which citizens and not preachers or priests ruled, he set out at length to found a new commonwealth of his own, which in time became known as the State of Connecticut. Hooker's migration, like that of Williams, marked an important milestone not only in the history of America but also in that of the world. It has been celebrated upon countless occasions in various parts of New England, and to its political significance there has been added through the mellowing of the years something of the spirit of poetry and legend. The Reverend Allen's description of the Hooker hegira catches something of the drama of the occasion:

> In the beautiful month of June in the year of our Lord 1636 might have been seen from the hills in the southeast of this town a strange phenomenon. It was a company of men, women and children—one

hundred in all—driving before them a herd of cattle, one hundred and sixty in number, which supplied them with milk on their long and toilsome pilgrimage. "They hewed their difficult way," says the historian J. S. Palfrey, "through thickets; and their simple engineering bridged with felled trees the streams which could not be forded. Tents and wagons protected them from rain and sheltered their sheep. Early berries which grew along the way furnished an agreeable variety to their diet. . . . It occupied a fortnight, though the distance was scarcely a hundred miles. Mrs. Hooker by reason of her illness was carried in a horse litter."

This Mrs. Hooker was the minister's wife, and this goodly company was composed of members of his congregation in Newton, now Cambridge, and of the neighboring churches of Dorchester and Watertown, and their destination was the fertile banks of the Connecticut, where they laid the foundations of three flourishing towns, Hartford, Whethersfield, and Winsor." [1]

The Connecticut constitution, the earliest and one of the most famous democratic documents in the world, found its genesis in the brain of Thomas Hooker, who, called "a Son of Thunder in the Pulpit," [2] declared in words rife with revolutionary challenge that "the foundation of authority is laid in the free consent of the people." It was Hooker's contention that God had endowed the populace with the indefeasible right to appoint or elect its own officers and magistrates. The people in his opinion were sovereign—not the king, not the magistrates, not the ecclesiastics.

### THE FIGHT AGAINST THE ECCLESIASTICS

Unlike Massachusetts, Connecticut did not require one to be a member of a church in order to possess the right of suffrage. Although Hooker himself was a devoutly religious man and a minister whose first thought was of God, he did not believe that preachers had any right to claim special privileges or demand political dictation over the community. He believed, like the Pilgrims, in the separation of church and state, and in the administration of his colony laymen and not clergymen dominated.

His attitude stands out in sharp contrast not only to that of the Massachusetts theocrats but also to that of the Eatonites who founded New Haven and delivered over the community, lock, stock, and barrel, to the ecclesiastics. Not only were church and state conjoined there, but it was the church that determined the life of the state. Only church members could vote. The constitution of the settlement declared that "The Word of God shall be the only rule attended unto in ordering the affairs of government."[3] Trial by jury was forbidden because it lacked Biblical precedent and authority.

The Hooker administration, on the other hand, was not only purely civil; it was also purely local and immediate. It succeeded in organizing itself without being bound by charter, patent, or royal decree. It was unindebted to London capitalists or churchmen. In a word, it was able to start, relatively speaking, from scratch and build itself upon a fresh foundation.

### A NEW EXPERIMENT

It was that fact which gave to the colony its uniqueness as a political experiment. Nothing like it had appeared in the old or the new world. Plymouth had been built about a democratic base, but its ties with the old world, with the capitalists who had lent it financial aid and whom it had to pay off before it could be emancipated from their control, fettered it with obligations which impeded its immediate independence and advance. Connecticut escaped all such commitments. Its founders ventured forth into the wilderness without concern for king, capitalists, or churchmen. They went as pioneers of a new freedom born of a country which proffered it as generously as it did the air, the forests, and the waters that indented and interlaced it. What they stood for was not to die like the theocratic organization of government inaugurated by the Massachusetts colony, but was to live on through the centuries, finding expression generations later in the political philosophy of Thomas Jefferson, and still later in that advocated by Woodrow Wilson and Franklin D. Roosevelt.

### FAITH IN DEMOCRACY

In brief, the evolution of this "new freedom" is not new but old. It was rooted inalienably in American soil. Thomas Hooker and Roger Williams were the apostles of it when it was nothing more than a nebulous aspiration. They nurtured it when it was heresy to believe in it, and they were unhesitatingly willing to be denounced as heretics in their defense of it. They believed in Jeffersonianism long before Jefferson was born, and in democracy long before it became recognized as the touchstone of progress. In fact, in their day, and for many days to follow, democracy was associated with sedition, and it was only through the struggle waged by such spiritual and political pioneers as Williams and Hooker that it finally became accepted as defensible doctrine.

Hooker not only advocated a civil state as opposed to an ecclesiastical one, and political democracy as the best bulwark of that state, but he went further and stressed decentralized as superior to centralized authority. Long before the battle over states' rights became a national issue, long before the problem of sovereignty assumed crucial significance in the nation, Hooker declared that the rights of local groups were indefeasible and must never be sacrificed to central authority. Rooted in Hooker's social philosophy was the conviction, which Jefferson was later to convert into a political principle, that only in local groups can the people exercise their rightful powers; the further away authority is removed from such groups, the further away the people are removed from sharing in the function and administration of government. John Cotton, who, ironically enough, had come over on the same boat with Hooker, advocated in Boston a philosophy that was antipodal. He believed in government from the top and not from the bottom. This conflict in their respective social philosophies, which led to Hooker's migration to Connecticut, has remained active in this country till today, changing and shifting in emphasis but unaltering in fundament.

Like Roger Williams, Hooker believed in dealing fairly and generously with the Indians, and from the very time he and his followers started forth on their trek through the Connecticut country, the Indians were recognized as the rightful owners of the territory; and it was from them, and not the predatory adventurers, who in many cases claimed ownership, that the land was purchased.[4] However, Hooker never won the friendship of the Indians as Williams did because he never knew them as well, never lived with them, never spoke their tongues. Though a nonconformist to the core, with the spirit of a rebel living in him, as his emigrations to Holland, then to Massachusetts, and finally to Connecticut so eloquently testify, Hooker never fraternized with the people in the mass as Williams did. He was a man of dignity, of discrimination, who exalted the populace but never became a part of it. Ideas, principles, doctrines absorbed and fascinated him more than people.

### WILLIAMS: THE MAN OF THE MASSES

Williams was different. He was truly a man of the masses. Born the son of a merchant tailor, he not only believed in the people but was one of them. His heart beat in unison with theirs. He rose above his father's class, but never beyond the people who constituted it. He never deserted it, never disdained it. He always carried himself humbly, and translated that humility into his doctrine. He never felt himself superior to anyone, Indians or white men. All were the product of God's creation, and in all inhered the right to worship God in their own individual ways. "No one," he declared, "should be bound to maintain a worship against his own consent."

Hooker believed in the importance of the church but not in theocracy. Williams didn't believe even in the church. He believed that churches and congregations were impediments, not aids, to man in his struggle for salvation. When he converted the Indians to Christianity, he refused to organize them into congregations as John Eliot and other missionaries did. He was satisfied with their simple conversion. If they came to know the true Christ, that was enough, for knowing Him was all that men needed to know. He was suspicious of all organizations that attempted to harness the individual in religious matters, aristocratic or theocratic. He believed that individual intuition or revelation was superior to priestly wisdom. If a simple, gentle, unlettered Indian made his peace with the Savior, Williams considered his act as significant as that of a John Cotton or an Anne Hutchinson. Differences between people revolved, in his eyes, not about their respective stations in life or their claims to knowledge or advanced intelligence, but about their "regeneration." "Regeneration," which meant becoming one with the Lord through repentance and conversion, was his constant shibboleth. He considered it "unlawful for an unregenerate Man to pray or a regenerate man to pray with him." The great object of all preaching and teaching was to make men "regenerate." Nothing else mattered. "Jesus Christ is King in his own Kingdom," John Callender wrote a century later, in exposition of Williams's doctrine, "and no others have authority over his Subjects in the Affairs of Conscience and eternal Salvation."[5] Callender's words captured exactly what Williams stood for and fought for all his life. There was no sovereign but Jesus Christ. Kings, queens, ecclesiastics, magistrates, governors might possess civil power, but that was where their power stopped. In religion no one possessed power but Christ Himself and the individual who had the spirit of Christ living in him.

## THE FIGHT FOR TOLERANCE

Williams's whole fight for tolerance when tolerance was viewed askance, and ofttimes as subversive, was based upon that conclusion. Williams's defense of political democracy was an outgrowth of his belief in religious democracy. While in England in 1654, during the early years of the Commonwealth, he made a plea for what was then known as absolute Voluntaryism, which really meant a plea for religious liberty as a social imperative. He urged that England establish "a true and absolute Soul-freedom to all the people of the land impartially; so that no person be forced to pray or pay, otherwise than as his Soul believeth and consenteth."[6] He was bitterly opposed to all the forms of intolerance and persecution that had become so widespread in New England. "We must not let goe for all the flea-bitings of the present afflictions, &c.," he declared, "having bought Truth deare we must not sell it cheape, not the least graine of it for the whole world; . . . least of all for the bitter sweetening of a little vanishing pleasure. For a little puffe of credit and reputation from the changeable breath of uncertaine sons of men."[7] His words are unforgettable. Never did he sell Truth cheap; never did he sell it at all. Truth was the "unsellable," priceless challenge of his career.

In short, he did not believe that the civil state had any right to coerce anyone to believe in any specific creed or doctrine. That choice belonged to the individual and to no one else. "It agreeth both with humane reason and naturall equity that every man worship God uncompelled and beleeve what he will," he declared, quoting an ancient thinker,[8] and later he argued with demonstrable clarity that all persecution was uncondonable. "I acknowledge that to molest any person, Jew or Gentile," he averred, "for either professing doctrine or practicing worship meerly religious or spirituall, it is to persecute him and such a person (whatever his doctrine or practice be true or false) suffereth persecution for conscience." [9]

Williams's enemies called him "a fire-brand"; his friends described him as "divinely mad." He was both. He was a fire-brand to those who believed in the old order of things, and "divinely mad" to those who believed in the new order of things. His three propositions, an apodictic separation from the Established Church, separation of church and state, and absolute "soul liberty," made him a revolutionary in his day, a fugleman of a new philosophy. The Pilgrims could accept his first two propositions, but not his third, and it was the third that resulted in his departure from Plymouth after he had sought it out as a refuge. His concept of "soul liberty" was more progressively circumferential than that of anyone else of his time. He left Salem because he "durst not officiate to an unseparated people"; he left Plymouth because he found that a "separated people" was lacking in the libertarian ideals in which he believed.

In the judgment of Cotton Mather, he was a madman, a wild, erratic personality, unamenable to reason. What was at stake was that Roger Williams did not believe in a theocracy; he did not believe in rule from the top, religious or civil. He believed essentially in rule from the bottom, by the people, who were the truest Christians in his eyes. It is no wonder, therefore, that the New England theocrats considered him a menace, an unholy terror, a hurricane of dissonance and unrest. Cotton Mather describes so well just how he and his colleagues felt about Roger Williams and the problem he created:

In the Year 1654 a certain windmill in the countries, whirling around with violence by reason of a violent storm then blowing, the stone at length by its rapid motion became so intensely hot as to fire the mill, from whence the flames being dispersed by the high winds did set a whole town on fire. But I can tell my reader that above twenty years before this there was a whole country in America like to be set on fire by the rapid motion of a windmill in the head of one particular man. Know then that about the year 1630 arrived here one Mr. Roger Williams, who being a preacher that had less light than fire in him, hath by his own sad example preached unto us the danger of that evil which the apostle mentions in Rom. 10, 2, "they have a zeal but not according to knowledge." [10]

Accepting Mather's words, Roger Williams was a Don Quixote of the seventeenth century, slashing, not tilting, at the windmills of the New England theocracy. Without a Sancho Panza, without a Dulcinea, Roger Williams flung himself at the windmills, broke them, and lived on to pick up their pieces, while the country itself lived on and later put them together.

## DEFENSE OF THE QUAKERS AND THE JEWS

Without doubt the tyrannies and persecutions which occurred in the Massachusetts Bay Colony broke Williams's heart and terrified his soul; after all, to see Quakers, Baptists, and Antinomians whipped and imprisoned, their ears chopped off and their bodies branded, and ofttimes even hanged, was enough to sicken and revolt men less sensitive and latitudinarian in their religious philosophy than Roger Williams. His reaction to it was violent. He would have none of it, and he made that clear in no ambiguous way. His defense of tolerance was cosmic. He excluded no man from it, regardless of religion, color, or nationality. In a day when Quakers were despised, imprisoned, mutilated, and hanged, Roger Williams defended them—and not without risks. But his tolerance did not stop with Christians. He was one of the few of his period who also defended the Jews. In England, when he was there, he opposed their exclusion. In Rhode Island, to which he had given birth, he welcomed them to become citizens. His aim was to break down the divisions between men. Living at the time he did, he was bound to think of such divisions as being fundamentally religious. But he believed so much in religion that he could not condemn the religion of a people who did not accept his own. Much as he would have liked to convert the Jews to Christianity, as he had done many of the Indians, he respected their right to their own belief, and he was willing, a century before Voltaire uttered his famous declaration, to sacrifice his life if necessary in defense of that conviction.* "I

* John Cotton, on the other hand, declared in his *Bloody Tenent Washed and Made White In the Blood,* which was a reply to Roger Williams's *Bloody Tenent of Persecution for Cause of Conscience,* that "if Idolaters and Seducers [meaning practically any religious

humbly conceded it to be the Duty of the Civil Magistrate to break down that superstitious wall of separation (as to Civil Things) between us Gentiles and the Jews," he declared while in England, "and freely (without this asking) to make way for their free and peaceable Habitation amongst us." He condemned in unmitigated language "the unchristian oppressions, incivilities and inhumanities of this Nation against the Jews."

Like all the other preachers of his time, Williams used the Bible as his immediate and impeccable reference. Quoting the Bible, he stressed the fact that Biblical writers have always been kind to the populace. He attacked the theocrats because they ignored, or attempted to blot out, that fact. In attack upon the persecutory tendencies of the Puritans, he declared that the apostle did not say, "You whom I send shall deliver the people (whom you ought to convert) unto Counsells and put them in Prisons and lead them to Presidents and Tribunall Seates and make their Religion Felony and Treason."[13] *

It would be a mistake to conclude that Roger Williams was a friend of the Jews, a friend of the Quakers. He was a friend of none of them and yet, in another sense, a friend of them all. He was a friend of liberty, liberty of conscience, liberty of worship. He had no particular affection for Jews, no prejudice in favor of Quakers, no predilection for heretics in general. His affection was for Christ and the sacredness of the individual, but at the same time he was convinced that Christ's way was to respect the individual's way—

group that disagreed with the Puritans] be tolerated to seduce the servants of Christ to pollution and Apostacy, the Church will stand guilty before God of the seduction and corruption of the people of God" (p. 50). Tolerance, in other words, was a vice rather than a virtue in the opinion of Cotton. Williams replied to Cotton in a most incisive and annihilating way in his *Bloody Tenent Yet More Bloody* (1652): "For if none be peaceable Subjects, loving neighbors faire dealers but such of Master Cotton's conscience and religion (which he conceives to be the only true religion) what will become of all other states, governments, cities, towns, peoples, families, neighbors upon the face of the earth? I say what will become of them especially if power were in Master Cotton's hand to deal with them as Wolves?"[11] Later, in the same Tenent, he states: "It is against civill justice for the civill state or officers thereof to deal so partially in matters of God as to permit to some the freedome of their consciences and worships but to curbe and suppress the consciences and souls of all others of their free-born people."[12]

* In his comment, included in the Fourth Paper, presented by Major Butler to the Honourable Committee of Parliament, 1652, he declared that "by the last Will and Testament of the Christ Jesus we find not the least title of Commission to the Civill Magistrate (as Civill) to judge and act in matters of his Spiritual Kingdom."[14]

that there was no way to salvation except through the individual.

In other words, this "young man of bright accomplishments but of unstable judgment,"[15] as Reverend Clark described him, was trying to find a road, a highway, on which all people could meet, notwithstanding their differences and disparities of creed and conviction. As a result, he succeeded in establishing in his colony the first home of freedom in the new world. It was one of the first homes of freedom anywhere in the world. The Dutch had opened up their country to refugees from various nations and were the first to exalt tolerance into a virtue. Roger Williams, however, surpassed them, and converted religious democracy into political democracy. He believed in people's right not only to worship freely, but also to vote freely, to share freely and equally in the organization and administration of the civil state.

Liberal as Williams's belief in freedom and democracy was, it must not be thought it had no limits. He was not anarchistic in his attitude. Like Christ, who said, "Render unto Caesar the things that are Caesar's and to God the things that are God's," he believed the civil state had its rights, which ought to be respected provided the state did not infringe upon the religious liberty of its citizens. In explanation of just how he stood in the state-church relationship, he wrote in 1655:

There goes many a ship to sea with many hundred souls in one ship, whose weal and woe is common, and is a true picture of a commonwealth, or a human combination or society. It hath fallen out some times, that both papists and protestants, Jews and Turks, may be embarked in one ship; upon which supposal I affirm, that all the liberty of conscience that ever I pleaded for turns upon these two things—that none of the papists, protestants, Jews or Turks be forced to come to the ship's prayers or worship, nor compelled from their own particular prayers or worship, if they practice any. I further add that I never denied that notwithstanding this liberty the commander of this ship ought to command the ship's course, yea, and also command that justice, peace and sobriety be kept and practiced both among the seamen and all the passengers. If any of the seamen refuse to perform their services, or passengers pay their freight; if any refuse to help, in person or purse, towards the common charges or defence; if any refuse to obey the common laws and orders of the ship, concerning their common peace or preservation; if any shall mutiny and rise against their commanders and officers; if any should preach or write that there ought to be no commanders or officers, because all are equal in Christ, therefore no masters nor officers, no laws nor orders, nor corrections nor punishments;—I say I never denied, but in such cases, whatever is pretended, the commander or commanders may judge, resist, compel, and punish such transgressors according to their deserts and merits. This is seriously and honestly minded, may if it so please the Father of lights, let in some light to such as willingly shut not their eyes.

Williams had joined the Baptist group—better known as Anabaptists in those days—as early as 1638, and had been baptized by Ezekiel Holyman; [16] later he himself baptized others. His relationship with the Baptists, however, was short-lived, and within a few months he was without a church again. He could not ally himself with any specific church for long because there was no church with doctrines sufficiently elastic, generous, or tolerant to suit him. After his Baptist experience, he became a Seeker, as many of the English Dissenters had already become, and to the end of his days he continued to *seek* for that which would bring him closest to Christ, in whom he believed and for whom he worked.

Such was the career of a man who, in more senses than one, can be called the first American—the first man in this new world to believe in, struggle for, and dedicate his life to the realization of what today is known and recognized as the American ideal: religious liberty, political freedom, and individual independence.*

* There is not space here to deal with the conflicts in all the colonies. Only those most significant in determining the destiny of the country have been treated in detail.

Nevertheless, New Hampshire should be mentioned (and even early Maine) because part of its history was involved in the same struggle which upset the career of the other colonies.

The territory which later became known as New Hampshire and Maine was granted originally to two men, Mason and Gorges, who divided it among themselves into what later became two colonies and eventually two states. The part which was east of the Piscataqua was called Maine, and the part to the west of the river and north of the Merrimac became New Hampshire (John M. Whiton, *Sketches of the History of New Hampshire* (1834), p. 10). Mason was familiarly known as the "father of New Hampshire," although he was far from a father to his colonists, whom he viewed as feudal tenants and servants and from whom he demanded feudal homage. Although John Wheelwright succeeded in organizing the first Congregational Church in the land, Mason's own inclinations were in favor of the Established Church and he did everything in his power to forward its interests.

Mason wanted to be a Proprietor in the Lord Baltimore, William Penn style, but the closeness of Massachusetts and the spirited opposition of his colonists prevented the realization of his dream. The control of the colony was eventually taken over by the Crown, "which constituted a president and council to govern the Province." (Jeremy Belknap, *History of New Hampshire* (1784; 1812 ed.), Vol. I, 139.)

The populace resented this shift of affairs and in more ways than one expressed its opposition. Massachusetts assumed control of the territory but, after a bitter conflict, it became a colony in itself, although it retained a great number of the Massachusetts traditions.

The same argument prevailed in New Hampshire as did in the other colonies in reference to the ownership and control of the land. Mason claimed the land as his own and gave orders to arrest, imprison, and even fire upon any individuals caught shooting animals on his territory or cutting down his timber. Naturally, the populace hated him. (*Ibid.*, p. 184.) When Mason assumed the title Lord Proprietor matters became even worse.

Mason and Gorges, in Maine, wanted to see an aristocratic government established, with the English King as its titular head. They advocated an Established Church, a loyalist clergy, and were even willing to accept Roman Catholics if they promised to support their regime. Mason was willing to sponsor the Established Church and outlaw the Dissenters. (Franklin B. Sanborn, *History of New Hampshire* (1904), p. 13.)

## THE GOVE REVOLT

As in the other colonies, when the Assembly was deprived of its power, or dissolved, the populace protested, and in Hampton and Exeter, Edward Gove led a revolt which turned into a fiasco.

Gove, for a time, was a Paul Revere of the period, riding from farm to farm, calling the farmers to resist the oppression of the king and the proprietor. His rallying cry was for "liberty and reformation" and it rang over the New Hampshire hills and valleys and vibrated in the hearts of the people. He carried arms wherever he rode, flourished them, and challenged the people to follow them.

His revolt, however, proved premature. The people were not ready for it. Gove was arrested, imprisoned, shipped to England, incarcerated in the Tower, and kept there for several years. Later, he was freed, and allowed to return to the colony and recover his estate. (Belknap, p. 195.)

## CHAPTER IX

# The Religious Equalitarians

IT IS customary to conclude that America is and always has been exclusively a land of individualism, of individualistic initiative, of individualistic aspiration. Without doubt a vast part of the hope and energy which have made this country into a nation has sprung from that source. Historians, sociologists, journalists, statesmen, demagogues, have asserted and affirmed that fact so continuously for centuries that it has become part of the great American legend, or what is more often called the great American Dream.

But that is only part of the case. This country has not only been a land to which men have migrated to acquire individual fortunes; it also has been a land to which people have come to plant and construct religious and economic utopias.

America, more than any other country in the world, has been the great magnet for utopians. These utopians have been conspicuous for ideas and ideals diametrically opposed to those that have been associated with the American Dream. The utopians also had a dream, but it was co-operative and not competitive, communal and not individualistic. They dreamed of an America in which men would be able to carve out the contours of a new society; they were convinced that the very newness and vastness of the American land lent itself to that accomplishment. They sought, each group in its own way, to realize that ideal. All these groups originated in the Old World and transported their idealistic doctrines across the sea in order to find better soil in which to fructify. Other groups later, springing out of the maturing adventurousness of eighteenth- and nineteenth-century ideas,* developing with pyrotechnic swiftness in the minds of the economic sansculottes of those days, multiplied across the length and breadth of the land.

* These groups will be dealt with in the second volume of this work.

### A NEGLECTED PART OF AMERICA

Those groups are as much a part of the history of this country as the more familiar record of the predatory achievements of the individualistic-minded groups and leaders. These groups are not all of America, but they are an important part of America—and, unfortunately, a most neglected part of America. Their co-operative philosophy represents as much of the American Dream as the competitive philosophy of the rest of the country.

America cannot be understood without understanding their role in its making, for it very well may be that ultimately, and long before this century is ended, it will be their philosophy, and not the individualistic one, that will triumph.

But there were other individuals, other sects, which were even more radical than Williams and his Rhode Island colony. They stood for all that Williams did—and more. To Williams's principle of political equality they added the proposition of economic equality, the right of every individual to an equal share in the economic wealth of the community.

In England these groups—Anabaptists, Quakers, Levellers, Barrowists, Millenarians, Ainsworthians, Diggers—clustered about the banner of Independency, and were the ones who drove the more conciliating and compromising Puritans further and further to the left, and eventually succeeded in having Charles I decapitated. Their ideas and convictions were by no means uniform; they often disagreed and conflicted with one another and could find unity only in opposition to a common foe.

### CHRISTIAN COMMUNISM

Many of these left-wing religious sects had retained certain of the communistic characteristics of the primitive and medieval Christian sects, and as late as the seventeenth century the Diggers, led by Winstanley, clung to a mystical, millenialist communism which terrified the ruling classes of that day. "At this very day," declared Winstanley, "the poor people are forced to work for 4 d. and corn is dear. And the tithing-priest stops their mouth and tells them that 'inward satisfaction of mind' was meant by the declaration, 'the poor shall inherit the earth.' I tell you the scripture is to be really and materially fulfilled. . . . You jeer at the name of Leveller. I tell you Jesus Christ is the Head Leveller. . . . The day of Judgment is begun . . . the poor people you oppress shall be the saviors of the land . . . and break to pieces the bands of property."

Many of the Anabaptists of that day were equally revolutionary in their declarations. Thomas Münzer, the Anabaptist leader, had endowed the movement with its communist challenge. Harrison's Fifth Monarchy Men were violent in their economic demands. There was even a left-wing element among the seventeenth-century Quakers. The whole period, which was marked by all the pains and penalties that are inevitably associated with the collapse of an old economy and the emergence of a new, was rife with radical protests and proclamations. The Ranters, Seekers, and Diggers,* as well as the Levellers, became hysterically vociferous in their denunciations of the existing order.

### QUAKERS AND ANABAPTISTS

In the American colonies it was mainly the Quakers and Anabaptists who represented that left extreme. While most of the Quakers and many of the Anabaptists were far from communistic in their economic convictions, and opposed to rather than in favor of Winstanley's declaration, the left elements among them had stamped them in Europe as menaces to the social order. The very fact that the Quakers refused to bow before civil or religious authority, and refused even to have ministers in their own meeting places, each Quaker being a minister in his own right, was enough to evoke a condemnation of them from both king and clergy. That stigma clung to them in the new world as well as the old.

In almost all the early colonies, Quakers and Anabaptists were viewed with suspicion, punished severely for the slightest infraction of rule or law, and banished whenever they became obstinate or vociferous in defense of their ideals. The treatment of the Anabaptists in England was scarcely any worse than their treatment in New England. Canards were invented to undermine their reputation,

* "No man shall have any more land than he can labour himself," the Diggers maintained, "or have others to labour with him in love, working together and eating bread together, as one of the tribes or families of Israel, neither giving hire nor taking hire."[1]

and villainies of the lowest order were perpetrated in order to destroy their influence. So egregious did the practices and persecutions become that the dissenting ministers in England arose to their defense and drafted a letter to the Governor of Massachusetts urging that he display more leniency in his treatment of the Anabaptists and free them from the prisons in which they were confined. The intervention proved futile. The Anabaptists were not discharged from prison, and the laws were not lightened in their behalf.

Cotton Mather's denunciation of the Quakers held equally true in his eyes for the Anabaptists:

> They induced many to oppose good order, sacred and civil. They manifested an intolerable contempt of authority. . . . I appeal to all the reasonable part of mankind whether the infant colonies had not cause to guard themselves against these dangerous villains.

Quakers and Anabaptists were anathema in the eyes of Mather not because they actually sowed disorder in the community but because their ideas carried that threat within them. As a matter of fact, the Quakers were the most peaceful of people, opposed to war and conflicts of all kinds, and eager to co-operate with anyone and everyone in the spread of Christ's gospel. They conflicted in their interpretation of what constituted Christ's gospel. The Quakers and Anabaptists, like many of the other insurgent revolutionary sects, and like many of the earlier medieval and pre-Reformation groups, believed in apostolic Christianity and revolted against the Christianity that had developed after the Church had become an organized institution. The Church, with its pyramidal officialdom, its intricate and sterile ritual, its mechanical techniques and tactics, had given a structural rigidity to religion. These insurgent groups hated that concept of a church. To them a church was a personal thing, a place simple as breath, intimate as pain. They would not call their gathering place a church; the very word was repulsive to them. After all, the Established Church had rid itself of little of the elaborate ritual and paraphernalia of the Roman Catholic Church. When they thought of a church, they thought of the Roman Catholic Church or the Established Church, and they would have none of either.

## OPPOSITION TO CHURCHES

But they were sceptical not only of churches but also of ministers.* They wanted neither. Any place where they gathered became sacred through their individual presence. They did not need or want stained glass windows, multicolored pulpits, bright shining rails, plush carpets of exotic weave, or any of the decorations and elaborate embellishments which made a church into a church in the eyes of the conventionally religious. These people met in humble places, ofttimes with only the earth as a resting place. If they were Quakers they bowed their heads in prayer,† without minister or deacon to

* Typical of this attitude are the words of the great Quaker George Fox, whom Cotton Mather spitefully and meanly called "that proud fool." [2] Worse than that, Mather declared that Fox could not write his own name (the battle of the *knows* against the *know-nots*) and that Fox's book *The Battledor* was not written by Fox, but "certain Jews were hired to do that work and had four score Pounds for their pains and a Dozen Bottles of Wine over and above."[3] That there was an element of antisemitism embodied in Mather's words is scarcely open to doubt.

Fox, describing his experiences in America, stated that at one place he heard that "some of the magistrates said amongst themselves, If they had money enough, they would hire me to be their minister: this was where they did not well understand us, or our principles . . . this thing, namely, hireing ministers, had spoiled many, by hindering them from improving their *own* talents; whereas our labour [that of the Quakers] is to bring everyone to their own Teacher [the inner light, inner monitor] in themselves."[4]

† The Quakers were determinedly and fanatically opposed to bowing or uncovering their heads, or bending their knees, to anyone but the Creator. All the uncovering, bowing, and bending which people were supposed to undergo before individuals of high rank they not only condemned but refused to participate in, even though at times it resulted in severe censure and punishment. They would bow only to God, not to man, be he lord, duke, or king.[5] They were democrats in life as well as in spirit, and objected to any and every form of adulation encouraged by aristocracy, theocracy, or bureaucracy.

Their insistence upon addressing each other as "thee" and "thou" did not have a dissimilar origin. Fox himself defended the custom, and declared that it was justifiable and by no means absurd to address an individual or a king by "thou"—that the Quakers refused to acquiesce in the prevailing habit, which sprang from the false affectations of men.[6]

In consonance with the same philosophy, the Quakers refused to take oaths, considering them offensive to God. The literature of the period is replete with attacks on the Quakers for their stand on this issue. The following passage, culled from a pamphlet of the early eighteenth century, is illustrative of how the non-Quaker elements viewed the Quakers in that connection:

"*Q.* Pray, tell me why thee and the rest of our Friends will not agree to take an Oath when it is so tender'd according to the known laws of the Kingdom?"

"*A.* Because our Lyes will pass muster as well or better without swearing than a Carnal Man's Words though never so true with a thousand oaths and curses."[7]

The pamphlet quoted from is bitterly satirical but little more. Other pamphlets of the day were violent in their hostility.

In addition, the Quakers did not believe in churches, for reasons given by George Fox: "The steeple houses and pulpits were offensive to my mind, because both priests and people called them the house of God, and idolized them; reckoning that God dwelt in the outward house. Whereas they should have looked for God and Christ to dwell in their hearts."

guide them, and spoke only when the Lord commanded them. They wanted no professionals, no clerics, no hierophantic bureaucrats, to lead them in prayers or to subdue them with sermons. If they wanted to pray, if they wanted to hear a sermon, they wanted that which sprang from the heart, not that which came from the lips of a paid ecclesiastic. If they were Anabaptists, "their preacher used a half a tub for a pulpit and was girded with a white cloth. Each one brought with him whatever food he had at home to eat and the leaders divided money amongst those who were poorer, saying that they imitated the life of the apostles and refused to enter the temples to partake of the Lord's Supper as it was a papistical ceremony."

## CHRISTIANITY VERSUS CHURCHIANITY

Like the early Christians of the apostolic era, these groups were democratically minded in the purest and holiest sense of the word. There was a halo, an element of glory, about their democratic vision. Democracy lived in them like a sacred light, radiating every sector of their personalities. They carried on the democratic ideal to which Christianity had given birth. It was "Churchianity," not Christianity, which destroyed that ideal. It was these groups, in their simple, lowly ways, that wanted to bring Christianity back to Christ, back to its original and pristine conception.

What Christianity brought to the world was the concept of democracy as a spiritual ultimate. It elevated the concept of man as man, regardless of his position in society, his wealth, his office in the state. It made all men equal in the eyes of the Lord. It condemned the rich and exalted the poor. Earlier religions had divided men off in the next world as well as this. Among many of the primitive peoples, the poor had no future at all after death.* Among

* Among the Tongans, the Maoris, and the Samoans, for example, the concept of the other world was one in which the rulers became immortal personalities in the next world, deities that ruled the sky as well as the earth, while the common people perished as so much scum, consumed by the sea, or swallowed up by the wind and the rain. Among the Leeward Islanders the same outlook prevailed. Only the chiefs and the more privileged members of society were able to enjoy the bliss of *Rohutu noanoa,* which was their heaven, "for only they could afford to pay the heavy charges which priests exacted for a passport to paradise; common folk seldom or never dreamed of attempting to procure for their relatives admission to the abode of bliss."[8]

Among the Marquesans the fate of the soul after death "was determined, not by moral considerations, not by the virtue or vice of the deceased, but by the rank he had occupied the Egyptians, the Pharaohs were embalmed and mummified for eternity; the commoners perished or, as in certain periods of the Egyptian religion, they were preserved merely to serve and wait upon the ruling class in its myriad functions. At one time the servants and slaves were killed at the master's death in order to provide for his existence in the next world.

Christ's message was different. He went farther than the Egyptians, farther than the Babylonians, farther than the Assyrians—farther than the Greeks. In Greece, for example, which is often credited with being the first country to give birth to the democratic idea, democracy really had little place. In Athens, the greatest of all cities at the time, only 9,000 out of a population of 515,000 in 300 B.C. could marry—or vote. The 506,000 were not freemen, not property owners.

## THE RISE AND FALL OF CHRISTIANITY

The challenge of Christianity from its inception down to the time when its doctrine crystallized into theological dogma was its revolutionary democratic content. It was that challenge which made it dangerous to the state and drove the Roman emperors to persecute it, in all the various and vicious ways they did, in an abortive attempt to stamp it out before its message spread to the masses and resulted in revolution. The Roman emperors did not attempt to suppress Christianity because of its religious content, but because of its political and economic threat. Roman civilization was full of too many Christs, too many messiahs of all kinds—Mithraic, Zoroastrian, Manichean—to be alarmed about another Savior born of the Jews. It was the revolutionary doctrine of this particular Christ, who associated with fishermen, carpenters, tradesmen, whores, that terrified the Romans and made them drive his followers to the hills and the catacombs and finally to the lions when they were captured. Eventually, when it was found that Christianity could not be conquered, it was bought out, compromised, vitiated, and conjoined to

in this life; people of quality went to the upper world, and common people to the lower, to Havaiki."[9]

It is pertinent to note here Fraser's statement that this belief in class immortality tended "to strengthen the respect for the government and to ensure the maintenance of law and order. Moreover, by lending a supernatural sanction to the rights of private property among all classes, it further contributed to abolish one of the most fruitful sources of discord and crime in the community."

the state. By the end of the third century, Christians were to be found in the high places, in royal circles, among the senators and equestrians, and scattered in many positions of importance throughout the Empire. It was this conversion of people of influence to the Christian cause that ultimately determined its victory over the Roman religion but, at the same time, diluted it of its original passion and purpose.*

## THE APOSTOLIC IDEALISTS

Thus died a great religion—but all its greatness did not die with it. The individuals, groups, sects, of apostolic times were not forgotten entirely. The purity of their challenge, the belief in man as man—as an individual—persisted, and down through the centuries men and women with true Christian dedication have taken up that challenge and, lifting and lighting it like a torch that has begun to burn out, have flung it in the faces of those who had tried to trample it into extinction. Those men, those groups, have always been a plague to the churchmen, the ecclesiastical functionaries and officials. They have always been embarrassing, and ofttimes harassing, reminders of an aspect of Christianity which is difficult—in fact, impossible—to reconcile with the Christian religion as an organized institution.

All through the Middle Ages Christian leaders and groups sprang up—Albigensians, Waldensians, Taborites, and many holy orders—determined to live the life of Christ and not that of the churchmen. Known mainly as primitive or apostolic Christians because they wanted to live the simple, unpretentious, communal life of the apostles, they indented the darkened corridors of medieval history with sudden and vivid sparks of illumination. Later, when their dream had been burnt to ashes by the extinguishing tyranny of the Catholic Church, new groups arose from the remains of the old. In England, France, Germany, Holland, these new groups revived the spirit of their predecessors.

The Quakers and Anabaptists who settled in America stemmed from this new revival. They believed in the apostolic idealism of their

* By the time the second century A.D. rolled around, Christianity had already begun to justify slavery.[10] Paul had already urged, "Servants, obey in all things your masters"; and Peter advised, "Servants, be subject to your masters with all fear."

predecessors, and loathed the absence of such idealism among their contemporaries. They wanted to co-operate and not compete, share and not hoard.

Naturally, such doctrines could not be tolerated in the new world any more than in the old. The John Cottons and the Cotton Mathers of New England,* who believed in an organized church and an organized Christianity, were intolerant of such apostolic Christians, who were naïve enough to believe that the original doctrines of Christ could be put into practice. As we have seen, they fought these groups tooth and nail, and considered no punishment too severe in their suppression.

### THE INNER LIGHT

"What!" Fox asks, "are all Christians priests? Yes. All Christians." Fox even went further and said not only that all men were priests, but also that "all women are priests," which indicated how inclusive the Quaker movement was in its ideology. Obviously the priests could not endure such heresy; it was a direct challenge to their power. Moreover, it was an immediate challenge to the power of the state as well, for the Quakers respected civil officials just as little as they did ecclesiastical. Like the Ranters and Levellers in England, and many other Dissenting groups, they set the individual conscience, the inward monitor, the inner light, above church and state.[12] They refused to listen to bishops or priests, governors or magistrates. They refused to listen to anything except their own consciences, their own intuitions.† They were the truest, most complete individualists to which the world has given birth. They exalted the individual above everything in the world: church, state, family. Without doubt, their zealotry at times, especially on the part of their more perfervid members, was unhappily hysterical and obnoxious. Neal tells about how at times "when a [Quaker] Man or Woman was moved by the Spirit of the Lord they would leave their Families and Employments and ramble over the whole Province to gain

* Cotton Mather himself, for instance, writing of the Quakers, declared that "if they had not been Mad they had been worthy to die." [11]

† In a letter to a London friend, Captain James Cudworth wrote on December 10, 1658, that "They [Quakers] deny the Holy Scriptures to be the only rule of their Faith and Manners and Advance their 'Light Within' in the place of it.... This 'Light Within' they affirm to be sufficient to Salvation without anything else." [13]

Proselytes," and how upon occasions to "cloath their Message with the greater Terrour they covered themselves with Sackcloth and put Ashes on their Heads."

They believed that Christ lived in every individual, and that the only thing the individual had to do was to discover, to live in rapport with, the Christ force dwelling in him. Everything was secondary to that reality. Religious canons, legal mandates, social customs, moral dicta, economic conventions, meant nothing to them. Individual salvation, which was something that happened within the individual, regardless of such outward factors, was everything.

Naturally such doctrine appealed more to the lower classes than to the upper. The former had nothing to lose from such convictions; the latter had much to lose if such convictions ever became dominant in the land. In England the Anabaptists, Ranters, Quakers were attacked as "unclean beasts," and whatever extremes of the vocabulary, unprintable as well as printable, could be mustered forth were employed as additional denunciations—not because these groups *were unclean*, but because they were intolerable to those who believed in the "law and order" of the status quo. In America, as was to be expected, the same reaction prevailed.

Fox's stand was a moderate one compared with that of many of his left-wing English apostles, and a most conservative one compared with that of his Dutch following, who advocated, with unhesitating gesture and with the effrontery of sanculottes, an equalitarian division of wealth.

## AGAINST LAW AND ORDER

In the light of these facts, it is not surprising that the Quakers fared ill in the new world, in which the dominant elements were law-abiding groups of a relatively conservative cast. The Puritans, and even the Pilgrims, believed in "law and order," however much they differed in its interpretation and application. The Anabaptists and Quakers did not believe in "law and order," or perhaps it would be better to say they did not believe in the "law and order" of the day. They believed in the "law and order" of the individual, not that of the church or state. Without doubt their religious beliefs, revolutionary in implication, were a menace to the more moderate and conservative groups which were in power in the New England colonies. Back in the Commonwealth days they had disclosed their insurgent tendencies. "Our most considerable enemies," Henry Cromwell wrote to Thurloe, "are the Quakers. Some of our soldiers have been perverted by them, and I think their principles and practices not very consistent with civil government."[14] In short, the Quakers, like the Communists immediately after the Bolshevik Revolution, were a most unhappy thorn in the side of both the conservative and the liberal groups in England as well as in America.

Up to that time, and unfortunately up till today, all government has been based upon force, however implicit, and it was force that the Quakers ineradicably opposed. They believed in goodness and generosity, in co-operation for a common end, and fought all those who believed in tyranny and suppression.

It is only by understanding these attitudes of the Quakers that one can understand the hostilities to them which developed in the new world, and the punishments visited upon them by the other Christian sects. Cotton Mather condemned them, as we have already shown, because he believed they were a menace to social tranquillity. His words condemning their religious attitude are most revealing:

> The Quakers made themselves to be Christs as truly as ever was Jesus the son of Mary....
>
> They say every day is the Lord's Day....
>
> And for prayer itself, they said all must cease from their own Words, from their own Time, and learn to be silent until the Spirit give them Utterance....[15]

### ANTAGONISM TOWARD ECCLESIASTICS

What Mather feared was that the Quakers' conviction that all men were Christs, that all men had the same Christ-fire burning in them, laymen as well as clerics, would result in a democratic levelling of the whole community, depriving the theocrats of their position of intellectual and social superiority. If cobblers and carpenters were as close to God and knew as much about God's word as ecclesiastics, which is what the Quakers and Anabaptists believed, then there would be no need for ecclesiastics at all (as the Quakers contended) and religion would become nothing more than a form of mass demonstration and dedication. This, in the eyes of Mather, a confirmed hierophant, was sacrilege. After all, Mather believed that laymen and clerics were different, and, what was more, that laymen were inferior to clerics. He would not go so far as the Catholics and contend that laymen couldn't understand the word of God except when it was interpreted for them by priests, but he would go so far as to say that laymen didn't know enough to interpret the Bible wisely without the aid of clerics. Above all, he couldn't endure Quakers who said that you didn't need clerics at all to understand the Bible or to know the way of God.

No better indictment of Mather's own philosophy was ever written than the one by himself in his *Magnalia Christi Americana*, wherein he attempts to describe the nature of the Quaker heresy. What he condemns is not the Quakers but himself, the Puritans, the New England theocracy. "The whole history of the Gospel," he writes, negativing the Quaker ideas, "they therefore beheld as acted over again every day as literally as ever it was in Palestine; and what befals this Principle in us they advanced as the Truth of Christ sacrificed for us, Dying, Rising and Sitting at the right hand of God and coming in Clouds to Judgment they set themselves hereupon to extinguish our whole Christian Religion for these airy Notions to succeed in the room thereof; they scoffed at our imagined God beyond the stars; and said our carnal Christ is utterly denied by the Law." [16]

His comment to the effect that the Quakers beheld Christianity "as acted over again every day" is illuminating: it exposes one of the main reasons why he opposed their tenets. The Quakers believed in Christianity as preached by Christ, which meant Christianity which was not only "acted over every day," but Christianity which believed in a social and communal order of things, Christianity which reached down to the lower levels of society and exalted them to the higher levels of authority. This was not only heresy; it was revolution.

### PERSECUTION OF THE QUAKERS

The punishments meted out to the Quakers were immediate and severe. When they were put on trial, their demeanor was unabashed and fearless. They answered questions with heroic intrepidity. It was impossible to intimidate or terrify them. When asked how they could prove that God had sent them to the new world, they replied with obliterating candor "that they had the same call which Abraham had to go out of his country," after which they were imprisoned, mutilated, and often hanged. A vast bonfire, in Hitlerian style, served as a means of destroying their literature, which was impressively prolific. Masters of vessels and ship captains were penalized a hundred pounds for bringing a Quaker to the country; they were fined five pounds for importing Quaker literature, and even more if they hazarded a defense of Quaker opinions; ordinary citizens were penalized forty shillings for every hour's entertainment given to a Quaker. The Quakers themselves had one ear cut off upon their first conviction, regardless of the nature of the crime, which ofttimes was one involving nothing more than a heretical assertion of argument; upon second conviction the other ear was severed, and upon the third their tongues were bored through with a molten iron.

Mary Wright, one of the courageous Quakers of her day, defied the court before which she was tried, declaring that she was a child of God and that the members of the court "thirsted for blood." She insisted that the members of the court should "repent of [their] bloodshed and cruelty and shedding the blood of the innocents." Her words, alas, were of no avail. Being a Quaker, she was found guilty and punished.

So widespread were these persecutions of the Quakers in England as well as in America that George Fox, the great Quaker leader, whose voice thundered up and down the highways and byways of the English countryside, made the pillory into a pulpit. Thereafter the pillory became a sacred symbol in Quaker lore. Revealingly enough, the more the Quakers were persecuted, the better they thrived.* Persecution endowed them with courage and an ever-deepening faith in the truth of their doctrines. It infused them with a belief that they were related to the early Christians who braved the lions rather than capitulate to the Caesars. To reach the gates

* "They gloried in their sufferings,"[17] Neal writes, "as for Cause of God and the Testimony of Jesus." Even after four of them were executed, their fortitude continued. In one case the Court was empowered to sell two people, Daniel and Provided Southick, for having sided "with the Quakers and absenting themselves from public Ordinances" among other things.[18]

of Zion they were willing to defy the devil and all his beasts of temptation, and battle against the preachers and priests who were nothing more than human wolves that had put on the sheep's clothing of ecclesiastics.

## ALL MEN ARE CHRISTS

Quaker doctrine undermined the structure of organized Christianity. It not only advocated the elimination of the clergy, but it also refused to accept the Scripture as final authority. Its final authority was the individual soul. It was "Christ in the heart," not "Christ in the Bible," that they revered. "They stiled those Blind Beasts and Liars who should say that the Scriptures reveal God: and confirm it," Mather writes, "the greatest Error in the World and the Crown of all errors to say the Scriptures are the rules for Christians." [19] They condemned those Christians, Mather goes on to say, "who were expecting the Christ's second Coming will be Personal. They said those Things called Ordinances as Baptism, Bread, and Wine, rose from the Pope's invention." [20] "Believing that Their Christ was not the carnal being worshipped by the Puritans or Pilgrims. He was a certain Heavenly Divine Body constituted of invisible Flesh, Blood and Bones." He came "from Heaven and did put that body into the other Body of all Nature . . . and this heavenly and spiritual Body . . . is the Man Christ . . . upon which accounts the Quakers made themselves to be Christ as ever was Jesus the son of Mary." [21]

If all men could be Christs, as the Quakers believed,* then all men could be, all men essentially were, equal. Divisions vanished between people, between women as well as men; rich people not only were no better than poor people but were worse if they did not share their wealth with them; preachers and magistrates, no longer superior to the rest of the community, were bereft of authority and power.†

* Jasper Danckaerts in his *Journal* (1679-1680) comments on the Quakers' tendency to think of themselves as Christs, Virgin Marys, and the like: "But what are not these people capable of who present themselves to be carried away as we have mentioned above; as well as others in this country who publish and declare, one, that she is Mary the mother of the Lord; another, that she is Mary Magdalen, and others that they are Martha, John, etc."[22]

† Writes Neal: "Another thing that disgusted the government of New-England was the stubborn and disrespectful behavior of the Quakers to Authority; it was a new thing in those

### CO-OPERATIVE ECONOMICS

Such beliefs, couched though they were in religious language, represented an implicit but unmistakable revolt against "law and order," the law and order of New England capitalist society. A carry-over from the precapitalist economics of the Middle Ages, such beliefs possessed enough dynamite in them to shatter the whole structure of the new economic order. They had to be fought; they had to be destroyed. After all, the Quakers were not only inveighing against the ecclesiastics and the magistrates, but also against the "devil-take-the-hindmost" economics which had become the fashion in the new as well as the old world. The Quakers objected to the competitive market wherein one bought cheap and sold dear, and insisted that the divorce between economics and ethics which inevitably resulted from that philosophy was disastrous to the soul and society.* For a long time, despite the economic losses which ensued, the Quakers insisted upon the "just price" in all their transactions. In brief, they insisted upon co-operation instead of competition in economic affairs.

Behind all the antagonism and hostility to the Quakers, then, was an economic as well as a religious conflict. The two, it is obvious, were inextricably interwoven, for economic ideas in those days found their social body in religious doctrine. Not only were the ministers convinced that if the Quakers ever became powerful they would be "ripe to cut throats," [25] but the magistrates were certain that they would redistribute the land. The Quakers who had fled to Holland, as we have seen, advocated that all wealth should be shared in common,[26] and many Quaker zealots in England as well as in America maintained that such a division of goods was imperative. The state, to be sure, as well as the church, could not afford to have such doctrine disseminated. It is no wonder, therefore, that Mather denounced the Quakers in such vituperative language, that Neal denounced their doctrine as "the Sink of all Heresies," [27] or that Josselyn spoke contemptuously of the "bottle-bellied Witches

Times to see People refuse the common Titles of Respect to their Superiors and deny them the ceremony of the Hat; this was apprehended to be a Denial of the Authority of the Civill Magistrate."[23]

* "O ye earthly-minded men," George Fox wrote, "give over oppressing these poor: exalt not yourselves above your fellow-creatures; for ye are all of one mould and blood."[24]

amongst the Quakers," [28] for these humble people were determined upon the most impossible and impracticable task: to prepare the world for Christ's rule.

### CORRUPTION OF THE IDEAL

What happened to the Quakers in America is what happens to every group when its leadership changes as its members become more prosperous. In England as well as America the old spirit which dominated the movement when its members came, as their enemies declared, from "the dregs of society," "the poor and the ignorant," vanished when those members became less poor and more learned, and when new members flocked into it from the more successful sections of society. Quakerism experienced something of the same disintegrative process that Christianity underwent during the century preceding the Council of Nicaea, when an increasing number of rich Romans forsook their old gods for the new god of the Christians. The entrance of such wealthier elements into any poor-man's movement is bound to undermine and vitiate its morale. This invasion of the richer elements began in England but soon spread to America. In this country another factor was at work that did more to hasten the dilution of Quaker doctrine than anything else; namely, the productivity of the land itself and the economic opportunities springing therefrom, which soon made poor Quakers into prosperous Quakers and prosperous Quakers into economic and political conservatives.

### QUAKERS AND THE SLAVE TRAFFIC

In time the Friends, as the Quakers prefer to be known, began not only to divorce themselves gradually from their co-operational concepts of economics, but even to participate in the slave traffic that became popular in those days. It was not long, as the more successful Quakers found that traffic increasingly profitable, before the majority of the Quakers in America came to condone slavery. As early as 1671 George Fox, while in the Barbados, had to deliver his worst attacks against his own followers because of their having succumbed to the slave traffic. Fox, one of the true descendants of Christ, a pure prophet if there ever was one, inveighed against this evil with all the mightiness of his power, which was so great in those times that it shook men's souls to their depths, challenged their consciences, and stirred them like some inward tocsin. His protests, followed by those of his unpolluted followers, rang down the years and, before long, revived a new sentiment in the movement. Agitation against slavery, inspired by his Isaiah-like fury, resulted finally in the development of an antislavery attitude among the Friends. His famous letter in 1657 "to Friends beyond the sea that have Blacks and Indian slaves" encouraged that attitude, but his sermons in the Barbados galvanized it into a dynamic challenge. His declaration that God has no respect for persons, classes, or nations, that the *gospel* belongs more to the slaves than to the enslavers, constituted part of the greatest social challenge of the era. If all Quakers did not heed it, many in time did, and within a few generations, under the later inspiration of John Woolman, Fox's fight achieved success.

Woolman, who came to America in 1742, was an even more effective force than Fox in fighting slavery in the new world. His peregrinations, punctuated by preachments more gentle than severe, all of which are recorded in his amazingly interesting and stimulating *Journal*, had a profound influence upon American Quakerdom and upon the American populace as a whole. A simple English clerk, who had refused years earlier to sign a bill of sale for a Negro woman, he became in America one of the earliest Abolitionists. It was mainly as a result of his work that the Friends came at length to abjure slavery and eliminate it from their way of life. In fact, without the challenge and inspiration of Fox and Woolman, it is doubtful whether the Quakers would ever have become the ardent Abolitionists they developed into in later years.

It should not be thought that all Quakers succumbed to the slavery traffic. Many of them, to be sure, remained poor, but even among the more prosperous there were those who clung with admirable tenacity to their idealism. As far back as 1688, in Germantown, at a meeting held at Richard Worrell's, the Friends went on record as being officially opposed to slavery as an institution.[29] This represents one of the earliest (if not the earliest) expressions of antislavery sentiment in the land, and even when, in the nineteenth century, the majority of the Quakers had turned from radicals into moderates, the greater number of them adopted an Abolitionist stand.*

No one can question the genuineness of the Quaker attitude toward Negro slavery even though many of the Quakers' followers, notwithstanding the challenge of their leaders, were loath to give up the traffic and some were willing to desert their faith in order to continue it. On the whole, however, the Quaker attitude toward downtrodden groups and peoples, oppressed or enslaved, was both sympathetic and magnanimous.

### ATTITUDE TOWARD THE INDIANS

In regard to the Indians, the Quakers were the most exemplary sect that settled in the new world. One of the outstanding reasons why the Puritans opposed the Quakers was that the latter treated the Indians as if they were human beings and not savages, equals and not inferiors. Added to everything else, this was just too much, and few of the Puritan leaders refrained from saying so—in language that was untrammeled and unmitigated in its condemnation.

Cotton Mather hated the Quakers for their attitude toward the Indians. Dominated by the dictates of his color and class, Mather considered the white men superior beings, ordained thus by God, and the Indians as savages, foreordained thus by God. So enraged was Mather by the attitude of the Quakers that he denounced them as "another sort of enemies, which may with very good reason be cast into the same History with them [the Indians]." [30] He condemns in particular a certain Tom Maule, who "sets himself to Defend the Indians in their bloody Villanies, and Revile the Countrey for Defending it self against them." This is not only heresy, in Mather's opinion, but treason.

Mather, endeavoring to attack the Quakers, sneers at their comment that "the Killing of the Indians or Murdering of them" is

* An interesting and important, but unanswerable, question would be to ask what position the Quakers would have adopted toward slavery in the nineteenth century had the majority of them been settled in the South, where the majority of every group, compelled by the logic of circumstance, economics, and geography, took the opposite stand. In the light of their earlier attitude toward the Indians, the *original* Quakers undoubtedly would have made more than a little effort to side with the Negroes.

evil. The Indians, in his eyes, are not human, at least not Christian, and although he does not urge their destruction, he does not hesitate to state that they have to be dealt with as savages and combatted at the point of arms when necessary. His hatred for Tom Maule is based primarily upon the latter's defense of the Indians. Maule had written, with candor and wisdom rare in New England in those days, that: "God hath well-rewarded the inhabitants of New England for their Unrighteous Dealings towards the Native Indians, whom now the Lord hath suffered to Reward the Inhabitants, with a double measure of Blood, by Fire and Sword." Such words, scorching with truth, made Mather writhe. There was no vituperation, in his opinion, violent enough to annihilate this Quaker maniac. Frothing with fury at a man who had the audacity to side with the Indians against the white men, he urged all New Englanders to use Tom Maule's name as "a proverb for lyar of the first Magnitude." To fail to do that, he declared, would be to "deprive their Language of one Significant Expression, which now offers itself unto them."

Mather was by no means the only one in New England who attacked the Quakers for their extreme friendliness toward the Indians. Mather's attitude was the familiar, the popular, one. Most of the New Englanders were willing enough to be friends with the Indians so long as they were able to gain something from that friendship and so long as the Indians did not interfere with their projects for expansion. The Quakers, as the Indians quickly realized, were different. They didn't use Indian friendship for their own advantage; their friendship, like that of Roger Williams, was principled, not opportunistic. They not only were fair in their dealings with the Indians but also refused to take up arms against them, and in those respects the Quakers remained consistent through the years. They were the Indians' best friends. And that was something the rest of the populace, which had fleeced, robbed, and slain the natives, could never understand; down the centuries they attacked the Quakers for their "treacherous" tendency. As late as 1764, in a pamphlet entitled *The Quaker Unmasked*, the Friends were satirized and condemned as allies of the Indians—and because the Quakers respected the Indians as human beings and would not slay them. The words of the pamphlet are interesting and revealing:

> Go but into the House of a Quaker and before they have Time to discover what you came for he will ask you with an affected Meekness, "Hast thee seen the Massacre of the Indians at Lancaster?"

What the author of the pamphlet, as well as most other white men, objected to, was the sympathy which the Quakers constantly showed toward the Indians.[31] That sympathy might easily enough be construed as sentimentality if it were not for the fact that the Quakers themselves never suffered the attacks and tortures from the Indians that other white settlers suffered. The Indians respected them because they respected the Indians, and therein is the answer.

Thomas Chalkley, a well-known Quaker in his day but now largely forgotten, describes in his *Journal*, in language simple as sound, clear as sight, how he and his friends spent their time among the Indians. His words reveal just why the Quakers experienced none of the difficulties with the Indians that the rest of the settlers had. The Indians to them were brothers, friends, compatriots of God. "We went on cheerfully, and with good will, and much love to the poor Indians," he writes, "and when we came, they received us kindly, treating us civilly in their way."[32] Hundreds of letters, articles, sermons, documents, reveal that attitude as common to all Quakers.

## WILLIAM PENN: THE COMPROMISER

When William Penn founded Pennsylvania, which soon became the great Quaker refuge, he gave that attitude official status. His treatment of the Indians was most laudable. He refused to allow any of his followers to take advantage of the ignorance of the natives and insisted that in all their transactions with them they be paid an "honest price" for whatever was purchased: land, furs, food. Penn himself, like most of the Quakers who followed him, was not the uncompromising idealist that George Fox and the earlier Quakers were; he was a good man but not a holy one. Although he had been expelled from Oxford because of his nonconformist convictions, and was imprisoned several times for his attacks upon the orthodox religious conceptions of the day, his later life did not conduce toward the continuance of such idealism. He never forgot that he was a Quaker, but he never attempted to advance Quakerism as radical doctrine. Beautiful and inspiring as were many of the sentiments expressed by him in his volume *No Cross, No Crown,* the fact remains that he became a compromiser who introduced the moderative attitude into the Quaker movement. He made Quakerism tolerable if not acceptable to Cotton Mather and other religious and political conservatives. As the Quakers became more conservative and less radical, the laws against them were either repealed or left unexecuted.

Nevertheless, Penn's attitude toward the Indians and the Negroes prevailed throughout the seventy years that the Friends were in power in Pennsylvania, just as the same attitude obtained in Rhode Island during the extended period when the Friends were dominant there; and if in other ways his Pennsylvania experiment, conceived with such high vision, faded into something unadventurous and prosaic, it must not be forgotten that it clung to more of its original convictions for a longer time than any of the other colonies.

Whatever may have been Penn's failures, and there were many, certain truths remained with him through the years, down to the time when his mind gave way and what was left of it resolved itself into incoherent gibberish and weird abracadabra. Even in the obliquity of his mania he continued to mouth recollections of what he had once believed and could not altogether forget. Never in his life did he fail to affirm, mad as well as sane, that "Christianity teacheth people to beat their swords into ploughshares, and their spears into pruning hooks, and to learn war no more; that so the wolf may lie down with the lamb, and the lion with the calf, and nothing that destroys be entertained in the hearts of the people." [33] He was a Quaker to the last, and it is to be greatly regretted that he did not live to realize more of his aspirations, especially his dream of a General Court or General Diet of international scope and influence, which would adjudicate economic and political relations between all countries, Oriental as well as Occidental. In this dream, which he voiced in his *Essay Towards the Present and Future Peace of Europe,* he anticipated the League of Nations conception which was to attract and absorb so many minds several centuries later.

### THE ANABAPTISTS

The career of the Anabaptists was similar in many respects to that of the Quakers. They were persecuted in Europe from the time of their inception, and that persecution persisted also in America when groups of them emigrated here. Over most of the old world they were hunted by ecclesiastical as well as civil authorities, imprisoned, scourged, branded, and often tortured to death. Their unweakening intransigence resulted almost in their extinction.

The Anabaptists were originally followers of Zwingli, and felt nothing but contempt for the doctrines of Luther and Calvin. They broke with Zwingli about 1525 over the issue of baptism, which they insisted upon as a necessary rite, and hence acquired the name of "rebaptizers" or Anabaptists. Their concept of "rebaptism" was most revolutionary, embodying as it did a complete condemnation of the ecclesiastical state. They insisted not only upon the separation of church and state, but also upon the destruction of all authoritarian power that conflicted with the freedom of faith of the individual.

It was not long before the movement spread rapidly throughout most of northern and central Europe, and by 1530 it had become such a force with the masses, who constituted its main following, that being a member of it inevitably meant exposing one's life to jeopardy. But the more dangerous opposition and persecution grew, the more fearless the movement became. Its leaders defied church and state in defense of their faith, which was most democratic. In Moravia, the movement was converted to communism by Jacob Huter, one of the leading Anabaptists of the time, and his followers were commonly known as Huterites.[34] Thomas Münzer adopted a similar position, as did a number of other leading Anabaptist figures.

In the uprising at Münster in 1534, Anabaptism excited international alarm. The people in Münster ejected the extant government, drove the ecclesiastical and civil authorities into retreat, and established a new government of their own based upon communist principles. The town was besieged and the people's government was overthrown, but the memory of the revolution did not perish. It was a source of inspiration to the Anabaptists, but a source of terror to those in authority everywhere. Although the Anabaptists never succeeded in controlling a whole city as the Taborites had dominated Prague a century earlier, their activity was more widespread and their influence more profound.

### THE HUTERIAN SECT

The Huterites established communist colonies in the Tyrol, Carinthia, and lower Austria, and many of these became conspicuous for their economic efficiency and scientific advances. In Moravia they bred the finest horses in Europe and manufactured woolens, linens, and cutlery of impeccable quality. Their physicians were among the best in Europe. Continued attacks, however, drove them from place to place, killing off many of them and effecting divisions among the remainder, a section of which in the nineteenth century finally found its way to America, settling in the James River valley in South Dakota. Through the years they clung to their nonresistance philosophy and were so persecuted by the Americans during the World War that they fled from their settlement to Canada. A remnant of them still remain in South Dakota, and their households continue to be models of efficiency and co-operation. They have adhered steadily to their communist ideals, and to this day their style of living in that respect has altered little. In their colonies everything is owned in common: land, tools, houses, furniture, and even clothes. Nothing is inheritable. Money cannot be lent out at interest, and all forms of life and property insurance are forbidden.[35] The lives of all the members of their communities are regulated in minute detail. Everyone, regardless of profession, must share in the manual labor of the community. Money does not circulate within the group but is used only in relations with the outside world.

All Huterian communities try to isolate themselves in territories as far away as possible from other people, that is "the outside world," in order to assure and insure their economic and spiritual independence. All reports of their economic activities in Canada and South Dakota prove how successful they have been. In Alberta "neighbors say the Huterian people get five bushels of grain to the acre more than others do," Bertha W. Clarke states.[36] And their social life has been no less successful than their economic life. Everyone in the community, including the preacher, is taught a trade, and everyone must do an equal share of the more arduous and unappealing tasks. Everyone, for instance, must be a stallboy, which is the most disagreeable job in the community, for one year of his life. The result of such discipline is that there is not, and never has been, an illiterate in any of the twenty-six Huterian communities (with the exception of one fellow who was born an imbecile), never a Huterian in an almshouse or in a jail, except those who went to jail as conscientious objectors during the World War. Not only did every Huterian refuse to join the armed forces of the nation, but all refused to perform any substitute services, and would not "don military uniform, or obey military commands when put in prison." [37] However odd many of their customs are, these people are sacrificially consistent in their practice of them. They will not allow a photograph to be taken of them because of God's commandment that "thou shalt not make unto thee any graven image or any likeness of anything that is in heaven above or that is in the earth beneath." Huterians frown upon the concept of romantic love, but all of them marry, and there are no divorces among them. Their philosophy of communism is based upon scriptural command: "And all who believed were together, and had all things in common; and sold their possessions and came, and divided them among all." (*Acts* 2: 44-45.)

## THE MORAVIANS

But more important than the Huterites were the Moravians and Mennonites, the latter belonging to the right wing of the Anabaptist movement. The Moravians, emanating from the Hussian revolt, from which Anabaptism sprang, soon became known as the United Brethren and, with the aid of Count Zinzendorf, who first welcomed them to his estates,[38] they ultimately succeeded in reaching and settling themselves in the new world. Zinzendorf was by no means the founder of Moravianism. He was a wealthy count who sympathized with the reformistic religious movements of his day, and who gave the Moravians haven when they were being mowed down by the artillery of their adversaries. It is said of Zinzendorf that when he was an undergrown, ascetic youth he scribbled messages to God on tiny scraps of paper and flung them to the winds, convinced that they would reach their heavenly destination. His pietistic convictions persisted, persecution ensued, and at length, along with the Moravians, he decided to hazard the wilds of America as a final alternative. The group landed in 1741 in Pennsylvania, which was inhabited at that time by "English, Swedish, and German Lutherans, and the Scotch, Dutch, and German Reformed [besides] Arminians, Baptists, Vereinigte Vlaaminger en Waterlander, Mennonites from Danzig, Arians, Socinians, Schwenckfelders, German Old Tunkers, New Tunkers, New Lights, Inspired Sabbatarians or Seventh Day Baptists, Hermits, Independents, and Free Thinkers." [39]

### A GENERAL ECONOMY

However individualistic the Moravians were in religious attitude, they were most co-operative in economic vision. They constantly stressed community of feeling as more important than individualistic aspiration, and made *Gemeinschaft* and *Gemeingeist* sacred words. In Bethlehem, which speedily became the matrix of Moravian life in America, a General Economy was established, the motto of which was: "We pray together, we labor together, we suffer together, we rejoice together." The concept of "together," or *togetherness*, was their unifying ideal. Although there was no hostility to the institution of marriage, as later we shall find existed among the Ephratists, men and women slept in separate quarters, and the family was relegated to a position of tertiary significance. Households were run upon a representative basis, with committees instead of individuals in charge of them. In fact, committees ran practically everything in the lives of these people—their trades and manufactures as well as their schools, kitchens, and churches.

The communal life adopted by the Moravians continued for only a brief period, after which they reverted to the individualistic pattern of existence. Unlike the Labadists and Ephratists,* and in the next century the New Harmony-ites, the Mormons, the Oneidists, and countless other groups, which perpetuated themselves as communal societies, the Moravians deserted their communism once the promise of the land encouraged that desertion. While it lasted, how-

* The Ephratists came into conflict with the Moravians over all kinds of matters, the sexual one being paramount. Beissel attacked the Moravians for exalting marriage, which the Ephratists discouraged.[40]

ever, the communism of the American Moravians was most comprehensive. It was an economic communism based upon spiritual support. No one was legally bound to anything. The community was opposed to binding anyone; the contracts were verbal, not written. Everyone donated himself to the general cause, the social objective of the community. The people "belonged to no man and therefore would accept no man's wages; for as they themselves said in the Brotherly Agreement of 1754, 'We all belong to the Saviour, as He is our Lord, and what we have, that all belongs to Him, and He shall dispose of it as it pleases Him.' "[41]

### THE FIRST COMMUNITY CHEST

The communism of the Moravians was, it is true, a feudal derivative, possessing the disadvantages as well as the advantages of its medieval precursors. All the business of the community was handled with remarkable expedition and efficiency. Those who joined the group did not surrender their possessions; they lent them to the community chest *without interest*, but were privileged to withdraw them at any time that they decided to leave the group. A valiant attempt was made to prevent the family from proving a stumbling block to the colony's success. Children were placed in a nursery, and their education was undertaken by special members selected by the group. The moral behavior of the unmarried and married was supervised with fanatic vigilance. The young men and women were subject to so many rules and regulations of behavior that it was practically impossible for them to see each other except under the most strict chaperonage. That Moravian youth ultimately revolted against this monastic discipline is not surprising—and when the revolt came it was most declarative.

### UNCOMPROMISING PACIFISTS

The Moravians, like the Quakers, were noncombatants, and upon all occasions they refused adamantly to serve in the militia or in any other armed group. They were persecuted for their pacifism and several times were exposed to violent attacks by the belligerent settlers. Nothing, however, could change their conviction on the issue. In the case of the Indians, their attitude was the same. Like Roger Williams and the Quakers, they made fast friends with the natives and would brook nothing that would disturb the tranquillity of their relationships. Zinzendorf, for instance, made several journeys among the Indians in a missionary capacity and was notably successful in his efforts to convert them to Christianity. As an outgrowth of the Count's efforts and those of other Moravians, Indian dictionaries were published, hymns and sermons were translated into the aboriginal dialects, and it was not long before the Indians felt that the Moravians were their spiritual brothers. A child of the Pietist tradition, Zinzendorf believed in the power of enthusiasm to evoke the religious energies within man, civilized or savage, and in his appeal to the Indians as well as to the white men, he always insisted that, as a first prerequisite to conversion, "The heart must burn." [42] It was not doctrine which counted, but the heart which was the touchstone of all things sacred. This belief made it possible for the Indians to feel closer to the Moravians than to the Pilgrims or Puritans. The same was true of the Negroes, whom the Moravians treated with equally tender and generous consideration. The Moravians were among the first groups in the new world to become interested in Negro education and to make a definite and concrete attempt to organize a Negro school and develop a program of Negro education.

### THE MENNONITE ASPIRATION

The Mennonites are a much better known sect than the Moravians, although the latter are a more interesting and challenging group in terms of social philosophy. The Mennonites never entertained a communal conception of society and lacked the imaginative audacity of the Moravians. Representing part of the pietistic, Anabaptist revolt against the formalism of conventional religion, the Mennonites emigrated to the new world in much the same spirit that the Quakers did, to find a place where pacifism was permissible doctrine and preachers and priests were unnecessary to religious worship. They were undeviatingly consistent in their opposition to Negro slavery and to any and all forms of militarism. Beyond these attitudes, however, their progressivism did not extend.

The Mennonites sprang up shortly after the Münster revolt, under the leadership of Menno Simons, a quondam priest who deserted Catholicism after coming into contact with the Anabaptists and rereading the New Testament, wherein he discovered abundant reasons why he should adopt the new religion. He was baptized into the new faith in 1536, and from that time on the section of the Anabaptist movement which he led became so influential, organizing new centers in so many places, that the followers of it soon became known as Mennonites.* A price was put upon Menno Simons's head by Charles V, and the former found it necessary to seek one refuge after another in order to escape capture. The more he was hunted, the more his co-laborers multiplied. He wrote pamphlets and tracts, one more controversial than another, and carried on extended debates with many of the leading theologians of the day, all in a determined attempt to spread the new gospel to which he was converted. Like all converts, he burned with a proselytizing enthusiasm which was unquenchable.

## PLOCKHOY'S DREAM

A century later, Cornelius Pieter Plockhoy, of Zeirek Zee, taking up the torch which Menno Simons had flung in the face of his enemies, attempted to establish a communist colony somewhere in England and Ireland during the days of Cromwell's Commonwealth. Cromwell, however, was deaf to the idea, and Plockhoy, as a last resort, obtained the support of the city of Amsterdam to settle a colony of Mennonites along the shores of Delaware Bay, which at that time was owned by the Dutch.

Once the group had arrived in America and become oriented, it swiftly divorced itself from Plockhoy's communist dream. Like the Plymouth group, it adopted a general economy of a co-operative character for a three-year period. After the three years had elapsed, property was no longer held in common, the general storehouse was given up, and all the rest of the co-operative features of the colony were gradually relinquished. Education, however, remained free for everybody, and no form of ecclesiastical taxation was allowed. In fact, there was only one place of worship permitted in the colony, but in that place everyone could worship as he pleased. To eliminate the possibility of dissension on this score, *no ordained clergyman was allowed to settle in the colony.*

* The followers of Menno Simons were first known as Menists before they became known as Mennonites.

This colony, however, was not long-lived. During the war between the English and the Dutch, the former destroyed the Plockhoy settlement, and what finally became of the majority of the settlers, with the exception of Plockhoy himself, is not known. As late as 1694 Plockhoy and his wife managed to reach Germantown, where they lived as a public charge the rest of their years.

Dead though the colony became, and forgotten for the most part though it is, we must still turn to it for the first public protest against slavery made in America.[43] * The Plockhoy Mennonites were absolute and uncompromising in their condemnation of slavery as an institution.

Later Mennonites settled mainly in Pennsylvania, where, inspired by the tolerance of William Penn, they felt certain they could find a permanent home. And they did. Back in Germany these Mennonites were "daily hunted with constables, and as many as they can get [were] taken prisoners."[44]

In America the Mennonites found life more tolerable. The destruction of Plockhoy's Delaware colony was political, not religious. The Pennsylvania Mennonite groups did not achieve anything resembling prosperity for many years, and then only after great sacrifice and arduous effort. A letter from one of the Pennsylvania settlers depicts how difficult life was for most of the group: "*I do not advise anyone to come here;* those who come ought to come after Christian deliberation with pure intentions and the fear of the Lord, so that the Lord may be their support; for before a man here reaches ease he must exercise patience, resignation, and industry, the one as much as the other."[45]

Notwithstanding the difficulties and distresses of the American environment, which made life such a severe task, the Mennonites in this country did escape the humiliations and oppressions of their European brethren, who were tyrannized over by taxes, prohibitions, and segregational laws.

Germantown became the Mennonite center. It was to Germantown that the great Quakers, George Fox and William Penn, made

* In that connection it also has been maintained that the Labadist colony in Maryland was the first group to denounce slavery (Matthew Page Andrews, *The Founding of Maryland,* p. 303), but in the light of the fact that Peter Sluyter, one of the Labadist leaders, later exploited slaves as viciously as any slave driver, it is difficult to accredit the Labadists with such exalted nobility of motive.

their missionary tour, which proved so successful. During and after that tour many Mennonites were converted to Quakerism, and those who were not were persuaded at least to look upon the Quakers as their friends.

### THE AMISH EXTREMISTS

The Mennonites were an exceptionally practical as well as a remarkably determined and courageous people. Even the Amish schism of 1693 was unable to impede their success. The Amish, who were more extreme than the rest of the Mennonite brethren, were forced to go their own way, and have persisted in it until the present time. The Mennonites believed in religious separatism, but did not insist upon economic or social separatism. The Amish, impractical idealists in a most practical land, insisted upon separatism in every aspect of life. They refused to deal with people not of their faith, would tolerate no social relations with them, and above all denounced any intermarriage with them. In short, the Amish, like the Huterites, were complete isolationists and believed in the absolute ostracism of all people who were not of them.

Although these people remain obscure in the history of this vast country, their ideas of toleration and pacifism may become the challenge of tomorrow. Their religious fanaticism may be viewed as pathetically anachronistic,* but their social ideals have gained rather than lost value through the years—especially in these late years when the dark cloud of intolerance and war has overshadowed the Western world. They have held to a belief, held it close and dear —a belief that many men have cherished but few have had the courage to cling to in the face of opposition and attack. Never have they budged, compromised, or surrendered their conviction that war is evil and that no righteous man should ever participate in it. In this belief they preceded Gandhi by centuries. They adhered to it as steadfastly in the recent World War as they had centuries before.

### THE FAMILISTS

In his *Rise and Progress of the People Called Quakers* Penn observed that it was from the Seekers and Ranters that the Quakers

* No doubt the Mennonites were the *Fundamentalists* of their time. They had little interest in either art or science, and their education, though most democratic, was exclusively religious.[46]

derived.[47] Describing these earlier sects, he wrote: "These people were called Seekers by some, and the Family of Love by others; because as they came to the knowledge of one another, they sometimes met together, not formally to pray or preach at appointed times or places, in their own wills, as in times past they were accustomed to do, but waited together in silence; and as any thing rose in any one of their minds that they thought savoured of a divine spring, they sometimes spoke."

The Familists, sometimes known as the Family of Love, had originated in Holland in 1555, and had exercised considerable influence over the nonconformist sects of the time.[48] Their founder, Henry Nicholas,* insisted that religion was based upon love and nothing more; all else was inconsequential. Theological hostilities, creedal conflicts, ritualistic differences, were the concern of those who did not know Christ, who were not at one with Christ, and who did not realize that Christ was love. The Bible itself, in Nicholas' eyes, was important only as an allegory and not as a source of divine authority. The only divine authority was love, love of Christ, which made the individual into one with Him. "The true Light is the everlasting life itself," Nicholas declared, "and shows itself through illuminated, i.e., godded men, for through such persons the most High is *manned* [incarnated] . . . [and] the person henceforth lives and walks in the Light in all love." Like most of the leaders of the dissenting, pietistic groups of the period, Nicholas believed that the true knowledge of Christ inhered in his *family* of disciples, who had a monopoly upon divine wisdom.

* There is considerable dispute concerning the actual origin of the Familists. Oliver, for example, states that they "owed their origin to David George, of Delft, an enthusiast who believed himself the Messiah. They branched off into the various sects of Grindletonians, Familists of the Mountains, of the Valleys, of Cape Order, of the Scattered Flock, etc. They renounced the principal doctrines of Christianity, which they held to be superseded by the advent of David George, and are said to have practiced among themselves the grossest libertinism."[49] From all extant evidence, however, it seems highly doubtful that the charge of libertinism could be substantiated. But according to Blunt "immorality was very common among them."[50] What Blunt meant by immorality is difficult to ascertain. He seemed to believe, as also did Baxter and Fox, the fact that the Familists were sceptical of the existence of heaven or hell was proof that they were "immoral." To a large extent the Familists' insistence upon interpreting Christian doctrine allegorically instead of literally led to such egregious misconstruction of their motives.

### ARRIVAL OF THE PLOUGH

Such doctrines, like those of the Quakers and Anabaptists, were too revolutionary in their implications to be tolerated by the Puritans, and when a handful of Husbandmen, which was still another name by which the Familists were known, arrived at the Bay Colony in June 1631, on a ship called *The Plough,* they were subjected to the strictest surveillance, Winthrop records, and when they "vanished away" no regrets were felt by the original colonists.[51] They represented contempt for outside authority, civil as well as religious, and were enemies of the Puritans and Pilgrims who believed in "law and order" in order to preserve the status quo.

### SAMUEL GORTON: THE FIREBRAND

Samuel Gorton, who was one of the leading firebrands of his day, did not stem officially from the Husbandmen or Familists. He was definitely influenced by them, however, and gave formidable voice to their creed.[52] Translated into political form, the doctrines of the Familists were potentially anarchist. The individual, in their eyes, had nothing to respect but himself; the protection of minorities was more important than the exaltation of majorities. The rights of the individual were supreme and indefeasible, and their best protection, Gorton contended in his *Simplicities Defense Against Seven Headed Policie,* was in the English common law, not in the new theocratic laws introduced by the New Englanders. He denied the power of the magistrates to sentence people for violating laws which they themselves had invented, and in the case of his servant, Mrs. Aldredge, who was tried for the crime of smiling in the meetinghouse during service, he attacked the Plymouth regime in language so turbulent and thunderous he was banished from the colony.

The history of Gorton's life was the record of an irrepressibly violent personality, acrid and contentious to the core. He was willing to brave any opposition in defense of his convictions. He believed that every man was a judge in himself, and needed no priest or preacher or magistrate to instruct him in what was right and good and just. "I thought myself as fitt and able to gouverne my selfe and family," he wrote, "as any that were then upon Rhode Island." [53] Although Edward Winslow described him and his followers as "unlearned men, the ablest [of whom] could not write true English,"[54] we know from better and less hostile authority that he was learned enough to read both the Old and New Testaments in their original tongues, and that he was able to write, as his own works eloquently attest, a vigorous if erratic and ofttimes obscure prose. Like most mystics, he believed in a fourth-dimensional universe, in which the fourth dimension was more important than all the other three. Calling himself "professor of the mysteries of Christ," he declared himself to be a minister, even though he had not had one day's theological training, and he defied anyone to challenge his right to function in that capacity. What the theocrats could not endure was that he would take upon himself, as Winslow described, "to interpret the most difficult places of Scripture and wrest them any way to serve [his] owne turne."[55] He despised the Puritans and Pilgrims because "the scope of their doctrine was bent only to maintain that outward form of worship which they had erected to themselves, tending only to outward carriage of one man toward another."[56]

From Plymouth Gorton went to Aquedneck, where he came into conflict with Mrs. Hutchinson's group, founded the town of Portsmouth, was banished from it shortly after; thence he ventured with a handful of disciples to Pawtucket, near Providence, where he came into conflict with none other than the great latitudinarian, Roger Williams. Very soon he attracted a considerable following, which in time caused so much conflict in the colony an armed group was sent out to subdue them. Gorton and twelve men "fortified themselves in one house . . . lined the walls with earth," to quote Winslow again, "and had made Flanckers and had provided victualls, &c, to indure a siege." In a few days they were forced to surrender, taken to Boston, imprisoned, and brought to trial. Winslow justifies this high-handed treatment of the Gortonites by declaring "they were no State or Body Politique, but a few fugitives living without law or government." It was just that fact which made them so dangerous to the authorities. They didn't believe in law—at least not in the law established in the New England territory—or in government.

### GORTON'S ATTACK ON THE THEOCRATS

Brought before the Church Assembly, Gorton fulminated against the whole New England hierarchy, declaring that all their "Ordinances, Ministers, and Sacraments, &c, were but men's inventions for shew and pomp" and described the magistracy among the Christians as "an idol." [57] Gorton's own words in that respect are significant: "They brought us forth," he wrote, "into their congregations to hear their ministers, which was meat to be digested, but only by the hearte or stomache of an ostrich." He and his followers objected strenuously to being forced to attend the church services. Such coercion violated the very principle of individual freedom—the fundamental principle of English common law. He condemned their hypocrisy: "But finding them to be a company of gross and dissembling hypocrits," he wrote, "that under the pretense of law and religion have done nothing else but gone about to establish themselves in ways to maintain their own vicious lusts, we renounced their diabolical practices." [58]

Every means was used to force Gorton and his followers to repent and promise to deport themselves in accordance with the law, but they were adamant. Finally they were sentenced to hard work, with an iron chain attached to one leg, and after serving a good six months' sentence, were banished "upon paine of death if they were found in any part of our jurisdiction."

The question that remains is: Why were Gorton and his little band treated in this manner? What constituted their crime? Why were they viewed as such a menace to New England society? Why did Roger Williams, the most tolerant and magnanimous of all New Englanders, oppose them? Williams's own words provide us with a clue. He attacked Gorton's "unclean and foul censures of all the Magistrates of this Country" and also his "denying all visible and externall Ordinances in depth of *Familisme*, against which I have a little disputed and written and shall (the Most High assisting) to death." [59] Williams believed in freedom of worship, in the right of the individual to believe what he wished, and was willing to do everything in his power to defend that right; but he did not believe in opposing, as the Familists did, the *existence* of the magistrates and ministers.

What Gorton denied most forcefully was the legitimacy of "self-constituted town government."[60] Throughout his career this spitfire libertarian continued his onslaughts upon New England governments wherever and whenever they violated individual rights and prerogatives. In the amazingly progressive Code of 1647, approved by the first General Assembly of the United Colony, Gorton's clever and cunning hand was present. There is abundant reason to believe that it was he more than anyone else who fought for the inclusion of the clause forbidding imprisonment for debt and for the astonishing statute against Negro slavery.[61] The statute is significant: "Whereas there is a common course practised amongst English men to buy negers, to the end that they may have them for service or slaves forever, for the preventinge of such practises among us, let it bee ordered that no black mankinde or white, being forced by covenant bond or otherwise, to serve any man or his assigns longer than ten yeares, or untill they come to be twentie four yeares of age, if they be taken in under fourteen. . . . And that man that will not let them goe free, or shall sell them away elsewhere . . . he shall forfeit to the Colony forty pounds."[62] Although the statute did not free Negroes immediately from their bondage, it was important because it guaranteed them the right of freedom within a relatively brief period of years. In fact, the white indentured servants fared little better at the time.

Despite all his Swedenborgian mysticism, Gorton was a profoundly practical man. Even in his *Commentary on the Lord's Prayer* he was realistic. In the main, it was an attack on "priestly mediations" and the whole business of priesthood as a form of social authority.[63] He loathed rites and ceremonies as much as he despised professional priests. All men, in his opinion, were or at least could be priests. He went as far as the Quakers in his insistence upon the fact that women as well as men could be teachers, preachers, and prophets. A John the Baptist of his era, he challenged all the prevailing conventions of his time and pointed a warning finger toward the future, which would give birth to a new vision of Christ and of society.

### RELIGIOUS UTOPIANS—THE LABADISTS

The American communist colonies date back to the seventeenth century. As far as can be discovered, the Labadists, who settled in

Maryland in the early half of that century, represent the first of these groups. Although short-lived, the colony is by no means insignificant. It realized, in practice as well as in theory, the communist ideal which the Diggers, left-wing Quakers, and certain other nonconformist groups had extolled. In other words, it was not an isolated, eccentric outgrowth, but part of the inevitable flowering of a widespread, fecund movement. It lifted the co-operative tendencies of medieval life to a higher and more modern level of expression. In striving to reconcile certain of the ideals of Christ within the frontiers of a co-operative society, it pointed the way toward a view of life which, within the next two centuries, was to become popular with reform as well as with religious groups.

## JEAN DE LABADIE

The Labadists derived their name from that of their founder, Jean de Labadie, a Jesuit who confounded the Catholic world by deserting the Church and becoming a Protestant minister. A friend of Richelieu, by virtue of his extraordinary oratorical gifts, Labadie could have won high honors by compromise. But that was impossible for him. Infused with the zeal of a Savonarola, this herb-eating zealot preferred revolt to compromise, and after being banished from France in 1657, he discovered refuge in various places before he finally went to Amsterdam, where he found his first opportunity to lay the groundwork of his conception of a communal society. He was invited to settle in England by John Milton, who was one of his admirers, but after continued correspondence Labadie decided against it.[64] Before he died, in 1674, his group had multiplied so rapidly that it not only had established itself in numerous communities but had even sent out missionaries to many parts of the world.

Jasper Danckaerts and Peter Sluyter were the missionaries who established the Labadist community on Bohemia Manor in Maryland. Bohemia Manor, near where Elkton, Maryland, is today, was owned by Augustine Herrman, an adventurer who, influenced by the fact that his son was a convert to the movement, offered part of his land as a settlement place for it in the new world.[65] The two Labadists immediately took advantage of Herrman's magnanimity, and shortly thereafter moved in upon his territory. The colony established itself within a relatively brief time. What the people built was a communist colony which was more advanced than any other colony in the country at the time and, perhaps, more advanced than any existing in Europe during the period. It was dedicated to a way of life which was so Christian that Christ himself, had He been alive, would have blessed it.

Following the precepts of Labadie, these disciples strove to erect in Maryland the structure of a communist society founded upon the equalitarianism of Christ. Without communism such equalitarianism was unattainable. They despised the religious equalitarians who thought Christ's ideals could be achieved in a competitive society. Danckaerts, for example, is most bitter in his condemnation of those Quaker groups which tried to reconcile their religious idealism with worldly acquisition and aggrandizement. He would not have his hundred Labadists in Bohemia Manor succumb to such hypocrisy and deception. From the very beginning of the colony, they pursued a communal way of life which was copied in the main from the mother church in Wieuwerd, Friesland, where the Labadist movement had its old-world center. It is important to remember that the Labadists were an international movement proliferating from Friesland. Everything they cultivated in the Maryland colony—tobacco, corn, flax, hemp—was grown co-operatively.[66] Like their founder, Jean de Labadie, many of the members of the sect heard strange sounds, and saw stranger visions, but never did they allow extravagances of hallucinatory zeal to interfere with their practical attitude toward economic life. Communism to them was a natural way of life, at least for Christians. They believed not in divisions between men but in the equality of men. They believed that life on this earth was nothing more than a preparation for life in the world hereafter, and that any attempts to establish differences between people in this world were futile. If there were differences to be established, they should be between people in the next world, not this. This world was temporary, contemporary, not eternal. In this world all should be equal, fair, co-operative. Christ, when he broke the loaves and fishes by the sea, had established that fact. He had shown that all should share alike, regardless of wealth or station—that all men essentially were of the same station, equal in the eyes of the Lord.

The Labadist community achieved during its heyday a remarkable degree of efficiency. Work was apportioned with engineering precision; each person had his assignment of work to do, in the laundry, the kitchen, the fields. Little time was wasted. Everyone who joined the colony surrendered all his possessions and gave them to the group. These people were *levellers* in the true tradition of Winstanley; they carried out in the new world what Winstanley had hoped to see realized in the old. "Haughtiness of the worldly spirit must be subdued" was their leading tenet, and they lived by it as well as swore by it.[67] Anyone suspected of the sin of pride was given the lowliest tasks in order to conquer his weakness. The refractory and recalcitrant were punished by reducing their allowance of clothing or "being placed lower down at the table."[68] Men and women were separated at meals and daily tasks so as to lessen the influence of the sex factor in their relationships, but at the same time women were endowed with the same rights as men and were in no respect reduced to a condition of inferiority.

## ATTITUDE TOWARD WOMEN AND MARRIAGE

There can be no doubt that the Labadists' attitude toward sex was fanatically ascetic. They insisted, in keeping with the ancient Biblical tradition, upon circumcision as a sacred rite. They did not prevent or even oppose marriages, but they definitely discouraged the sexual relations. In the first place, they believed that any Labadist married to a wife or husband who was not a Labadist should separate immediately and annul the marriage.* In fact, any Labadist married to a person who was not a Labadist was not considered married at all. The pair, in the eyes of the Labadists, were living in sin. Peter Dittleback's experiences, as recorded in his *Vernal en Val Labadisten,* disclose even more of the Labadist attitude toward sex and marriage. Dittleback tells about an experience the wife of one of his friends had in the colony; she was castigated severely for kissing her children, because such a gesture betrayed "fleshly cleavings," and later was reprimanded harshly for nursing her child at her breast. After a time an attempt was made to convince the husband that his wife, because of her physical desire for him, was a harlot. The husband,

* Both Petrus Bayard and Ephraim Herrman (son of Augustine Herrman) separated from their wives after they joined the Labadists.

however, refused to be persuaded by such arguments, and after a prolonged debate about the matter left the colony and returned to Holland.

Samuel Brownas, who visited the colony in 1702, discovered it to be a most original and exciting enterprise. Like others he comments upon the attitude toward women and observes that "the women eat by themselves, and the men by themselves, having all things in common respecting their household affairs, so that none could claim any more rights than another to any part of their flock, whether in trade or husbandry."[69] He also notes that, like the Quakers, the colony believed in prayer only when it sprang spontaneously from the individual: they distrusted the official prayers of the hierophants and the conventional conception of undertaking to pray at regular times according to the demands of the ritual. They believed that secret silent prayer was superior to public prayer, and exalted those that were holy in their hearts rather than those who were sanctimonious in public appearance and gesture.

Despite their peculiarities and eccentricities of behavior and philosophy, the Labadists succeeded in doing more work in one day than other groups of similar size managed to do in three or four. What wrecked them was the economic voracity of one of their leaders, Peter Sluyter, and the failure of their mother colony in Holland, which proved a death knell to the whole communal experiment. Before long Sluyter became the dominant proprietor of the lands, and though he later divided up the property between several of the remaining members of the colony, he became a wealthy proprietor in his own right. So decisive was this change in the status of the group that five years after Sluyter's death, in 1722, the colony ceased to exist.[70]

## THE EPHRATA COMMONWEALTH

Of a little later origin, but much more significant and much longer-lived, was the Ephrata colony founded in Pennsylvania shortly after the first quarter of the eighteenth century. Two members of the Ephrata group journeyed to the Labadist colony, which was then in a moribund stage, to discover how life fared with their fellow-utopians.[71] Isaac von Bebern, one of the pair, was a Hollander, who had become so wealthy as a result of communal life in the Surinam that he was eager to examine communism among the North Americans. He was most unhappy to discover what had happened to the Labadist colony, but that in no sense deterred him from belief in what the Ephratists could achieve with their venture. As a matter of fact, it is possible that it was the Labadists who inspired Conrad Beissel, who accompanied von Bebern in the visit to the Maryland colony, with a vision of what could be done with his followers if they did not succumb to certain of the temptations which had undermined the Labadist experiment.

### BEISSEL: THE FOUNDER

Conrad Beissel, who was the founder of the Ephrata colony, had been born in Germany in 1690, become apprenticed to a baker as a young man, acquired an aptitude for the violin, and finally, after a series of mishaps and misfortunes, set sail for the new world in 1720. A fight with the wife of his employer led him to detest womankind and convinced him that man's salvation lay in celibacy, which ideal prevailed in the Ephrata colony throughout his dominance. The inception of the colony can be traced to 1724, when Beissel, disillusioned with the Dunkers whom he had joined shortly after the arrived in America, was baptized along with six of his followers in the Pequea River by Rev. Peter Baker.[72] The group maintained themselves at Mill Creek for a while, then moved three miles north, and seven years later ventured into the territory known today as Tunkerstown, or Ephrata, which has always been celebrated as the center of their colony.

### KELPIUS: THE RELIGIEUSE

As early as 1694 John Kelpius, an oblique-eyed religieuse, had founded a celibate, co-operative colony which had become known as *The Woman in the Wilderness*, but it had died a premature death.*

* Kelpius, a native of Siebenbuergen, was a man of great scholarly accomplishments, the master of three languages, and a most learned correspondent whose letters retain interest even today. There are two explanations of how the colony got its name. One explanation is that it was called the Woman in the Wilderness because all the members were single men and the ridge upon which they settled was a wilderness at the time. The other explanation is that the colonists believed in the imminent arrival of the millennium "when the woman mentioned in the Book of Revelation should come up from the wilderness leaning on the arm of her beloved and deliver the church." [73] In terms of sheer learning, the colony was perhaps the most erudite in the new world. Their mastery of languages was phe-

Beissel's Ephrata colony not only carried on the Kelpius tradition but added to it. Beissel believed in more than celibacy; he believed also in communism, and there was not a little of the adventist psychology intersticed among his sexual and economic ideals. While Beissel did not make marriage entirely impossible among his followers, the fact remains that during the first twenty years of the colony there were "only two marriages in the congregation, and those were of persons of advanced years." [74] Beissel, like many others of his time, believed that Christ's return was imminent, and that what the human race—or at least the limited sections of it which he could contact—had to do was to prepare for that miracle. He was not so wild-visioned as Miller and his Millerites, who a century later believed implicitly in that miracle and, in 1843, perturbed the entire world with their proclamations about the Second Advent, preparing Elysian robes and gathering on roofs and mountain tops in anticipation of their supernal ascent.[75] What Beissel believed was that man was living in ways that were evil and that he had to repair those ways in order to save himself from the abysms of temptation and destruction.

The first way to begin that reparation, Beissel contended, was sexual celibacy; the second way was economic communism. In brief, he was opposed to the sexual and economic freedoms of his time, especially to those that led man to love the flesh more than the spirit, and he devoted his life to those ideals. There were scandals associated with Beissel, one suit on the part of a sister of the community to the effect that he was the father of her child, but all extant evidence indicates that such attacks and allegations were motivated by envy or malevolence and not by fact. Whatever he failed in cannot be attributed to lack of devotion or sacrifice on his part, because his entire life was spent in pursuit of ideals.

At all events the Ephrata group, under the hegemony of Conrad

nomenal, prodigious. Their dedication to celibacy was absolute until Kelpius died, after which the colony gradually dissolved, some members wandering off to new places, others marrying, and the rest adopting a less rigid and fanatic way of life.

Kelpius has had many admirers, as also has the colony itself. The colony was praised unreservedly by everyone for its good works in helping the poor. Whittier's three lines in praise of Kelpius are most interesting in capturing something of the quality of the man:

"Or Painful Kelpius from his hermit den,
By Wissahickon, maddest of good men,
Dreamed o'er the Chiliast dreams of Petersen."

Beissel, who was known as the *Vorsteher*, or Superintendent, built up in a relatively short period of years a colony which survived almost all the communist colonies on this hemisphere.

### CENOBITIC IDEALISTS

Beissel was devoted to the cenobitic ideal. He insisted upon celibacy for both sexes because he believed true communism could not be achieved otherwise. When men and women loved each other as individuals, and as members of families, such an ideal was impossible. It was bound to be vitiated, traduced, by the nature of the circumstances. Beissel went even further in his insistence upon points of dress and appearance. What he aimed at was a simplicity of attire that would remove every possible form of sexual attraction—remove as far as possible the semblance of the human body.

Like the ancient Catholic orders of monastic character, he believed that the human body was seductive, and that the best way to eliminate its enamoring and inveigling qualities was ecclesiastical decree. He insisted in keeping with many of the older monastic orders, that the main thing to do was to conceal the body, its lines, its contours, its seductions; and this is mainly why priests, sisters, and nuns wear such dress today.

"It was resolved to muffle the mortal body" (it must not be forgotten that the Ephrata group believed in the close arrival of Christ, which was the conception of all Adventists) in such a style and in such a garment as would fit it for its immediate transportation to the skies and the eternal hereafter.[76] The group adopted what was fairly close to a Capuchin costume, a surplice that extended to the feet, with an apron front and a veil behind, and in which no one could distinguish sex from sex. In a word, the people were to be considered a *sexless* colony, pure as light, clean as rain.

### COMMUNIST ECONOMY

One of the rules of the group was that whenever a person joined it he had to surrender all his worldly goods to it. The admission of Sigmund Landert, a wealthy widower, resulted in the construction of an additional house of prayer, and that of Benedict Yuchly in the erection of a convent upon a near-by hill, which shortly became known as Zion Hill. From that time on, which was in the spring of

1738, the Ephrata colonists were often known as the Zionitic Brotherhood.[77] No one in the colony had any advantages over the other, no matter how much they had originally contributed to the community on joining it. Moreover, if they left the order they could not take their possessions back. Brother Lamech's description of how they worked is interesting: "They drew their cart themselves, and were their own horses; when they travelled, they went heavily laden like camels, and sometimes the whole Brotherhood might be seen trooping down the hill of Zion." [78]

The colony soon became so successful that it began to lend money out, and, as Brother Lamech says, "it is likely that if God had not destroyed this economy, the Brethren would by this time have ships upon the sea." A mill was purchased, a vast orchard was developed, a vineyard was begun, and for a considerable time Ephrata was one of the most thriving industrial communities in the country. It was not long before there were flour and grist mills, a saw mill, an oil mill, a paper mill, and a tannery; pottery manufacture was started, basket making became an important occupation, and at length a printing plant was established which published over fifty volumes, among them being the popular *Wunderspiel*, *Man's Fall*, and what is today their famous hymnal.[79] Ephrata printing became renowned throughout the land. The colony was also very musical. It organized singing schools, encouraged hymn composition; and that aspect of it is still preserved today by the Snow Hill group, or Nunnery, which is located not far from Waynesboro, Pennsylvania. The Snow Hill people, descendants of the Ephrata colony, strive to keep alive Ephrata music, which is as inimitable as the masses of Palestrina.

Busy as the colony was with its agrarian and industrial tasks, it never lacked time to devote to reading, writing and studying. Its whole life was routinized in such a fashion that it was impossible to waste time. The members worked all day long, with the exception of the time consumed in eating, and then from seven to nine at night they read, wrote, or studied; from nine to twelve they slept; they arose at midnight, spent an hour at song service, or matin, as they called it (they detested the word *mass*), slept again, woke once more at five, celebrated another matin, and then went to work afterwards until nine in the morning, when breakfast was served. Such was the life of these simple, solemn folk, who believed that Christ was a communist and that to be Christians they had to be communists too.

In the first place it must not be forgotten they were one of the most long-lived co-operative colonies in the new world. Survivors of them are living yet, and their music is preserved by votaries in Snow Hill who still believe it is the most beautiful music that has ever been composed. Although we may admit that it is inferior to many Catholic masses, as also to the masses of Bach, there is a quality about it which is unique, subtle, and sublime. Something undoubtedly lived in the Ephrata people that was rare, communicative in the higher and finer sense of the word, and that has lived on, like an echo that cannot be forgotten, in the lives of those people who eventually took over their land and occupied what was once the original colony.

A great fire which destroyed their best farms and industries played havoc with their plans and reduced their aspirations to a nullity. Even Peter Miller, who was one of the most brilliant men to join the group, was forced to confess that, though the colony by that time had grown to more than three hundred, it was practically impossible to continue it under communist auspices.

In a letter which Peter Miller wrote to Benjamin Franklin, he confesses, in simple, succinct language, what happened to the Ephratists; namely, that "the Genius of the Americans [was] bound another way." Peter Miller lamented that fact beyond words. It broke up his life because he believed in a different ideal. His ideal was a cenobitic one, in which the individual sacrificed himself, his family, and everyone, no matter how precious, in behalf of Christian communism, which he considered the gateway to the future life.

Ephrata, or at least a remnant of it, remains for scholar and tourists, but little of it remains in the essential sense of the word. Those who go to it as on a pilgrimage find little to convey the original spirit of the place. Nevertheless, as one of the most long-lived communist colonies in the new world it will always be remembered by those who cherish a co-operative way of life as superior to a competitive one.

## COMMUNISM: MEDIEVAL AND MODERN

All these communist and semi-communist groups which believed in the creation of a co-operative world grew out of a philosophy that was medieval. Their communism was largely rustic, not urban; it was a communism of peasants, small tradesmen, and scattered artisans. They believed like the Waldensians, the Cathari,* the Taborites, in communal economics, and were opposed to the individualistic economics of the modern world. They were as unacquisitive and unaggressive as the new capitalist elements were acquisitive and aggressive. All that went to make modern capitalist society—initiative, selfishness, accumulative aspiration, and other extensions of the "buying cheap and selling dear" philosophy—was anathema to them. They would have none of it.

Noble and exalted as their philosophy was, it is important for us not to forget that it was unadapted to the needs of the new age. Good, gentle, and humanitarian as their communism was, it was definitely lacking in that individualistic incentive necessary to the social and economic progress of industrial civilization.† Their communism insisted that men surrender their individual wealth to the community, not in order that all men should benefit from it, but because it was good for man's soul not to possess wealth. It exalted poverty as a good and wealth as an evil. After all, Christ had advised the rich man's son to give up his possessions for the sake of his soul, and they believed in Christ and the application of his doctrines. Even among the artisans, particularly the weavers, the same philosophy prevailed. The artisans, who dominated large sections of the Catharian movement, were interested in wresting wealth and power from the merchants who, as commercial capitalists, were exploiting them, but they were not concerned with communism of production because they still owned their tools of production.

It was not until the invention of power machinery, when the tools of production fell into the hands of the industrial capitalists, that anything like the theory of modern communism or socialism ‡ could

* The Cathari carried these beliefs to an incredible extreme. They even refused to believe that Christ had ever been an earthly man, and insisted that his body was created in heaven and emerged not from Mary's womb but from her ear. They even went so far as to exalt death by voluntary starvation as the highest ideal. They were opposed to the acquisition of wealth, to the delights of food, and to the pleasures of sex.

† Even Kropotkin, who extolled peasant communism in his book *Mutual Aid,* was forced to admit that it did not encourage intellectual advance or scientific progress.

‡ I have used the words communism and socialism interchangeably here, as representative of a co-operative economy based upon an industrial structure. The differences in theory and tactic that have developed between communists and socialists within the last twenty years do not fall within the radius of this discussion.

crystallize. Modern communism is based upon the co-operative ownership of the means of production as well as of those of distribution.

In other words, medieval communism was based upon religious idealism instead of economic reform. It believed in the subjugation of the individual rather than in the conquest of the economic order in which he lived. In short, it was spiritual rather than material. Modern communism, on the other hand, is material rather than spiritual. It does not exalt poverty as an ideal but condemns it as an evil. It aims not to encourage poverty but to eradicate it. Medieval communism sought to escape the world, and most of the colonies embodying its philosophy shut themselves off from the other members of humankind because they believed the rest of the world was unimportant and would be destroyed when the millennium arrived. Modern communism is just the opposite: it wants to conquer the world, not to shut itself away from it. It is a product of capitalist society, is based not upon artisan and peasant elements but upon those of an organized proletariat which has developed the trade union into its major weapon. It is interested in economic advance, not mystical purity.

Admirably intentioned though these religious communal groups were—Ephratists, Huterians, and Mennonites, as well as the European groups and orders—their economic outlook was unprogressive. Out of them it would have been impossible to develop the industrial and scientific societies of our day; invention, initiative, speculation—all prerequisites of modern civilization—were discouraged by them. They were not interested in such advance. Had they succeeded in dominating the country, they would have impeded the progress of the people.

In America of the seventeenth and eighteenth centuries, individualism was more important than communism in the development and exploitation of the country; the communism that evidenced itself in the various groups and communities which have been described in the preceding pages was too limited by religious absolutism and the ingrownness of a peasant economy to cultivate those qualities that were necessary to the advance of the nation. The America we know today could never have evolved from such communities as the Labadists and the Ephratists, which represented the segregated and isolated aspirations of sects.

Communism, in the modern sense of the word, is possible only when an industrial proletariat is born which is determined to wrest the tools of production from the hands of individuals and place them in the hands of the state. Nevertheless the old communal groups, ineffectual though they were in the realization of their ambitions, held aloft a social ideal which has acquired more meaning today than it had in the past, when peasants and artisans adopted it as part of their religion. It was impossible at that time to convert communism into economic fact, except as an agrarian reality. Today, with the industrial proletariat which has emerged wherever the machine has become dominant, communism has become an attainable reality, with progressive instead of retrogressive economic potentialities.

It would be wrong to belittle the efforts of these early communal groups. They represent the matrix of those ideas which were to color and compel so much of the thought of the world. It is impossible to understand the contradictions and paradoxes underlying American social philosophy without an awareness of the significant role that these communal groups and colonies played in shaping the character and determining the spirit of the country.

# BOOK II

## CHAPTER X

# Virginia: The Cradle of Conflict

*Why, they are a race of convicts, and ought to be thankful for anything we allow them short of hanging.*

—DR. SAMUEL JOHNSON

*Let not the meannesse of the word Fish distaste you, for it will afford as good Golde as the mines of Guinea.*

—CAPTAIN JOHN SMITH

THE MEN who founded Virginia were not without vision. They lacked in large part the religious idealism of the early New England settlers, but they had another idealism of their own. Although Sir Walter Raleigh and Captain John Smith were adventurers and buccaneers, they were men who were dominated also by a dream. Their dream was not that of a religious utopia but that of an international empire with England as its radiant center. They were nationalists at a time when nationalism in Europe had scarcely developed beyond a fumbling, foetal thing. Their nationalism was truly national, and not confined to town, city, or metropolis. "I shall yet live to see it an Englishe nation," Raleigh declared not only about Virginia but about the whole new land, the extensity of which he was unaware, but the richness of which he believed was greater than all the resources of India.

The ambitions of Venice had been commercial, not colonial. The Venetians believed in conquest, exploitation, and expansion of enterprise, but not in despatching their own citizens into strange lands in order to make them over in the Venetian image. They were content with the economic fats and gravies which they derived from such places. They had lost the nationalistic fervor and aspiration of their Roman forebears.

It was the English who recovered that old Roman spirit, and who in time were to make the English empire into the great successor of the Roman. Such men as Sir Walter Raleigh and Captain John

Smith were the early leaders who spurred England on toward that destiny. The founders of the New England colonies were governed by a different ambition. They were interested not in dreams of empire but in religious freedom. Their concept of freedom, as we have seen, was not extremely elastic, but at least it was freedom from the dictation and tyranny of the Established Church. America beckoned to them; it offered them that freedom. America beckoned also to Sir Walter Raleigh and Captain John Smith, but for a different reason: because it promised to add to English power and to convert the country from an island into an empire.

That difference was significant.

The majority of the colonists in both New England and Virginia came to the new world for the same reason; namely, to improve their lot, to find fortune in a land which promised not to be so unfortunate as the one they had left. The leaders of the respective colonies, however, were different. And leadership in those days, no less than in ours, was determinative. The leaders gave form to colonial enterprise and organization, endowed it with the virtues as well as the vices of their past. The leaders of the early Southern colonies were men of different stature if not different stock from those who founded the New England colonies. Sir Walter Raleigh died before his dream of Virginia could be realized, died before he could know the final destiny of the colony. Captain John Smith, after a hard and bitter battle against adversaries and adversities, found himself an outcast in the colony which he had done so much to found and perpetuate, and consequently spent most of his later years in New England instead of Virginia. Both, however, were men who loved fighting for fighting's sake, adventurers in the truest sense of the word, who shared little of the lower middle-class Dissenter psychology which dominated New England. They preferred the looser and flamboyant way of life of the aristocracy.* Smith himself made the mistake of allying himself with the king's party rather than with that of the populace, and this error expedited his political demise.

Both men, however, left the stamp of their personalities upon the colony of which they were the fathers.

* It should be remembered that Sir Walter Raleigh was not a born aristocrat. It was only after his naval victories and piracies that he was knighted by the Queen.

## THE F. F. V.'S

Although New England as well as Virginia suffered from the presence of irresponsible and criminal elements, the latter colony was more afflicted with them than the former. Cotton Mather, and even the less prominent Puritan hierarchs, might rail and rant against the undisciplined servantry, denounce their sins of omission as well as commission, attack their ingratitudes and disobediences, but they were faced with a gentler and more manageable populace than that which inhabited Virginia. In class status, there was little difference between the poorer elements which migrated to both places. Indentured servantry prevailed in New England as well as Virginia. The piratical and unmitigatedly commercial nature of the Virginia enterprise, however, attracted to it a disproportionately large part of the vagrant and lawless sections of the English populace. New England was less infected with that virus. Although the Plymouth and Massachusetts Bay groups were by no means untainted by the economic motivation, they combined with it a religiosity which determined to a large extent the nature of the indentured menials and laborers who set sail with them. In brief, unmoral and vicious though many of them proved to be, they were indubitably superior to the lower-class elements which settled in Virginia.

"The people that are said to inhabit the Colonie," a sixteenth-century commentator notes, "are the most of them the very scum and off-scouring of our nation.* Vagrants or condemned persons, or such others as by the looseness and viciousness of their lives have disabled themselves to subsist any longer in their nation; and when they come thither either know not how, or will not betake themselves to any sober, industrious course of living." Over two-thirds of the early Virginian population were indentured, and three-fourths of the total population were illiterate. So many "convicts and felons" were foisted upon the colony that the House of Burgesses had to enact a law in 1670 to prohibit their increase. The law, which was denounced by the king, commented upon "the great number of felons and other despe-

* Daniel Defoe in his novel *Moll Flanders* comments on the fact that the people who founded Virginia "were of two sorts: either, 1st, such as were brought over by masters of ships to be sold as servants; or, 2nd, such as are transported after having been found guilty of crimes punishable with death."

rate villains sent hither from the several prisons of England"—and, ironically enough, many of the most illustrious of the F. F. V.'s (Famous Families of Virginia) are reformed descendants of that tribe. On the upper side of the scale, the English aristocratic element, minute though it was in numbers, was far more influential in the life of Virginia than it ever was in Massachusetts. However much Massachusetts suffered at times from court officials and plenipotentiaries, it seldom allowed them to influence the pattern of its behavior. In Virginia the opposite occurred. Governor Berkeley, for example, was more than a governor. He was a dictator in the fullest sense of the word.

At a time when the citizens of New England were forced to bow and kneel as the theocracy commanded, Governor Berkeley, as aristocratic as a Roman senator, declared that "ministers should pray oftener and preach less." He would abide nothing that was even suggestively theocratic in his regime. Like the English aristocrats, he believed in the supremacy of the Established Church, and the Established Church in England as well as America was always subservient to the political machine. Besides, the Established Church, supported by the more successful and prosperous members of the community, was ever more eager to condone than to condemn. There was nothing severe, harsh, or sadistic about its philosophy. It fitted its doctrines to the measurements of its followers.

### THE CELESTIAL ASSES

It is not surprising, therefore, that Virginia, and later on the rest of the plantationist South, became notorious for its horse-racing, gambling, card-playing, swearing parsons. These men were men of the people, no better and sometimes a little worse than their parishioners. They were not hierophants in the Cotton or Mather tradition; they were American fragments, blurred by distance, of the gayer type of English curates. They believed like all those who administered to the religious needs of the more aristocratic, or more prosperous, members of the community that it was better for men to enjoy life than to deny it, better to add to its charms than subtract from them. There was nothing of the Lollard tradition in their outlook. They would have been aliens in the home of Goldsmith's Vicar of Wakefield, whose adoration of virtue would have struck them as pathetically naïve and absurd. It was nothing for these parsons to arrange their services to fit in with the hunting habits of their flock, or with the demands of their horse-racing enthusiasts. They were as much at home on a racetrack or in a tavern as in the pupit. In the famous old church on Miles River, in Maryland, which was not different from Virginia in that respect, the preacher and the congregation repaired to the horse-races immediately after the service terminated.

"The lives of the planters in Maryland and Virginia are very godless and profane," Danckaerts wrote in his *Journal*. "They listen neither to God nor his Commandments, and have neither church nor cloister. Sometimes there is someone who is called a minister, who does not as elsewhere serve in one place, for in all Virginia and Maryland there is not a city or village . . . but travels for profit, and for that purpose visits the plantations through the country, and there addresses the people; . . . you often hear that these ministers are worse than anybody else, yea, are an abomination." [1]

One of the key facts in this connection, as Danckaerts stresses, is the geography involved. The fact that most of the Southern colonies built themselves around plantations rather than villages, towns, and cities had a great deal to do with the nature of the clergy. In the first place, it prevented the clergy from getting a throttle-hold upon the populace, and in the second place it converted a large number of clergymen into traveling salesmen with the *gospel* as their commodity.

"Clergymen . . . should be persons that have read and seen something of the world," Hugh Jones declared in his description of what the wealthier Virginians preferred their ministers to be. He added that they should also "have studied Man and business in some measure as well as books; they may eat like Gentlemen, and be facetious and good-humored without too much freedom and licentiousness; they may be good scholars without being cynics, as they may be good Christians without appearing stoics." [2] This attitude eventually gave birth to a contempt for clergymen which made many of the upper-class Southerners describe them as "celestial asses."

These were the clergymen of the upper classes, not the lower. They were obviously inferior in both intellectual and moral status to the New England clergymen—which explains in part why New

England culture in the seventeenth and eighteenth centuries was so much richer than the Virginian. The Puritan theocrats and even a number of the Pilgrim preachers were men of exceptional ability and of fairly wide intellectual interests. Several were Oxford graduates, and a considerable number of them were men of high training. Cotton Mather, for example, delved into the eccentric science of his time and encouraged people to record their scientific observations and discoveries. At a period when such matters scarcely had been freed of the trappings of magic, the New England clergy came out in defense of vaccination, and defied the prescientific objections to it that were raised by many medical men of the day.

In other words, the clergymen who served the interests of the dominant group in New England were exemplary insofar as knowledge and conduct were concerned; the clergymen who served the dominant group in Virginia were the opposite. Moreover, the clergy which served the regnant element in New England also served all other groups, whereas the clergymen who served the same group in the South could never function in that comprehensive capacity. The latter served a class, not classes. It served the aristocracy and the aristocracy alone, and was unconcerned with the middle class, which had a different clergy entirely and exclusively its own.

New England, as we have seen, was by no means unified in religious conviction. To begin with, there was the division between the Pilgrims and the Puritans; there were also the divisions occasioned by Roger Williams and Thomas Hooker; in addition, there were the lesser and more sectarian divisions instigated by the Quakers, Anabaptists, Familists, and their ilk. Nevertheless, these divisions though numerous were divisions within a class, not within classes. In the main, they were divisions within the middle class, the Puritans representing the upper middle class and the Pilgrims and the rest of the Dissenters representing divers and peripheral aspects of the lower middle class. As middle-class groups, however, they stood as one in their opposition to horse-racing, dancing, gambling, card-playing, and kindred vices of the aristocracy. However much they disagreed with one another or fought with one another over Scriptural interpretation, they never failed to recognize their common foe: papacy in religion, with all the vestiges of it that were retained by the Established Church.

In short, all middle-class religions of that day were based upon a stern, ascetic ethic; upper-class religions were more liberal and generous in ethical outlook.

### DIFFERENCES BETWEEN VIRGINIA AND MASSACHUSETTS

What made Virginia different from New England was not the fact that the majority of the people who settled in the two places were different, but that the dominant groups involved were different. "If New England be called a Receptacle of Dissenters and an Amsterdam of Religion," Hugh Jones wrote in 1724, "Pennsylvania a Nursery of Quakers, Maryland the Retirement of Roman Catholics, North Carolina the Refuge of Run-Aways, and South Carolina the Delight of Buccaneers and Pyrates, Virginia may be justly esteemed the happy Retreat of true Britons, true Churchmen for the most part." [3]

What Hugh Jones was saying was not an untruth; it was simply a part-truth. He was not wrong in his general description of the leaders of the respective colonies; he was wrong in his description of the majority of people in the respective colonies. Without going into a detailed analysis of his errors, it is patent, from all the evidence which has been gathered since that time, that New England was far from "an Amsterdam of Religion." The Massachusetts Bay group exiled Roger Williams, Thomas Hooker, and their numerous followers, and even the Pilgrims fought Samuel Gorton and many of the Quakers and Anabaptists. It is patent that Virginia was also far from a "happy Retreat of true Britons, true Churchmen for the most part." As a matter of fact, Virginia was not essentially "the happy Retreat of true Britons, true Churchmen for the most part," but of people who were very closely allied to those who settled in New England.

The tradesmen, shopkeepers, butchers, bakers, candlestick-makers, and sub-underlings who made up the colonists who deposited themselves in New England were indubitably similar to those who found a landing place in Virginia. They were largely of lower middle-class or menial origin. The lower middle-class elements were religious, honest, fanatical; the menials, who still retained a Fourth Estate psychology, emulative of the aristocrats, were loose, irresponsible, and wanton. Added together, the middle-class elements were in the majority, but in the government and administration of a community it is not the majority that rules, but the dominant minority.

In New England the dominant minority was anti-Established Church in conviction; in Virginia, on the contrary, the dominant minority was pro-Established Church. The Puritans in New England might declare, as they often did, in language vibrant and thunderous, that they wanted not to separate from the Established Church but merely to *purify* it, yet they *established* a church of their own shortly after they landed on these shores, and made it completely independent of the Established Church of England. This was one of their first and most final acts. No American church thereafter in New England ever allied itself with the Established Church tradition.

On the other hand, all the early churches opened in Virginia were hardly more than carbon copies of the Established Church of England. This was because the founders of Virginia, beginning with Sir Walter Raleigh and Captain John Smith, were adventurers, soldiers of fortune, who accepted the religion of their time—which was that of the Established Church—and were unconcerned with the conflicts, battles, and schismatic dissensions which then raged within the religious world. They were not religious men in the Dissenter or Puritan tradition, but at the same time they were not irreligious. Religion for them was a form, a function, something which they could have lived without easily enough, but which, since they had lived with it all their lives, they saw no reason to renounce. They naturally accepted, for opportunistic reasons, the most convenient religion of their day, the one backed by the state: namely, that of the Church of England. The main fact is that, in contrast to the nonconformist groups and sects, they never lived religiously and never tried to; religion to them was a side-line, something which you revered but never practiced except on Sundays, and certainly never allowed to interfere with your work or destiny.

Not only was this the religious attitude of Sir Walter Raleigh, to whom Virginia was more of a vision than a reality, and of Captain John Smith; it also was that of Governor Berkeley and his entourage and of most of the Established Church members who hazarded life on these shores. They believed in religion, all of them, but it was a religion which was part of life, not all of life. With the

New England nonconformists, Dissenter and Puritan, religion *was* life, or at least was involved in all the details of life, and definitely was a way of life in itself.

That difference was decisive in determining the contrasting psychologies which evolved in Massachusetts and Virginia.

### PURITANISM IN THE SOUTH

A mistake, however, that is most common is to conclude that all Virginia was composed of the same pattern. That the ruling group in Virginia was different from the ruling group in Massachusetts is undebatable. The rest of Virginia, on the other hand, was like the rest of Massachusetts. The *populace* in both regions belonged to the same economic class; the more fortunate elements among it, the Third Estate, were just as stern, severe, and ascetic as the Plymouth Dissenters. The poorer elements, the Fourth Estate, made up of indentured servants, criminals, idlers, petty adventurers, discharged soldiers, unskilled artisans, irresponsible ne'er-do-wells, imbecilic menials, and whatnot, were familiar in both colonies. The Fourth Estate, however, played no role in the determination of the life of the country. Fourth Estaters liked their own kind and also the wealthy class, the aristocrats; they couldn't abide the Third Estate upstarts, the cheap chiselers, the rainy-day savers, the hoarders, who represented in their eyes the non-tipping, non-spendthrifty middle class, from whom they gained or profited not at all. It was only later, with the appearance of the industrial proletariat, that the Fourth Estate acquired significance and influence in history.

The small fellows, the middle class, the Third Estate, constituted the bulk of the population of both Virginia and Massachusetts. They not only represented the majority of the populace—this had never happened in any other country in the world prior to this time—but they also represented a most formidable and formative part of its life. In Virginia, for example, they did not control the way of life of all Virginians; the aristocrats were more important in that respect. But they could exercise a significant influence over the lives of most of the community. The influence of the aristocrats stopped with those who adopted their philosophy and with those Fourth Estate underlings who were willing to support it so long as they could eke a living from it. The influence of the middle-class elements was more extensive and intensive. The Virginia middle class resembled the New England middle class in both character and conviction.

We constantly hear of how dour, repressive, and fanatical the Pilgrims and Puritans were, but we hear little of how widespread those same traits were in Virginia. A cursory glance at the laws passed by the first representative Assembly in Virginia is sufficient to illustrate the similarity of moral outlook which prevailed among the middle classes in the Northern as well as in the Southern colony:

Against Idleness, Gaming, Drunkeness and Excesse in apparell the Assembly hath enacted as followeth:

First in the detestation of Idleness be it enacted, that if any men be founde to live as an Idler or renagate, though a freedman, it shal be lawfull for that Incorporation or Plantation to which he belongeth to appoint him a Mr to serve for wages, till he shewe apparant signes of amendment.

Against gaming at dice & Cardes be it ordained by this present assembly that the winner or winners shall lose all his or their winninges and both winners and loosers shall forfaicte ten shillings a man, one ten shillings whereof to go to the discoverer, and the rest to charitable & pious uses in the Incorporation where the faulte is committed.

Against drunkenness be it also decreed that if any private person be found culpable thereof, for the first time he is to be reprooved privately by the Minister, the second time publiquely, the thirde time to lye in boltes 12 howers in the house of the Provost Marshall & to paye his fee, and if he still continue in that vice, to undergo suche severe punishment as the Governo' and Counsell of Estate shall thinke fitt to be inflicted on him. But if any officer offende in this crime, the first time he shall receive a reproof from the Governor, the second time he shall openly be reprooved in the church by the minister, and the third time he shall first be committed and then degraded. Provided it be understood that the Governo' hath always power to restore him when he shall, in his discretion thinke fitte.

Against excesse in apparell that every man be cessed in the churche for all publique contributions, if he be unmarried according to his owne apparrell, if he be married according to his owne and his wives, or either of their apparrell. . . .[4]

But it might be argued that such laws were more moral than religious, and that when it came to religious issues the Virginians were less zealous than the New Englanders. The facts in the case, however, allow for no such illation. A few quotations from other laws will be sufficient proof:

That no man speake impiously or maliciously against the holy and blessed Trinity, upon paine of death.

That no man blaspheme Gods holy name upon paine of death, or use unlawful oaths . . . , curse . . . , upon paine of severe punishment for the first offence so committed, and for the second, to have a bodkin thrust through his tongue.

Everie man and woman duly twice a day upon the first towling of the Bell shall upon working daies repaire unto the Church, to hear divine Service upon paine of losing his or her dayes allowance for the first omission, for the second to be whipt, and for the third to be condemned to the Gallies for six Moneths.[5]

The same attitude prevailed toward dancing. As late as 1691, three men were arrested "for fiddling and dancing on the Sabbath."[6] Literature itself was looked upon with affection only by the aristocratic exiles or by those Englishmen, scions of the aristocratic tradition, who flocked about Berkeley. Even in the eighteenth century, when the structure of Southern society had already begun to alter, the petty bourgeois contempt for *belles lettres* persisted, as references in *The Virginia Gazette* testify. Even after this petty-bourgeois philosophy had been superseded by the semifeudal plantation one, the attitude toward the artist as an individual did not become very laudatory. It was easier to appreciate art than to appreciate the artist. Indeed, even today the individual artist in the South is looked upon with scarcely less contempt than his seventeenth- and eighteenth-century predecessors. In general, a man who turned to literature in the old days was viewed as one who could not succeed in more "honorable callings." *

Altogether, then, the South, particularly Virginia, in its middle-class aspects, was so little different from New England that the gen-

* For further details concerning this attitude, see the author's *Liberation of American Literature*, pp. 91-103.

eral tendency to construe them as contrasts is unfair to fact and reason. In both communities, as has been evidenced from the preceding quotations, resemblances, not differences, were more conspicuous. In every sense the Virginia middle class was just as rigid, just as narrow-minded, just as myopic, as that of New England. In some ways, it was even more rigid in its *puritanism* than the New England Puritans. Nothing evidences that better than the delightfully interesting account of the tragic fate of Honest Jack Pamflino, which is recorded in the *Virginia Gazette:*

Honest Jack Pamflino informs me that in the year 1718 he made his address to a Prude; that he observed a strict decorum at his first Approach. . . . At his first visit he remark'd that more Time was emploied to keep her Feet from peeping from under her petticoat and examining the Pins of her Neck-Handkerchief lest one of them should be displac'd. . . . He came away satisfy'd with his Conduct and in a short time paid his Devoirs to the Lady again: The Discourse running upon the News of the Town he unluckily related the Fact of a certain Lady's losing her Garter in the Drawing-Room: Upon which she flew out of Company in a great Passion, and was about a Fortnight before she would be reconcil'd to receive another visit from him. The day before the Marriage being fix'd, honest Jack thought himself sure of his Mistress; but unfortunately happened to praise the Fashion of the Ladies wearing their Stays low before; which exasperated the Virtuous Dame in such a manner that she . . . discarded her Lover, never to see him again.

'Tis strange! We do not give ourselves Leave to consult Nature a little more: we could never thus degenerate into the stupidity of Brutes, nor become such refined Fools. But the Prejudice of Education is so prevalent that few are able to walk by their own Light.[7]

In the treatment of adultery both colonies were equally severe. In Virginia we discover that:

He or she that can be lawfully convict of Adultery shall be punished with death . . . and know ye that he or shee that shall commit fornication and evident proof made thereof, for their first fault shall be whipt, for their second they shall be whipt, and for their third they shall be whipt three times a weeke for one month, and ask publique forgiveness in the Assembly of the Congregation.[8]

More than that, we find the Virginians as harsh in the matter of illegitimacy as the New Englanders. "If a woman [servant] gave birth to a bastard," Virginia law declared, "the sheriff, as soon as he learned of the fact, was required to arrest her and whip her on the bare back until blood came." [9] Of course, there were cases in which the *Scarlet Letter* tradition was qualified by economic considerations. In that connection, the case of Katherine Higgins, of York, is very much to point:

> Katherine Higgins, of York, having borne a child out of wedlock, was ordered to receive thirty nine lashes. To secure remission of this part of her punishment, John Page, her master, gave the vestrymen assurance that he would deliver to the parish in providing food and clothing for the bastard.[10]

Other cases are equally illustrative. Two maids who became pregnant at sea were "ordered to be sent back again." [11] Robert Sweet, an undistinguished Virginian, was commanded "to do penance in church according to the laws of England for getting a negroe woman with child and the woman whipt." [12] A remarkable revelation of how the church was willing to take economic advantage of immorality is evident in the statute put into effect in December 1662, declaring "that each woman's servant gott with child by her master shall after her time by indenture or custome is expired be by the churchwardens of the parish where she lived . . . sold for two yeares, and the tobacco to be imployed by the vestry for the use of the parish." [13] All these laws were products of the same middle-class psychology that dominated in Massachusetts.

If this middle class had been able to dictate to Virginians as successfully as it did to Massachusians, there would have been little difference between the colonies.

When all is said, however, the middle class did not rule for a long time in Virginia. It succeeded in leaving its impress upon the laws and statutes of the state, but once royal authority intervened and Berkeley was made governor, that ceased. In other words, before Berkeley the middle class ruled, or at least its ideals and philosophy ruled; after Berkeley the laws expressive of the middle class were not abrogated but they were gradually ignored.

The economic struggle involved was simple. The wealthier adventurers and planters, dominated mainly by the aristocrats, became immersed in the commercial ventures of the day, particularly with fur trading, which paid larger profits than any other form of enterprise. It was out of fur trading that the earliest fortunes were accumulated in this country. The less wealthy earned their living from the land; they represented the landed element, from whom the petty tradesmen and other middlemen derived most of their livelihood; eventually, however, as the frontier was shoved farther westward, it was this landed group which became so powerful that in 1828 it elected Andrew Jackson President of the nation.

### SANDYS' REVOLT

The struggle of the Virginians against paying taxes imposed by the king, or by any of his representatives, was a carry-over from the struggle which had begun in England over a century before—the struggle between the middle class and the Crown over the right of the latter to levy taxes against commercial and colonial enterprises. Certain aristocrats, like Sir Thomas Wentworth, Sir John Eliot, and Sir Edwin Sandys, supported the middle class in its struggle. They represented the left wing of the aristocracy, the more progressive elements among it, who realized that something new was happening to the world and that kings and queens and their ambassadors were powerless to stop it. Many of the descendants of these aristocrats later became active in the Whig party. They knew that the king had no vision of the value of the colonies as commercial projects; he was interested in them only to the extent that he could impose taxes and customs duties upon them.

It was this lack of vision on the part of the Crown and the conflict which resulted from it that ultimately caused the American Revolution and gave birth to the United States of America.

Sandys was one of the first persons to give body and force to that conflict. He was one of the first leaders to declare himself in favor of protecting "the right of the subject against the encroachments of the Crown." He was a libertarian by principle. His belief in liberty, to be sure, did not extend to the commoners, the indentured servants, and other bondsmen. His belief in liberty was confined to that of freemen. For those freemen, however, he was willing to fight and did fight throughout most of his career. Long before the Revolutionary War, Sandys adopted the position which was later to become that of the rebellious Americans of the eighteenth century; namely, that of insisting that the right to create laws, redress grievances, institute taxation, inhered in Parliament and not in the king. The king was perfectly correct in those early days in accusing Sandys of sedition, for it was out of the seditionary doctrines of this determined, recalcitrant Englishman that the spirit of revolution matured in the new world. It was Nathaniel Bacon, not many years later, who was to translate those doctrines into actual practice, and after Bacon it was Thomas Jefferson and Andrew Jackson who were to write them into the spirit of the new and independent nation.

Sandys believed that the *new* England which was founded in this *new* world was to be truly new. He wanted it to achieve the freedom and tolerance that were absent from the old country. He wanted men to govern themselves and not be governed by the presumptuous and arbitrary authority of a remote monarch. It was not without reason, therefore, that James I declared, when the officers of the Virginia Company were chosen: "Elect the Devil treasurer, if you will, but not Sir Edwin Sandys." The man elected, however—the Earl of Southampton, Shakespeare's patron—was equally antipathetic to royal authority. Both men, Sir Edwin Sandys and the Earl of Southampton, swiftly became known as patriots—part, to be sure, of the Patriot party—and it was their patriotism that ultimately became identified with the national patriotism of the colonies. The arrest of the two men was inevitable.

### VIRGINIA MORE ADVANCED THAN MASSACHUSETTS

During the period of their domination of the London Company, *Virginia represented the most interesting and striking political experiment in the new world. It was far more advanced than New England in political philosophy*. It had rid itself of all remnants of religious domination; its doors were open to every variety of Dissenter: Anabaptist, Quaker, Brownist. Besides, it had become so bold as to challenge the political authority of the king. It was back in the old country, however, that those freedoms were acquired, and from there derived. The liberal aristocrats, led by Sandys and Southampton, were glad to join forces with the middle class in its struggle to free itself from the fetters of royal authority. They both wanted freedom from royal censure, freedom from royal taxation, freedom from royal dictation.

Sandys and Southampton were torchbearers in this struggle, and it is to them that we must turn to envisage the first revolt waged on this continent against royal oppression. What the American "minutemen" fought for a century and a half later found its first political expression in this revolt, led by these two fuglemen of a new order. Other men were to dramatize this conflict in divers ways, but the Sandys revolt was what gave it its original formulation.

### SANDYS' PHILOSOPHY

Sir Edwin Sandys was one of the most admirable and challenging men of his time. His interest in Virginia dated back to those early and mischievous days when the colony was almost as amorphous as mist. All attempts to settle in Virginia before had proved fruitless. New England then was little more than a dream nurtured in the spiritual womb of the future. Although a member of the Church of England (the Established Church), Sandys believed in "the emancipation of the human mind" and was "at harte opposed to the government of a monarchie." [14] Sandys was also influenced by the Genevan doctrines of his day. At one time he said that "if God from heaven did constitute and direct a frame of government on Earth, it was that of Geneva." He was a good friend of Brewster and many other of the Pilgrims. It was owing to his good offices that the Pilgrims set sail for Virginia instead of New England, and it was through no fault of his that they landed by miscalculation upon the desolate shores of a more northern country.

He was eager to aid any individual, any group, ally himself with any force, that inscribed liberty upon its banner.* His draft of the charter, which finally was submitted to the king by Sir Francis Bacon, constitutes one of the most remarkable documents in the history of liberal thought. The subsequent charter, also drafted by Sandys, was no less progressive. Sandys' aim was to establish a truly free and popular government, in which the people would have "no government putt upon them but by their own consente." So bitter did

* So consistent and circumferential was his liberalism that he even opposed (and he was one of the first to do so) the introduction of Negro slaves into Virginia.[15]

James I become in his opposition to Sandys and his liberal clique that there came a time when he decided to sell Virginia and the Bermudas to Spain, and if it had not been for the vigilance of the Patriot party he would have done so.[16] Even after the king had imprisoned Sandys, the latter's friends continued their opposition to the Crown, and on the floor of the House of Commons demanded the right of every man to freedom of speech and conscience.

### FIRST AMERICAN REVOLT OCCURS IN ENGLAND

Thus it was in England that the first American revolt occurred. It was the English Patriot party which led that revolt and gave a charter to the colony that made it into a "dangerous seminary of sedition." Even after the king got rid of Sandys and seized control of the colony himself, the Virginia assembly declared, contrary to the king's wishes, that "The Governor shall not lay taxes or impositions upon the colony, their lands or commodities other way than by the authority of the general assembly." Sandys' influence at the time was stronger than that of the Crown, and it was not an easy task for the latter to eradicate it. In fact, it never did succeed in eradicating it, because it was irrepressible as a storm. In time it bred a Bacon, and later still a Patrick Henry, a Washington, and a Jefferson.

In the struggle against Sandys and his Patriot party, James I was forced to resort to the theory of the "divine right of kings" as a justification of his procedure. The king, appointed by God, was infallible and unassailable. Needless to say, the opposition fought this theory with unremitting determination and fury. In the end it was their will that prevailed against that of the Crown. It was their will that, over a century later, voiced itself in the political logic and oratorical challenge of Burke, Pitt, and other leaders of the Whig party.

Sandys himself declared that monarchy "had its origin in election," which in those days was revolutionary doctrine indeed. It took no less a man than Thomas Hobbes to attempt to refute it in his masterly but unconvincing volume *The Leviathan.* The battle was between Parliament and the Crown, and had Parliament won at that time, there is little doubt that there never would have been an American Revolutionary War. The United States today, in that event, would be similar to Canada. It was the victory of the king, who adjourned Parliament and revoked the Virginia charter, that paved the way for the revolutionary developments which followed in all the colonies. What Sandys had insisted upon had been that the colonists "be free from customs for twenty-one years, and from taxes (save import duties) forever."[17] Emancipated from such burdens, the colonists would have faced no necessity to wage a revolutionary war against the mother country.

The defeat of Sandys led ultimately to the defeat of the Crown in the American Revolution—which means that in the end it was Sandys and not the Crown that was victorious.

### BACON'S REBELLION

It can be said without exaggeration that the beginning of the struggle that was to dominate the history of this country down till today found its first formulation in the shots fired by the followers of Bacon in their rebellion against Berkeley. Bacon stands out as a great symbol in the history of the American people. It is not Virginia which he represents, not any particular colony, but all the colonies that were eventually to constitute the new nation. He stood for the small man, the man who had little but wanted more, the man who had found it impossible to get more than a little in the *old* world, but who believed it was possible to get a little more in the *new* world.

Berkeley, like the rest of the aristocrats who settled in Virginia, soon realized that the best living at that time was not to be derived from the land. Wealth in the new world was far more easily acquired in trade than in agriculture. The trade which excited and challenged the interests and investments of the wealthier groups in Virginia was the fur trade. The Dutch had made fortunes from the fur trade in earlier years, and the English had bought furs from the Dutch because they had no fur supply of their own. But now the English learned that they could build up a fur trade of their own, and defeat the Dutch in the industry.

Berkeley was more concerned with furs than with the theater, dancing, clothes, or any other of the divers cultural interests of the period. The result was that he bent all his energies, as did his henchmen, to make the fur trade in Virginia the success that it rapidly became.

Berkeley was not interested in the independent settlers, the small farmers, who made the land into a fetish. He could not sympathize with their childish concern for the soil. Like all other English aristocrats, he had known the land as something which not only bore fruit but also made it possible for the owner of it to live in opulence and splendor. Merely to work it as the American middle-class colonists did, just to make a livelihood from it and use it as a protection "against a rainy day," was something which he didn't, couldn't, fathom. Consequently he could never understand the interests, needs, demands, of the small farmers who ultimately rose in arms against him, when Bacon challenged them into action.

### A SMALL-FARMER REVOLT

Bacon believed in those small farmers, believed in their simple, stable, independent form of existence. He distrusted the aristocrats on the one side and the traders on the other. Like Thomas Jefferson, of whom he was the spiritual father, he believed that "a man's house is his castle" and his farm his empire. A hundred years before the Declaration of Independence was signed, he waged a rebellion dedicated to the overthrow of monarchy, autocracy, and oligarchy, and the establishment of democracy.

Much has been written attacking Bacon for his hostility to the Indians, and many writers have maintained that it was that hostility which was the basis of his rebellion. The facts in the case, however, disprove this contention. Bacon's hostility toward the Indians resulted from the fact that Berkeley and his whole governing clique refused to protect the small farmer from Indian attacks. Berkeley's associates made most of their money trading trinkets, liquor, and firearms to the Indians for furs. Naturally they were more concerned with maintaining happy relationships with the red men than they were in defending the interests of the small farmers in the backlands. Finding my "country was basely for a small and sordid gain betraied," Bacon declared, "and y lives and fortunes of y poor inhabitants wretchedly sacrificed, [I] resolved to stand up in this ruinous gap; and rath expose my life and fortune to all hazards than basely desert my post and by soe bad an example make desolate a whole country." [18]

### DEMOCRACY TRIUMPHS

That Bacon was fighting for more than protection for the small farmers against the Indians is evidenced in the laws which were passed during that brief interval when he achieved power. Those laws restored the rights that Berkeley had stolen from the populace. One of the first things that Bacon did, after he had beaten Berkeley and acquired power, *was to repeal the statute preventing freemen from having the right to vote in the election of the Burgesses. He likewise restored democracy in the churches by endowing the "freeholders and freemen of every parish within this country" with the right to elect the vestries of the church.* In addition, the law stated that "such election of a vestrie [was] to be made once in every three yeares."

*All Bacon's laws were based upon that same principle of quick turnover in the seats of power.* He was afraid of power when it became invested over an extended period in the hands of an individual or a group. Even in the case of sheriffs, he was equally severe in this respect. "No person whatsoever within this country," his Act V stated, "shall exercise, hold and enjoy the office of sherriffe or under sherriffe more than one yeare successively." Even the army was purged of its aristocratic privileges and powers. The first act passed by him stated "that the soldiers for greater encouragement have free liberty to nominate theire owne officers, Provided they choose them among the militia officers belonging to their own respective counties." Moreover, he also insisted, contrary to Berkeley's procedure, that whatever taxes were levied, the "Chancillors and Ministers families" had to pay them as well as the rest of the people.

All this most advanced and progressive legislation was an outgrowth of the economic struggle extant at the time. The Berkeleyan oligarchy had imposed such unjust and heavy taxes upon the people that revolt had begun to ferment within the colony even before Bacon raised his voice in protest against the government. The people who rallied immediately behind Bacon were not only the small farmers but also the freemen who were without any land at all but, nevertheless, had to pay their share of the intolerable taxes. It had been possible for Berkeley to impose these taxes only because he had succeeded in putting an end to the popular elections of the Burgesses.*

## FRANCHISE RESTORED

It is inevitable, therefore, that one of the first things that Bacon did was to give back the franchise to the populace.†

Few men of the time had more friends and, at the same time, more enemies than Nathaniel Bacon. Although he "had the honour to be descended from an Ancient and Honourable Family,"[21] his sympathies were always with the underdogs rather than the top dogs. It should be made clear, however, that such people as the indentured servants and the Negro slaves, members of the Fourth Estate, did not fall within the scope of his underdog conception. His underdogs were the small landowning farmers and the impoverished freemen whose *interests* he understood and was willing to defend with his life. The *interests* of the servants and the slaves were not his interests. He was as willing as the next man to employ or exploit them.‡

Consequently it was not the servants or slaves who fought by Bacon's side when he drove Governor Berkeley from his gubernatorial fortress, but the propertied farmers and propertyless freemen. They viewed Bacon, tall, slender, black-haired, melancholy man that he was, as a hero, a frontier Galahad. They realized that he was willing to give his life for them, and they in turn were willing to give their lives for him. He was a reticent, simple man, given to few words, and they admired him for it. A letter which Bacon's wife wrote to her sister on June 29, 1676, describes their allegiance in simple, touching words:

> After Mr. Bacon was come in hee was forced to keep a guard of soldiers about his house, for the Govern[or] would certainly have had

* It must always be borne in mind that the Burgesses from the early history of the colony were "to be freely elected by the inhabitants thereof" and that in the first representative assembly convened in Jamestown that democracy prevailed.[19]

† In the report of the king's investigators, Thomas Ludwell and Robert Smith, it was stated that Bacon's Rebellion did not spring from the upper classes, but "from the poverty and uneasyness of some of the meanest whose discontent render them easyer to be misled." [20]

‡ This attitude toward servants, unfortunate though it was, should not be condemned without qualification. After all, men are the product of their times, and servitude in Bacon's day was a relatively unchallenged reality. Even Roger Williams, with all his nobility of spirit, did not free the indentured servants, although he did his best to mitigate their suffering and to shorten their period of indenture.

his life taken away privately, if hee would have had opportunity; but the country does so really love him; that they would not leave him alone anywhere; there was not anybody against him but the Govern[or] and a few of his great men, which have gott their Estates by the Govern[or]. I doe verily believe that rather than hee should come to any hurt by the Governour or anybody else they would most of them willingly lose their lives.

In another letter, that of An. Cotton, we discover an additional evidence of Bacon's popularity:

It is but the tother day that I did see N. B. in the condition of a tratour, to be tryed for his life; who but a few days before was judged the most accomplished Genman in Virginia to serve his King and countrey, at the councill table, or to put a stop to the insolenceies of the Heathen.[22]

The records of the day and later days are replete with letters, articles, and documents extolling and condemning Bacon.* In short, he was a man to whom no one could be indifferent. He immediately awakened either friendship or enmity. He knew little of the subtlety

* Among the worst attacks upon Bacon was that of Thomas Mathew, who declared: "As for Mr. Bacon, fame did lay to his charge the having run out his patrimony in England except what he brought to Virginia, which together made him suspected of casting an eye to search for retrievement in the troubled waters of popular discontent, wanting patience to wait the death of his oppulent cousin, old Collo. Bacon, whose estate he had expected to inherit." [23]

In direct repudiation of Mathew's account is that of John Day Burke: "After having laid in a competent stock of general learning, he had given a professional direction to his mind, by passing the necessary number of terms at the inns of courts, when he arrived in Virginia with the reputation of commanding talents and considerable legal erudition." [24] Then, too, there is the eulogy running thus: "He was a man of quality and merit, brave and eloquent, became much endeared, not so much for what he had yet done as the cause of their affections, as for what they expected he would do to deserve their devotion; while with no common zeale they sent up their reiterated prayers, first to himselfe, and next to heaven, that he may become their guardian angel, to protect them from the cruelties of the Indians, against whom this Gentleman had a perfect antipathy." [25]

One of the most vivid, though far from accurate, accounts of Bacon's Rebellion is to be found in *Strange News From Virginia,* 1677, in which the author describes in graphic detail the beginning, development, and progress of the rebellion, with dramatic accounts of how "the Governour thereupon ordered an allarm to be beaten through the whole town, which took so hot that Bacon thinking himself not secure whilst he remained there within reach of their Fort, immediately commanded his men aboard and tow'd his Sloop up river"; other episodes recounting different aspects of the rebellion are treated with equal vividness. The author, an anti-Bacon man, is happy to state that "these Virginia troubles were put a "stop to" by "the death of this Nathaniel Bacon, the great Molestor of the quiet of this miserable Nation," and then adds, by way of complete annihilation, that this Mr. Bacon was a very hard drinker and that he dyed by imbibing or taking too much Brandy." The author and finesse of diplomacy; he spoke his words simply and bluntly, as in his famous reply to Berkeley, in which he attacked the parsons who backed the Crown against the people, upbraided those in authority who exploited the people, assailed those who had acquired vast estates by favoritism and fraud and had sucked up the wealth of the colony, and unhesitantly declared that it was his duty as a human being, a citizen of Virginia, to right those wrongs by force if necessary. Bacon resorted to force against Berkeley only after the latter made it inevitable. Berkeley had played with Bacon the way a cat does with a mouse, tried to bargain him off to no avail, made him promises which he never kept, striven to trick him, resorted to every conceivable maneuver and stratagem, but Bacon knew what he wanted and knew how to get it.

The great tragedy is that after he got it, he died, prematurely, and it was not long before much that he had done was undone.

### FROM REBEL TO HERO

Nathaniel Bacon bears no comparison in early American history. When, on a fine spring day, with the assembly still sitting, he marched into Jamestown at the head of over five hundred soldiers, he was a rebel; within a few days he became a hero. In one sense, in his fight for democracy as a legal and political principle, he is more like Roger Williams than anyone else in the seventeenth century;

is fair enough to admit, however, that it is possible that Bacon was not guilty of such libational excesses, but was certainly guilty of "juvenile extravagances" despite his "great natural parts." [26]

Among other comments on Bacon, the following verse is illustrative of a sentiment which later came to be shared by many:

Wrapt in their little God of Strife,
He was (to draw him to the life)
From Head to Foot scarce nine-pin high,
Nor half so thick as Magogg's Thigh.
The Male-contents with one Consent
Brave Not with Praises compliment;
Then to Sir William recommend him
As qualified, would he send him
With force their Gen'ralissimo
'Gainst their Ocanackeean Foe;
But Will that better knew than they
The Indian Game he had to play,
Would not on any Motives yield,
To let Nat govern in the field;
And in derision bid them nim'ly,
"Go smoak their Bacon in the Chimney." [27]

but he was without Williams's fundamental and far-sweeping belief in religious freedom and humanitarianism. Religion with Bacon, as with most Virginians of the upper crust, was a minor matter. Religion was a vital concern for Williams and for Hooker and for Gorton, and also for the power-obsessed theocrats of Massachusetts; it was not a vital concern for upper-class Virginians who accepted the Established Church with something of the same nonchalance that the Catholics in France today accept the Roman Catholic Church.

In New England economic struggles appeared in religious garb; in Virginia they required no garb at all. They appeared as they were—economic conflicts which demanded political action. Religion played but a little role in their determination.

Bacon was not a great thinker, not a great politician. He lacked the perspicacity of Jefferson, was unendowed with the vision of utopian planners and schemers, but he had a dogged faith in the individual and an inspired belief in the virtues of independence, wheresoever or howsoever derived. The rebellion he led was directed not only against Berkeley but also against the king [28] and against the Parliament of the time which submitted to the dictates of the king, and it was his rebellion that prepared the ground for the more successful rebellion waged a century later when the colonies were strong enough to resist the power of the monarch.

## TOBACCO: THE NEW KING

During all this early period in Virginia history it was tobacco that was the real king—not the King of England or the aristocracy from which the king sprang. As was pointed out earlier, the aristocracy was not a solid bloc, not a unified, inviolable class. On the contrary, it was divided, as are all classes, and the more farsighted of it sided with the middle class; a century later that aristocracy found itself scissored even more when considerable sections of it allied themselves with the Whig party in opposition to the Tories. By the time the nineteenth century achieved maturity, with Disraeli and his cohorts at the ramparts, the aristocracy had become more progressive in humanitarian legislation than the Whigs.

But that is not our story. We are concerned here with what happened in the seventeenth century.

The battle that raged then was between two commodities: tobacco and fur. The landed elements of the population were concerned mainly with tobacco production; the commercial elements, which included the aristocrats of that time, were concerned with fur. Tobacco had become more than the main commodity of the colony; it had become the source and medium of exchange. One bartered away one's resources, determined one's income, paid one's servants, acquired distinction with one's fellows, in accordance with how much tobacco one possessed.

Tobacco was one of the first contributions of the new world to the old. Explorers and colonists had hazarded the seas in hopes of discovering in the new country the incalculable sources of wealth which had been promised them by the legends and prophecies of political soothsayers. Tobacco soon became, in those days, as precious as gold because it could be sold for prices that were truly golden.

## A HOLY HERB

Tobacco provides but one of many instances in modern history in which a luxury commodity has played a determining role in the development of an economy. For a time tobacco, despite its attractive virtues, became a subject of bitter dispute within the English realm. James I denounced smoking it as a "vile and stinking custome... loathsome to the eye, hateful to the Nose, harmful to the brains, dangerous to the Lungs," although he was perfectly willing to accept and insist upon the duties which he imposed upon its sale.*

* George Arents, in an article in *The South Atlantic Quarterly* (April 1938), recounts in amusing and arresting detail the attitudes that prevailed toward tobacco in those early days. He points out that the American Indians were the first people to use tobacco and that they used it for hedonistic and ritualistic reasons. His article is replete with allusions of all varieties, including the famous Earl of Essex poem, two lines of which run: "If I cannot have honey, bewitching tobacco, I will turn to thee." His description of the tobacco teachers of the fifteenth and sixteenth centuries is informing and delightful. Apparently, then, in England, and no doubt in many other countries, there were these teachers who instructed young men how to smoke a pipe or cigar, how to inhale the smoke and then exhale it graciously and generously, forming it into rings and other fancy designs. It is interesting to note, as Mr. Arents states, that nowhere in Shakespeare is there mention of "the weed," although Bacon showed considerable concern for its cultivation. Also there is the memorable picture of Sir Walter Raleigh stopping to light his pipe and take a final whiff before exposing his head to the executioner.

Tobacco, to be sure, was supposed to have been known among the Chinese "from time immemorial," as their pipes suggest.[29]

Every schoolchild knows about the use of tobacco as a pipe of peace, a token of friendship. We know little, however, about how intricately tobacco was employed in so many ways. There were special pipes among the Indians for all variety of purposes: peace,

Physicians and politicians vied with one another in denouncing it as a loathsome weed, a breeder of filth and disease, but the colonists continued to produce it in prodigious proportions, unfazed by the warnings and homilies of the moralists. For a long time it became necessary to defend the use of tobacco as a medicinal substance, and during that period various governors of Virginia attempted to restrict its growth. Later, however, it became a "holy herb" and soon was recommended by medical men and laymen in England as well as in America as a panacea for all ills.[32] In time the "holy herb" became the dominant, if not the exclusive, product of Virginia, and it is around the history of tobacco that so much of Virginian history inevitably radiates. As early as 1629, 1,500,000 pounds of it were exported.[33] From that point on Virginia proceeded to produce tobacco in uneconomical superfluity. In 1676 Virginia paid over $750,000 (£150,000) to the king for import duties on tobacco. At the time of the Revolutionary War tobacco constituted more than three-quarters of the goods exported from Virginia. Preachers were paid in tobacco, teachers were paid in it, as also were clerks, sheriffs, judges.* Tobacco was better than coin; at least one could buy more with it. After John Rolfe discovered that Virginia leaf was as good to smoke as Spanish

war, love, religion. Originally, no doubt, smoking was confined to medicine men, sorcerers, priests, prophets.

Among Indians like the Crow, raising tobacco was considered a sacred privilege, associated with divinity.

"The natives of northern and central South America and the West Indies," Ralph Linton states, "were cigar smokers. The Central Americans and Mexicans were predominantly cigarette smokers. The North American Indians, with the exception of the Pueblo tribes of the Southwest, were exclusively pipe smokers." [30]

One of the most interesting aspects of tobacco use is to be found in the custom of the Central Algonquins, who flung tobacco into rivers and lakes and every liquid place in order to quiet the rages of the water gods.

Professor Weiner contends that the tobacco plant was introduced into America by the African Negroes, and it is impossible to disprove his illation. He shows that pipes were found among the ancient Romans and that smoking was even common to the Persians and Syrians. All other collected evidence, however, lends little support to his contention. That the word tobacco (associated though it is with the word nicotine, derived from the name of the Frenchman, Jean Nicotine, Ambassador to Portugal, who was one of the first Europeans to attempt to cultivate the herb on European soil) originated from the early West Indian name of the "pronged stick" can scarcely be denied.[31]

* In New England laws were first passed limiting the production of tobacco, and in one year all retail trade in it was prohibited. Smoking in public in New England was regarded as a crime, and a severe penalty was meted out to all offenders. In certain places a physician had to prescribe tobacco as a medicament before it could be smoked with impunity. Using tobacco on the Sabbath Day was a crime of the gravest order.

leaf, Virginian history assumed a different and more prosperous character.

It was not long before tobacco became an industry with the usual triad of producers, middlemen, and buyers; and the middleman, characteristically and customarily, acquired the largest profits. Often he succeeded in making as much as 50 per cent profit, which reduced the planter to second place and the buyer to third place in the industry. The planter became little more than an appendage of the merchant, and the buyer was placed in a position equally helpless. The buyer had to pay the prices the merchant demanded.

However much the middleman cheated the producers and exploited the consumers, tobacco continued to be the witching charm of the new world, and before long hundreds and then thousands of emigrants came to Virginia in hopes of cultivating it. It was a "charmed weed," an agricultural miracle.*

In a few years the *weed* became so charmed and magical that it was necessary to curb its production. In 1666 Berkeley and Charles Calvert of Maryland insisted that tobacco planting should cease.[36] As early as 1639, Governor Sir Francis Wyatt had urged a careful inspection of all tobacco and the destruction by burning of all that was below the first grade.[37] In short, what had happened was an overproduction of tobacco, and in order to keep the price up to a level at which profit could be made from the crop, it was imperative that its production be decreased.

This was equivalent to introducing what today is known as the AAA technique; namely, the technique of limiting production in order to maintain or raise prices.

### THE PLANT-CUTTERS' REBELLION

The rebellion that occurred during the regime of Governor Culpeper revolved about the issue of production limitation.

Culpeper was even less astute than Berkeley in gauging situations and measuring the response of the populace. As a matter of fact, he

* So much of a miracle was it that "ninety agreeable persons, young and incorrupt," sailed from the old country to the new, to become wives of Virginians for 120 pounds of tobacco apiece, and several years later another shipload of maids came for 150 pounds of tobacco.[34] "Thus Virginia having to itself and Maryland," Hugh Jones wrote, "the staple Commodity of Tobacco, has a great Advantage of all other Plantations on the Continent for the Encouragement of the Crown." [35]

had less interest in the colony than Berkeley; so little concerned was he with its fate that he didn't go to Virginia until the second year after his appointment, and even then it was only because of royal pressure that he finally set sail. It was unfortunate for him that he arrived in Virginia just at a time when the tobacco industry was at its lowest ebb. Everyone in the colony was clamoring for something to be done, and the spirit of violence was in the air. The crusading *vigilante* psychology had begun to overrun the land. Men and women set out with knives, axes, and every other variety of instrument to destroy all semblance of the tobacco crop. Through the night and into the day they worked, knifing, slashing, rooting up whatever remained of the tobacco stalks. Robert Beverley, a friend of the departed Berkeley, was accused of supporting the revolt, and was imprisoned for it. Later, after having escaped once and been recaptured, and after putting up $50,000 bail, he was exculpated from any connection with the crime.

Culpeper, however, went after the other vandals with a firm and furious hand, arrested them in their homes, hideouts, and obscure retreats, and then arraigned them not for the crime they had committed but for *treason*, and had two of them hanged. He had a genius for doing things wrong. In addition, he tried to collect the quitrents, which were of a most onerous variety, and before he was aware of it he had all the poorer groups lined up against him in violent opposition.[38]

This plant-cutters' rebellion, as it was called, was, next to Bacon's Rebellion, the most important rebellion in early Virginia history. Culpeper's words, describing the people engaged in it, are graphic:

> That there were many persons Engaged in it (Plant-cutting) who though they knew they did amisse, Did not thinke or intend to commit Treason, but only to raise the price of Tobacco, and were inveighed to doe the same by letters from such Merchants in England as had bought Great Quantities thereof at Home, and . . . had interest enough with them to persuade them to it, with a Designe of Gaine to themselves not the Planters.[39]

Culpeper knew that the populace was involved in it, knew that it was in their own economic interests that they set upon the destruction of the tobacco crop, but in his own eyes he had no choice but to suppress, imprison, and hang the culprits. He knew that once the wild fury of destruction had spread throughout the colony, the tobacco owners themselves, once their own crop was destroyed, would make one with the rioters and destroy the crops of their neighbors—that the frenzy of destruction was in the very air that men breathed. Before Culpeper succeeded in quelling the rebellion, vast quantities of tobacco were destroyed.[40] It was the fear of a repetition of Bacon's Rebellion that drove the government to such vicious extremities of repression.[41]

The rebellion was inspired by the small tobacco producers, who insisted that Culpeper pass a law enforcing a reduction in tobacco cultivation. Only by such a reduction, they were convinced, could the price of tobacco be raised. It was Culpeper's refusal to accede to their demand that caused the riots and depredations.*

What Culpeper succeeded in doing, by his arbitrary acts, was to unite all Virginians in common opposition to the king. It was this common opposition that a century later made Virginia one of the first colonies to clamor for independence from England and to lend its power in support of the American Revolution. Many of the same aristocrats who had backed Berkeley against Bacon, which meant the Crown against the populace, now joined the populace in its opposition to Culpeper in order to present a united front against the king. In short, the king became the common enemy of the colony, and men who once thought themselves above the people became advocates of the people's cause.

* The situation today is appallingly similar. As *The New Republic,* in a sound editorial, writes, describing the status of the farmer today: "The farmers are poor because they grow too much; the city people are too poor to buy all that the farmers grow; Congress votes to compensate the poor farmers at the expense of the city people, while for the sake of economy it cuts relief and plans to starve hundreds of thousands who already haven't enough money to buy what the farmers grow. And meanwhile, we plan to defend democracy by battleships and airplanes."[42]

## CHAPTER XI

# Maryland: The Free State

*What doubt then can bee made, but many thousands of Soules may be brought to Christ by this most glorious Enterprise; and it may indeed bee called glorious, seeing it is the saving of Soules, which was the work of Christ, the King of Glory.*

—From A Declaration of the Lord Baltimore's Plantation in Maryland; wherein is set forth how Englishmen may become Angels, the King's Dominions be extended and the adventurers attain Land and Gear; together with other advantages of that Sweet Land. 1633.

MARYLANDERS are wont to refer to their state as "the free state," a euphemism which, surprising though it may seem, grew out of the Prohibition conflict when the *Baltimore Sun*, in a sardonic editorial in 1923, suggested that the state secede from the Union. Centuries before, however, Maryland was viewed as a "free colony" because it was putatively founded upon the principle of religious freedom. In the seventeenth century freedom meant chiefly one thing, religious freedom, which implied the right of everyone to worship in any way he pleased. Political freedom in those days meant little. Even when granted it meant freedom not for *all* the people but only for those who owned property and who, therefore, were entitled to that privilege. Religious freedom was rooted in deeper soil.

But Maryland's religious freedom was unhappily circumscribed in scope. It included freedom of worship only for those who believed in the divinity of Christ and the Trinitarian conception of Christianity.

### TREATMENT OF THE JEWS

Maryland freedom did not extend to Jews, who found their life in the province far from felicitous. Naturally Jews kept away from the territory, and during the colonial period it is doubtful whether more than two score of them ever made it their permanent home. Atheists, agnostics, sceptics, Mohammedans, Buddhists, and other religionists who did not accept the Trinitarian creed suffered from the same economic and political limitation.

In the case of the Jews, there can be no doubt that Cecilius Calvert definitely aimed to exclude them from the province,[1] which explains why they never settled in the colony in any great number, as they did in South Carolina, Georgia, and New York. No Jews were allowed to hold office or vote. All during the colonial period the life of Jews in Maryland was extremely hazardous. According to the Toleration Act of 1649, anyone not believing in the divinity of Christ could be punished with death. Even the revision of that Act in 1723 did not remove that punishment, but reserved it for the third offense. For the first offense the victim had his tongue bored through, and for the second he had the letter *B* burnt on his forehead. The well-known Jew, Jacob Lombrozo, managed to escape the extremity of those punishments, but was imprisoned for suggesting that Christ did not rise from the dead after his crucifixion.[2] * Even after the American Revolution Jews were still deprived of rights of citizenship.[3] It was not until 1818 that they acquired those rights.

## FREEDOM FOR THE CATHOLICS

The fact is that Maryland became known as a "free colony" only because it was the only province, with the exception of Pennsylvania, in which Roman Catholics were allowed complete liberty of worship.[4] The battle which the Established Church carried on against the Dissenters was uncompromisingly vigorous, but the one which it waged against the Catholics was far more fierce and bitter. After all, Catholicism was viewed as a foreign religion, whereas Puritanism was an indubitable English product. Catholicism was the religion of Spain and France, both enemies of the English Crown, and to combat them in the new world as well as the old the co-operation of all Englishmen was imperative. It is not surprising, therefore, that in many of the colonies most forms of religious worship other than the Cath-

* Lombrozo was released later when Richard Cromwell became Protector. The new Protector granted a general pardon, and Lombrozo found himself released as a result.

olic were permitted. The Catholics were political as well as religious opponents, and were fought, persecuted, and suppressed upon every possible occasion.

Maryland stood out from the other colonies because it opened its doors to all Catholics who sought a haven in the new world.* Its founder, George Calvert, was a converted Catholic, and he was determined that Maryland was to be the one colony in which Catholicism would have an unmolested home in the new hemisphere. He was made a noble by the king, first Sir George and, later, in 1625, Lord Baltimore; it is under the latter title that he is known as the founder of Maryland. Despite his interest in colonization, and his two trips to the new world, he never lived to see the colony, whose largest city still bears his name. His son, Cecilius, the second Lord Baltimore, shared a similar fate. Like his father, however, he urged the colonists to "be very careful to preserve unity and peace" on shipboard as well as on land, and assured them that only in that way could the settlement succeed. The first of the family to land in Maryland, which was named in honor of the Queen, was Cecilius's son, Leonard Calvert, who for all practical purposes was the first ruler of the colony.

George Calvert, reactionary in most respects, was progressive in one; namely, in his belief in tolerance for all Christians—but for no one else. He insisted upon Catholics and Protestants living side by side, each respecting the other, and each practicing his own religion without interfering with that of the other, or with that of anyone else.

### PERSECUTION OF THE QUAKERS

That this relative tolerance did not last can be blamed not upon the founder of the colony but on conditions in England and on the general tendency of most of the colonies to suppress all groups that threatened to disturb the peace. The Quakers were the first to be persecuted, and upon occasion were banished from the colony.[6] As elsewhere, the Quakers were accused of being a "people of no religion,"[7] a calumniating lot who were so opposed to all forms of ecclesiasticism that they were little more than heathen. As in other

* During the period of the Commonwealth, even Maryland passed a law forbidding Catholic worship. The Maryland Assembly in 1654 passed a law stating that "none who professed and exercised the Popish religion could be protected in this province."[5]

colonies, the Quakers in Maryland refused "to take oath" or doff their hats in court, because they believed such acts to be sacrilegious. In addition they asserted, in words barbed with defiance, that they would not fight or bear arms under any condition or circumstance. They were men of God and not vassals of the state. Because of such attitudes, in one year forty of them were punished, many by public whipping.[8] Yet they claimed that they "were governed by God's laws and the light within and not by Man's laws." Whereupon the rulers of the colony declared them "Rebbels and Traitors," and ordered them "to leave the territory within a year." [9]

### VIRGIN MARY EXALTED

In all the colonies there were laws against blasphemy, but only in Maryland did those laws include violations of the Catholic credo. Anyone uttering "reproachful words or speeches concerning the blessed Virgin Mary, the Mother of our Saviour," the Maryland law read, "was to be fined severely, and lacking money for the fine, to be publicly whipped and imprisoned"; upon second offense the fine or punishment was to be doubled, and if the party was found guilty a third time he was to be expelled from the colony.[10] This provision was unique. In no other colony did the Virgin Mary occupy such an exalted and sacred station.

Although the Catholics, owing to the favoritism of the Calvert family, held high places in Maryland, and priests in education as well as religion exercised an influence far beyond that exercised by Catholics in other colonies, the colony itself never became Catholic. The Jesuits supported the project, lent their energies to help it succeed, but they could not dictate to it once it established itself in the new world. The Calverts themselves fought the Jesuit attempt to dominate the colony,[11] and later the Puritan elements drove the Jesuit fathers from the province. The majority of the people were Protestants, and remained so through the mischievous march of the years. In later decades they became a thorn in the side of the Catholics, and when conditions in England changed with the advent of Cromwell to power at the middle of the century, and afterwards with the coming of William of Orange in 1688, they reduced the Catholic dream of a Maryland utopia into a mutilated recollection.

### TOBACCO: "THE CURRANT COYNE"

Like Virginia, Maryland was a tobacco colony. Tobacco not only was its main product but was the product by which all other products were measured. It was God, King, Master. "Tobacco is the currant coyne of Mary-land," wrote George Alsop, "and will sooner purchase Commodities from the Merchant than money." [12] * There was also business in furs and meat, but tobacco was the staple commodity. The people were taxed in terms of tobacco; their wealth was gauged in relation to it; the colony was run according to its standards.[14] Cotton was not planted until the very end of the seventeenth century, and even then there was an objection to it because it would compete with and injure tobacco production. It was only after tobacco was produced in superfluity that the cultivation of cotton, hemp, and flax was undertaken.

### A MEDIEVAL DICTATORSHIP

The political structure of the colony was the most backward structure in all the settlements. It resembled a medieval kingdom more than a modern state. All power inhered in the proprietor, who possessed absolute sovereignty. He was the dictator over the economic and political destiny of the colony; he made laws, issued writs, and determined the life and death of the inhabitants. The latter had no more rights than the subjects of a feudal lord. Indeed, the whole colony was organized about a medieval manor system,[15] and the class divisions were no less marked than they had been in feudal Europe.

In no other colony did the people possess less economic and political freedom. The charter rights granted to the Baltimore family endowed it with the power to regulate trade, tax arbitrarily, and claim possession of all mines or other resources discovered in the domain. Judges and state officials were appointed by the proprietor, in whom inhered all final authority. Even the Assembly, which consisted exclusively of property owners, had no rights of its own and could be called or adjourned at the governor's discretion.

As in other colonies, it was the Assembly that gave voice to the people's cause and that, after a long struggle, succeeded in under-

* "For one hundred and fifty years tobacco was the staple of Maryland's economic life." [13]

mining the power of the proprietor and, ultimately, in making Maryland into a democratic state. The Baltimore family never had an easy time of it in Maryland. Beginning with the conflict with Claiborne, who was a Virginian with an inveterate hatred for Catholicism, the family had to fight continuously in order to maintain its sovereignty. Claiborne's hostility was more personal and religious than political, and in the battle over Kent Island that ensued he did not hesitate to turn the conflict into actual war. The battle between Claiborne's fleet and that of the proprietor was one of the first open wars undertaken in the colony. Claiborne was defeated in this struggle, but a few years later, while Leonard Calvert was in England, he recaptured Kent Island, and a blustering buccaneer, Captain Ingle, seized Saint Mary's. It took the Baltimore family two years before they could recover their possessions.

Claiborne and Ingle, however, did not lead popular revolts. Their interest was not in the populace but in possessions and power.

### THE DAVYES AND PATE REVOLT

The abortive revolt led by Davyes and Pate was the first revolt concerned with the emancipation of the populace from the aristocratic rule of the Baltimore family. Inspired by Bacon, Davyes and his followers published a proclamation condemning the governor. They were bitterly opposed to Lord Baltimore's disenfranchisement of the freemen and to the impossible taxes that were levied as severely upon the poor as upon the rich. The Davyes group were denounced as rebels and were set upon by the proprietor's forces, and Davyes and Pate were hanged shortly after their capture. The episode created considerable bitterness in the colony and augmented the hostility that the people felt toward the dictatorship the Baltimores had established.

The Baltimore family did not realize that with the defeat of the Davyes group it had won only a Pyrrhic victory. It did not understand that upon every front it was fighting a losing battle, that the whole direction of economic enterprise and political philosophy was antagonistic to its outlook. Its vision of life was feudal, and it was unaware that this vision was growing anachronistic. Consequently it misconstrued as rebellious almost every suggestion of popular protest and opposition. In order to quell any incipient challenge to its authority, it had passed a law as early as 1649 forbidding freedom of speech and threatening any offenders with the most dire punishments: cropping the ears, branding the forehead, severing hands, and in the worst cases, indefinitely prolonged imprisonment or banishment from the province.

### FENDALL'S REBELLION

The result was inevitable. Few colonies were so torn with discord as Maryland during the seventeenth century. Following Davyes and Pate came Fendall and Coode, both of whom Lord Baltimore denounced as "Rank Baconists." The proprietor was convinced that Fendall was connected with Bacon and had aided him in the latter's revolt in Virginia. "This Fendall has a great influence on, and interest in, most of the Rascales in the North parts of Virginia," Lord Baltimore declared, convinced that Fendall had made those associations during the time when he was first forced to leave the Maryland colony.[16]

Bacon's rebellion proved an inspiration to most of the rebellions that followed in the new world; it represented a danger signal to those in power: governors, proprietors, and king. After Bacon, anyone who was connected with a group opposed to those in authority was condemned as a Baconist. Bacon's name became a symbol. It inspired fear among the upper classes and courage among the lower. It was a challenge to protest and action.

Fendall fought in Maryland for essentially the same things Bacon battled for in Virginia. Claiborne and Ingle had been involved in the religious issue: Protestants versus Catholics. Fendall had little concern for religious differences; one of the leaders in Fendall's movement, for instance, was Gerrard, a Catholic. Fendall's movement was a popular one. It was opposed to the authoritarian regime set up by the Baltimore family, and insisted that the people themselves should determine what taxes they were to pay to the proprietor. Fendall's appeal to the people was enough to brand him in the eyes of the Calverts as a dangerous agitator and rebel. They did not believe in the people, but in themselves, in the superiority of their power over that of the populace. Fendall believed in the superiority of the populace over the proprietor.

### THE PURITAN INFLUENCE

In his first insurgent adventure, Josias Fendall, functioning as the leader of the Puritans, was unable to effect many important changes in the organization of the colony. It is a curious and ironic fact that he was made ruler of Maryland by none other than the Calvert family, and the actual words transferring that power to him are still interesting:

> Caecilius Absolute Lord and Proprietary.... And we do heerby Nominate Constitute and Appoint Josias Fendall of the Province of Maryland in America Gent: Our Lieutennant and Chiefe Governor of the Said Province of Maryland....[17]

He did not achieve power until 1656, during Cromwell's rulership in England, and he lost it in 1660 upon the restoration of Charles II, who saw to it that Lord Baltimore regained his supremacy in the province. Lord Baltimore retaliated by denying the vote to an even larger percentage of the populace and threatened to have Fendall executed. The populace, however, was so hostile to the procedure that the proprietor relented, and after having sentenced Fendall and his two main followers, Gerrard and Hatch, to banishment, he reduced their punishment and merely insisted that thereafter they should not be able to hold office.[18] From then on Charles Calvert attempted to throttle every expression of popular sentiment. He not only insisted that no one could vote who possessed less than fifty acres of land, but also deprived the more unfortunate groups of rights they had previously possessed. He converted the *Council* into a family circle. In addition he revoked laws that had been passed by the Assembly, and antagonized the majority of the people by his high-handed tactics. Even in those dark parlous days when Fendall lived in a state of obloquy, he was not inactive. He continued to be the mouthpiece of the populace, and the Baltimore regime never ceased to fear him. He constantly urged the freemen of Maryland to limit the power of the proprietor.

In his struggle against the Baltimore family Fendall met with bitter opposition, but he refused to give up the battle. In 1681 the proprietor had a law passed that forbade the dissemination of false news, which meant news that aimed to evoke unrest and revolt in the colony. The law was directed mainly at Fendall and Coode, an ex-clergyman, who joined the former governor in a revolt against the proprietor. The death of Bacon had heartened Lord Baltimore in his belief that the rebellious elements in the colonies would no longer hazard an attack upon those in power. The revolt of Fendall and Coode, however, soon disillusioned the proprietor in that regard. "Had not these three persons been secured in time [Fendall, Coode, Godfrey]," he wrote in a letter to William Blathwait, "you would have heard of another Bacon." [19]

### MOTHER EATS CHILD

It was Bacon's ghost that haunted the ruling class throughout the South during the colonial period. To rid the land of potential Bacons, to suppress them if possible before they could attract a following, to imprison or banish them if they did acquire influence, was the determined aim of those in power. The records of those days, written mainly by people in sympathy with the ruling class, are replete with annihilatory attacks upon the character of these early rebels.* The conditions of the populace encouraged rebellion. Danckaerts provides a terrifyingly realistic description of the economic status of the colony. After upbraiding the masters for debauching themselves with liquor every time a boat arrives, he tells about the famine that overtook the province and of the scores of people who perished from it. His account of the mother who was so hungry that she killed her own child and devoured it, urging her neighbors to pursue the same course, is unforgettable. Her speech at the time when she was hanged is most revealing; she did not beg for mercy, for she considered herself innocent of any crime. She put the blame upon the governor, who created the conditions of starvation that made the murder a cruel necessity.[21]

What Fendall and Coode were attempting to do was to carry out to a triumphant conclusion the unsuccessful rebellion of Davyes and Pate. Their central conception was to transfer power from the proprietor to the Assembly, which meant changing minority rule into majority rule, autocracy into democracy. They believed that by this

* Even later historians have perpetuated that tendency. R. G. Thwaites,[20] for example, does not hesitate to call Fendall "an unworthy rogue," and others have described him in equally unfavorable language.

means it would be possible to improve the economic conditions of the people and make Maryland a happy colony.

### NO TAXATION WITHOUT REPRESENTATION

Philip Calvert accused Fendall of "telling the people they were fools to pay taxes," and also of defending freedom of speech by his remark "Now nothing was treason . . . a man might say anything." [22] These were dangerous doctrines in those days, and Fendall paid a grave penalty for daring to give voice to them. He meant not that people were "fools to pay taxes" but that they were fools to pay those taxes which they themselves did not vote for and levy.

The plans of the revolt were disclosed to the proprietor by two judges whom Fendall approached, and also by a sea captain who, forced to land his ship in Virginia, accidentally learned of the scheme. Colonel Darrall was despatched with ten men to arrest the conspirators, and within a short time Fendall and Coode, who for a moment threatened to fight his way to freedom, were in prison, and shortly thereafter they were brought to trial. The jury was for both of these "two Rank Baconists," but the judges, appointees of the proprietor, were against them. Coode's membership in the lower house of the Assembly helped him to win his acquittal. Fendall, however, was "fined forty thousand pounds of tobacco and banished forever from the province." [23]

All the precautions taken by the Baltimore family to protect their interests, however, were insufficient to save them from downfall. Even Charles Calvert's decree denying suffrage to any man who possessed less than fifty acres of land failed to subdue the populace. Discontent mounted, and when James II abdicated in 1688 and was succeeded by William of Orange and his wife Mary, the populace broke forth once more in revolt, led again by none other than the irrepressible Coode. A spy was sent to discover more details of the revolt, but he was captured by Coode and imprisoned.[24] Major Sewall and Colonel Darrall were dispatched to capture Coode, but found that the people believed in him and were willing to fight to resist his capture. A little later Colonel Jowles, the general of the army of Maryland, joined Coode; then the latter became invincible.

### CODE'S TRIUMPH

Coode's revolt sprang from the same basis that the previous revolts had sprung from, and it succeeded because the turn in English affairs was propitious. Coode's organization was called "An Association in arms for the defense of the Protestant Religion and for Asserting the Right of King William and Queen Mary to the Province of Maryland and all the English Dominions." [25] James II had been a Catholic, and William and Mary were Protestants; so it was natural that the revolutionary party should introduce the religious issue into their attack. Fundamentally this was the same political struggle for power that had been waged by insurrectionary predecessors of Coode.

Coode and his followers were patriots, not rebels. Their association was led by high-minded, not low-minded, people. Among them were Chesseldine, the speaker in the lower house of the Assembly; Jowles, a military officer; Blackiston, quondam Collector of the King's Customs; and other men of prominence, such as Warren, Beal, and Addison.[26] Coode was condemned by the Calvert clique as "insolent and flagitious," [27] "an apostate clergyman of profligate life and foul and blasphemous speech," [28] but he had little difficulty this time in overthrowing the Proprietary Government, which he did on August 1, 1689. The Baltimores and their Council were unable to provide serious resistance to this popular movement and went down in quick defeat, despite the fact that shortly before they had distributed arms only to "such hands as shall faithfully serve the King, your Lordship and the Country." [29] But the king the Baltimores were supporting was James II, whose abdication effected their defeat.

John Coode in his account of the revolt stressed the "Injustice and Tyranny under which we (people of Maryland) groan . . . the absolute Authority exercised over us (by the Proprietor, and by the greatest part of the Inhabitants) in the Seizure of their persons, Forfeiture and Loss of their Goods." [30] Coode naturally took advantage of the change in the English situation, attacked the Baltimore family for its support of James II, and announced that his cohorts would overthrow the Catholics and convert the colony into a Protestant one under the rulership of "the King and Queen's most Excellent Majesties," William and Mary, who succeeded to the throne after

James II fled. In building up his cause Coode resorted to religious arguments in his condemnation of the proprietor, assailed the latter's regime as one of "Popish idolatry and Superstition," and asserted that Maryland could never be a happy colony until it had rid itself of all its Catholic vestiges.

The curious thing is that the colony had "Thirty Protestants to one Papist," [31] but owing to the authority of the Baltimore family, the Protestants had been inclined to consider themselves an inferior element, and, like all such groups, had invented complexes and compulsions of a psychopathic character. Coode, who originally had been a Roman Catholic before he was converted into a Protestant, strove to free the colony from that phobia. He inspired the Protestants to stand upon their own legs, to struggle for their own rights, and to refuse to capitulate to Catholic tyranny. Undoubtedly he exaggerated Catholic influence and power, and in the fury of strife he resorted to propagandistic extremes in his attacks upon the Papists and their pretensions to final authority. At the same time there is little reason to believe that it was he who conjured up the rumor that the Catholics were allying themselves with the Indians in preparation for an attack upon the province. Whatever Coode's defects, and no doubt there were many, he did not have to adopt such a procedure at that time, when the reaction against the Baltimore family was so immediate and unequivocal.

In 1691 Sir Lionel Copley was appointed the new governor of the colony, to assume authority the next year. This ended for the time being the conflict between the rulers and the people.

Few if any other colonies had so stormy a history as Maryland, a history in which there were so many conflicts, insurrections, and revolts in such a short span of years. Unquestionably the tyranny of the Calverts, made possible by the medieval charter granted the family by the Crown, was mainly responsible for the unrest in the colony. After the Baltimore family was removed from power and the charter was repudiated, life in the province at last became relatively peaceful and felicitous.

## INTRODUCTION OF SLAVERY

As in other colonies, the lower classes, or the Fourth Estate, were treated in Maryland as if they were physical scum. White and black slavery existed in the province just as it did in all the other Southern colonies. As far as can be discovered, the first Negroes were brought to Maryland in 1642, when Governor Calvert purchased thirteen slaves, to be delivered to St. Mary's.[32] The proprietor, interested in the fur trade, discouraged Indian slavery because he was eager to cement a strong friendship between his settlement and the natives. Representing the prevailing attitude, William Bullock urged that under no conditions should Indians be allowed to "come into your houses, neither admit more of them than you can master." [33]

The white slaves, or indentured servants as they are better known, in Maryland were subjected to the most severe and ruthless discipline. In few colonies were their punishments so merciless. The penalty for attempting to escape was death. More than that, anyone who aided a white slave to escape was to "suffer paines of death and after his due debts paid, shall forfeit all his lands and goods and chattells." [34]

In 1671 an act was passed which extended the service of white slaves from four to five years.[35] These slaves were forbidden to drink, gamble, barter, trade, or wander about except with the permission of their owners. Any of them found "Bartering and Tradeing and Gaming" . . . [was to] receive on the bare back Thirty Stripes. . . . For a second offense Thirty Stripes and shall (also) be burned on the shoulder in forme of the Letter *R*." [36] Any woman giving birth to an illegitimate child was subject to an indefinite extension of her slavery, the number of years to be determined by the convenience of the Court.[37] This law naturally encouraged masters to seduce their female slaves in order to prolong their years of servitude. An extremely pathetic aspect of that law was to be found in the proviso that all children born of white women whose fathers were Negroes were to be considered as slaves all the rest of their lives. Moreover, the white women were forced to "serve the master of such slave during the life of her husband . . . and their issues shall be slaves." [38]

For a time, according to the law passed in 1640, each indentured servant was to be endowed at the end of his service with fifty acres of land. Soon after that law was repealed, and it was declared that "for the future there shall be nothing allowed to any servant at the end or Expiracon of his or their service." [39] Those under age, as was provided, were to serve even longer years, depending upon their age at the time. Those who were sixteen, for example, were to serve until they were twenty-six years of age.[40]

### LIFE OF THE SLAVES

Jasper Danckaerts, the communist, was one of the founders of the Labadist colony, which was located in Maryland on Hermann's Bohemia Manor. Danckaerts commented upon the lives of the indentured servants that were imported into the province in order to plant "that vile tobacco, which all vanishes into smoke." [41] He also described the kind of life which these slaves had to endure: "their usual food . . . is nothing but maize bread to eat, and water to drink, which sometimes is not very good and scarcely enough for life, yet they are compelled to work hard." [42] Both whites and blacks, he stated, were sold to the highest bidders. The owners discriminated very little between them, and when they did it was in favor of the blacks; the whites had relatively few years to serve as slaves, whereas the blacks were bound by life. *Naturally the slave owners exploited the whites and strove as far as they could to work them to death, since they would be of no further use once they were disenslaved.* The blacks, on the other hand, were treated more kindly because, being lifelong slaves, they were exploitable until death. Danckaerts tells a pathetic story about a master who, realizing that one of his white slaves was dying, forced him to dig his own grave, "in which he was to be laid a few days afterwards, in order not to busy any of the others with it, they having their hands full in attending to the tobacco." [43]

For a time there was considerable hostility on the part of the planters toward the conversion of the Negroes to Christianity; later that hostility lessened and the Negroes were allowed to become Christians, but at the same time a law was passed stating "That where any Negro or Negroes Slave or Slaves being in Servitude or bondage is, are, or shall become Christians . . . is not to amount to . . . a manumicon or freeing." * [44] Moreover, the testimony of Negroes was not accepted as legal evidence; the Negro was not a person but a pawn, a chattel. Ministers and magistrates were forbidden to marry whites

* In this connection, it is a curious fact that Maryland at that time had a person who was called a "Thief-catcher," and who challenged Danckaerts and his friends because they were viewed as "foreigners and travelers." [45]

and blacks even though there were children involved. By an act passed in 1715, a free Negro or mulatto who married a white was subject to lifelong slavery.

Despite these traditions and laws, Maryland was one of the first colonies to organize an anti-slavery society. In 1789 The Maryland Society for Promoting the Abolition of Slavery and the Relief of Poor Negroes and Others Unlawfully Held in Bondage was founded. Its work was most progressive. Baltimore became its center, and it labored for the abolition of slavery "by silent and gradual steps, with the consent of the owner."

## THE MARYLAND PARSON

Unfortunately the Maryland clergy was little more than a pawn in the hands of the masters. Few states, with the possible exception of North Carolina, have possessed clergymen as ignorant, ineffectual, and corrupt as those that exploited Maryland. Almost everyone who visited the province denounced them as irresponsible and idiotic.[46] In the main, they were itinerant ecclesiastics who traveled for profit, and all reports indicate that their moral practices were even worse than those of their listeners. The Maryland parson, to be sure, had already become a subject of ridicule all along the Atlantic seaboard. In one case a profligate rector threatened to shoot anyone who dared to expel him from his church.[47]

Most of the Maryland parsons were happy-go-lucky fellows, ne'er-do-wells who preferred gaming and drinking to preaching, and who were perfectly willing to arrange their services to fit the hunting, fishing, and horse-racing interests of the planters. In the old church on Miles River, pastor and congregation hastened together to the horse races which followed the services. The Jesuits were different, but their philosophy of rule or ruin had antagonized the Protestant populace and even evoked the opposition of the Baltimore family, Catholic though it was, with the result that the Jesuit influence dwindled instead of multiplied through the years. The Protestant clergy, however, was even worse. "In this Province," wrote Rev. John Yeo, "and in them at least twenty thousand Soules and but three Protestant ministers of us that are Conformable to the Doctrine and Discipline of the Church of England." [48]

To Thomas Bray must go the credit for encouraging the first public libraries in the colonies. Bray believed that libraries would prove "a necessary encouragement" to ministers, who need books to inspire them with ideas for their sermons, and also would be valuable to the lay public, which is interested in "the pursuit of useful knowledge, as well Natural as Divine." In addition he urged the introduction of free schools, which would enroll not only white students but also Indians, in order to convert the latter to Christianity.[49] For a long time, however, only one school was definitely known in Maryland: King William's at Annapolis, now St. John's.[50] At the time when Bray wrote, at the close of the seventeenth century, he noted that there were sixteen Church of England ministers in Maryland and sixteen libraries. The number of clergymen, it is obvious, had not increased greatly since 1676, when the Rev. Yeo, as noted above, had estimated there were only three Church of England men in the colony.

### ATTITUDE TOWARD WOMEN

Unprogressive though Maryland was in so many respects, it must be given credit for having had the first woman lawyer in the new world. Margaret Brent appears in the Maryland records as an attorney on February 16, 1647, in connection with a deal involving the sale of "One Browne Cow."[51] Later she functioned as executrix of Leonard Calvert's estate. Verlinda Stone, though illiterate, opened in Annapolis the first printing press in the colony. At the time of the Revolutionary War, Baltimore had a woman in charge of its post office. As far as can be discovered, however, these women did nothing to aid their sex in its struggle for equality before the law. Women in Maryland, as in the other colonies, were subject to the same punishments as men but were not entitled to the same privileges. When convicted of crime, they were often forced to "stand naked in the Pillory," as was Blanche Howell, who also had both ears cut off.[52] They had no political or economic rights, and in marriage had even less rights. Women who were servants were forbidden to marry free men except with the approval of their owners; a law was passed in 1777 fining ministers fifty pounds for marrying women servants and freemen, or men servants and freewomen. There were ducking stools for gossipy women, but not for gossipy men. The Baptists in other colonies as well as in Maryland refused to allow women to pray in public, or to permit them to vote on religious matters. Bastardy was considered one of the grave crimes of the day, and in most cases it was the woman who suffered for it. She was forced to pay an impossible fine or be lashed twenty-five times, and, if she was indentured, she had to serve an additional year of slavery. If the father of the child was her owner, she was not required to spend extra time in his service, but was turned over to the parish, which sold her to a different owner for another year.

The spread of bigamy, sodomy, and bastardy in Maryland moved a Church of England minister to denounce the colony as "a Sodom of uncleanness, and a pest house of iniquity," but there is nothing on record indicating that this rector or any other ecclesiastic ever took up the cudgels in defense of women in such matters. In the vast majority of cases it was the woman and not the man who paid the penalty for the dereliction from conventional mores; no one raised a voice to aid her.

Many women were kidnapped and sold like chattels once they arrived in the province, but, as in the other colonies, they had no recourse to law or justice to rescue themselves from their unfortunate and dismal fate. Eben. Cook wrote a number of interesting verses about such women, and the following, a reply that his chamber-maid gave him, in which she calls herself "a *slave* for twice two year," is extraordinarily interesting and revealing:

Curious to know from whence she came,
I prest her to declare her name.
She blushing, seemed to hide her eyes,
And thus in civil terms replies,
"In better times, e'er to this land
I was unhappily trepanned,
Perchance as well I did appear
As any Lord or Lady here,
Not then a slave for twice two year,
My cloaths were fashionably new,
Nor were my shifts of linnen blue;

But things are changed, now at the Hoe
I daily work and barefoot go;
In weeding corn or feeding swine
I spend my melancholy time." [53] *

Cook was the son of an Englishman of wealth, and in his "Sot-Weed Factor" (sot-weed was a common name for tobacco), he depicted in diverting and sometimes devastating style a number of his experiences in Maryland. He had a quick eye and an even quicker ear, and little escaped his satire upon the colony. His lines describing a quarrel between several Maryland women are excellent in exposing the false claims to aristocratic lineage made by many of the early female settlers:

D—m you, says one, though now so brave,
I knew you late a four-years' slave;
What if for Planter's wife you go,
Nature designed you for the hoe.
Rot you, replies the other straight,
The captain kissed you for his freight;
And if the truth was known aright,
And how you walked the streets by night,
You'd blush (if one could blush) for shame,
Who from Bridewell or New Gate came.[57]

At length, disgusted with the colony, Cook penned the last two lines of his poem:

May wrath divine then lay those regions waste
Where no man's faithful nor a woman chaste.[58]

* Cook's picture of Annapolis at that time is worth quoting:

"Up to Annapolis I went,
A city situate on a plain,
Where scarce a house will keep out rain;
The buildings framed with cypress rare,
Resembles much of our Southwark Fair." [54]

By the middle of the eighteenth century Annapolis had developed into a town of magnifying proportions. Sports and other amusements multiplied. Horse-racing, cockfighting, and fox-hunting were the most popular diversions. In addition, the first theater in America was opened in 1752 in Annapolis.[55] A printing press was brought to Annapolis in 1726, and in 1745 the first issue of *The Maryland Gazette* was issued there.[56]

Negro women, it is scarcely necessary to say, were treated far worse than white women. Most of them were worked inordinately hard, and many of them were seduced by their masters. Such seduction had already become an old Southern custom; the vastness of our mulatto population is the best illustration of that custom. For a period Negroes were forbidden to marry, and even later, when marriages among them were allowed, marriages were not widely encouraged. Negro women were viewed not as human beings but as forms of property which happened to exist in female form.

### CULTURAL BACKWARDNESS

Even after the Baltimore family lost its rights to the colony and the colony became a royal province, the economic and social status of the populace did not improve. It continued to provide good revenues for the proprietor's family—although the Baltimores lost their control over the government, they did not lose their claim to the soil—but not a very prosperous way of life for the majority of the people. Unlike New England, where towns multiplied in number and expanded in size and became centripetal forces in the organization of colonial life, Maryland and Virginia cultivated no towns at all. What towns they had were little more than magnified market-places, customs ports, exchange emporia, with an indented fringe of stores, warehouses, bars, gambling joints, and cheap brothels; nothing of genuine town life clung to such unruly and haphazard places. Marylanders and Virginians did not want to live in them. They lived on farms and plantations, in little clover-leafed hamlets or patchy villages, isolated from the contacts and intimacies which endow real town life with a sense of civic concern and pride.

It was that difference which mainly accounts for the retarded social development of Maryland, which prevented that land, during the colonial period, from making considerable cultural advance.

## CHAPTER XII

# Slavery: Black and White

*If I could find a Negro who knew Greek syntax, I should believe that the Negro was a human being and ought to be treated as a man.*

—CALHOUN

*We are indebted to the Negro for the very keystone of our modern civilization, and we owe to him the discovery of iron.*

—EMILE TORDAY

### WHITE SERVITUDE

It is customary to think of slavery in America in terms of the Negro, but slavery here has been white as well as black. Black slavery differed from white slavery mainly in regard to duration. In the beginning, to be sure, many Negro slaves were bound only by the laws of indenture and were allowed their freedom after they had worked out their time of service. These emancipated Negroes were free to buy property, purchase servants and slaves of their own, and were entitled to all the laws of protection possessed by the white freemen of the colony. It was not until after 1640 that life-long slavery of the Negroes became an established and unalterable custom.[1]

While white slaves, better known as indentured servants or redemptioners, were not subjected to all the brutalities and barbarities that oppressed black slaves, they suffered much at the hands of their masters. What is commonly known as servitude in the early history of this country was that condition of enslavement to which men and women were driven in order to pay for their transportation from the old world to the new. They became the servants, or slaves, of those men who advanced the money for their passage. These people became known by various names in different colonies; the names that persisted longest were "indentured servants" and "redemptioners." The period of servitude was not always the same, but in most cases it averaged between four and seven years.*

That period could be extended, however, as it often was, when an indentured servant became stubborn, insolent, or refractory.† Some servants, for such reasons, were forced to remain with their masters for an appalling number of years. In many cases the cause adjudged by the court for the extension of such servitude was a deliberate result of machinations on the part of the master. It is not surprising, therefore, that many indentured servants ran away from their owners and went to live with the Indians.

Both white and black slavery in the early years of this country was not confined to one section or territory. New Englanders as well as Virginians and Carolinians owned both white and black slaves and exploited them with equal cruelty. The New England and Middle Atlantic colonies maintained white slavery as long as the South; as late as 1831, in Philadelphia, there is a record of an indentured servant being bound to a master. The Northern colonies abandoned black slavery at an earlier period than the Southern, mainly because they found it unprofitable. They discovered it was far more profitable for them to capture, steal, and buy slaves, and then sell them to New England dealers and merchants.

The white slave group ‡ was made up of the poorer classes; many were rogues, criminals, beggars, ne'er-do-wells, delinquents, but many more were just simple, honest folk who were willing to sell themselves, and even their children, into servitude for the chance to succeed in a new land, a land beyond the horizons which they knew —the farther away the better, the newer the sweeter. Conditions in the England they knew had nothing of charm or wonder to hold

* Periods of servitude varied in different states. In New Jersey, for those above twenty-one it was approximately four years; in Maryland, it was five years above twenty-two and six years between eighteen and twenty-two; in New England, especially in Massachusetts and Rhode Island, seven years was more common. In almost all colonies children above five had to serve until the age of twenty-one.

† The General Court at Annapolis, for example, on July 9, 1640, ordered two runaway servants to be punished by whipping and "to serve out their time and add a year to their master to recompense his loss by their absence." At a court held the following week, the master of certain runaways was given a year's additional service "or longer if said master shall see cause." [2]

‡ In a conventional sense, it may be unfair to refer to the *indentured servants* and *redemptioners* as white slaves. Their extension of servitude in the majority of cases was limited: from four to seven years.

them. What they had known had been distress, sorrow, bitterness, poverty; at the worst, it could not be worse in this new land, which might be, perchance, if the words they had heard about it were true, "the green and pleasant land" of Blake's dream.

Although the famous upper-class Virginian Robert Beverley declared that the servants and slaves were not worked "so hard, nor so many hours in a Day, as the Husbandmen and Day-Labourers in England," it was not long before the underdogs realized that the new land for their kind was not much better than the old. In an interesting letter, written as late as 1792, we discover a revealing picture of what the indentured servants had to endure:

*Negroes being a property for life, the death of slaves in the prime of youth or strength is a material loss to the proprietor; they are, therefore, almost in every instance, under more comfortable circumstances than the miserable European, over whom the rigid planter exercises an inflexible severity. They are strained to the utmost to perform their allotted labour; ... they groan beneath a worse than Egyptian bondage.*[3] *

## HANGING BETTER THAN TRANSPORTATION TO THE NEW WORLD

The fact that a certain percentage of these servants were criminals † caused their masters to treat them as a class, regardless of their individual experience and training, and to bear down upon them as if they were all felons. Many criminals, to be sure, having heard of the type of life they would have to endure as white slaves in Virginia or in any other of the colonies, flatly refused to change their form of imprisonment for the servitude they would have to submit to in the new world. In another London letter, the writer speaks of "convicts who rather chose to undergo the severest penalties of the law, than endure the hardships which are annexed to their situation, during the state of servitude on this side of the Atlantic." Then, too, there is the case of Philip Gibson, "who had been con-

* John Fiske admits that though the lives of the indentured servants were protected by law, the laws were seldom put into effect. It was rarely possible to get a verdict against the master. He confesses that "the condition of the former [the white slave] seems to have been nearly as miserable as that of the latter [the negro slave]."[4]

† In King Charles II's *Instructions for the Councill appointed for Forraigne Plantacons* (1660), he urges that "vagrants and others who remaine here noxious and unprofitable, may be soe transplanted to the general advantage of the publique as well as the particular commoditie of our Forraine Plantacons."

demned to death for a street robbery [but] would not accept the offer of fourteen years transportation, and insisted on his former sentence, which was that he be hanged."[5]

### EXTREMITIES OF LABOR AND SERVITUDE

The largest number of indentured servants came from among the paupers and convicts of England and Ireland, with interspersed handfuls from Wales, France, and Sweden, and with occasional Jews intersticed within the mass. In order to prevent these white slaves from escaping, the death penalty was prescribed.[6] The enslaved people were forced to perform military duty as one of their paramount services; many of them were required, before they sailed, to sign papers in which they consented to be soldiers as well as servants in the colonies in which they landed.

The conditions of passage to which these people were subjected were unbelievably horrifying and hideous. "As we descended the side of this hulk, a most revolting scene of want and misery presented itself," Henry Bradshaw Fearon remarks, describing the arrival in Philadelphia of an Amsterdam brig loaded with Dutch slaves or *redemptioners*. "The eye involuntarily turned for some relief from the horrible picture of human suffering, which this living sepulchre afforded," he goes on to add. "The deck was filthy. The cooking, washing, and necessary departments were close together. Such is the mercenary barbarity of the Americans who are engaged in this trade, that they crammed into one of those vessels 500 passengers, 30 of whom died on the passage."[7]

Many of the redemptioners were whipped to death, and in order to protect the masters in that event, in 1662 a law was passed by the Assembly "prohibiting private burial of servants or others, because of the occasion thus given for much scandal against divers persons . . . of being guilty of their deaths."[8] The indentured servant was not viewed as a human being with rights inherent in his own personality; he was part of an estate. In an act passed in 1711, for instance, it was definitely stipulated that all indentured servants should continue to work out their period of servitude even after the master who had bought them had died.

All sorts of tricks and deceptions were resorted to in order to attract people to Virginia and the rest of the colonies in those days.

Redemptioners were needed to maintain the economy, which had not advanced far enough to be able to thrive upon free labor. London companies made all kinds of outlandish, impossible promises to those who would emigrate to the new country; some of the promises included houses, gardens, orchards, fine clothes, ornaments, and gleaming jewels as part of the reward. When the emigrants arrived, however, they found that they "were marched to their daily work in squads and companies under officers and the severest penalties were prescribed for a breach of discipline or neglect of duty ... neglect of labor was to be punished by galley service from one to three years. Penal servitude was also instituted; for 'petty offenses' they worked 'as slaves in irons for a term of years.' The planters affirm that there were 'continual whippings, and extraordinary punishments' such as hanging, shooting, breaking on the wheel and even burning alive."[9]

Even toward the felons who came over, however, preferences were shown, as the following item from the *Virginia Gazette* clearly shows:

> On Monday the 17th, early in the Morning the Felons ordered for Transportation set out from Newgate; Those of the common sort were conducted on Foot by a proper Guard ... and put on Board a Ship ... bound to His Majesties Plantation in America; but the Felons of Distinction had a little more Respect shown to them; Mr. Wreathack, the Attorney and Mr. Ruffhead, the Butcher ... and Mr. Bird, the Bailiff ... went in a Hackney Coach ... and as they pay for their Passage it is supposed that as soon as they land they will be set at Liberty instead of being sold as Felons usually are: Thus by the wholesome Laws of this Country a Criminal who has Money... may blunt the Edge of Justice and make That his Happiness which the law designs as his Punishment.[10]

## KIDNAPPING OF CHILDREN

When there were not enough free people to venture voluntarily into the new world under such a condition of servitude, and there were not enough felons to fill the quota, the companies and their captains resorted to either kidnapping or child seduction. Kidnapping was a familiar procedure; in fact, it became so lucrative a business that the court ladies and noblemen found it a most profitable investment. The technique of attracting children into the holds of ships with all variety of false promises became a subtle and sinister occupation. Sympathetic ballads were even sung about these defenseless children, the following being one of the most interesting and touching:

> When we came to Virginia . . .
> Where the captain he stands with a cane in his hands,
> And our aching hearts before him doth stand,
> With tears in our eyes in a foreign land,
> Was sold for a slave in Virginia.[11]

Edward Neill tells how one hundred children were sent over by the London Company itself upon one occasion, and how the next spring one hundred more were demanded. The boys became indentured servants, or "apprentices" as they were euphemistically described, until twenty-one years of age, and girls till the same age except in cases in which they married earlier. Since the majority of the children shipped over or kidnapped were about twelve years of age, they had to serve approximately nine years of hard servitude.[12] The traffic in maidens at the time became so horrifying that, in one parish alone, forty young girls fled from their homes and hid themselves in out-of-the-way places where they could not be traced and captured.

### SAIL ON!

Letters and diaries of the day record how the indentured people, young and old, were treated on shipboard. John Harrower's *Diary* is full of accounts of an unsuccessful mutiny, sickness, suffering, and all the daily tribulations of life on a white-slave ship. His description of an experience with the "Soul drivers" is worth quoting:

> This day severalls came on bd. to purchase servts Indentures and among them there was two Soul drivers. They are men who make it their business to go on bd. all ships who have in either Servants or Convicts and buy sometimes the whole and sometimes a parcell of them as they can agree and then they drive them through the Country like a parcell of Sheep until they can sell them to advantage, but (this time) all went away without buying any.[13]

Virginia and the other Southern colonies were not the only culprits in this traffic. Every colony, even Roger Williams's Rhode Island, was involved in it. The New Englanders were never averse to slavery, white or black. They not only sold black slaves to the Southern colonies but bought them themselves. The *Boston News-Letter* is replete with announcements and advertisements of slaves, black as well as white. Citation of a few of them should suffice to show how active the New Englanders were in the business:

Two Negro men and one Negro woman and Child to be sold by Mr. John Colman, Merchant....[14]

A Negro Woman Slave about 22 years of Age, to be sold by Mr. Nicholas Boone, Bookseller, and to be seen at the London Coffee-House.[15]

A Surranam India Woman and Child about five years old, to be Sold. Inquire of John Campbell, Postmaster of Boston, and know further.[16]

A Molatto Man-Servant aged about eighteen years to be sold....[17]

Such commerce was not confined to black and Indian slaves. It also included the indentured servants, and the newspaper items regarding them are no less revealing of New England psychology:

A Servant Maid's Time for four years to be sold: Inquire at the Post Office in Boston and know further.[18]

Ran away from his Master, Seth Sweetzer of Charlestown, in New England, August 15, 1703. A young man named John Logen, about 19 years of Age, of a middle Stature, black hair, by occupation a Taylor. ... Whoever shall take him up, and convey him safe to his above-said Master, shall have Four Pounds reward.[19]

Ran away at Boston about three weeks ago from his Master, Capt. Samuel Rymes, Commander of the Barbadoes Merchant, a Manservant named Joseph Ingerson, aged about 22 years....[20]

Ran away from his Master George Short of Boston, Taylor on the Lord's day night the 5th Currant, two servant Lads aged about fourteen years....[21]

A servant maid about 18 Years of Age fit for any family Business, her time to be disposed of for Five Years.[22]

## THE REDEMPTIONERS

If we turn to Pennsylvania, we find a similar picture. There the *redemptioners* were treated with equal brutality. As in the other colonies, wives were often separated from their husbands, and children from their parents,*[23] at public sales when families were divided by auctioneers, captains, and shippers. "Their fellow black slave was often treated better, for he was a slave for life," Louis P. Henninghausen writes, "and it was in the interest of the master to treat him well to preserve him, whilst the poor Redemptioner was a slave for a number of years only, and all his vital force worked out of him during the years of his service."

That a vast number of these redemptioners were robbed of what little they had by captains, entrepreneurs, and agents can no longer be denied.[24] No attempt was ever made to protect them from such exploitation. They were crowded into the holds of ships and subjected to all the suffocating and annihilating congestions of the unhappy way of life forced upon them. The result was that a considerable percentage of them died before they ever saw the new world, and many others when they arrived were little more than disease carriers and breeders. In less than one year during the period over two thousand were buried in the sea.[25] †

In brief, the people on board who were redemptioners or indentures were at the mercy of the captain or his agents, and had no recourse to law or any other source for defense. They were the victims of circumstance, namely, the circumstance of their dependence upon those who had the right to sell them to the highest bidder. In

* Louis P. Henninghausen, in his *German Society of Maryland* (pp. 80-81), describes one such separation thus: "The Ship was crowded and the register was engaged in making out and signing apprenticeship contracts in one part of the ship, when a Mr. W. Denny, a farmer from Queen Anne County, seeing the Brenning boys, was so pleased with their appearance that he offered the captain of the ship a liberal sum of money to buy them as redemptioners. The captain accepted the money, and the farmer, without having them bound and indentured by Mr. Thomsen, and without the parents understanding what was going on with their children, placed the boys in his boat, which was laying alongside of the ship, and shoved off. The mother seeing her only children carried thus away, cried and lamented crazed with grief and anguish. Mr. Thomsen called to Mr. Denny and ordered him to bring back the boys. He would return him the money he paid, but neither the order of this officer nor the piteous cries and lamentations of the mother and father of the boys made an impression on the farmer. It was a clear case of kidnapping. To make matters worse, the bereaved and grief-stricken parents were afterwards sold to a farmer in Pennsylvania where they bitterly bewailed the loss of their children."

† Geiser tells also of other voyages, the one undertaken by Scot, who "chartered a ship to transport 130 passengers to East Jersey in 1685, lost thirty-five during the voyage, by deaths, and there is no account of any unusual accident to the vessel or to the passengers." In another case a ship lost 100 out of 150 passengers because of starvation.[26] One vessel arriving in Philadelphia in 1745 landed only 50 survivors from a group of 400, most of them redemptioners or indentures.

unadulterated language, what this meant was that they were slaves, slaves of those who owned them. They didn't have to be slaves for life, as the Negroes did, but they had to be slaves for as long as they had contracted.* In Virginia, for example, these white slaves could not even marry without the consent of their masters. In 1643 a law was passed providing that any man servant guilty of marrying without the consent of his master should have to serve the latter an extra year for the offense, and in the case of the woman the time extension was doubled.[28]

### THE WHITE-SLAVE SHIPS

These slave ships were literal prisons in which men, women, and children grew sick, suffered, and died. Even the galleys were not much worse. There were no doctors on most of the ships, and even when there were, their interest in the propertyless redemptioners was less than little. The following report of what these white slaves had to endure is illustrative of how they were treated by the captains, companies, or individuals who bought and owned them:

"After fourteen days had elapsed, the captain informed them that they would get nothing to eat except bread and meat. After this last person received two biscuits, one pint of water and the eighth part of a pound of meat per day . . . the hunger was so great on board that all the bones about the ship were hunted up by them, pounded with a hammer and eaten; and what is more lamentable, some of the deceased persons, not many hours before their death, crawled on their hands and feet to the captain and begged him, for God's sake, to give them a mouthful of bread, or a drop of water, to keep them from perishing, but their

* In that connection there is an account which is too irresistible not to repeat:

"About the year 1795 the trade was almost abandoned. It is related of a soul-driver named McCullaugh, who became noted in the trade, that he made several trips to Europe and gathered droves of redemptioners for the American market. On one occasion McCullaugh was outwitted by a man called 'Terry,' who was one of the herd of human chattels, and who contrived to be the last offered for sale. 'Terry' was Irish and McCullaugh was Irish, too. One night 'Terry' and his master lodged at a tavern, the landlord of which was ignorant of the fact that one of the strangers was a redemptioner. In the morning the young Irishman arose early and contrived to sell his master to the landlord. Pocketing the money, he casually informed the landlord that his new servant, still asleep in an upper room, although tolerably clever in other respects, was rather saucy and a little given to lying. In fact, he had presumption enough at times to indeavor to pass himself off as a freeman, and that possibly he might represent himself as such to his new owner. By the time the soul-driver was up and doing and the landlord undeceived, the son of Erin had gained such a start that pursuit was impossible."[27]

supplications were in vain; he most obstinately refused, and thus did they perish."

Of the four hundred Palatines who sailed for New York in 1709, twenty per cent died on the voyage. The number of deaths in fifteen vessels, in 1738, are estimated at from 1600 to 2000. As late as 1818, Fearon, an English traveler in America, visiting a ship lying in the harbor at Philadelphia, observes "that they crammed into one of those vessels 500 passengers, eighty of whom died on the passage."

Many a time parents are compelled to see their children miserably suffer and die from hunger, thirst and sickness, and then see them cast into the sea. I witnessed such a misery in no less than thirty-two children in our ship all of whom were thrown into the sea. . . . Children who have not yet had the measles or smallpox generally get them on board the ship, and mostly die of them . . . sometimes whole families die in quick succession; so that often many dead persons lie in the berth beside the living ones, especially when contagious diseases have broken out on board the ship.[29]

The living were forced to sleep next to the dead.[30] Once the ship arrived, and the dead were carried off and buried in the dirt lands beyond the immediate boundaries of the city, the ship itself became a butcher stall, a marketplace, and dozens of slave purchasers, hungry for profits, would leap upon it, survey the slaves, tweak their noses, rough their skins, stare into their eyes, to discover whether they would be good purchases, good investments.

The people were, to put it simply, so much cattle. Parents sold away their children for their own freedom, and other parents leased themselves out for longer times so that their children could be free. Families were divided on all sides, husbands from wives, children from parents, for economic gain. An interesting incidence of how tragic this business could become is evidenced by the following case:

A gentleman of this city [Philadelphia] wanted an old couple to take care of his house;—a man, his wife, and his daughter were offered to him for sale; he purchased them. They proved to be his father, his mother, and his sister.[31]

The state was so concerned with the perpetuity of this white slavery that it did everything in its power to defend it. People like

Benjamin Franklin, much later, even speculated in the "racket." In New Jersey, for one state, a law passed in 1713 stipulated that slaves that ran away from their masters should have their time of service doubled and should have to pay all the expenses incurred in their capture and restoration to their owners.[32] Even William Penn, humanitarian though he was, suggested a statute that would not only punish the slaves that ran away but also "any that shall Inveigle any servant to goe from his master." [33] *

The whole structure of American society in those days was based upon slavery. The North was not different from the South. It was only later, much later, that slavery became a color fact: the Negroes becoming the major victims. In the beginning, whites as well as blacks were involved in it. Whites were bought and sold like so much butcher's meat in Holland, in England, in Ireland, before they ever set sail for the new world. They were weighed, examined, tested like horses, and were bought in accordance with what their flesh, as working assets, was worth.

The records of this white-slave business are infinite. It is hard to believe today that a country which has become so noted for its democratic and libertarian doctrines could have been founded upon such a mercenary and servile basis. Yet the whole country at the time was the same; no colonies disdained or scorned the practice.

But it was not only England that participated in this traffic; most of Europe was involved. In every country humble people were willing to sell their present, bodies and all, for the future. The idea of becoming indentured servants did not terrify them. They were scarcely more than that in the old world. What was physical freedom if it didn't include economic freedom? Of what value was it to be able to move about freely if you also starved freely? Nation, country, race, had nothing to do with such matters. So men of all nations, all countries, all races, flocked to America.

"About 1500 people, men, women, and children," Bernard Roman writes, "were deluded away from their native country, where they

* In this connection the court records of New Amsterdam include a striking case which illustrates how the indentured elements were dealt with then: "A servant lad being imprisoned for stealing a ring, and refusing to tell where he concealed it, was ordered to be privately whipped. After this punishment, he still refused to disclose the stolen article. The court then ordered that a year be added to the time of his indenture, and that the master should have the liberty of selling him to Virginia or any other colony." [34]

lived at home in the plentiful cornfields and vineyards of Greece and Italy, to this place, where instead of plenty they found want to its last degree, instead of promised fields a dreary wilderness; instead of a grateful soil a barren arid sand; and in addition to their misery, were obliged to indent themselves, their wives and children for many years."[35]

Mittleberger tells us about the people from Holland who were "packed densely, like herrings, so to say, in the large sea vessels ... one person receiving a place of scarcely 2 feet width and 6 feet length ... the lice abound so frightfully, especially on sick people, that they can be scraped off the body."[36] Their suffering on shipboard, Diffenderfer asserts, "equals all the horrors of the 'middle passage' during the African slave traffic."[37]

The final irony of it all is that many of the "best" Americans speculated in this white-slave racket. Ministers, lawyers, doctors, statesmen, were engaged in it, for it was one of the most profitable investments of the time.

### BLACK SLAVERY

Black slavery is predominantly associated with the South because it thrived best there. It was tried in various other parts of the country, but without marked success. As a matter of fact, it was not a success in the South until after the invention of the cotton gin in 1794. Prior to that time, the price of slaves was relatively low, and slavery as an institution was on the decline. Curiously enough, the leading antislavery societies of the eighteenth century originated in the South and not in the North, and all through that century it became a not uncommon event for wealthy Southerners to include a clause in their wills freeing some, if not all, of their slaves. George Washington and Thomas Jefferson were among those who pursued that practice. In 1786 George Washington declared that he hoped that some plan might be devised "by which slavery [might] be abolished by slow, sure, and imperceptible degrees." In his will he stated:

> Upon the decease of my wife it is my will and desire that all the slaves which I hold in my own right shall receive their freedom—To emancipate them during her life would, tho earnestly wished by me, be

attended with such insuperable difficulties, on account of their intermixture of marriages with the Dower negroes, as to excite the most painful sensations—if not disagreeable consequences. . . . And whereas among those who will receive freedom according to this devise there may be some who from old age, or bodily infirmities & others who on account of their infancy . . . will be unable to support themselves, it is my will and desire that all who come under the first and second description shall be comfortably cloathed and fed by my heirs while they live and that such of the latter description as have no parents living, or if living are unable or unwilling to provide for them, shall be bound by the Court until they shall arrive at the age of twenty five years. . . .

Thomas Jefferson, because he died bankrupt, did not manumit many of his slaves in his will, but he fought against slavery upon numerous occasions, and in the Ordinance for the Northwest Territory he made a provision, which was finally adopted in 1787, that slavery should not exist therein after 1800.

In the seventeenth and eighteenth centuries slavery was a moot subject. Men argued pro and con about it without becoming violent or vicious. It had not yet struck close enough to their pocketbooks. Holding slaves in those days was as much a luxury as a necessity. It was not until the nineteenth century that it became a reality over which men could not remain calm; by that time it had become a fighting issue.

### SLAVERY ORDAINED BY THE BIBLE

While many Southerners were vociferous in their condemnation of slavery in the seventeenth and eighteenth centuries, many Northerners justified it as an institution sanctioned by God. In reply to Samuel Sewall's contention in *The Selling of Joseph* that "it would conduce more to the Welfare of the Province to have White Servants for a Term of Years than to have Slaves for Life,"[38] John Saffin declared the Bible had ordained slavery, that "the Israelites were forbidden (ordinarily) to make Bond Men and Women of their own nation, but of Strangers they might. The words run thus (*Levit.* 25, 44), 'Both thy Bond Men and thy Bond Maids which thou shalt have shall be of the Heathen that are round about you: of them shall you Buy Bond men and Bond maids,' &c. See also I

*Cor.* 12, 13. 'Whether we be Bond or Free,' which shows that in the times of the New Testament there were Bond men also." [39] Many others voiced similar sentiments in New England.

If slavery had proved as economically adaptable in the North as in the South, the institution would have become as deep-rooted there and would have been just as hard to root out. In fact, if that had happened there would probably never have been a Civil War. The chances are that, without slavery as a form of emotional dynamite, the economic differences between the two regions could have been straightened out without a military conflict. It was slavery that provoked the hysterical antagonisms and finally precipitated the country into the crisis. Underlying the struggle, to be sure, was the economic conflict between two productive systems, one industrial and the other agrarian, and contingent upon that was the political conflict that resolved itself into the issue of "states' rights," over which so much ink was spilled; but beneath it all, like a deep undercurrent which swells into a typhoon, was the challenge of slavery.*

As we have seen, black slaves were not the only slaves in the new world. The English under Cromwell had sold the captured Irish into slavery, and many Englishmen made their living hunting for children in Ireland to sell as slaves in the West Indies. At times, too, Englishmen themselves were sold; the record of the seventy Englishmen transported to the West Indies "for 1,550 pound weight of sugar a piece, more or less," is pathetically illustrative of that practice.[40] But horrible as was this white-slave traffic, it was far less horrible than the black-slave traffic.

### NEGROES AS COMMODITIES

It is easier for men to be cruel to people unlike themselves, whom they consider a different and inferior species, than to men of their own kind. Negroes were not men in the eyes of the whites who captured, bought, and sold them; they belonged to a different realm of reality, a lower and subhuman kingdom of existence. They were a little better than animals, but not much; they were treated, con-

* A detailed analysis of the conflict between the North and the South, dealing with its economic, political, and moral causes and effects, will appear in the second volume of this work.

sequently, more like animals than men. That statement, however, demands modification. Animals that were high-priced and difficult to procure were treated far better than blacks, who were not so high-priced and not so difficult to get. The Negro was a commodity, as were trinkets, tobacco, and fish, and his value was what he could be sold for on the auction block. When the price was low, antislavery sentiment in the South was by no means uncommon; when the price was high, antislavery sentiment lessened, if it did not abate. At the Constitutional Convention it was Virginia and not New England that stood out in most firm and direct opposition to an extension of the time allowed for noninterference with the slave trade. Before the invention of the cotton gin the slave sold for relatively low figures. In the seventeenth century slaves sold for as little as $100 to $150. The slaves brought over by the *White Horse*, the first American slave vessel dispatched direct from New York to Africa, sold on the average for $125.[41] In the middle of the eighteenth century, George Washington purchased slaves for $250 and $300. By 1803, after the invention of the cotton gin, the price of slaves had soared to $400 and $600, and by 1856 they were selling for as high as $1,642. In Louisiana the *Herald* of Lake Providence listed sales of Negro men as ranging from $1,500 to $1,635, of Negro women and girls from $1,250 to $1,550. In 1859 a Negro slave was sold for as much as $2,850.[42]

What the Negroes endured in this wholesale campaign to use them like animals is something that almost forbids belief. The treatment of the Jews in Egypt, the slaves in Babylon, the helots in Greece, was gentle and generous in comparison. The deals undertaken in Africa itself, with raids, invasions, and wars of an unspeakably ruthless character, represent the white man in one of his darkest and evilest roles. Helpless, defenseless blacks were pounced upon, shot at, snatched from their ancient homes, chained, whiplashed, spiritually broken, dragged onto vessels, and crowded, scores upon scores on top of one another, into ship pens infinitely more forbidding than the horrid prophecies of their medicine men. En route, all of them suffered; those taken with disease were flung overboard; many others died; those who reached the new world were introduced to a form of living death. Noah Webster, describing the misery of the Negroes as slaves, tells of the West Indian Negroes who "consider death as a deliverance from servitude and the restoration to their native country. Hence their funerals are seasons of joy and festivity, and are attended with dancing." [43]

Few tragedies in the world have been comparable to that experienced by the Negroes in this coercive transplantation to a white man's land—a transplantation that resulted in the degradation of white men as well as black. "Slavery," Noah Webster declared, "necessarily enervates the vigor of the human mind in all climates and among all nations." [44] Many Englishmen, as well as many Americans, at that time adopted the same stand. Thomas Day, an Englishman, assured one of his American friends who was contemplating freeing his slaves that "slavery is a crime so monstrous against the human species that all those who practice it deserve to be extirpated from the earth." [45]

### PURITANS ACTIVE IN THE SLAVE TRADE

It should not be thought that all those engaged in the inhuman trade were vicious persons, as cruel and remorseless as recidivists. Many of them were devout Puritans, church members with a flair for the sacred, who speculated in slave traffic simply because it was a lucrative way of making a living. Undoubtedly many of them were good to their wives and children, treated animals kindly, and helped cripples across a muddy road. What they did was to separate into logic-tight compartments their business life from their personal life. Buying and selling slaves was an occupation, just as fishing was. If men in high places, like Cromwell, could sell white men into slavery, they could see no reason why they couldn't do the same with blacks. Slavery was too ancient and too common an institution to make men shrink, especially when the Bible could be adduced in its defense and when men could justify their consciences by convincing themselves that they were making it possible for the slaves to achieve Christian salvation.

Most of the Negroes sold to the American slave traders belonged to the less cultured elements of the African populace. Nevertheless, among the Negro slaves brought to America there were many with extraordinary talent and more than a handful who spoke a number of languages. Josselyn tells us of the Negress who "had been a

Queen in her own Countrey," indicating that higher-class as well as lower-class Negroes were brought to these shores.

### JOB OF BOONDA

Best known, perhaps, of the higher-ranking and more intelligent Negroes sold into slavery in this country was Job of Boonda. Job was "the son of Solomon Dgiallo, the High Priest of Boonda in the country of Foota, Africa."[46] Job studied with Prince Sambo, who later became the King of Fouta; he learned to read the Koran, married twice, and had children by both wives. He was set upon by the Mandingoes, enemies of his tribe, sold by them to an English trader, and after a harrowing sea trip found himself in Annapolis, where as a slave he was forced to work in the tobacco fields for Mr. Tolsey, his master. He escaped, was caught, and imprisoned. He wrote to his father a letter in Arabic which finally reached the hands of General Oglethorpe, who had it translated at Oxford and, shortly thereafter, had the youth ransomed and brought as a free man to England. In the latter country Job became immediately popular with the aristocracy, was wined, dined, and feted, and even persuaded to catalogue the Arabic manuscripts in the British Museum. The next year he returned in triumph to his native land.

### THE PLIGHT OF THE NEGRO

There is a general conviction, perpetuated by many of our more sentimental historians, that the Negro was docile and subservient by nature and, therefore, ideally adapted to slavery. Actually the Negro did not accept his slavery with anything like the compliance suggested by such historians. He revolted against it from the very beginning, and the history of his revolts constitutes one of the most interesting and revealing aspects of our history.

When the Negroes first landed upon these shores they knew nothing of the land to which they had been brought. The Indian had known this land for centuries. It was far easier to enslave people to a soil to which they were strangers than it was to enslave the Indians, who had known the country from their birth and whose fathers had lived upon the land for countless centuries. The Negroes had never known the land, but they adapted themselves to it so successfully that today there are more Negroes in America than there are Irish in Ireland or Jews in the entire world. What is more pertinent, if not more astonishing, is that the Negro represents one-tenth of the total population of the United States, constituting a greater minority than any other people in the nation.*

### FIRST ARRIVAL OF THE NEGROES

When the first Negroes landed upon these shores is still difficult to ascertain. Most historians, relying upon Captain Smith's quotation from John Rolfe's letter, have concluded that 1619 was the year when the first Negro slaves made their appearance in the new world. A closer reading of the letter, however, provides no such evidence. Before the "Negars" could be purchased, the captain of the ship "had sett saile and was gone out of the Bay." [48] That the first Negroes arrived some time early in the 1620's there can be no doubt, but those Negroes were not purchased as lifelong slaves. They were bought as the white slaves of that day were bought; namely, as *indentures*. It was not until two decades later that blacks were sold into perpetual slavery.

Many people, like George Fox, thought that the best way to rid the land of Negro slavery was to convert the blacks into indentured slaves. "It will doubtless be very acceptable to the Lord," he wrote, "if it be that masters of Families here would deal so with their servants, the Negroes and blacks whom they have bought with their Money to let them go free after a considerable Term of Years if they have served them faithfully." [49] Noah Webster thought the best plan was "to raise the slaves by gradual means to the condition of free tenants." [50]

It was after the Negroes were made lifelong slaves that indentured servitude decreased.[51] In the North and in the Middle Atlantic states indentured slavery continued because bond slavery had no root there. In the South, on the contrary, the Negroes became so preferred that in the year 1705, for instance, over 1,800 were brought into the Virginia colony. In 1708 there were only 18,000 white tithables and 12,000 Negroes in the colony.[52] It was in this competitive numerical battle that the race feeling in the South began.

* When "hundreds of the English settlers had died of the 'plague,' every one of the blacks was alive and contented . . . if they suffered in the winter, there is no record of the fact." [47]

The organization of the Royal African Company in the seventeenth century gave official sanction to slavery enterprises. It was not a battle over slaves so much as it was in the beginning a conflict with the Dutch, who were the greatest slave traders of the times; the brother of Governor Berkeley, George Berkeley, was a heavy stockholder in the company, which was evaluated at the time at £96,000. Later it was fear of France that made many Englishmen justify slavery as a necessary institution. In a most interesting letter of a British merchant, written as late as December 11, 1744, and addressed to the king, we discover the following observation: "But if the whole Negroe Trade be thrown into the hands of our Rivals, and our Colonies are to depend on the Labour of the White Men to supply their Place, they will either soon be undone or shake off their Dependency on the Crown of England."[53]

Dozens and hundreds of clergymen disapproved of slavery and gave the best energies of their lives to fighting it. In the beginning the preachers, ministers, and priests had to fight against the planters, who were opposed not only to teaching the Negroes Christianity but also to teaching them ideas of liberty, freedom, and independence. The Reverend Morgan Godwyn, for instance, asserted that the bringing of Christianity to the Negroes would be sufficient to quiet and pacify their souls. "There are some thousands of them," Godwyn wrote, "who understand English no more than our own People, and who if baptized would be rendered dutifully docile and subservient."[54] He also commented on the talents of the Negroes, indicating that they were far from being the backward people they had always been assumed to be. "As to their (alike pretended) stupidity," he states, "there is as little truth therein: divers of them being known and confessed by their Owners to be extraordinary Ingenious, and even to exceed many of the English." A little later John Burke stated that "in vain does philosophy object to the abstracting capacity of the Negro; whilst experience records a thousand instances of strong, intellectual vigor, of ardent and generous attachment."[55] Nevertheless, the whites in the South refused to regard the Negroes as men. Abraham Lincoln, as late as October 18, 1858, still found it necessary to declare in his letter to the Hon. J. N. Brown that "I have made it equally plain that I think the

Negro is included in the word 'Men' used in the Declaration of Independence."

### NEGROES APPEAL TO THEIR MASTERS

The natural reaction to such slavery was revolt, but many of the Negroes preferred the method of supplication to that of active resistance, and among the documents of the time a number are to be discovered which reveal that attitude. In 1783, for example, the Quakers addressed a special plea in behalf of the Negro cause. What they said remains to this day illuminating and memorable. The first thing they stressed was that the slave raids undertaken by the white men in Africa were resulting in the destruction of the felicity and progress of the black peoples. "This traffick," their argument runs, "is the principal source of the destructive wars which prevail among these unhappy people, and is attended with consequences the mere recital of which is shocking to humanity. The violent separation of the dearest relatives, the tears of conjugal and parental affection, the reluctance of the slaves to a voyage from which they can have no prospect of returning must present scenes of distress which would pierce the heart of any in whom the principles of humanity are not wholly effaced."[56] Other sections of this document emphasize the fact that "in procuring slaves from the coast of Africa, many children are stolen privately," and that slaves "are sold to the highest bidder and branded with a hot iron." In 1793 the Negroes themselves made a direct appeal to their masters to consider the black man as a human being, equipped with intelligence and potentialities which rivaled if not equaled those of the white race. They headed their appeal with the words: "An Address to those who keep slaves and approve the practice." And what they said in that appeal is worth quoting:

> You try what you can to prevent our rising from the state of barbarism you represent us to be in, but we can tell you from a degree of experience that a black man, although reduced to the most abject state human nature is capable of, short of real madness, can think, reflect and feel injuries. . . . We believe that if you would try the experiment of taking a few black children and cultivating their minds with the same care and let them have the same prospect in view as to living in the world

as you would wish for your children, you would find upon a trial that they were not inferior in mental endowments.

The man must be wilfully blind and extremely partial that cannot see the contrary effects of liberty and slavery upon the mind of man.[57]

## THE NEGRO REVOLTS

But not all Negroes were so supplicatory and obsequious. Many were resistant, recalcitrant, and revolutionary. Anthony Benezet quotes an old slave trader who later came to regret the nature of his ways and was eager to do penance for them, averring that he wanted to contribute "all in [his] power towards the good of mankind by inspiring any of its individuals with a suitable abhorrence for that detestable practice of trading in our fellow-creatures":

I was ordered to go up the country a considerable distance upon having notice from one of the Negro Kings that he had a parcel of Slaves to dispose of. I received my instructions and went, carrying with me an account of such goods we had on board to exchange for the Slaves we intended to purchase; upon being introduced I presented him with a small case of Spirits, a Gun, and some trifles, which having accepted and understood by an interpretor what goods we had, the next day was appointed for viewing the slaves, we found about two hundred confined in one place. But here now I shall relate the affecting sight which I there beheld, the silent sorrow which appeared in the countenance of the afflicted father, the painful anguish of the tender mother expecting to be forever separated from their tender offspring. . . . I purchased eleven who I conducted by two by two to our ship. Being but a small vessel (ninety ton) we soon purchased our cargo consisting of a hundred and seventy Slaves . . . shackled two and two together, pent up within the narrow confines of the main deck with the complicated distress of sickness, chains and contempt; deprived of every fond and social tie and in a great measure reduced to a state of desparation. We had not been a fortnight at Sea before the fatal consequences of this despair appeared, they formed a design of recovering their natural right liberty by raising and murdering every man on board . . . the plot was discovered; the ringleader tied by the two thumbs over the barricado door; at Sun rise received a number of lashes and in this situation he remained till Sun set exposed to the insults and barbarity of the brutal crew of Sailors with full leave to exercise their cruelty at pleasure: The consequence was the next morning the miserable sufferer was found dead. . . . The next victim was a youth who from too strong a sense of his misery refused nourishment and died disregarded and unnoticed till the hogs had fed on part of his flesh.[58]

In the seventeenth century there were not enough Negroes in the colonies to inspire organized revolts. In 1670 Negroes constituted only five per cent of the population of Virginia; in 1715, on the other hand, they represented over one-third of the colony. In South Carolina an even greater increase occurred; by 1740, the blacks, who had been in a minority the century previous, became four times more numerous than whites. Consequently, prior to the dawn of the eighteenth century, Negroes would flee from their masters and, sometimes as individuals and sometimes as groups, struggle to make their way into the Spanish territories, where they knew they would be safe. Few reached there; most were captured and slain before they could escape from British-owned soil.

It was only after the Negroes became sufficiently numerous to offer concerted opposition—which became the case in Virginia and the Carolinas in the eighteenth century—that they became a threat to white supremacy. From that time on, Negro revolts became mass phenomena and, as such, sources of great terror to the whites. In 1739 a revolt took place on the Stone plantation, which was near Charleston, South Carolina, and before many days had passed the forty or fifty slaves who had initiated the rebellion were joined by scores more. *En masse* they marched upon the country, plundering, pillaging, and burning, and land, houses, crops, and cattle fell to their hands. Slave owners were killed—all save one, who was known by everyone as a kindly man who had been good to his slaves. The rebels were later overtaken by the whites and massacred. Those who were not shot were "hang'd and some Gibbeth alive."[59] The whites were so frightened by the revolt that in 1743 a law was passed which stated that all white men who attended places of worship had to carry a weapon of defense "with at least six charges of gun-powder and ball," and that any who failed in this respect were to pay a fine of twenty shillings. In North Carolina a law was passed forbidding Negroes to assemble and subjecting them to the punishment of death if they in any way discussed or plotted a revolt.

The next year, despite the new laws and statutes, another Negro revolt occurred in South Carolina, but it was squelched rapidly. Abortive revolts ensued in other colonies. Earlier still in New York, in 1712, a revolt occurred in which the Negroes, after having burned a house and barricaded themselves against attack, were overwhelmed by the soldiery, but not before a number of them had shot themselves and their wives and some had slit their own throats. In New York in 1741 the discovery of a "Negro plot," involving a Roman Catholic, Ury, and a number of other whites, resulted in a wholesale slaughter of suspects. Over one hundred fifty Negroes and a score of whites were jailed; four of the whites and eighteen of the blacks were hanged, and thirteen of the blacks were burned at the stake.[60] The excitement of the populace, egged on by a factitious fear of Popery and Spain, was incorrigibly maniacal. In Louisiana, in 1795, a revolt was planned by a combination of whites and blacks, but internal disagreements thwarted its realization.

### THE GABRIEL, VESEY, AND TURNER INSURRECTIONS

One of the better known and more celebrated revolts was that led by the Negro Gabriel, a Virginian slave who gathered over a thousand Negroes behind him and who was determined to advance upon the city of Richmond. A series of adverse circumstances resulted in the defeat of his revolt and the capture of his followers. An outstanding aspect of the revolt was that it was imbued with the French ideals of "liberty, equality, and fraternity," and its leaders were agreed that no Frenchmen were to be attacked, nor were any Quakers or Methodists, because both of those denominations had revealed a marked hostility to slavery.[61]

In 1801 and 1802, in 1811 and 1816, there were insurrections, and in 1822 Denmark Vesey, a free Negro, attempted the greatest revolt of the period. The plan was to set fire to the city of Charleston, seize the arsenal, and give the arms to the rebels, after which the whites who resisted were to be shot. If the plans of the revolt had not been betrayed by one of the household slaves, the revolt might have succeeded and the Negroes might have acquired possession of the city. That they could have held it for long is exceedingly problematical; whites from surrounding territories and even adjacent states would have banded together and eventually conquered them. The end result of the plot was that only fifteen of the conspirators were caught. The leaders died courageously, convinced that they had but begun to ignite the spirit of revolt among their people.

The final revolt of consequence was that led by Nat Turner, a Bible-inspired black who tore up and down some twenty miles of territory with a hundred Negroes, burning a number of houses, killing several scores of people, and alarming a nation. Turner had only five followers when he started his revolt, and not one of them had any ammunition. He was a mystic, however, and had had a vision which told him that God was on his side and that his followers would multiply. "I am told to slay all the whites we encounter," he declared to his men, "without regard to age or sex. We have no arms and ammunition, but we will find these in the houses of our oppressors; and as we go on, others can join us." [62] Turner's leading follower, Will, whose wife had been sold to "nigger traders," was the best fighter of the group and, when ambushed, he killed three white men before he himself was shot.

The Turner revolt filled the whole South with terror. Negroes sprang up on every side to join this man who called himself "The Black Moses," and whites fled anxiously from place to place in search of protection. Three thousand troops were summoned to arms, and the militia of all the surrounding counties were called into action. Once the rebellion was quelled, the whites turned upon the Negroes with unspeakable ferocity, and for weeks afterward there was not a black whose life was safe. Innocent as well as guilty suffered from the holocaust of vengeance. Judges were afraid to acquit an innocent Negro lest the populace take the law into its own hands and initiate lynch rule. Heads of Negroes "were stuck up on poles, and for weeks their grinning skulls remained, a warning to all who should undertake a similar plot. With the same purpose, the captain of the marines, as they [the soldiery] marched through Vicksville on their way home, bore upon his sword the head of a rebel." [63] Nat Turner and three of his leading followers were hanged. The body of Turner was not buried, but was skinned, and mementos and souvenirs were made from his flesh. There are people in the South today who still claim to have purses made from Turner's hide.[64]

These revolts are only the better known ones, those that were most widely discussed. In addition, there were multitudes of minor revolts, some squelched before they began, others throttled at the very start, and still others broken before they could acquire momentum.

### CHALLENGE OF THE ABOLITIONISTS

Just prior to the Civil War, in the 1850's in particular, the struggles between the blacks and the whites became even more critical. As the fight between the free-state men and the slave-state men became increasingly violent, the Negro was drawn inevitably into the conflict. The rousing challenge of the Abolitionists, the organization of the Underground Railway, inspired the black man with new and more substantial hopes for freedom. A new horizon was opening up for him, disclosing the vistas of a fresh and free life. Whites were allying themselves with him; societies were being organized for his protection, education, and emancipation. For the first time since his transportation from African soil he found it possible to think of himself as a man, a human being, an individual. Instead of revolting blindly against his oppressors, he now worked in organized groups, the purpose of which was to overthrow the slave regime. Members of his race became leaders, prophets, martyrs, legendary heroes. They dedicated themselves to the great cause of manumission, to the vision of an unfettered and unoppressed people. They were black avatars of a new race of men.

Negro women like Harriet Tubman and Linda Brent became warriors in the cause. Gun in hand, and endowed with all the grit and stamina of a martyr, Harriet Tubman consecrated her life to freeing her black brethren. Lovejoy gave his life, and Garrison jeopardized his own upon many occasions, in the same struggle, but their efforts were no greater than those of the more advanced blacks who forsook homesteads, deserted wives and families, and stopped at nothing in their determined endeavor to emancipate their people.

When the Civil War came, the Negro played a far more important role than usually has been recognized. He was active as an organizer as well as a fighter. He worked with his fellow slaves, agitated against their submission to their masters, and persuaded them to join the Northern armies. Before the end of the Civil War the Negroes had a number of regiments in the field, and their efficiency as well as their bravery was attested by almost all military authorities. Colonel T. W. Higginson stated that "it would have been madness to attempt with the bravest of white troops what he successfully accomplished with the black," because the blacks were fighting for freedom, whereas the whites were fighting for a diversity of reasons, none of which was so important.[65] The Negroes in the battlefield and the Negroes back in the corn and cotton fields were most important in assisting the North to overcome the South. It is only today that we are beginning to appreciate this fact; hitherto we assumed that the role of the Negro in the Civil War was insignificant. Lincoln himself admitted "that but for the assistance given by the Negroes, the North might have been lost."[66]

### THE BETRAYAL OF THE NEGRO

What the Negroes were co-operating in was the overthrow of Southern feudalism. If the North had supported them in their struggle, feudalism would have been wiped out of the South as completely as it was out of France after the French Revolution of 1789. What happened was that the North used the Negroes in the struggle to defeat the South, aided them for a period, and then abandoned them to the Southern reactionaries, who very soon reduced the Negroes to a state of economic subservience scarcely superior to that which they had known before the Civil War. The result was that the "freed" Negro in the South was unutterably miserable and oppressed. He was introduced into a new form of slavery worse than wage slavery. The whites had been subjected to ordinary wage slavery for generations; this new slavery was wage slavery with a color incubus which has continued down till today. In pre-Civil War days the Negro had been bought and sold like a chattel, but he had at least been provided with a house to live in and food to eat; in post-Civil War days he was not bought and sold, but he was not provided with food or shelter. Worse than that, he was discriminated against by white employers and found it more difficult to support himself economically than in the days of slavery.

In time the Negro has made his adjustments to this new order of society, but to this day he remains a slave to white prejudice and conventions and discovers it insuperably difficult to establish himself economically and prove his genius.

## CHAPTER XIII

# The Carolinas: A House Divided

*I believe this [North Carolina] is the only metropolis in the Christian or Mohametan world where there is neither church, chapel, mosque, synagogue, or any other place of public worship of any sect or religion whatsoever.*

—WILLIAM BYRD

It is a curious historical irony that the colony which was looked upon as the worst in the South—in fact, the worst in the country—at the time of the Revolutionary War has become the leading state in the South today. That state is North Carolina. Even now, if a South Carolinian is asked if he is from North Carolina he will wince, shudder, and inform his questioner in emphatic language that neither he nor his relatives nor his ancestors ever derived from that state. Throughout most of the South, North Carolina is considered the "white trash" state, South Carolina the aristocratic. That conviction persists even today among Southerners, despite the fact that North Carolina with its universities, magazines, libraries, and writers has far surpassed its sister state in cultural progress.

The origin of that difference can be traced to colonial days, when the structure of the two states created definite economic and social contrasts. The geographic character of North Carolina encouraged small farms and discouraged large plantations, whereas in South Carolina large plantations and large plantation owners dominated the land. During the colonial period practically all South Carolina's political and cultural life radiated from Charleston, which early became one of the most important cities along the Atlantic seaboard.

### THE FARMERS OF CATAWBA

North Carolina had no Charleston; in fact, for many years it had no cities at all. Its population was too dispersed to cultivate an urban center, and even its town life lagged far behind that of other colonies. Altogether it was a decentralized instead of a centralized colony, and it remained so for many generations. It was a small farmers' utopia. There were no large plantation owners to oppress the small farmers, and few conniving middlemen to rob them of whatever profits they could derive from their products. They realized, in those early days, something of what Jefferson envisaged many decades later as an ultimate ideal; namely, that of having every farmer possess a plot of land that was exclusively his own and that could not be invaded by state or nation. These farmers of Catawba—a name by which North Carolina was also known and by which the significant American novelist, Thomas Wolfe, later popularized the state—were recalcitrant, independent, and democratic. They had respect for nothing but themselves; they despised hereditary rank and plutocratic privilege and would have none of them. In that sense they came closer than any other coastal colony to the psychology of the Western frontier.

But such a psychology, born though it is of the spirit of independence, has drawbacks which are most unhappy. It is an insuperable handicap to intellectual and cultural advance. The best proof of that is to be discovered in the fact that there were no schools or newspapers in North Carolina until after the middle of the eighteenth century. The people of the colony felt no need for such things. They were almost complete isolationists; the outside world meant little to them. What faint contact they had with it they achieved through Virginia, from which they received mail little more than half a dozen times a year. They had no mail system of their own. They had few courts and even fewer churches, both of which they disregarded and discouraged. In court and church they indulged themselves as at a circus, crooking their legs upon chairs, benches, tables, and the backs of pews, spitting upon floors, smoking corncob pipes, gabbling out of turn, and leaving when they desired. William Byrd described the courthouse as "having much of the air of a common tobacco house." The judges were scarcely any better than the prisoners; many of the former drank openly during trials, and when such trials were held at taverns, which was not uncommon, they ofttimes swilled themselves into a stupor.

## RELIGIOUS TOLERATION

The main gain from this frontier informality was religious toleration. North Carolina, like Rhode Island in the North, became a haven for Quakers, Anabaptists, and divers types of heretical Christians. All found an unmolested, congenial meeting place in the colony. Undoubtedly there was in those days a greater admixture of different peoples—Germans, French, Swiss, Scotch, Moravians—in North Carolina than in any other colony. Preachers were scarce; so the people could worship as they pleased. It was a paradise for the Quakers, who were opposed to preachers on principle. This religious attitude was a corollary of the economic freedom and individual independence of the North Carolinian settlers. All three were a gift of geography.

"As for the Constitution of this Government," John Lawson wrote, back in the second decade of the eighteenth century, "it is so mild and easy, in respect to the Properties and Liberties of a Subject, that without rehearsing the Particulars, I say once and for all, it is the mildest and best established Government in the World, and the Place where any Man may peaceably enjoy his own without being invaded by another. Rank and superiority ever giving Place to Justice and Equity, which is the Golden Rule that every Government ought to be built upon and regulated by." [1]

What Lawson wrote was true. It was not true because North Carolinians were different in background or tradition from the settlers in other colonies, as many historians have asserted—notably John Fiske, who insisted that they were a biologically inferior group, lawless, shiftless, and lacking in the virtues and values of civilization.[2] It was the different form of economic life necessitated by telluric factors that caused the dissimilarity.

The people of both North Carolina and South Carolina constituted what many have called the backwash of Virginia. In the last analysis, however, the majority of the people who founded all three colonies were not widely unlike in social lineage or economic status. In Oglethorpe's own words, "it is most certain that the... [natives?] of Carolina in our Days have exactly answer'd in all respects the Descriptions we have of the Inhabitants of Virginia when we first got footing there in the Beginning of the last Century." [3] The fact is that after Bacon's group lost power in Virginia many of the best of the rebellious elements retreated into North Carolina. The number of English aristocrats who actually settled and stayed in South Carolina was even fewer than in Virginia, and there, as we have seen, the number was very small. What in time made the settlers in these colonies unlike in divers ways was conditions of environment, variations of economic life, not differences of social or biological heritage.

North Carolinians were more contemptuous of authority than other colonists because the nature of their land inspired that attitude. Scattered as they were, it was difficult for any central government to discipline or control them. They could defy the government, refuse to pay taxes, and even revolt with relative impunity. They were "rarely guilty of making any court to their governors," William Byrd writes, "but treat them with all the excesses of freedom and familiarity. They are of the opinion their rulers would be apt to grow insolent if they grew rich, and for that reason take care to keep them poorer." [4]

Although the Church of England had been foisted upon the colony as the official church, the people opposed paying any taxes toward its support. Consequently it was not until 1732 that a regular Church of England minister settled in the colony.[5] It was with considerable dismay that George Fox, who ventured into Albemarle in 1672, confessed that he could find no places of worship in the land. Others who explored the territory discovered the same thing. "I believe this is the only metropolis in the Christian or Mohametan world," William Byrd wrote, "where there is neither church, chapel, mosque, synagogue, or any other place of public worship of any sect or religion whatsoever." [6]

North Carolina in those days was the only colony in which complete religious freedom existed. Even Rhode Island, from which the Familists had been routed, did not offer such extremity of toleration. Maryland, later to be known as the "free state," never proffered such freedom to its inhabitants in colonial days.

Had North Carolina been a centralized instead of a decentralized colony, had its topography encouraged a plantation instead of a small-farm economy, its early freedom and religious toleration would never have been achieved. It represented the best and at the same time the worst in seventeenth-century democracy—the best in the sense of individual independence, the worst in the sense of social retardation and stagnation.

Such freedom did not exist at that time in South Carolina, where the Church of England hierophants made a determined and vigorous attempt to dictate the religious beliefs of the colony. It was possible for them to make that attempt only because the colony was a centripetal entity. Charleston was its hub, and the villages, towns, and plantations which made up the rest of the colony were but spokes radiating from it. Under such circumstances it is not difficult for ecclesiastics to control a community. Fortunately, however, South Carolina was settled by so many foreign elements—French Huguenots, Irish Protestants, German Lutherans, as well as English Dissenters and Established Churchmen—that no single denomination could acquire religious supremacy. Shortly after the beginning of the eighteenth century toleration ensued.

### CHARLESTON: THE CULTURAL MECCA OF THE SOUTH

South Carolina was a most religious community as compared with North Carolina. The indifference to churches and clergymen that prevailed in North Carolina had no parallel in the sister state. In South Carolina people lived closer together; even the plantations found their selling and buying center in one place—Charleston. In time there grew up a plantation aristocracy which invested a considerable part of its surplus wealth in the cultivation and expansion of the city. The original plantation owners in South Carolina were in the main as uneducated and unrefined as the small farmers in North Carolina, but as their wealth accumulated they found that they could afford to send their sons and daughters to study in the colleges and universities in England and sometimes on the Continent. It was these later generations that made Charleston the great cultural Mecca of the South.

The small farmers in North Carolina were unable to derive enough from their limited possessions to create a landed aristocracy or send their children to Europe for their education. They remained on the whole the same untutored lower middle-class people they had been from the start. Their economy did not encourage the accumulation of vast wealth, the creation of cities, or the acquisition of culture. This was not due to the fact that they dawdled away their lives, as William Byrd declared, "through an aversion to labor," [7] but to the circumscription of their territory and the constrictions of their economy.

## LOCKE'S CONSTITUTIONS

Both Carolinas started out with the same Constitution, which was drawn up in 1669 by John Locke, then secretary to Lord Ashley. Locke at that time had not yet developed those revolutionary concepts of government for which later he was to win international renown. Nevertheless, he was even then far more liberal than most of his contemporaries. He was hemmed in on all sides by a regime that was quick to take offense at the most microscopical violation of its authority. There was enough liberalism alive still in the Restoration England of that day, however, for him to be able to insert a number of clauses in the Carolina Constitutions—known as The Fundamental Constitutions of Carolina—that were most advanced and progressive.

The first of those clauses was Number 97, which guaranteed religious freedom to everyone, even to slaves. Locke went so far as to declare that any violation of religious liberty was tantamount to an "Offense to Almighty God." Dissenters, Quakers, Jews, were all allowed to worship as they pleased. In fact, Locke wrote, "any seven or more Persons agreeing to any religion shall constitute a Church or Profession, to which they shall give some name to distinguish it from others."[8] Locke's hope, to be sure, was that all dissident religious sects would be so impressed by this evidence of latitudinarianism that they would be "won over to embrace and unfeignedly receive the Truth," which meant the *truth* of the Established Church, regnant in England at the time he drafted his constitutions. The only limitations imposed upon the populace were that agreement should be unanimous as follows: (1) "There is a God; (2) That God is publickly to be worshipped; (3) That it is lawful and the Duty of every man being thereunto called by those that Govern to bear witness to the truth."[9] In addition, no one was permitted to "disturb or molest any religious assembly." Furthermore, Locke added, in Clause 107, "it shall be lawful for slaves as well as others to enter themselves and be of what Church or Profession any of them shall think best, and thereof be as fully members as any Freeman." This proviso alone endowed the Constitutions with lasting significance.

The next clause that represented an important advance at the time was the one guaranteeing trial by jury. "Each jury," Clause 69 stated, "shall consist of twelve men and it shall not be necessary they should all agree, but the verdict shall be according to the Consent of the Majority." In the light of the royal acts of the time, and the treatment of prisoners in England as well as on the Continent, this provision was extremely progressive. It protected the individual from the arbitrary power of authority. Neither king, noble, nor governor could imprison an individual without trial. The jury, not the monarch or any other person in power, was to judge his case.

There were other valuable clauses, such as those providing for the registration of marriages, childbirths, and deaths, and for the recording of biennial parliaments, land titles, and taxes. Altogether the Constitutions were most carefully prepared documents, in which few details of organization or administration were neglected.

### OPPOSITION TO DEMOCRACY

Other items, however, were far from advanced. In the first place, Locke drafted the Constitutions so that the government of the Carolinas would "be made most agreeable to the Monarchy" and in order that it could avoid "erecting a numerous Democracy." He insisted, it is true, upon the existence of a parliament "consisting of the Landgraves and one freeholder out of every precinct, chosen by the freeholders. They shall sit all together in one room and have, every member, one vote." This parliament, however, was far from a popular assembly. Only freeholders and persons owning five hundred acres of land could vote. The Landgraves, for example, were to constitute "the hereditary Nobility of the Province" (Clause 9), and each Landgrave was not only to be a member of Parliament but also to have "four Baronies and each Cassique two Baronies hereditarily and unalterably annexed to and settled upon the said Dignity." It is important to point out, however, that white slaves, once they had worked out their term of service, were to possess the right of suffrage after they had occupied the grants of land promised them by the proprietors. Members of Parliament, on the other hand, could be chosen only from those "who hath less than five hundred Acres of Freehold within the Precinct for which he is chosen" (Clause 72). This provision was to protect the power of the property owners and save the land from the horrors of democracy, which then was a word as terrifying as communism is to the property owners of today. More than that, Locke provided, with callous unconcern for the populace, that "all wrecks, mines, minerals, quarries of gems, and precious stones, with Pearl-fishing, whale-fishing and half of all Ambergreece by whomsoever found shall wholly belong to the Lords Proprietors" (Clause 114).

Locke's Constitutions were, in other words, a mixture of the old and the new, the past and the present; they espoused neither, but catered to both in theory as well as practice. Locke defended the concept of "hereditary Nobility" on the one hand and, on the other, advocated the electoral and judicial reforms proposed by the middle classes. He clung to Monarchy as a guiding concept, but insisted that it should be restricted instead of absolute. In brief, Locke was a middle-of-the-road man, whose heart was with the future but whose head knew better than to disregard or dismiss the present or the past. Even later, in his *Two Treatises of Government*, in which he justified the American Revolution, he was careful not to challenge the economic principles of capitalist society. He believed in the defense of life, liberty, and property. In fact, in places he thrust his main emphasis upon property: "Man hath by nature a power . . . to preserve his property—that is, his life, liberty, and estate." [10] It was Rousseau, in the next century, who endowed Locke's doctrine with revolutionary intensity and challenge, and converted it into a forthright attack upon property.

Nevertheless, it must not be forgotten that Locke gave lifeblood to American revolutionary doctrine and infused it with the spirit that was later to find voice in the Declaration of Independence.* Before the American Revolution, Locke's words that no government must "raise taxes on the property of the people without the consent of the people given by themselves or their deputies" had inspired

* There are several passages in his *Letter Concerning Toleration* which undoubtedly influenced Jefferson when he wrote the Declaration of Independence. Locke had declared earlier that "the people [are] more disposed to suffer than right themselves by resistance," and then added, "but if a long train of abuses, prevarications and ordinances all pointing the same way make the design visible to the people . . . it is not to be wondered that they should then rise themselves and endeavor to put the rule into the hands which may secure to them the ends for which government was first erected." [11]

the "No Taxation without Representation" cry of the rebellious colonies.

In the Carolinas, Locke's Constitutions had awakened no such response, because they belonged to a different epoch. Locke himself at that time had not matured as a political philosopher; besides, he was handicapped as a secretary to Ashley and could introduce into the Constitutions only those clauses which he was sure would escape the censure of his superiors. As it was, the Constitutions survived for a very short period. They were revised a number of times; five editions appeared, the last in 1698, before they finally were discarded.

What remained of them was the liberal clauses on toleration, trial by jury, and parliamentary privilege, which ultimately became part of the tradition of the nation.

### LOCKE'S HEREDITARY NOBILITY

Locke's "hereditary nobility" had little appeal in North Carolina, where the governor and council were elected by the colony itself and where "the Governour [was] to rule but three years, and then learn to obey."[12] Even during that period the governor possessed no right to levy taxes or modify or repeal laws except with the consent of the Assembly.* North Carolinians were determined that the people and not the king or proprietors were to rule. From the time when the first Virginians emigrated to the Albemarle, as early as 1650,† and began what later was to become known as North Carolina, a spirit of independence prevailed in the colony. This territory, originally part of the Virginia grant of 1606—once called "New Brittaine" by Bland, who was one of the first to explore it, and often referred to also as Florida in those days—was granted to eight English courtiers by Charles II shortly after his restoration as King of England. Robert Heath, to whom the territory had first

* In a letter written to "The Right Honourable the Lords of Trade & Plantation, Governor Burrington" stated that "the inhabitants of North Carolina . . . always behaved insolently to their Governours, some they have imprisoned, drove others out of the Country, at other times sett up two or three supported by Men under Arms, all Governours that ever were in this Province lived in fear of the People (except myself) and Dreaded their Assemblys.

"The People are neither to be cajoled or outwitted, whenever a Governour attempts to effect anything by these means, he will loose his Labour and show his Ignorance."[13]

† Ashley River, lower Carolina, was not settled until April, 1670.[14]

been granted, found himself robbed of his possession. But these English courtiers did not succeed very well in making over the colony in the image of their aspirations. Their memory is best preserved in the names of counties, towns, rivers, and sounds such as Albemarle, Ashley, Carteret, Berkeley, Clarendon.

### THE LAND OF MILK AND HONEY

What the courtiers did succeed in doing was to populate the territory by offering all kinds of promises to prospective settlers. Pamphlets were published, not at all dissimilar to the publicity material issued today, in an attempt to attract people to the colony. Robert Horne, in one of the most arresting of such publications, described the "full and free Liberty of Conscience granted to all," the "freedom from Custom . . . for 7 years" that "Every Free-man and Free woman that transport themselves and Servants by the 25 of March next, being 1667, shall have for himself, Wife, Children and Men-servants, for each 100 Acres of Land for Him and his Heirs for ever, and for every Woman-servant and Slave 50 Acres, paying at most ½ d. per acre per annum."[15] In a later passage, Horne added this interesting item: "If any Maid or single Woman have a desire to go over, they will think themselves in the Golden Age, when Men paid a Dowry for their Wives; for if they but be Civil, and under 50 years of Age, some honest Man or other will purchase them for their Wives." Other writers stressed the superior climate of "New Brittaine" (Carolina), pointing out that it was more temperate than "that the English now inhabite," "that tobacco there grows larger and more in quantity," and that tobacco "Pipes have beene seene among these Indians tipt with silver, and they weare Copper Plates about their necks: They have two Crops of Indian Corne Yearley, whereas Virginia hath but one."[16] Samuel Wilson declared that an "Ox is raised at almost as little expense in Carolina, as a Hen is in England . . . and it hath by experience been found that Beef will take salt at Ashly-River any Month in the Year, and save very well," "that Ewes have most commonly two or three Lambs at a time," and that "Hogs increase in Carolina abundantly."[17] Another inducement which was most attractive was the act prohibiting the suing of any citizen of North Carolina for five years, and also exempting all settlers from paying any tax levies or customs duties for one year after their arrival.[18] South Carolina not only agreed with its sister state in that provision, but in addition passed an act suspending foreign debts.[19]

More important than all the above provisions were those guaranteeing men servants at the expiration of their service a grant of "100 Acres of land and his heirs for ever," each paying only a pittance per acre; the result was that more indentured servants succeeded in establishing themselves as free men and successful property owners in the Carolinas than in most of the other colonies. "Land is not wanting for men in Carolina," Governor Burrington wrote, "but men for land." In time the attractions of the new territory brought men to the land in encouraging abundance.

Governor Burrington, despite the attacks upon him, was conspicuous for laying out roads and constructing bridges throughout the territory. He was instructed to invite merchants to the colony to increase trade and to begin traffic with the Royal African Company for slaves. He and those who followed him were so successful that within a relatively short time the number of white and black slaves in North Carolina became so prodigious as to outnumber the free population.[20]

This brings us to a consideration which it would be unfair to avoid. We have spoken much about the North Carolinian belief in democracy and independence, and yet it would be incorrect to assume that this meant democracy and independence for all; it definitely did not. It meant democracy and independence for freemen, as they were then called, for holders of property, but not for indentured servants or black slaves. Indentured servants were very important in North Carolinian economic life. Some of them, notably Andrew Johnson, succeeded in becoming important figures in the colony and nation afterwards. The majority of them, however, suffered from the same handicaps, punishments, and oppression that their fellow victims underwent in other colonies. When a runaway indentured servant was caught in North Carolina, an iron collar was placed about his neck, and ofttimes he was branded in characteristic and decisive New England style.[21] North Carolinian democracy extended, in short, to those who were part of it, the freemen of the community, and there it stopped. The less successful sections of it represented the debased coin of the new political currency.

## JOHN CULPEPER'S REVOLT

In South Carolina, as we have seen, the divisions between people and classes were even more marked than in North Carolina, and it is not surprising, therefore, that the first of the rebellions against established authority should occur in that colony. The man who led the first rebellion was John Culpeper,* who had come to South Carolina from the Barbados in 1671.[22] He was the Surveyor-General of South Carolina, and in that capacity mapped out the city of Charleston. Unfortunately Culpeper had to flee from South Carolina before his architectural plans could be executed. In the confusion his work was "whollie miscarried and lost." [23] He came over into Carolina, according to one report, with Governor Sayle, and from that time on became active in state affairs.[24]

There can be no question that in his struggle to defend the poor against the rich he was the Nathaniel Bacon of the Carolinas. All his enemies, who spared no epithets of denunciation when they referred to him, agreed that his main purpose was "to cause the poor to plunder the rich." [25] The first rebellion he encouraged, which he carried on in co-operation with O'Sullivan, was in South Carolina, then still known as the Ashley River settlement, but there he was defeated and had to flee from the colony in order to escape being hanged.† He retreated to North Carolina, where he led a successful revolt and managed, with his followers, to stay in power for two years.

Without doubt the success of Bacon's Rebellion in Virginia inspired Culpeper with a belief that a rebellion could triumph in North Carolina. Hating the parties in power with no less vigor than Bacon did those in Virginia, Culpeper bided his time until the moment arrived when he could deliver a death blow to the regime. In the meanwhile, he propagandized against the injustices and intolerances of Miller, the president of the Council, and its members, and it was not long before the populace was won to his side. Eastchurch, the governor, had gone to England to discuss ways and means of improving the economic affairs of the colony, and had allowed Miller to function in his capacity until he returned. Miller, about as diplomatic as a

* His name is spelled Culpepper, also, but the Culpeper form is more familiar.

† One report has it that he came from New England, where he was also mixed up in rebellious activities.[26]

German warlord, taxed the people harshly, threatened to raise the quitrents, and made life painfully uncertain and miserable for most of the colonists. When a New England trader, Gillam, arrived with a cargo of various clothes and foodstuffs, he was arrested by Miller and allowed his freedom only when he had paid a bill amounting to one thousand pounds. Gillam immediately declared he would leave the colony without selling it a single thing. Miller continued to denounce him as a smuggler and was eager to drive him from the colony without delay. The people of the colony, however, felt differently about the matter. They wanted the things which Gillam had brought, and the fact that the man was a smuggler made them want them even more, because they knew they could get them without having to pay the exorbitant taxes that would be imposed upon them by the government.

### CULPEPER TAKES THE LEAD

At that point the people took up arms against the government, and, led by Culpeper, started a revolt which resulted in the imprisonment of Miller and six members of the Council. They also seized "all the writings belonging to ye Prop. and all the tobacco and writings belonging to ye King's Customes, employing ye King's Tobacco towards ye charge of maintaining and supporting their unlawful actions." [27] Culpeper then set up a government of the people, in which he assumed the office of Collector of the Customs. Culpeper's enemies swear that he took this office in order to enrich himself at the expense of the populace, but there is no record or document that would confirm that conclusion.

The battle here was the same one that was constantly waged throughout early American history and that found its culmination in the American Revolution. It was the battle against royal or aristocratic authority in defense of democratic economic privilege on the part of the colonists. They wanted to make as much as they could from what they had, and did not want to see their hard-earned gains liquidated by internal taxes or external customs duties, or be forced to limit their enterprise in accordance with the demands of English economy. They were fundamentally interested in emancipating themselves from such burdens and conscriptions and were always willing to fight to attain that end. All that later became known as the struggle of democracy against autocracy, of the people against the king, sprang from this fundamental economic conflict. The concept of liberty, melodramatized so effectively in the eighteenth century by Patrick Henry in his cry "Give me liberty or give me death," burgeoned from the same soil.

It was about this struggle that American economic life revolved prior to the Revolutionary War. The white slaves, exploited though they were by the freemen, did not revolt, for they continuously entertained hope that they, too, would become freemen and property owners themselves. They all had, secreted in their souls, the lower middle-class aspirations of the individual farm owner or shopkeeper. The black slaves, as we have shown, revolted because they possessed no such hope, but their revolts were suppressed with appalling expedition.

John Culpeper, like Nathaniel Bacon, was not interested in the indentured servants or black slaves; he was interested in the freemen of the time, who had something to lose from the tyranny of the proprietors. It was those freemen who supported him in his revolt and made it possible for him to establish a tax-free government for a period of two years. Those men were made of the same stuff as the "minutemen" of Lexington who began the Revolutionary War a century later. They admired Culpeper and were willing to fight for him, because he believed in them and their demands. Culpeper established a government that was *their* government, "and according to their own Modell." [28] He set about getting goods for them as cheaply as possible, without taxes or duties to increase their price, and refused to allow the proprietors or any of their representatives to live upon the backs of the colonists. He ignored the English laws that forbade the populace from undertaking manufactures which existed in England. He was not terrified by the presence of smugglers who sold goods cheaper to the settlers than they could ever get them from England or Virginia, where duties were scarcely less exorbitant. He was interested, in a word, in making the colonists, and not the proprietors, rich.

### CULPEPER LEAVES FOR ENGLAND

When the former Governor Eastchurch attempted to return to the colony the next year, the people kept him out by force of arms.

They preferred the Culpeper regime. Eastchurch made a valiant effort to get the Governor of Virginia to assist him, but died before he could make an attack upon the colony. The situation created by the threat of attack made the colonists believe that the best policy would be for Culpeper to go to England and try to persuade the king to accept the extant government. Culpeper set out for the Old Country but, once he landed there, discovered that Miller, who had escaped from his confinement, had already prejudiced the authorities against the insurgent government. Culpeper made a bold defense of the revolt, explained its purpose, attacked Miller for what he had done to tax and oppress the people, pointing out that the latter had refused to allow the populace to elect a free assembly, had fined and imprisoned most arbitrarily some of the best men in the territory, and had cheated the colony of 130,000 pounds weight of tobacco.* Furthermore, he gave assurance that the affairs of the colony in the future would be managed in such a way as to effect the happiest relations between the two countries. The lords-proprietors listened to Culpeper patiently and tacitly approved of his propositions, but shortly afterward he was arrested on board the vessel that was carrying him back to North Carolina. He was indicted for high treason, and in the case which followed, Lord Shaftesbury, one of the great English liberals of the time, came out in defense of him and, after most disputatious sessions, succeeded in gaining his acquittal.

### SETH SOTHEL'S STRUGGLES FOR POPULAR CONTROL

After Culpeper's acquittal, the proprietors decided they had to have a governor in North Carolina upon whom they could depend not only to preserve law and order but also to gain the support of the populace. Their choice proved to be, from their point of view, an exceedingly mischievous one. Seth Sothel, whom they chose because he had just bought Lord Clarendon's eighth of the colony, turned out to be a stormy petrel, whose attitude toward their property was far from reverent. His trip over to the colony was as tempestuous as his later career proved. He was captured by the pirates of Argier, and it was only after devious negotiations, which extended over three years, that it was arranged for him to be exchanged "for one

* The fact that Miller, after being given another post, finally spent his last years in jail, is ample evidence of the man's corruptibility.[29]

Hadgamore, late Commander of the Tiger, or Argier, or one Buffilo Ball."[30] Not long after his arrival he stirred up the hostility of a large part of the colony, was arrested and threatened with deportation to England, but succeeded in persuading the settlers to give him a trial before the Assembly. The Assembly, dominated by his enemies, demanded his resignation from the gubernatorial office and insisted that he leave the colony within a year. Sothel had come with a certificate of authority, dated September 1681, stating that he was "one of the true and absolute Props. of the Province of Carolina," with the command that everyone was "to obey him as such if there be no elder Prop. than himself." His expulsion resulted from connivances on the part of his adversaries.

## SOTHEL RETREATS TO SOUTH CAROLINA

But Sothel was not an easily defeated man. He left North Carolina, went to South Carolina, and there managed to become governor and maintain power for a couple of years. He achieved the governorship by arousing the populace to fight against the injustices of the regime of Governor Colleton, whom Sothel replaced. Colleton, like Miller in North Carolina, was an inconsiderate and unwise man. He was unconcerned with the populace and insensitive to its discontent and misery. He tried to coerce the people to pay up all their arrears in quitrents, imposed severe taxes, finally summoned the militia, and declared martial law in the colony.[31] This gesture inspired such hostility on all sides that, when the Assembly met, it removed James Colleton from office and banished him from the land. It was at this time that Seth Sothel, who had led the opposition against Colleton, was chosen governor of the colony. Sothel remained a popular governor for a year, but later was attacked by his enemies for various crimes of an extortionate nature, and it was urged that he be shipped back to England. He left the colony, however, not at the command of the people, but at that of the proprietors, because they feared that he was undermining their authority as well as threatening that of the king.[32]

## SOTHEL'S INTEREST IN POPULAR LEGISLATION

In the main, the people who attacked Sothel while he was alive, and who wrote about him after his death, were reactionaries who were totally out of sympathy with his theory of government. Sothel, like Culpeper, was interested in extending popular control, in amplifying the power of the people. The liberality of the laws he was instrumental in having enacted unequivocally testified to his progressivism.[33] He was continuously concerned with fulfilling the aims and desires of the people. His concept of the people was far less limited than that of most governors of his day. He did not feel that the English represented all the people. He gave equal rights to the French and Swiss and other non-English groups, encouraging them to feel that they were as much a part of the colony as the English; he admitted them as citizens, and endowed them with the same rights as every English-born person. In addition he even passed an act favorable to the Negro slaves. This act provided for the protection and comfort of the slaves and for harsh punishment for anyone who killed a slave.

After the proprietors, unsympathetic with his advanced ideas, robbed him of his office, he retreated to his estate in North Carolina, where he died several years later.[34]

Few colonies suffered as much conflict and turmoil as the Carolinas, and it was only after the proprietors surrendered the colony to the Crown in 1729 that anything resembling order was established in the land. The king granted £5,000 to each of the proprietors, and the Council of North Carolina addressed a letter to the king declaring that it was "with the greatest Pleasure we receive the Notice of your Majesty's having taken this Government under Your Immediate direction."

Later years, however, were to prove that the king could be as unwise, as unjust, and as oppressive as the proprietors, and that there was no satisfactory solution to the problem but complete severance of all dependence upon the mother country.

### RICE: THE NEW KING

It was in 1693, about which time the two sister colonies began to be known as North and South Carolina, that rice, which soon was to become the most staple commodity of the state, was first planted in North Carolina. A captain of a ship that had recently left Madagascar gave the governor some rice as a present and described in vivid detail what an important food it was in Eastern countries. This rice was planted and began to grow, and after several years the colonists learned how to beat and clean it so that it became an extraordinarily valuable and salable commodity. Thus North Carolina, which began as the third tobacco colony, became a rice-producing territory. But South Carolina followed suit, and it was not long before rice became the main staple of both colonies. The tobacco market being overcrowded by Maryland and Virginia, both of which produced tobacco in appalling superfluity, the inhabitants of the two Carolinas naturally became elated at the prospect of controlling a market with which no other colony could compete. For over a century the citizens of both colonies rhapsodized about the virtues of rice in almost the same way that contemporary publicity and advertising men do about the products they are trying to sell. "In every point of view," one writer declared, "it is of more value than mines of gold and silver." [35] Rice was recommended as being the most digestible of all foods, as the only food which toothless septuagenarians could imbibe with impunity, and an ideal food for dyspeptics and gastritic hypochondriacs. Others declared it was better than bread and in every way an excellent substitute for it. Besides, rice, unlike flour, was transportable to any part of the world without injury to its substance. As one observer, Mr. S. G. Stoney, wittily declared, "it was rice and not righteousness that brought respectability to Charleston." Charleston became the center of the rice industry.

There can be little doubt that rice has been one of the main staples of the race since its dawn. In China rice and agriculture are the same, and in many languages rice stands for the same word as food.[36] The Carolinians and later the Georgians were the first peoples in the new world to cultivate rice as a staple commodity. In time South Carolina became the leader in its production, Georgia achieved second place, and North Carolina third. The warmer climate, better rivers, and superior swamp land made South Carolina and Georgia forge ahead of North Carolina.

In time more rice was being produced "than we had ships to transport," Governor Sothel reported,[37] and rice soon became the accepted form of money just as tobacco was in Virginia. People dealt in rice, thought in terms of rice, used rice for marital as well as commercial transactions, and paid clergymen, officials, laborers, and servants with it.

### INDIGO: THE NEW DREAM

In the middle of the eighteenth century, however, a new product arose which for a time threatened to supplant rice as the main staple of the deeper South. That product was indigo. Indigo was needed as a clothing dye in a Europe which lamented the monotony of its cloths. From India blue vegetable dyes had been procured, but at an excessive cost. Indigo could dye many stuffs blue: cloths of divers varieties, silks and other stuffs. Besides, indigo could be shipped at a cost incalculably less than that for rice.[38] So profitable did indigo production become that, at the time of the Revolutionary War, nine hundred pounds of indigo were exported from the Carolinas.[39] In addition, indigo could be raised more cheaply than rice. It took thirty slaves, attended by an overseer, to produce a good crop of rice, whereas "an Acre of good Land may produce about Eighty Pounds weight of good Indigo; and one slave may manage two Acres and upwards, and raise provisions besides, and have all the Winter Months to saw Lumber and be otherwise employed." [40]

In the cultivation of both rice and indigo, black slaves were ruthlessly exploited. In South Carolina, for instance, the planters worked the Negroes almost to death, and treated them with unmitigated cruelty—which accounts in part for the fact that South Carolinian Negroes were so constantly rebellious, and that South Carolina always kept a large militia ready to suppress any suggestion of resistance on the part of the blacks. For a long time, Negro labor in the rice fields was entirely manual. It was such fiercely exhausting work that it ofttimes resulted in premature death on the part of the men, and sterility on the part of the women.[41]

Rice and indigo continued to be the main products of the Carolinas, and also of Georgia, until the Revolutionary War. After the War, however, rice and indigo, as well as tobacco, began to lose their value as profitable industries. England had crippled the American indigo market by purchasing most of its indigo from India. Rice production became less profitable, too, as the narrowness of the market became definitely recognizable. Tobacco long before had ceased to be the magic plant, and overproduction had caused a sharp decline in its value.

It was at this time that black slavery began to lose its appeal in the South and antislavery societies were organized. With the decline of the rice, indigo, and tobacco industries, Negro slaves were no longer a great necessity.

If it had not been for Whitney's invention of the cotton gin in 1794, there would never have been a Civil War in this country. Whitney's invention revolutionized Southern industry, made cotton the South's main crop, and revived slavery as a profitable institution. From that time on, slavery was defended by Southerners as the *sine qua non* of their economic life, and when put to the test, they were willing to fight to preserve it.

Before Whitney's invention, the manufacture of cotton was largely domestic.[42] Planters, however, had been raising it for generations, and as early as the beginning of the eighteenth century North Carolina raised enough to provide "one-fifth of the [colonial] population with clothing." [43] Many South Carolinians at that time were devoting large sections of their plantations to its production.

After the invention of the cotton gin, however, cotton became as popular a product in the South as rice in China.

### PRIBER'S UTOPIA

North Carolina and South Carolina were unlike the Northern colonies in that they had no groups of a communal variety living among them. They were settled almost exclusively by colonists with an individualistic psychology. The only deviation from that psychology was found in a man named Priber, who succeeded in doing more to terrify the South Carolinians than any other individual of his time. Although Priber cannot be called "the first American communist," as one essayist described him,[44] he can certainly be credited as the first American communist in the deeper South. As we have already observed, communist Labadists had settled in Maryland a good while before. Priber, however, came over to the new world not as a member of a group but as an independent individual. "A little ugly Man, (but) a very extraordinary Kind of Creature," [45] he impressed people by his persuasive personality and acute mind rather than his appearance. He was an expert linguist, speaking over five languages, and he was a most advanced thinker. In France he developed his social philosophy which, in many respects, anticipated that of Rousseau. He not only believed in a communist society, and in the organization of communist colonies wherever they could be established, but also was in favor of communal marriages (as later the Oneida group was to advocate and practice). Though generally regarded as a German Jesuit, he was said to be definitely antagonistic to all religions.[46] "He proposed to them a new System, or Plan of Government," Ludovick Grant, an Indian trader, declared, "that all things should be common amongst them, that even their wives should be so, and that the Children should be looked upon as the Children of the Public and taken care of as such and not by their natural parents." [47] He was driven out of France by the authorities, fled to England, and not much later emigrated to South Carolina. Like Culpeper and Sothel, he found life in Charleston (then Charles Town) intolerable. The South Carolinians were unreceptive to his ideas, scorned him as an eccentric, and finally forced him to leave the city.

### PRIBER JOINS THE INDIANS

After his expulsion from Charleston, the great adventure in his life began. He headed straightway for the Indians, and within a relatively short period became one of them. Since most of the Indians had lived in communal ways for centuries, he had little difficulty in converting them to his philosophy. Unlike most white men who went to live among the Indians, Priber forsook his colonial dress and attired himself like the other natives. When he was captured later, he was attired in a "deerskin jacket, a flap before and behind his privates, with morgissons, or deerskin pumps, or sandals, which were laced in the Indian manner, on his feet and ankles." [48]

The Cherokees, with whom Priber settled, were fascinated by his conception of an Indian utopia, in which all the adjacent Indian tribes would combine into a vast federation, with the capital at Great Tellico, in Tennessee.[49] Priber was a precursor of Tecumseh in this vision.

Naturally, the English considered Priber a dangerous enemy. Anyone striving to band the natives together in any such federation was an adversary who had to be destroyed. A number of attempts were made to capture him, but for a long time they went without success. For to begin with, this man who had preached, according to Antoine Bonnefoy, "that each should contribute to the good of society as he could," was adopted as a member of the tribe, and any attempt to capture him, therefore, became a tribal and not an individual matter. When Ludovick Grant was sent to the Cherokees to investigate his activities, and to seize him if possible and return him to Charleston, he discovered that Priber was uncapturable. Priber had so inoculated the Indians with the idea that they should never surrender their lands, never capitulate to the Europeans, that Grant had a hard time of it while he was with the tribe. In fact, it was at this time that the Indians wrote a most defiant letter to the South Carolinian government defending their rights and warning the colonists not to violate them. The letter, incidentally, was signed by Priber as prime minister. Grant, upon later instructions, made even more valiant attempts to capture the man, but as he himself wrote, "found that he was well apprized of my design, and laughed at me, desiring me to try in so insolent a manner that I could hardly bear with it." [50] After Grant's failure several other persons were sent in an endeavor "to decoy and draw him out of Town, but all in vain."

## THE ENGLISH CAPTURE PRIBER

One of the difficulties that all these people encountered was to single out Priber from the rest of the Indians. He ate, drank, and slept with them as one of their tribe, painted himself as they did, wore the same clothes, and in general was indistinguishable from the rest of the tribe.[51] The book he wrote, over which he gloried in the face of his enemies, was lost, and the city of the west, of which he dreamed, was never built. Accused by the English of plotting with the French,* he really plotted with no one but the Indians themselves, and then but to educate them in a higher way of life and to emancipate them from their white oppressors. It is doubtful whether he would ever have been captured had it not been for the perfidy of the Creeks, who turned him over to the English. The Creeks, to be sure, were less acquainted with his doctrines than the Cherokees, and it was not extremely difficult to bribe them into such treachery.

* Such accusations were numerous. The English considered anyone who sided with the Indians as in the pay of French interests, especially if the Indians gave them any trouble or balked at their propositions.[52]

### A UTOPIAN REVOLUTIONARY

Priber was as revolutionary a figure in the new world as Rousseau later proved to be in the old. He was one of the utopian socialists, as much deserving of the name as Saint-Simon, Pierre La Roux, and Fourier. It is by no means improbable that had his book on the theme been saved, we should find in it today many of the same arguments and sentiments that made those other social dreamers famous. His *city of the sun* was never erected upon the Cusawatee, but neither was that of Campanello ever given a brick-and-mortar foundation. At least Priber brought into being what no other socialist at that time had ever achieved: a society that aspired toward socialist ideals, even though it did not attain all of them. He managed to have a Cherokee chief crowned as king of the "Cherokee Confederacy," had himself appointed as prime minister or royal secretary, and at Kashita set about realizing his communist dream.[53] The place, he decided, was to be called "Paradice."

Unlike most men, Priber maintained a stoical attitude even in defeat and imprisonment, and confounded his enemies by his philosophic imperturbability. Surrendered into English hands by the Creeks, he was put into jail, and there he died. The Cherokees were highly aroused by his capture, but were unable to achieve his release. In jail in Frederica, Georgia, Priber was visited by many of the colonists and, without exception, he impressed them all as a most exceptional and distinguished man. He ate little, thought a great deal, and was never in despair at his lot. "It is folly," he declared, "to repine at one's lot in life; my mind soars above misfortune; in this cell I can enjoy more real happiness than it is possible to do in the busy scenes of life. Reflecting upon past events, digesting former studies, keep me fully employed, whilst health and abundant spirits allow me no anxious, no uneasy moments; I suffer, though a friend to the natural rights of mankind—though an enemy to tyranny, usurpation, and oppression—and what is more, I can forgive and pray for those that injure me; I am a Christian and Christian principles always promote internal felicity." *

* There seems to be some doubt about Priber's religious attitude. In the letter from Frederica, Georgia, the statement was definitely made that Priber was opposed to all religions, particularly the Protestant. From the above quotation, however, taken from the *Annual Register*,[54] it would appear that he still adhered to certain Christian principles.

So even in imprisonment and later at his death, Priber did not break down, did not surrender his principles, did not deny his dream. Like Thomas Paine in later years, he clung to what he believed even when the rest of mankind was against him, and was willing to die in full faith that one day the world would do justice to him and to his vision.

## CHAPTER XIV

# Georgia: The Charity Colony

*My brother and I took boat and passing by Savannah, went up to pay our first visit in America to the poor Heathens.*

—JOHN WESLEY

*This confirms me in the opinion I have entertained for a long time, that Georgia never can or will be a flourishing province without Negroes are allowed.*

·GEORGE WHITEFIELD

GEORGIA was the only colony founded in the new world in the name of charity. James Oglethorpe, an ex-army officer, conceived the idea of freeing the English jails of the insolvent debtors that overcrowded them and converting the prisoners into colonists, and thus saving them from the deteriorating influence of prison life and, at the same time, assisting in providing in the colonies a military outpost against the Spaniards, who were threatening to engulf the Carolinian territory. The place to which Oglethorpe planned despatching these prisoners was to be called Georgia, in honor of King George II. One of his aims was to make it a buffer colony for South Carolina, protecting the older colony from Indians as well as Spaniards.

Although Oglethorpe actually succeeded in his plan and did settle Georgia with a small army of debtors, only a third of them remained in the colony. Not over twenty-five hundred people came over as *charity colonists.*[1] Ironically enough, as long as the experiment with these debtors continued, the colony failed to thrive, and it was only later, when all vestiges of Oglethorpe's experiment had been abandoned, that Georgia became a prosperous colony.

From its very inception, Georgia was completely controlled by the trustees, possessing no popular assembly or legislature or any other of the democratic privileges of the more advanced colonies. The fact that Georgia remained an unprogressive colony for so many years was accounted by many as due to the denial of those liberties that were granted in other colonies.[2] Military drill was made part of the daily procedure, and the whole colony was organized upon a martial basis. Since such a large number of the colonists were ex-prisoners, Oglethorpe insisted upon the prohibition of intoxicating liquors and the exclusion of black slaves. The members of the corporation were prevented from "holding any office of profit, or receiving any salary, fees, perquisite or profit whatsoever."

### OPPOSITION TO SLAVERY

The opposition to slavery, however, was not precisely humanitarian. Since most of the colonists were ex-jailbirds, they would have no money with which to buy slaves, and then, too, it was thought that the presence of slaves might incline the settlers to indolence. Besides, the staples that were to be cultivated in Georgia, particularly silk, made slavery additionally inexpedient. Again, black slaves could not be used as soldiers, and one of the important objectives of the colony, as we have seen, was to provide a good military defense against all adversaries. Finally, Oglethorpe himself was not antagonistic to slavery on principle. He owned a plantation in South Carolina upon which black slaves worked, and he was also connected with the Royal African Company, which made its main profits from the slave trade.

### A FUTURE EDEN

Unlike the poor people who settled in the earlier colonies and who had to "indenture" themselves for a span of years in order to pay for their transportation, the prospective Georgians were "carried gratis to a Land of Liberty and Plenty, where they immediately [found] themselves in Possession of a competent Estate."[3] In "Such an Air and Soil [which] can only be describ'd by a Poetical Pen," as Oglethorpe depicted Georgia, men could have land "for nothing; and that land is so fertile that . . . they receive a hundred fold increase for taking very little Pains."[4] In short, their passage to this "future Eden" was paid for, bestowed upon them as a gift, and all they had to do, aside from surrendering their claim to democratic privileges, was to sign papers and be shipped to this "most delightful country in the universe."[5]

Numerous pamphlets were published exalting the virtues of this new colony; one called it a "paradise, with all her virgin beauties," and others made it into a land of incomparable charm and magnificence. The Georgians "have the finest Land on all the Continent," declared one writer, and added that "it will not be long before their silk and wine manufactures will be brought both to perfection." [6] Practically every hyperbole of description was resorted to in the publicity "build-up" of the colony.

Beneath all this propaganda and underlying all Oglethorpe's philanthropy were transparent political and economic motivations. Georgian settlers were to be carried over free of transportation charges, primarily because they were to be soldiers who would dedicate their lives to the protection of the South Carolinian frontier.* The transportation charges were not too much to pay for colonists who could serve such an important purpose, especially since Philip II had proclaimed himself monarch of North America and had taken possession of the whole continent in the name of the King of Spain.

Apart from such obvious imperialist aims, Georgia also attracted the king and many Englishmen of wealth because it promised the production of raw silk as fine in "strength and Beauty as the Silk of Italy." [7] In the past, French silks had been used mainly in England. Georgia now, it was hoped, would provide such perfect silks that such French importations would become superfluous. Besides, the Georgia enthusiasts declared, "it will provide a new or additional employment for at least twenty thousand People in Georgia for about four Months in the Year during the Silk season; and at least twenty thousand more of our Poor here all the Year round in working the Raw Silk." [8] Oglethorpe himself had declared that "we shall be their market for great quantities of silk; perhaps (also) for wine, oil, cotton, drugs, dyeing stuffs, and many other lesser commodities." As a result of the silk manufactures of Georgia, it was believed that over fifty thousand people in both England and Ireland would be employed in converting the raw silk into wearable materials.[9] By this means, it was calculated, the Georgians could grow rich and the English could live better at less expense.

It was the tropical nature of Georgia's climate that led most of its original colonists to believe that silk production could be undertaken

* The Moravians, who were pacifists, refused to bear arms. So martial-minded was Georgia that the majority of the colonists threatened to massacre the Moravians, who thereupon left the colony and began their trek northward.

at a great profit. Influenced by these fabulous promises of an economic utopia, people from a number of lands flooded into Georgia: Swiss, German, Scotch, and English, and before long Georgia was a center of many nations and languages.

Unfortunately neither the climate nor the soil proved as conducive to silk production as had been expected,[10] nor did wine turn out to be a profitable product. The colony, bereft of its economic dream, stumbled and floundered about and almost lost its last legs of stability. What saved it was the development of rice production, which established the colony upon a new and more solid economic foundation.

Before that there had actually been rumors that the colony was extinct. The population had decreased at such an appalling rate that by 1740 even its sponsors had begun to give up hope for its survival. "The Colony is reduced to one-sixth of its former number," David Douglass, William Sterling, and Thomas Baillie wrote to the trustees in 1740. They went on to note that "the few who remain are in a starving and despicable condition." [11] Many Georgians retreated in desperation to Charleston, where, one observer notes, fifty "died in Misery and Want and most of them [were] buried at the Publick Charge." [12] * *The London Journal* (Oct. 26, 1734) described this exodus of Georgians to South Carolina as a daily occurrence.

## INTRODUCTION OF SLAVERY

The introduction of slavery in 1750 expedited rice production enormously, and shortly thereafter Georgia came back to life as an active, busy, growing colony. By this time it had disencumbered itself of its idealistic attitudes and outlooks and had become like all the other colonies. In addition to permitting slavery within its boundaries, it also opened its doors to the liquor traffic. It is true that before the sale of liquor was made legal in Georgia, bootleg joints had sprung up in many places, and there the settlers had been able to buy rum in plenitude. No Georgia jury at the time would convict settlers for buying it or the owners for selling it. Benjamin Martyn even went so far as to state that rum was drunk to such excess one year that "many of the People were thrown into burning Fevers, which carried off several." [14]

* A great number of these Georgians who fled to South Carolina were indentured servants.[13]

As its production increased, rice soon became an exportable item, and thus made for increased prosperity for the colony. For the first time in years new settlers came to Georgia, and it began to extend and expand its domain. Before slavery had been allowed in the colony, Georgian settlers had been wont to toast each other at their parties in favor of "the one thing [slavery] needful," and after slavery was introduced there was no colonist who dared to condemn it.

### WHITEFIELD EXTOLS SLAVERY

Even George Whitefield, the renowned Methodist preacher, whose evangelism electrified the land and who became such a good friend of Benjamin Franklin, extolled slavery as an institution. Without a spiritual blush, he gave slavery his benediction and urged that Georgia introduce it without delay. In a letter to the trustees he declared that his land in Georgia had suffered from the absence of Negro slaves to cultivate it. White hands had proved deplorably inefficient. Consequently he had purchased lands in South Carolina "where Negroes are allowed." These lands proved immediately prosperous, and Whitefield gave credit at once to God and slavery. "Blessed be God," he wrote, "this plantation has succeeded; and though at present I have only eight working hands, yet in all probability there will be more raised in one year, and with a quarter the expense" than was produced in several years on his Georgia possessions. "This confirms me in the opinion I have entertained for a long time," he concluded, "that Georgia never can or will be a flourishing province without Negroes are allowed." [15]

With the advent of slavery in Georgia, the colonists took the same precautions the South Carolinians did to discourage and suppress Negro revolts.[16] The Slave Code of 1755 included a military patrol system within its provisions. As in South Carolina, the colony was divided up into military units with commanders who could draft at immediate notice all male settlers between sixteen and sixty years of age. Their power over the Negroes was reprehensively extreme. They could invade Negro homes without a warrant, search for concealed weapons, and punish and even murder Negroes with impunity.

Georgia was never notable for generosity in the treatment of culprits, no matter how minor their offenses. "The Georgia Stocks,

Whipping-Post and Log-House soon were famous in Carolina," writes an observer whom we have cited before, "and everywhere else in America, where the Name of the Province was heard of, the very Thoughts of coming to the Colony became a Terror to People's Minds." [17] The author then notes that "for some Time there were more Imprisonments, Whippings, etc., of white People in that Colony of Liberty than in all British America besides." [18]

### RELIGION FOR THE HEATHEN

Viewed as the most backward of all the colonies at the time—a distinction to which Georgia is no longer entitled, now that in recent days Mississippi has displaced it as tail-end competitor—it was natural for evangelical missionaries to set out to save its unsanctified soul. The Rev. Mr. John Wesley, then a member of the Established Church but later to found the Methodist Church, and his less illustrious brother, decided upon "passing by Savannah . . . to pay our first visit in America to the poor Heathens." [19] Savannah at that time was far from a metropolis. A few years earlier a traveler had described Savannah, then spelled "Savanna," as "a very pleasant Town, very regularly laid out, and they have now at least 40 Houses in it." [20] Wesley went about his Savannah mission with great determination and expedition. On the boat he began to study German in order to convert the Moravians, twenty-six of whom were on board. He thought very highly of the Germans because they were so much more co-operative and so much less independent than the English. He was happily surprised when he found the Georgians immediately responsive to his gospel. The sight of the people "crowding into the church, [and] the deep Attention with which they received the Word and the Seriousness that afterwards sat on all their Faces," [21] delighted and encouraged him profoundly. Wesley had set out, as he declared in his *Diary*, "not to gain the Dung or Dress of Riches or Honour, but . . . to live wholly in the Glory of God," and in Georgia he found his reward.

Wesley, to be sure, like most clergymen, was too easily convinced by what he saw to give sufficient significance to that which he couldn't see. He saw only the church-going Georgians, not the rest of the colony, which was as little interested in religion as most of the North Carolinians of the time. The fact that a church and a clergyman's parish house were scheduled to be the first buildings erected in the colony was proof not that the settlers were interested in religion but that the trustees were determined to encourage them to be so interested—if possible.[22] Wesley notes in his *Diary* that one Georgian said to him: "I like nothing you do, all your sermons are satires upon particular persons. Therefore, I will never hear you again. . . . Indeed there is neither man nor woman in the town who minds a word you say!"[23]

Most Georgians were not pious. Of all the settlers the Moravians, who as we have seen were practically driven out of the colony, were the most zealous. After them the Scotch Presbyterians were the most devout. The Established Church, to be sure, was the official church, but its members, as in the other Southern colonies, were more economic-minded than soul-minded. Their religion was more of a property safeguard than a spiritual protection.

### ANTI-SEMITISM IN GEORGIA

The problem of anti-Semitism was not a new one in the colonies. In Georgia, however, it developed into a definite and decisive issue. The colony had been founded upon the principle of religious freedom, and the trustees could not summon up any legitimate reason why Jews should not settle in its territory. Nevertheless, when they learned that two groups of Jews, one from Germany and the other from Portugal, planned to emigrate to Georgia, they became most anxious and alarmed lest this would prove to be "of prejudice to the Trade and Welfare of the Colony."[24] The trustees insisted that these Jewish immigrants should be given a discouraging reception when they arrived, and that every effort should be made to rid the colony of them at the first opportunity. They were not to be given any of the guarantees and privileges of other settlers and were to be thwarted on every side so that they would speedily recognize that their presence was unwelcome. The trustees were particularly concerned with dispelling the idea that they were trying to "make a Jews' colony of Georgia."[25]

Oglethorpe, sharing none of their apprehensions on that score, welcomed the Jews immediately upon their arrival, honored them with grants of land, allowed them to erect a temple and to participate in the life of the colony. Moreover, Oglethorpe wrote long letters of praise about the excellent conduct of the Jews and the important role they played in the life of the colony, singling out in particular a Jewish doctor who was the principal physician and whose efforts had proved very efficacious in saving lives during one of the gravest epidemics the settlers had faced. In that connection the trustees had written Oglethorpe, expressing their gratitude to the physician for his good work, but urging that he not be favored by any grant of land. They were willing to have him rewarded handsomely in any way except a territorial one, because the latter meant that he would become an ineradicable part of the colony.

This anti-Semitic attitude, which Oglethorpe himself opposed, led many of the Jews to migrate into South Carolina, primarily into Charleston, where they found a more welcome environment. Only three Jewish families remained in Georgia,[26] but their descendants were conspicuously influential in the life of the colony, many of them in time becoming important personages and officials.

### A PLANTATION ECONOMY

Georgia began to prosper after it gave up its hope of becoming the silk paradise of the new world. When Oglethorpe went to England in 1734, for instance, that hope was so high that he carried with him, for the queen, a dress manufactured from Georgia silk, and this was declared by the court to be superior to that of any other country. But now Georgia became a rice-and-indigo colony. From this time on Georgian products were valued as highly in all markets, foreign as well as domestic, as those of other colonies; and later, with the magnification of the cotton industry after Eli Whitney's invention, Georgia developed a plantation system and a plantation aristocracy. In the cities, which were little more than expanded towns in those days, there were saddlers, candlestick-makers, shopkeepers, soap-batters, shoemakers, tanners, boatmen, and a curious combination of middlemen and frontier tradesmen. The plantations lived like vast, earthy dinosaurs, isolated from the rest of the economy. They were cities in themselves until the time came when they had to sell their products, whereupon they disentangled and stretched out their monstrous limbs and gobbled up all they could from the surrounding environment.

The plantation, not the city, became the center of Georgian economy—as it did also of most of the Southern economy. Even the coming of the railroad was unable to break up the domination of the plantation aristocracy. It might have ended the fight between Charleston and Savannah and shifted power to Atlanta, but it could not destroy the power of the land over commerce and industry. Only the destruction of the whole plantation economy could achieve that end, and it took the Civil War to accomplish it.

# BOOK III

## CHAPTER XV

# New York: Knickerbocker Unchained

*Some have said* IT IS NOT THE BUSINESS OF PRIVATE MEN TO MEDDLE WITH GOVERNMENT.... *Since it is the great design of this paper to maintain and explain the glorious Principles of Liberty, and to expose the Arts of those who would darken or destroy them, I shall here particularly shew the Wickedness and Stupidity of the above saying.... To say that private Men have nothing to do with Government is to say that private Men have nothing to do with their own Happiness and Misery.*

—JOHN PETER ZENGER, *New York Weekly Journal,* 1733

COLUMBUS set out for India but discovered America; Henry Hudson, an Englishman in the employ of the Dutch, set out for Cathay but discovered Manhattan.

On his first trip, undertaken in search of a short northwest route to the wonderland of China, Hudson got no farther than Spitzbergen; on his second, still in search of the same land of spice and gold, he succeeded in reaching Nova Zembla; on his third voyage, dedicated to the same explorative aspiration, he discovered the river that still bears his name.[1]

Unlike Columbus, Hudson did not make his discovery by accident. Quarrels and threatened mutiny by his crew, which was half Dutch and half English, forced him for the third time to abandon his Oriental objective in the northern waters and, guided by the maps of Captain John Smith, to head for the strange, uncharted territory sandwiched in between New England and Virginia. Hudson was an explorer rather than a colonizer, so he made no attempt to establish a settlement in the territory after he had discovered it. When he returned to Amsterdam, he described the wonders of the new country in fascinating detail, expatiating upon its rare and rich possessions, and urging the Dutch West India Company to dispatch colonists immediately to its shores. "It is as pleasant a land as one can tread upon," he wrote, "very abundant in all kinds of timber suitable for shipbuilding and for making large casks... copper must exist there, and iron likewise. . . . It seems to lack nothing that is needful for the subsistence of man, except domestic cattle, which it would be easy to carry there; and besides producing many things of which our own country is destitute."

His relations with the Indians were not unfriendly, although upon one occasion the natives, in two overcrowded canoes, launched an attack upon Hudson's vessel and did not retreat until several of them had been shot.[2]

### HUDSON'S TRAGIC FATE

Like Columbus, Hudson suffered a most tragic fate. On his fourth voyage he met his death because his passion for exploration and discovery was insatiable. After he discovered Hudson Bay, he wanted to pursue it far into the interior, to trace its inlets and islets and investigate the unknown lands against which it washed. His crew, however, was opposed to such a project and mutinied against him.

Columbus sent back to Europe in irons was hardly a more pitiable figure than Hudson attacked by his sailors, disarmed, and set adrift in an open boat on the hazardous waters of the bay he had discovered. His son and seven sailors were also abandoned with him. The picture of Hudson "in his coat of many colors," sitting in a tiny shallop with this handful of men, watching the vessel he commanded sail away from him, is unforgettably tragic. This was a sad, bitter end for a man who had explored so many parts of the earth, ventured into multitudinous seas—even into those in the topmost part of the planet—and whose name was known and admired throughout the civilized world. What happened to Hudson and his hapless group, left without food or drink or any other necessities of life, is unknown. The only evidence to indicate that they ever reached land is that of Captain James, who, when he was on Charlton Island in the winter of 1631-1632, discovered a serried line of stakes thrust into the ground. The way the stakes had been cut showed the use of a European ax, and it is possible that they were driven in by the forsaken Hudson band.[3]

After Hudson's discovery of the Hudson River, the Dutch made Manhattan—which derived its name from the Indian tribe, the Manhattes, who lived down toward the mouth of the river—their first possession in the northern part of the new continent. They bought the whole island of Manhattan from the Indians for what amounted to approximately twenty-four dollars' worth of glittering gewgaws and trinkets. They retained it until 1664, when the English seized it; they recaptured it in 1673, but lost it back to the English the next year, and this event put an end to their colonial career in North America.

## THE SWEEP OF DUTCH POWER

Originally the Dutch West India Company had been far more interested in promoting Brazil than in maintaining the New Netherlands. The Dutch had fought off both the Spanish and the Portuguese in their struggle to acquire hegemony over this rich South American possession. Only after they were beaten in their Latin American struggle did they give adequate attention to their Manhattan colony, but by that time it was too late. New Amsterdam and the whole New Netherlands territory were too little developed and too sparsely populated to make it possible for the Dutch to withstand British encroachments and attacks.

Brazil, with its illimitable resources, was superior to the New Netherlands and promised forms of wealth far surpassing those of the North American colony. If the Dutch had not lost Brazil, it is doubtful whether they would ever have expended much energy for their Manhattan colony. Brazil was gigantic, vast as water, virile as soil, a combination and composite of both elements at their highest potency.

Few people remember today that it was Holland which inherited the power and glory of Venice, Florence, Naples, those magnificent Italian cities which, in the fifteenth century, had ruled the Mediterranean and dominated most of the civilized world. When Holland became the queen of European nations, the grandeur and gilt of those cities had already begun to rust; they had become little more than pathetic reminders of vanished triumphs. Holland, great marine nation that it was in those days, challenged the international sovereignty of Spain and Portugal, and established herself as a conquering empire.

Her metropolis, Amsterdam, was one of the largest cities in the world, possessing a population of over 250,000, which was incredibly gigantic at that time. It was far larger and far more impressive than London. When the Pilgrim fathers fled from England to Holland, they knew that they were emigrating to a better place. Amsterdam was the leading city of Europe at that time. It was the center of European culture. The University of Leyden was so superior to Oxford that the Dutch would sneer when the two institutions were compared. The Dutch were, in fact, more literate and intelligent than any other Continental nation. Their religious attitudes were more tolerant and progressive than those of Spain, Portugal, France, or England; their politics were more democratic than those of other lands; their science was the most advanced of the day: for instance, Holland had made great progress in the study of disease and hygiene, in engineering and agriculture, all of which other nations were later to profit from and copy. In art, by the middle of the seventeenth century, Holland paced every nation with her Frans Hals, Jan Van Goyen, Jan Vermeer, and, above all, Rembrandt.

### HOLLAND: CULTURAL CYNOSURE

It was this Holland that led Europe in cultural progress for over a century. Holland's pre-eminence in culture dates from her pre-eminence in commerce. Ironically enough, commerce and conquest tend to obliterate the culture of the conquered but to advance the culture of the conquerors. Conquest provides increased wealth, more jobs, superior living conditions for the populace, a more intelligent and generous ruling class, different contacts, fresh impetus, new aspiration. Increase in trade also creates increase in tolerance, which, in the case of Holland, is the main reason that the early English Dissenters decided to flee to Holland rather than to any other European country.

As Miriam Beard in a most striking study has pointed out, the Dutch were "universal middlemen," irrepressible and ineluctable tradesmen and entrepreneurs.[4] They were at that time, as Defoe declared, "the Carryeres of the World," "the middle Persons in Trade, the Factors and Brokers of Europe."[5] They were the first of the modern capitalist nations to learn the truth of the precept that *to buy cheap and sell dear* was the secret of all successful enterprise. The Dutch were never so interested in conquering lands in a geographic sense as they were in controlling them in a commercial capacity. In the early seventeenth century the Dutch claimed a fleet of over 35,000 vessels, and boasted of building 2,000 new ships every year.[6] They not only owned two-thirds of the ships of Europe but also controlled the shipbuilding industry of the world. They possessed the necessary raw materials, the technical skill, and the capital requisite for such enterprise. When nations wanted to wage naval wars they had to go to the Dutch for their ships, and in more than one instance kings bought full-fledged navies from Dutch shipbuilders in order to wage war on Holland and its colonies.[7]

### THE MIDAS-TOUCH OF THE DUTCHMEN

Dutch ships encircled the continents, and Dutch traders appeared in all ports, gobbling up trade along every river, sea, and ocean in the new world as well as the old. No land, no nation, no race, however remote or strange, escaped the Midas-touch of the Dutchman. He was intimate with Indian maharajahs, Japanese samurai, African kings, Brazilian chiefs, Russian merchants—intimate with everyone and anyone in all the divers corners of the universe who had something to sell which he wanted to buy and which he could sell for a higher price to someone else.

Thus Holland, a quondam paradise for fishermen, became a new utopia for merchants and financiers.

The New Netherlands, of which New Amsterdam became the matrix, was but one of the extensions of the Hollander's empire. Being more of a trader than a colonist, the Dutchman never succeeded in building up his North American possession into an expanding and significant settlement. That task remained for the English. When the English conquered the territory in 1664, the population of "Greater New York" was approximately 1,500, only 350 of whom were adult males,[8] and the total population of the whole province was less than 8,000, a large part of which was not Dutch. The Dutchmen preferred their own country, and relatively few of them migrated to this new land of wilderness. After all, in their home country they had most of the advantages and privileges which the English lacked—and which inspired the latter to settle in America. The Flemings and Walloons, who had sought refuge in Holland during the wars and persecutions of the period, made up a large percentage of the contingent dispatched to the new world by the

Dutch West Indies Company. As exiles from their native lands, they were less reluctant than the native Dutchman to leave Holland and hazard their fortunes in unknown parts. The Walloons came over in 1624, dividing into three groups: one group founding Fort Orange, the second settling along the Delaware River, and the third making Long Island its new home. Another dissident group that came to the province were the Huguenots. The first Huguenot family came from Amsterdam, where it had fled to escape French persecution. Later a whole band of Huguenots arrived and before long a Huguenot settlement developed in New Rochelle.[9] * At one time there were over a score of languages spoken in the province.

### THE BATTLE FOR RELIGIOUS LIBERTY

In the new world the Dutch West India Company revealed little interest in religious affairs. The Dutch Reformed Church became the established ecclesiastical body, being privileged to tax everyone in the colony in support of its work.[13] But there its authority stopped. Dutch clergymen, like Dutch merchants, were more interested in the financial than the spiritual, and once the tax was paid they were blithely content to allow the populace to worship as it pleased. Perpetuating the tradition of their mother country, they defended tolerance as a principle, and English Dissenters of every variety, even Quakers, were permitted to organize and open churches in the province. Only Catholics found themselves suppressed in that respect.

Although Catholics were not welcome, New Amsterdam became a refuge for heretics and iconoclasts of the most extreme and fantastic type. In Maryland Quakers and Jews were both persecuted; in New York those groups were unmolested. When Peter Stuyvesant and his council attempted to expel the Jews from New Amsterdam in 1655, the Dutch West India Company immediately blocked his efforts, and Stuyvesant had to capitulate on the issue.[14]

* Westchester was a "howling wilderness" when the Huguenots made their settlement there. The Huguenots had also established settlements in New Oxford, Mass., at Narragansett, Rhode Island, and New Paltz, N. Y.[10] Jacob Leisler, whose mother was of Huguenot ancestry, was instrumental in aiding them in planning and founding their New Rochelle colony. In fact, when John Pell sold the New Rochelle territory he deeded it to Jacob Leisler.[11] Most of these Huguenots, driven out of France by the Catholic regime, were superior to the majority of the Dutch and English settlers in intelligence, wealth and breeding.[12]

More important than Stuyvesant's capitulation was the Makemie trial, which occurred long after the Dutch had surrendered the province to the English. The Right Reverend Francis Makemie, an itinerant Presbyterian, unhesitatingly violated the governor's instructions that no pastor could preach in the colony without license or specific permission, and was arrested and brought to trial—which was precisely what he desired. His case immediately became a *cause célèbre*. Three of the leading lawyers of the province, all Episcopalians, defended him. Makemie declared with most challenging candor that he had no respect for royal instructions. "Your instructions," he said to the governor, "are no law to me."

The trial became famous because it involved the whole question of freedom of religious worship, and Makemie's acquittal marked a milestone in the history of religious liberty in the State of New York. More than that, it signified a successful challenge to royal authority, and gave the Crown a foretaste of what it later was going to be forced to swallow in the American Revolution.[15]

In addition, the Dutch opened a series of public schools in most of the towns in the province—an innovation of great significance. After the English secured control of the colony, the public school system was abandoned.

### STUYVESANT: THE DICTATOR

Peter Stuyvesant was one of the most unwise, perverse, and pathetic of tyrants, who, afflicted with a wooden leg, made his mind into an extension of that leg. The inferiority complex born of his physical incapacity translated itself into his mental outlook, and he "took out" on the community what he could not "take out" on God. He destroyed all the freedom that existed before he was appointed governor and destroyed all that Holland had stood for throughout the world by making the Dutch colony the opposite of what it had striven to be.

In defense of Stuyvesant, who had made a good record as governor of Curaçao, it must be admitted that the colony was on the decline when he took office, and that in order to save it from dissolution he was forced to encourage all kinds of emigrants from the New Haven colony: "noble or ignoble, freeman or slave, debtor or creditor, yea, to the lowest prisoner included."[16] Although the

Dutch had finally beaten the Indians in a fierce war, the colony was so exhausted from the conflict that not even Peter Stuyvesant was able to make it stand on its own legs. Like his predecessors, Wouter Van Twiller and William Kieft, Stuyvesant allowed the settlers no political freedom, declaring that if he did so it would result in putting mad dogs into office. The advisory council was nothing more than a shock-absorber for the discontent rife in the colony. It had no official power and was disregarded by Kieft as well as Stuyvesant. There were several attempts on the part of the advisory council to convert its discontent and protest into action, the best known being that led by Vander Donck, a challenging, vitriolic lawyer, but none of them was effectual. The autocracy remained.

It was this failure of the Dutch to establish harmony within the colony that caused so much dissension and hastened the defeat of their regime.

## II

The English changed considerably the character of the colony. The Dutch had set up patroonships, discouraged free ownership of the land by the people, and encouraged tenancy, whereas the English colonies offered free grants of land to the settlers as an incentive to settlement. Naturally, the population of the English colonies multiplied much faster than that of the Dutch colonies, and within a fairly short period New York under English rule was on its way to being one of the leading provinces. When the English seized control of the province, there were only eighteen sloops and boats in the harbor of New York, by which name New Amsterdam became known after the Dutch lost control of it; before the close of the century that number had leaped to over one hundred and fifty vessels.[17]

The political governorship of the colony did not improve, however; it remained as tyrannical under the Duke of York as it had been under the Dutch West India Company. Like Lord Baltimore in Maryland, the Duke was opposed to popular bodies because they carried within them the seeds of revolt. He was prepared to rule with a gentle but firm hand, provided the colonists did not challenge his authority. His representatives, Colonel Nicholls, Major Andros, Thomas Dongan, were all loyal to his interests, but in being so undeviatingly loyal they aroused the ire of the majority of the colony.

## LEISLER'S REVOLT

New York's economic life centered about fur trading, fishing, especially whaling, commerce, and agriculture. Flour soon became more important than fur, and the flour barrel developed into the great symbol of New York's commerce. The merchants and fur traders, however, acquired the larger share of the wealth of the colony, purchased vast estates, and exploited the smaller tradesmen, shopkeepers, farmers, fishermen, and workers. The latter groups resented this exploitation as much as they did the tyranny of the proprietor, and protested against it frequently and vigorously. As early as 1674, there was a demand on the part of the corn and wine porters for a closed-shop agreement with their employers. In 1684 the New York City carmen went on strike. Other protests and strikes ensued. Finally, in 1689, the hostility of the populace assumed revolutionary proportions, and a party under the leadership of Jacob Leisler marched into the streets, captured the Fort of New York, and overthrew the government.

The abdication of James II in 1688 aided this revolt as well as those in the other colonies. It released the pent-up energies of economic protest, afforded an outlet for political discontent, and whipped up the fires of rebellion. Embroiled in all this hurly-burly of social conflict was the exacerbating factor of religion. James II had been a Papist and had placed Papists in important offices in the colony; the Protestants, embittered by such Catholic favoritism, were quick to oppose it once William and Mary became sovereigns of England. Consequently, religion was a motivating factor in stirring the impoverished colonists against the wealthy Catholics the king had put into high office.

Captain Jacob Leisler, the leader of the rebellion which still bears his name, was concerned with the religious issue but more concerned with the economic one. Leisler was a German merchant,* imbued with a passionate desire for justice. He had been born in Germany and had come to the new world as a soldier in the employ of the Dutch West India Company.[19] His enemies declared that his motive

* Leisler's name appeared among "a list of soldiers embarked for New Netherland in The Ship Otter—27th April 1660—as Jacob Loyseler, from Francfort." [18]

for revolt was personal, that he "had a ship loaden with wines, the customs whereof amounted to upwards of one hundred Pounds; payment of this he utterly refused, alledging the Collector being a Papist was not qualified to receive it, denying the then power to be legal." [20] His later acts, however, disprove that contention. Few men have conducted themselves in turbulent situations more admirably than Leisler. "It was never known in the Memory of Man," one of Captain Leisler's defenders avowed, "that ever a Revolution or change of Government was more regular." [21] Even Kiliaan Van Rensselaer declared, in an affidavit, that Leisler "acted and acquitted himself as a brave soldier." [22] *

Leisler was a man of great energy and political genius. It was he who improved the fort, bulwarked it with new protections, multiplied its extensions, and altogether made it well-nigh impregnable.[24] He was so popular with the people that he was able to keep them in control throughout the crisis. His enemies declared that he encouraged the populace to violence, but there is no evidence to confirm that conclusion. "Nor were the People drunk or mad," writes an observer, "for no Man, Woman or Child was hurt . . . even in the very Convulsion of changing the Government." [25]

That fact is very significant. Few revolts or revolutions, even though within so limited a territory, have been achieved in such a bloodless fashion. Leisler's leadership accounted for that happy anomaly. Unlike most leaders, he did not alter his attitude or action after he secured power. He translated his belief in democracy into practice shortly after his victory. The free men were given voting power, representatives were elected, and a committee of safety was created, of which Captain Leisler as commander-in-chief was the guiding force. A declaration was swiftly drawn up, signed by the majority of the populace, and forwarded to the Prince of Orange. On December 10 letters were received, delivered by a person named Riggs, "fully confirming Captain Leisler in the Government." [26]

* It is only fair to add that Charles M. Andrews is by no means so favorably impressed by Leisler. After crediting him with "courage, capacity for work, a forceful personality, and no little organizing ability," he denounces him as "domineering, revengeful, and often demagogic." [23] Andrews's conclusions however, are governed in considerable degree by his general sympathy with the status quo and his lack of appreciation of the rebels and radicals and, to quote him again, the "roving agitators of the time."

Leisler's regime lasted for over a year. Aside from the fact that for a time he had to force a number of merchants to contribute part of their goods in support of the government and the populace, and to imprison a few plutocrats, his rule was relatively uncoercive and unoppressive. He even contemplated a plan of invading Canada and converting it into an English territory. He was in touch with the Maryland revolutionist Coode and with most other leaders of the populace in different colonies.*

### CLERGY AGAINST LEISLER

The Dutch clergy, which had allied itself with the wealthy classes in the fight against Leisler, found itself in a most embarrassing situation when the latter struck back and effected a division in its ranks. For a time it looked as if the two factions would annihilate each other. When the ministers failed even then to cease their attacks, Leisler adopted such forthright methods that a number of the ecclesiastics fled to other places. When Leisler was tried later, it was the clergy which demanded no mercy for him and hastened his execution.

When Major Ingoldesby arrived, preceding, as commander of the troops, the newly appointed Governor Sloughter, Captain Leisler refused to surrender the fort to him until he was shown papers proving that the new king, William of Orange, in whose name Leisler had established his government, had empowered him with the right to rule. In a courteous letter Leisler explained to Major Ingoldesby that the king had entrusted him with the government of the colony, and that until the king instructed him to relinquish his

* This letter[27] which Leisler wrote to the Assembly of Maryland and was answered by Coode is most significant:

"A: 1689 29th Sept
in the Fort of N. Y.

"Gentlemen:

I have received your acceptable letter the 18th of this instant and communicated as directed, wee have considered the contents with due affection and returne you many thanks for your friendly and neighborly advice, and embrace with all our hearts your offers of a mutuall and amiable correspondence with you which we shall labour to keep and preserve inviolable towards you, and without fail shall omitt nothing that may appeare any wayes to your interest peace and welfare as we also doe with Boston and Connecticut colony being of the same opinion with you, *that it is the onely meanes to preserve their Maj: intrest and to prevent the papists and popishly evill affected adversaries to effect and bring to pass their wicked intents and designes against their maies loyal protestant subjects throw all his dominions in these parts of America, as we have good cause to suspect with you by severall deposi-*

office, he had no choice but to remain in it. Leisler's declaration of protest against Ingoldesby deserves quotation:

Whereas almighty God through his wonderfull mercy hath raised up their Majties King William and Queen Mary to be ye glorious instruments of delivering their Kingdoms & Dominions both Church & State from ye imposition of ye romish religion and illegal and arbitrary power exerced under ye unhappy reigne of ye late King James which hath appeared in a more than ordinary measure within this province of New Yorke under ye Governmt of Col. Dongan . . . a professed papist who together with seven councellors had power to make laws raise and levy taxes & transport ye inhabitants out of this province without having any regard to advice or consent of ye representatives of ye people, which said power was continued & augmented by Commission from ye sd King James appointing Sr Edmund Andros governor of this province as well as New England . . . who together with thirty odd Councellors of which seven made a Quorum did act accordingly and proceed in ye vigorous prosecution of pernicious practices within said province. . . .

Whereupon many of ye good inhabitants of this province (zealous for the protestant religion and rejoicing at so glorious an accession) to

*tions and circumstances before us relating.* It is three weeks agoe that I heard of some of your Papist grandees to be at Philadelphia expecting them nearer these parts to conferr with some of our Papists, and for some bad designe, for the which I made all the Inquisition imaginable with resolution to secure them well if I had found them, but I beleeve hearing the absence of Col Dongon he was at Rhoad Island where Sir Edmund Andross arryved the same tyme, having made his escape from Boston where he is now in fast hold again, the sd dongan is now in these parts again, he hes ranged all the country and is mott daily by several where it may be also they may come, I shall omitt nothing if I heare of them to secure them, gott a printed proclamation from new England the 21 June of their Maies King William and Queen Mary to be Queen of Scotland but have seen no proclamation thereof as yet, I have detained here a wholl week Mr. William Hinson and John Hinson expecting to get some part advice from Albany of the negotiations between the agents of new England and the Sinicks and Mohacks but understand onely that they have treated and are of good intelligence the said Indians have open war with the french and their Indianes to have for certain kild and taken prisoners about 500 french men women and children they give quarters but to very few but torture them as their customary way, the city of Albany suffers the late King James souldiers there to keep the fort by themselves and are payed with faire words, there is brought a letter to me by one of the old soldiers directed to him by the commander of the sd fort he offers him a sergeants place and desires him to list for the service of King William and Mary soe many soldiers as he can gett of Major Brockhouse and Capt Baisters companies, both rank papists and to send them to him but two or three at the tyme which is very suspicious . . ." Etc.

Col. Coode Nov. 26, 1689 writes to Leisler:[28]

". . . Your great ciuilitie I have communicated and represented to all our friends here who are extremely glad of so neer and convenient a friendship, especially since our circumstances are so alike, and ye common danger so equally threatening. . . ."

discover their loyalty taking incouragement from his highness ye Prince of Orange . . . his excellent memoriall and declarations, did secure his majestys fort displace and disenable ye lieutt Governor & his Councill and Militia settled by the authority of said King James in so much that a stop was put to their further proceedings to prosecute their majties & to preserve in their loyalty did Elect representatives for each county in their province who assisted forthwith to proclaim their Majties William & Mary King & Queen of England, France & Ireland & ye territories thereunto belonging according to forme and becoming ceremonies in opposicon to ye present power &ca who used their utmost art and diligence to prevent it making farther necessary steps for securing ye sd fort City and Province in behalfe of their sd Majties untill their Royall pleasure should be known concerning us which accordingly arrived ye 10th December, 1689, his majties letter bearing date July ye 30 foregoing directed to Francis Nicholson, Esq. & in his absence to such for ye time being take care for preserving ye peace and administering ye Govmt of ye sd Province. . . .[29]

Leisler even went so far as to offer Ingoldesby and his men housing quarters and food and every other convenience and protection necessary until the arrival of the governor.[30]

Ingoldesby was furious, and denounced Leisler in most threatening language, but the latter remained adamant and refused to surrender the fort. When Colonel Sloughter came over, however, with papers from the king, Leisler turned over the fort to him immediately. Leisler's letter to Sloughter merits rereading:

Fort William, March 12th, 1690

Sir,

Though your Excellency's absence & ye exorbitances of Major Ingoldesby (encouraging ye malice of Papists & other ennemies to their Majties accession to the Crowne whatever they now pretend) Things are brought into such a disorder and evil Crisis which threatned the destrucon of this province . . . it is impossible to continue in this state many days without blood shed which so happily hitherto has escaped it . . . pray God Send your Excellency amongst us Spedily . . . as it is our longing expectation So it shall be ye dayly prayers of your Excellcy's most humble servant

Jacob Leisler.[31]

Leisler had two interests: one, to protect the people from the oppression and exploitation of the wealthy landowners and merchants, which meant replacing autocracy with democracy; and the other, to rule in the name of William of Orange, in whose Protestant leadership he believed. Leisler was definitely opposed to papal domination in politics and enthusiastically welcomed the coming of William and Mary to the throne of England. Like many others of that day, he associated Catholicism with autocracy and Protestantism with democracy.

### SLOUGHTER VERSUS LEISLER

Colonel Sloughter distrusted Leisler's aims and questioned his integrity. After all, Leisler had not only ruled in the name of William of Orange but had also arrested certain rich men and challenged the authority of the propertied classes, and might very well repeat that challenge at some later time. It did not take the new governor, who had allied himself with the aristocratic groups, very long to put Leisler and his leading followers on trial and to convict Leisler and Milbourne of high treason. Despite their conviction, they were to be reprieved until the king's decision on the case was known. Sloughter, however, would abide no such delay, and during a fit of inebriation signed their death warrants and saw that they were executed at once. The jury that convicted Leisler was picked precisely for that purpose and was filled with men who were anti-Leisler by conviction. Sloughter not only was drunk when he signed the death warrant but had also been bribed with a large sum of money to sign it.[32]

### LEISLER ACQUITTED BY PARLIAMENT

The dark days that followed were not greatly lightened when Sloughter died of alcoholism, for his successors, Ingoldesby and Fletcher, were no less reactionary in their politics. Leisler's execution caused much discontent in the colony and the new rulers found themselves very unpopular. Leisler had won the support of the people because they believed in him, trusted him, and he in turn had believed in them and trusted them.* They did not believe

* Letter From a Gentlemen of the City of New York to Another Concerning Troubles which happened in that Province in the Time of the Late Happy Revolution (1698):

"I cannot but admire to hear that some Gentlemen stil have a good opinion of the late in or trust the new governors, and they were happy on the day when they learned that an act of Parliament had been passed acquitting Leisler of the high treason of which he had been charged, and restoring his estates to his heirs. The act even went so far as to defend the legality of Leisler's refusal to surrender the fort to Major Ingoldesby, on which score his conviction had been mainly based.

In later years Leisler's name has become increasingly respected and revered, and monuments have been erected in his honor, whereas those who executed him have been largely forgotten except in the microscopical footnotes of history.

But Leisler's name was not only a memory; it also lived in the political changes he effected, especially in the elected assembly which he introduced, and which the new governors dared not destroy.

## III

### THE NEGRO CONSPIRACY

For a considerable time after Leisler's revolt, New York succeeded in fitting itself into certain convenient grooves, in which all trace of friction was removed. The English expanded the colony, gave it more vital and vibrant initiative, infused it with new economic resolve. It was not long before they transformed it from a commercial into an agricultural venture. The Dutch had been interested in making a prosperous trading center; the English succeeded in developing a thriving colony.

Whatever unrest prevailed among the populace in the immediate years that followed was bottled up by the authorities and failed to find an outlet of social expression. The only protests that found voice were among the Negroes, who resented the treatment they were subjected to by their masters. Northerners were no more gentle in their treatment of slaves, white or black, than Southerners. As early as 1712, a group of black slaves went berserk, set a house on

disorders committed by Capt. Jacob Leisler and his accomplices, in New York as if they had been for his Majesties Service, and the security of that Province, and that such monstrous Falsehoods do find credit. That the Persons before in Commisson and did labour to oppose and prevent those disorders were Jacobites Persons ill affected to the Happy Revolution in England. . . ."

fire, and killed the whites as they fled from the flaming structure. The twenty-one Negroes captured were all executed immediately, the leader being burned to death in slow, intermittent flames.

In 1741 the Negroes were accused of undertaking an insurrection, and thereupon followed an era of hysteria and violence which paralleled that of New England during the witchcraft craze. People lost their poise, imagined impossible things, contrived fables, fantasies, rumors, and before long half the white population was convinced that the Negroes were going to destroy the city and incinerate every white inhabitant into so much ash. How it all began is known, but after the beginning most of what happened is still dubious. What is definitely known is that there was a robbery at Mr. Hogg's, from whose place were stolen "divers pieces of linen and other goods, and severeal silver coins, chiefly Spanish . . . to the value of 60 pounds and upwards." [33]

### RACE-RIOT MANIA

The robbery, it would appear from all available evidence, was accomplished by a youth named Wilson, scarcely eighteen years of age, who instructed certain of the slaves, Caesar, Prince, and Cuffee, and urged them to steal the money of their master. That the robbery occurred is indisputable. But after the robbery the whole town went insane, and no Negro's life was secure. Mary Burton, an indentured servant, swore that Peggy, a white woman, slept with Caesar, a Negro, and that ignited the baser and more vicious passions of the populace. Miss Burton also alleged that John Hughson, her master, a tavern keeper, was in league with thieves and constantly received stolen goods from numerous sources. She declared she had heard conversations between the group which betrayed their guilt for the fires that had been started in various parts of the city. When several fires did break out within the next few days, they were blamed upon the Negroes, and the hostility to the blacks became maniacal. Everyone quoted Mary Burton's assertion that Negroes had threatened to burn the fort and that they were going to set fire to the whole town, and that her master had guns and swords secreted in his house. With appalling expedition Caesar and Prince were executed.[34]

Another person, Mrs. Earle, swore that, looking out of her window, she had heard several Negroes say "with a vapouring sort of air" that they were going to consign the whole town to flames. Others supplied additional information equally unauthentic and unfactual. The whole city was like a vast grapevine, rumors spreading from tendril to branch, until the populace did not know what to expect, but was willing to cherish the newest bud that was born. Every Negro became suspect, regardless of his personality or conviction. Black became an odious color, a word white men swore at, denounced, loathed. To be black was to be vicious, criminal. Innocent people suffered even more than guilty in this holocaust of persecution. Negroes sought out every hiding place, every haunt, every crevice of escape, but many of them succumbed to the onslaught, sacrifices to the mania of the populace.

The tragedy of the whole episode is that a simple robbery was exaggerated into a racial issue. Undoubtedly certain Negroes were involved in the crime, but whites had been involved in many crimes before and nothing had been made of it. This crime was different. It was an issue of masters versus slaves, and nothing could be more fundamental.

Fires somehow by their very intensity add to the emotion of an episode, and it was not long before they became synonymous with Negroes, and everyone who saw a spout of smoke in a kitchen was certain that a Negro was hidden in the stove. Quick's fire was succeeded by that of Ben Thomas, and then that of Mrs. Hilton. In Joseph Murray's stable coals were found beneath the haystack, but no one ever discovered who put them there. Other fires occurred, and as the number multiplied, the blacks were blamed for them all, and a lynching psychology infected the populace.[35]

Innocent Negroes were seized upon the streets, attacked, beaten, mutilated, jailed, and then third-degreed. But nothing of a conspiracy could be learned from them. Rewards were offered by the government, promises multiplied, in order to get some Negro to testify against his race. But the Negroes were as stolid as Indians, impenetrably and imperviously silent; there was no Judas in their midst.

The whites were convinced that the Negroes had conceived of a design to "destroy this city by Fire and massacre the Inhabitants: That Fire was to be put to several Quarters of the Town at one and the same time: That the English Church was to be set on Fire at a time when 'twas most likely there would be the fullest Congregation and the Avenues from the Church were to be guarded ... in order to butcher those that should attempt to escape the flames."[36] The whole picture was conjured up by the morbific imaginations of the whites, who were terrified lest the Negroes wreak vengeance upon them for the crimes they had committed against the black people in the city. The court trial was a frame-up; the evidence was wretchedly slight and unconvincing, and if the jurors had been calm and composed, no conviction would have resulted. But the jurors were excited. They had heard that on Saint Patrick's night the Negroes had plotted to burn up the town and assassinate the inhabitants, and that was enough to spur them to a vicious verdict. Two whites were executed—Hughson, the tavern keeper, and Ury, the Catholic priest. Twelve Negroes were burned alive and eighteen hanged, and over seventy were shipped to Madeira, Hispaniola, where they were sold into slavery.[37]

A valiant effort was made by the court to pin a large part of the guilt upon the Catholics. The priest, John Ury, was exploited as a symbol, and his execution was hailed as a victory of Protestantism over Catholicism in the province. Ury was accused of having sworn in the conspirators, whom Hughson had already provided with arms —especially knives, "for those Weapons would make no noise." The truth of the matter is that there was no conspiracy at all, that Hughson and Ury were no more guilty of the crime for which they were hanged than Sacco and Vanzetti were of the one for which they were electrocuted. The whites and Negroes who lost their lives in this putative conspiracy were victims of the same type of mob mania that consumed the lives of so many innocent persons in Massachusetts during the witchcraft craze.

## IV

### PETER ZENGER: THE LIBERTARIAN

Like other colonies, New York was rife with rumors, antagonisms, and feuds, some economic, some political, some religious. New York and Maryland were the most despotic and authoritarian of the colonies because both were owned by individuals, or proprietors. This authoritarianism pervaded the whole colony: governors, generals, mayors, and all that ollapodridic composite of functionaries became infected with its virus. They sought to dominate rather than to govern.

As we have already seen, Makemie had to endure a court trial, to suffer all the opprobrium and obloquy involved, before the issue of religious freedom could be finally established in the province. But Makemie's struggle was far less severe than that experienced by John Peter Zenger, who carried his battle against authoritarian tyranny into the journalistic realm. Zenger did for the press what Makemie did for religion: he secured for it that freedom from governmental intervention which has given it the distinction, prestige, and significance lacking in the press of so many countries in Europe.

At a time when newspapers were still in an embryonic stage and their future dubious, Zenger was determined to endow them with an importance they had lacked before. He made his paper, the *New York Weekly Journal*, an exciting publication, pregnant with challenge, succulent with news, brilliant, witty, sardonic. People read it because they liked it, and also because they had to read it to keep up with the times. Zenger knew how to write and knew what to write about. He wrote freely, as if the world were his empire, without fear of kings, queens, or governors. He wrote almost as if he knew, subconsciously, that in time the newspaper would be more powerful than kings, queens, or governors.

Zenger was imprisoned on November 17, 1734, because he printed remarks and animadversions about Governor Cosby, who lacked a sense of humor, a sense of proportion, and most other senses. Zenger objected to Governor Cosby's avarice, and said so in unmixed and unmincing words. For Cosby was a Jimmie Walker, without grace of wit or suavity of gesture. He was a domineering man and was determined to have no one criticize him as an official or as an individual.[38] He hated Zenger because the latter attacked him and threatened his authority. Besides, he remembered the king's advice:

> Forasmuch as great inconvenience may arise by the liberty of printing within our province of New York, you are to provide, by all necessary orders, that no person keep any press for printing; nor that any book,

pamphlet, or other matters whatsoever, be printed without your especial leave and license be first obtained.

At a meeting of a committee of the Council on October 17, 1734, an attempt was made to have several issues of Zenger's papers "burned by the Hands of the common Hangman," because they contained "many things derogatory of the dignity of His Majesty's Government . . . [and tended] to raise Seditions and Tumults among the People thereof."[39] The Committee adjourned, however, and "did not attend the Burning of the Papers." The sheriff had to get his own Negro to burn them for him.[40]

The lawyers who defended Zenger, James Alexander and William Smith, were as courageous as their client. If James Alexander and William Smith had not volunteered originally to serve as Zenger's lawyers, and been followed by Andrew Hamilton, it is doubtful whether Zenger would have been acquitted, and a generation or more might have elapsed before the right to a free press was guaranteed in the new world. Governor Cosby had been bitterly opposed to Alexander because the latter had continuously challenged his gubernatorial authority. Alexander was even accused of inspiring the people of New Jersey to rebellion, and he had actually been eliminated from the New Jersey council for that reason. In the Zenger case Alexander and Smith were so determined to prevent the state from convicting their client that they were disbarred by the judge and were not able to regain their right to practice their profession for over two years. Zenger's case was more important to them, however, than the right to practice law, and at no time did they falter in their conviction.

After they were disbarred the veteran lawyer, Andrew Hamilton, who was noted for his liberal attitude, was called in to support Zenger's cause. A fervid and fierce believer in the freedom of the press, Hamilton delivered a noble defense of the New York publisher. Eighty years old at the time, he crowned the sunset of his life with this great victory. The closing part of his speech rings with a challenge as vital as Patrick Henry's "Give me liberty or give me death":

You see I labor under the weight of many years, and am borne down by many infirmities of body; yet old and weak as I am, I should think it my duty, if required, to go to the utmost part of the land, where my service could be of any use in assisting to quench the flame of prosecutions . . . to deprive a people of the right of remonstrating (and complaining, too,) of the arbitrary attempts of men in power.

While in jail Zenger was treated with marked discourtesy. He was forbidden to have pen or paper, and was not allowed to converse with other prisoners. When he was brought into the courtroom, he was viewed as a doomed figure. The trial, however, soon revealed him as a hero instead of a martyr. Accused of "Libelling His Excellency, the Governor of New York," he defied the governor or the state or anyone else to prove that he had made one false statement in his charges. "I will agree that if he [the State's Attorney] can prove the Facts charged upon us to be false," Andrew Hamilton avowed, "I will own them to be scandalous, seditious and a Libel . . . but we will save Mr. Attorney the Trouble of proving a negative and take the *Onus probandi* upon ourselves and prove those very papers that are called Libels to be TRUE."

### ZENGER'S CHALLENGE

Zenger's challenge rang down the halls of the courthouse and out into the streets of the city, and through the centers of the world. From that time on he could not be silenced. He had sounded the tocsin of revolt, and his words were to be repeated upon the lips of millions. The jury acquitted him immediately, and the courtroom rang with applause.

"I think every Man of Common Sense," Zenger had written in his paper, "will judge that he is an Enemy to his King and Country who pleads for any Restraint upon the Press . . . but to grant Liberty only for Praise, Flattery and Panegyric, with a Restraint on every Thing which happens to be offensive and disagreeable to those who are at any time in Power is absurd, servile and rediculous."[41] In a less turbulent period, Zenger was saying the things which later Tom Paine was to fling into the faces of the reactionaries at the time of the American Revolution. If Zenger lacked the eloquence of Paine, he did not lack his sincerity or courage. "It is the great design of this paper," Zenger declared in words anticipating and adumbrating Paine, "to maintain and explain the glorious Principles of Liberty and to expose the Arts of those who would darken or destroy them."[42] It was at great hazard that Zenger printed such words, for they were tinged with the spirit of revolt and aroused the active hostility of the economic royalists. But week after week Zenger continued his attacks upon every suggestion or semblance of tyranny, determined to keep this country free of its menace. "Despotic and arbitrary power is always hated in a free Country," he asserted, and at another time added that "when People are taught to reverence Butchers, Robbers, and Tyrants under the reverenced name of Rulers . . . then there is a confirmed and accomplished Servitude. . . . This is the height of human Slavery."[43]

It was the fight waged by Peter Zenger, Thomas Paine, Philip Freneau, and their followers that gave to American democracy such singular force and solidity. They carried on the fight which Bacon, Culpeper, Fendall, and Leisler had begun. They were great liberals at a time when liberalism was radical doctrine. They identified themselves with the people, proclaimed themselves democrats, and attacked the aristocrats and plutocrats. To be a democrat then was like being a Communist today.

Zenger, Paine, and Freneau in their day were prophets of a new economic and political order, and if Zenger was not the greatest of these fuglemen, he was one of the earliest and one of the most courageous.

It was not until the coming of the machine and modern capitalism, with the creation of an industrial proletariat and the institution of wage slavery, that a different type of social prophet was born, who believed in a collective instead of an individualistic form of society. It was not the task of Zenger, Paine, and Freneau to work for a collective society. It was their task to free the rising capitalist order of the vestiges of feudal tyranny and to encourage an individualistic attitude in economics and a democratic one in politics.

## CHAPTER XVI

# Pennsylvania: The Peace State

*That all persons living in the province who confess and acknowledge the one Almighty and Eternal God to be the Creator, Upholder, and Ruler of the World, and that hold themselves obliged in conscience to live peaceably and justly in civil society, shall in no way be molested or prejudiced for their religious persuasion or practise in matters of faith and worship, nor shall they be compelled at any time to frequent or maintain any religious worship place or ministry what soever.*

—35th Clause in Penn's Laws for State of Pennsylvania

ALTHOUGH Maryland was founded by Catholics, it never allowed them the continued freedom that they possessed in Pennsylvania. No colony proferred such a happy haven for Papists as Pennsylvania. During the Protestant rebellions in Maryland, it was not uncommon for Catholics to flee to Pennsylvania for refuge.[1] Even New York, which did not molest Jews or Quakers, did not give Catholics religious liberty. The only limitation imposed upon Catholics in Pennsylvania was that which prevented them from holding office. In order to hold office in the colony it was necessary to deny papal supremacy, and that no Catholic could do.

Whatever else Penn failed in, he succeeded in making his colony celebrated for the rare virtues of peace and toleration. Penn's pledge to preserve religious freedom in his province is notable for both its wisdom and its challenge. "Because the happiness of Mankind depends so much upon the enjoying of Liberty of their Consciences," Penn declared, "I do hereby solemnly declare, promise and grant for me, my heirs and assigns, that the first article of this charter, relating to liberty of Conscience, and every part and clause therein, according to the true intent and meaning thereof shall be kept and remain without any alteration, inviolably forever."

William Penn was a man of noble intent, of inspired wisdom, who met his spiritual Waterloo in his attempt to reconcile his ideals with realities.* Like all other men, he was a product of temperament and circumstance. By temperament he was romantic, idealistic, fanatical; by circumstance he was rich, powerful, authoritarian. He was ahead of his time in religious vision and in his belief in the essential goodness and wisdom of man, but behind his time in his conception of government and of popular sovereignty. Like many other men, Penn was a dual personality. No one spoke more nobly than he and yet at times no one acted more ignobly than he. He wanted to disseminate happiness but failed in his aim. To the end of his days he knew that his colony had been a failure—a failure in the ideals that he exalted. The failure resulted not from the loss of his ideals, which he retained to the last, but because of his inability to adjust those ideals to the practical realities of frontier life. Possessing wisdom, he wanted to spread it; possessing wealth, he wanted to retain it. Exemplifying the Biblical statement that "money is the root of all evil," he discovered it impossible to adopt procedures or to venture in directions that threatened his control of the colony.

Penn was far more puritanic than the Puritans in his attitude toward life, and he fought with unremitting determination all those upper middle-class and aristocratic tendencies which wealth encouraged. When some of the Quakers who became wealthy began to wear exciting and enchanting clothes, Penn condemned them, asking, "How many pieces of riband and what feathers, lacebands and the like did Adam and Eve wear in paradise, or out of it?" Penn, wealthy though he was, was not concerned with such gaudy trifles. He desired a simple way of life, and if at times he deviated from it, it was by accident rather than by design. Penn, like Fox and later Woolman, was opposed to dancing, play-acting, cards, gambling, drink—in fact, to all forms of diversion which might lend a mundane joy to existence.† "How many plays did Jesus Christ and his apostles recreate themselves at?" Penn asked, and then proceeded to denounce every variety of artistry and artifice practiced at the time. These were the words of the courageous William Penn, who refused

* This chapter will not contain an extended account of Penn's life or of the activities of the Quakers, because most of that material can be found in the earlier chapter "The Religious Equalitarians," in the section on the Quakers.

† Penn did have a wine cellar and at times did offer alcoholic stimulants to his friends, but no one ever saw him drink them himself nor was he ever known to have been under their influence.

to uncover his head in the presence of the king, and who suffered imprisonment in the Tower because of his convictions.

The Quakers, as we have seen, were Dissenters of a different order and denomination. Originally they had been more revolutionary in their economics than most of the other Dissenter groups; they had believed in communism at times and had continuously fought all attempts on the part of the rich to suppress the poor. When Penn joined the Friends, they had already begun to modify their beliefs; many of the society had acquired wealth and station and preferred to maintain rather than destroy the prevailing economic order.

### WILLIAM PENN: THE PROPRIETOR

Penn was less interested in wealth than in power, but it was the power of a father and not that of a plutocrat that he wanted. He was the kind of man who would have made a good king but a bad administrator; he did not want much for himself, but he did want to determine what others were to get. He was a paternalist by instinct and spirit.* He made little, if any, money from his colonial venture, although his heirs profited greatly from it.

From the moment he stepped upon American soil in New Castle, October 28, 1682, Penn believed that he knew better than the people what was to be done, and he objected to those who preferred the populace to the proprietor. He strove to retain his original prerogative, oppose popular threats at his authority, and rule with Christian magnanimity and paternalistic sagacity. When the representatives of the people challenged his power, he compromised for a time, declared that if in the charter "there be anything that jarrs, alter it, if you want a law for this or that, prepare it." Later, however, when the members of the Assembly in their new charter insisted upon certain changes in land tenure and contract, Penn, fearing such invasion of his rights, revised the document, which was then passed by the Assembly and remained for almost a century the established law of the colony.

* "Though good laws do well," wrote Penn, "good men do better, for good laws may want good men, and be abolished or evaded by ill men; but good men will never want good laws nor suffer ill ones . . . liberty without obedience is confusion, and obedience without liberty is slavery."

### PENN'S FAILURE

Penn was confronted with an ancient contradiction, and history has made him pay a severe penalty for it. He was a man of wealth, who believed in the principle of poverty. Buddha, Assisi, Kropotkin solved that contradiction by surrendering their wealth and adopting the life of poverty of their fellow men. Penn did not possess such greatness. He held on to his wealth,* but at the same time wanted to do all he could for his fellow men. Wealth, however, is too heavy an albatross for men of vision to bear; they know that they must either fling it off or succumb to its influence. Penn succumbed. He did his best to make his colony a utopia of peace and prosperity, a political oasis in the new world, but he failed because the power born of his wealth was too great to surrender. Benjamin Franklin phrased it well when he described the change that came over Penn after he came to America: "Less of the Man of God now appeared, and more of the man of the world." [3] †

Penn's failure was not singular. All other Quakers who acquired wealth failed in the same way. The poor Quakers, on the other hand, clung to their original beliefs and principles, and Penn had his difficulties with them as well as with the rest of the settlers. Since they did not believe in church or churchmen, they saw no reason to believe in governments or governors. "Friends here," wrote Logan to Penn, "think government so ill-fitted to their principles," [4] and then proceeded to expatiate upon the obstinacy of the Friends, as well as the rest of the populace, regarding the payment of the taxes imposed upon them. In fact, Logan, who was Penn's representative and who never failed to protect the latter's interests, went so far as to endorse Penn's suggestion that a bargain "be made with the Crown." If Penn could not collect their taxes, perhaps the Crown could: such was Logan's logic. But Penn was still hopeful of getting the colony out of the red by other maneuvers. His first hope was to monopolize the fur trade, but Logan soon warned him that this would be impossible.[5]

* In 1699 Penn occupied in America an 8,000-acre estate, upon which was erected a magnificent house that cost over $35,000. In that house he entertained his guests in most handsome and lavish fashion.[2]

† The book in all likelihood was written by the English Lawyer, Richard Jackson, but was definitely sponsored by Franklin.

### HIS SYBARITIC WAY OF LIFE

It is difficult to judge a man such as Penn, for he represented more exasperating paradoxes of behavior than most men of his time. He preached poverty and asceticism and yet lived in a mansion embellished in extravagant style; he ate off silver dishes, kept a cellar of fine wines, ales, and cider,* provided an elegant coach and a stable of horses for his family, wore expensive wigs, and dressed himself and his relatives in the latest ingenuities of style of the day.[7] At the same time he tried to instruct his followers to deny such luxuries as evidences of weakness and sin. Then again he insisted with a determination even exceeding that of Lord Baltimore upon the collection of quitrents, and down until 1884 his heirs succeeded in forcing the state of Pennsylvania to pay them for their property claims.

On the other hand, it must be admitted in Penn's defense that he declared that "I propose that which is extraordinary, to leave myself and my successors no power of doing mischief." Unfortunately he never converted his promise into practice, but there can be little doubt that he at the time meant what he said. Besides, he was the first of the proprietors to prohibit imprisonment for minor debts or minor crimes. In religion a similar contradiction existed. In favor of complete freedom of worship, as he avowed, he nevertheless would not open the doors of his colony to non-Christians, and this meant the exclusion of the Jews.[8] Over a century passed before Catholics could hold office in the colony or Jews become citizens. Again, unlike any other proprietor, Penn reprinted the *Magna Charta* and other documents upon which British liberty was based, so that his colonists would remember the origins of their freedom. The franchise he granted his colony, lacking though it was in certain economic liberties, was "twice as liberal as [that of] Connecticut, the most democratic of the other colonies, and with ten times the voting power of old England."[9] So liberal were his decrees that at the time of the Revolutionary War most Pennsylvanians could find little reason to grow enthusiastic about fighting for liberty, and the colony entered the fray with marked reluctance.

These are a few, and the most fundamental, of the contradictions

* In Watson's *Annals*[6] a writer remarks upon Penn's sybaritic form of life, declaring that "his suite is equivalent to that of the Great Mogul."

vital in the career of William Penn and the history of his colony.

In terms of the colony itself, the struggle was resolved into the conflict, first, over the rights and powers of the Assembly, and second, over the quitrent issue.

## II

### THE ASSEMBLY ISSUE: DAVID LLOYD, THE CHAMPION

The man who gave Penn most trouble was David Lloyd. Lloyd was in all likelihood a relative of Thomas Lloyd; the latter was president of the council when Penn left the province in 1684. Both of the Lloyds believed in the democratic instead of the aristocratic tradition, but it was David who, during most of his life, fought the more decisively for it.

David Lloyd, born in Wales in 1656, was sent over by Penn to be his attorney-general in Pennsylvania. Penn never suspected that Lloyd would turn against him and defend the people's cause against that of the proprietor. Lloyd made the mistake of believing that when Penn said, "We lay a foundation for after-ages to understand their liberty as men and Christians, that they may not be brought into bondage but by their own consent, for we put the power in the people," he meant to put such ideas into practice.

Lloyd proved to be the greatest lawyer in Pennsylvania, the most eloquent and effective statesman of his day; and he was the most formidable opponent of William Penn. It was through his leadership that an independent Assembly was finally acquired, that Negro slavery was successfully combated, that the courts were reformed, and that power was placed in the hands of the people instead of the proprietor.

Logan, vigilant in everything concerning the prosperity of Penn's plans, was convinced that David Lloyd, who had been the leader of the Assembly, was a dangerous man not easily to be dismissed. In 1703 he had written Penn stating that "as for David Lloyd, he must be in (the Assembly) therefore resolve, as honorably as possible, to fall in with him, it being as things stand, of absolute necessity." [10]

Lloyd was not a Bacon or a Zenger, but he did believe that *the Assembly* should be superior to the dictates of the proprietor, and he carried on a long, bitter fight in defense of his conviction. Though he lacked the heroic proportions of certain of his predecessors, who challenged royal and proprietary power, he was not less vigorous and determined in the pursuance of his aim.* His victory was due to his amazing and admirable pertinacity. Nothing daunted him. He knew that he was working for a popular cause, and even when the outlook was darkest, he persevered in his battle, and not in vain. Eventually Lloyd won; the council, which had been Penn's personal instrument, and which he had packed with rich men as well as personal friends, was dissolved, and the Assembly acquired the authority and power for which Lloyd had fought.

Logan had realized, as he wrote to Penn in 1702, that he was "universally found fault with by the common vogue of the country," and Lloyd, aware of that discontent, profited from it. Logan had tried previously to prevent an election by refusing to allow the Assembly to meet, explaining his action to Penn as necessary to avoid the legislative difficulties and disputes that it would create. "All our study," Logan stated, "should be only to preserve peace and good order and prevent occasions of complaint." He was especially concerned in discouraging the lower counties, which later achieved their independence and became Delaware, from revolt. Penn himself, a year earlier in a letter to Logan, had advised that he "had rather the lower counties began with me than I with them" and had also urged Logan to "ply David Lloyd discreetly (and dispose) him to a proprietary plan." Penn by this time feared Lloyd and was glad to make a compromise that would satisfy and pacify him. But Lloyd wanted more than Penn was willing to grant, and it was only after a turbulently protracted struggle that Penn was forced to admit defeat and grant power to the Assembly, which Lloyd defended.

Lloyd's battle for the rights of the Assembly was an old one. It was an essential part of the struggle of the populace against the proprietors and the Crown. The whole future of American democracy was involved in it. Should the Assembly, which came closest to representing the will of the populace, be superior in power to the proprietor or not? That was the issue, and Lloyd said that the Assembly should have that superiority.

The Pennsylvania Assembly, like those in other colonies, was not a democratic body. Democracy has always been relative, and whether

* Bolles, an advocate of Penn and of Lloyd, writes of the latter as follows: "He had been born out of due time for the most brilliant display of his abilities. Had he lived amidst the Revolutionary storm, he would have been one of the leaders, perhaps the greatest of all, in fertility of resource and audacity of execution." [11]

we ever get pure democracy is still a moot question. The struggle to get more democracy, however, has always been a noble one, because it means that more individuals, more people, have something to say about what they need, want, do. The fight for rights of assembly in the various colonies was not a fight for the fourth estate but for the third. Nathaniel Bacon, as has been previously noted, never fought for landless farmers, indentured servants, or black slaves; he was not interested in them. Bacon was interested, as also was Lloyd, in the freemen, the freeholders, those who had some land, some property, some privilege, whose rights had been violated by governor, proprietor, or king. He wanted them to have a lever of opposition, a pivot of protection, against the ruling authority or class that controlled the mechanics of society.

Lloyd was waging the same democratic fight * that all opposition-

* Mr. Andrews differs in this regard, refusing to give Lloyd the credit he deserves for the struggle he waged against ruling class power. Mr. Andrews is a great scholar, but painfully conservative in his opinions, as is evinced in his attitude not only toward Lloyd but also toward Leisler and other oppositionists in the various colonies. Another conservative historian who attacks Lloyd is William Robert Shepherd, who describes him as "an ambitious and somewhat unscrupulous party leader, who lost no opportunity to oppose and perplex the proprietor."[12] Dr. Shepherd sentimentalizes over Penn, and, as overwhelming proof of his bias against anything popular or opposed to the interests of the proprietor, he sneers at the important constitution of 1701, which under Lloyd's leadership was actually wrested from Penn, as "scarcely worthy of examination, except as showing the advance of the assembly from a mere ratifying body to a position equal with the governor in legislative power." Again, later, he shows his lack of sympathy with the populace and exaggerated sympathy for Penn and all those in authority. "To pacify them (the people)," Shepherd writes, "he (Penn) had granted a charter of exceptional privileges. Would they value it? Would they recognize and appreciate his kindness?"[13] The fact of the matter is that Penn gave the people the charter not out of the kindness of his heart but because he was forced to do so by the threat of political pressure and potential revolt.

More liberal historians have written of David Lloyd in an antipodal spirit, praising him for his courage and sagacity. Lawrence Lewis, Jr., for instance, writes that "David Lloyd (was) ever watchful and jealous of the public interests.... No epithet was in their minds (the minds of his enemies) too harsh to be applied to him, and no motive too base to be attributed as the mainspring of his actions. Neither the intensity of his partisan feelings, the rash and impetuous character of his actions, nor the repeated slanders and sneers of his enemies can avail to hide from the discriminating eye of the unprejudiced observer his abilities, his virtues, and his usefulness to the community."[14] Lewis even gives credit to Lloyd for "most of the important court laws passed up to the date of his death," and adds that "few of the early colonists of this Province deserve the thanks and remembrance of posterity more than David Lloyd."[15]

Rufus M. Jones, the great authority on the Quakers, observes that "the leader of the opposition (to the Proprietary party) was David Lloyd, a Welshman of remarkable ability. His standing as a Friend was better than Logan's. He was fully devoted to their extreme views concerning war and oaths. He was an intense democrat, a stout champion of popular rights... who marshalled the country Friends against the aristocratic tendencies of the proprietary party, and opposed with vigour and success any increase of its prerogatives."[16]

ists were in those days against the authority of proprietor or king. He had no vision of democracy in its present form. After all, we must not forget that as late as 1842 all people were not able to vote in Rhode Island (the free state founded by Roger Williams) and that Thomas Dorr was jailed because he battled for that significant right; it is important to remember that after the Constitutional Convention the vote was granted to scarcely more than one-fifth of the population.

Democracy in this country has been a gradual evolutionary process, a slow, accumulative development. What democracy we have was attained only through struggle. Those in power never grant rights and privileges to those who are not in power unless the latter struggle for them. American democracy today is a result of that struggle. Democracy is a dynamic and not a static concept. Today we have political democracy; tomorrow, it is to be hoped, we shall have industrial democracy. Whether we get it or not will be determined by the success of the struggle to extend political freedom to include economic freedom. At the present time the future of industrial democracy is in the hands of the labor movement; in David Lloyd's day it was in the hands of the freemen. The freemen were not battling for those who were not freemen, but in their endeavor to defend and promote their own ends they also advanced the interests of their economic inferiors and prepared the way for the democracy of our day.

### THE CONTRADICTION OF THE REVOLUTIONARY WAR

To understand the early history of this country, it is necessary to bear in mind that there were two struggles in progress before the Revolutionary War: first, that of the landed proprietors and wealthy merchants against the Crown and its representatives, and second, that of the underprivileged freemen against the oppressive proprietors and exploitive merchants. The Revolutionary War was inspired and sponsored by the proprietors and merchants whose ends it served. The prosperous landed gentry and the rich merchants had everything to gain from the war—freedom from British taxation, escape from constrictions of enterprise, an unhampered market, an untrammeled sea. The freemen had relatively little to gain from the war. Their conflict was more often with the proprietor than with the king—with laws, charters, constitutions, which favored the landlords and commercial barons. The freemen supported the Revolutionary War only because the dominant groups made appeals, adopted slogans, guaranteed profits, advocated programs, that promised freemen advantages they had not possessed before. Even at that, as we shall see later, the freemen did not plunge themselves into the War with any great enthusiasm, and the fourth estate was not concerned with it at all. Little did it care whether it was ruled by the Crown or the colonists: it would be oppressed and exploited equally by both.

The proprietors and merchants, however, converted the issue into a social challenge, and men like Thomas Paine and Philip Freneau, prophets of a new society, endowed it with a significance that aroused and stirred the hearts and souls of men.

After the Revolutionary War the conflicts in the country changed; the fight against England was over, but it was supplanted by the strife between the North and the South and the battle between capital and labor. The Civil War solved the first conflict, which was between an industrial and an agrarian economy, between a wage-slave and a bond-slave regime. After the Civil War the struggle between capital and labor became paramount, and to this day it has continued with increasing and exacerbated intensity.

### DAVID LLOYD'S STRUGGLE

David Lloyd could not have foreseen this. He was a reasonably simple, humble, courageous man, living at the end of the seventeenth and the early part of the eighteenth century, when industrial machinery was still undeveloped and an industrial proletariat still unborn. He was interested in forcing Penn to surrender part of his proprietary power and give it to the Assembly, which was the only popular body in the colony.

Several successive charters had to be wrung from Penn before representative government was gained in the province. To the end Penn insisted upon retaining his right to veto any laws the Assembly passed, but the latter body would not grant him the privilege. Upon one occasion the Assembly attacked Penn for having forced it to accept the Charter of 1683 and for refusing to allow it to be changed or amended.[17]

### STRUGGLE FOR FREEDOM OF PRESS

Penn's fight against the rising tide of popular influence was directed not only against Lloyd. He had Anthony Weston lashed for having made certain political suggestions of a popular character to the council; he suppressed Atken's *Almanac* because it printed an attack upon him, and confiscated William Bradford's printing press because of adverse remarks upon his government.[18] He censured Joseph Growden, a leading citizen, for publishing and distributing *The Frame of Government*.[19] He even went so far as to condemn the free use of the printing press.

Bradford's case preceded that of Zenger and, therefore, can be regarded as the first battle waged in the colonies in favor of freedom of the press. Bradford, a humble printer with a flair for truth, hazarded among other things the publication of various pamphlets of George Keith, the iconoclastic and heterodox Quaker. Not only was Bradford arrested but his whole printing establishment was confiscated. When he was tried, Bradford refused to have a lawyer argue his cause; with characteristic frontier defiance he defended himself. Pleading "not guilty," he challenged the jury to convict him of a crime of which he was innocent—spreading false doctrine. What he published was truth, and until it had been proved not to be truth he was an innocent man. The jury was impressed by his challenge and could not agree upon a verdict; Bradford was thereupon discharged, a stronger and freer man.

Born in 1663, Bradford lived to the rare old age of eighty-nine, happy to the end of his days in this triumph over Penn's tyranny.

In the end, the people's cause, backed by Lloyd, was victorious, Penn's authority was checked and curbed, and Pennsylvania entered a new and more liberal period. No better proof of the democratic nature of Lloyd's struggle is to be found than in the revealing words of Governor Evans (1706), who was opposed to Lloyd and sympathetic to Penn:

> The people forced Penn to rob himself of his rights in the Government, and in his property, and that David Lloyd was at the head of it, and he and his associates meant by it to overthrow the fundamentals of the English Constitution and establish a Government more nearly like a republic.[20]

DEMOCRACY VERSUS ARISTOCRACY

*In short, Lloyd was fighting for a republic, Penn for a continuation of the monarchy with himself as aristocratic proprietor.*

It is no wonder, then, that when Lloyd wrote to his friends in England, begging them to intercede with the queen because William Penn had done nothing "for (their) relief," [21] Penn denounced him as a man without religion or principles "but that of his (own) interest and revenge." [22] On another occasion Penn called Lloyd "a self-interested tool . . . that owes his bread to me, too." [23]

*It is to Lloyd that most credit belongs for endowing the Assembly with power and infusing the constitution of the colony with democratic challenge.* Lloyd not only won independence for the Assembly but succeeded in destroying the influence of the council, which Penn had originally invested with superior if not sovereign authority.

Lloyd's battle had been against the party of the proprietor, led by Penn's friend and representative, James Logan, who through a long span of years fought Lloyd with every weapon at his command. Both men were Quakers, but that did not lessen the struggle between them. The conflict, however, was more economic and political than personal and individual. It was rooted in the class struggle that was being waged between the paternalistic interests of Penn and the independent interests of the lower middle class, which was the rising economic class of the time. Penn clung to all the vestiges of the baronial tradition; Lloyd, advocating the cause of the lower middle class, was eager to destroy such anachronistic appendages, remove power from Penn, and transfer it to the people.

Although Penn had been robbed of control over his colony at the time of the accession of William and Mary, and Benjamin Fletcher had been made governor-in-chief, he regained control of it later, and despite his attempt to sell it before he died, his wife succeeded in thwarting his aim and kept it in the possession of the family for generations after.

Pennsylvania rapidly became one of the most prosperous colonies on the Atlantic seaboard. "It is not to the fertility of our soil that we ought chiefly to attribute the great progress this province has made," Andrew Hamilton, one of the best lawyers in the colony, declared; "it is practically and almost wholly owing to the excellency of our Constitution." [24] The excellency of the Constitution was due not to Penn or Logan or Fletcher, but to David Lloyd.

In his old age, Lloyd made peace with Penn and accepted in 1717 the chief justiceship of the province, which he retained until his death in 1731.

An illustration of the democratic spirit that Lloyd encouraged is to be discovered in the statement of the Assembly in 1739, when it refused to pass a bill initiated by the governor to provide for militia:

> If we have committed any mistakes, the time draws near in which our constituents, if they think it necessary, may amend their choice, and the time also draws nigh in which your [counselors' and governor's] mistakes may be amended by a succeeding Governor. Permit us to congratulate our country on both.[25]

### THE SLAVERY ISSUE

That democratic spirit manifested itself also in the early opposition to black slavery in the colony. The Quakers, as we have seen, were among the first to condemn slavery as an institution, even though many of them did little more than urge its gradual abolition. Penn, for example, never advocated the manumission of slaves, but in his will he arranged to have his own slaves set free at his death.[26] He did encourage good treatment of slaves, and was known to have been most kind to his own. Even George Fox, as has already been noted, did not demand the immediate cessation of black slavery, but suggested its evolutionary demise. The German leader, Pastorius, had denounced slavery as early as 1688. Many other groups soon joined in a chorus of denunciation.* Again, one of the leaders who did most in defense of antislavery sentiment was David Lloyd, who was ever in the forefront of every melioristic conception or action.[27] It was not until 1758, however, that the Quakers as a group went on record as being definitely opposed to slavery, and it was as late as 1775 before they took action against members of their group

* Other details concerning the attitude of the Quakers toward slavery are to be found in the Quaker section in the chapter "Religious Equalitarians."

who owned slaves. "Such members as continued to hold slaves," it was decided, "are to be testified against as other transgressors are by the rules of our Discipline for other immoral, unjust, and reproachful conduct." During the Revolutionary War the last black slaves in Pennsylvania were emancipated.

In fairness to fact, it should be noted that Negro slavery existed in Pennsylvania before it was settled by William Penn and his followers,[28] that William Penn himself in a letter to his steward at Pennsburg (his Pennsylvania estate) advised that it would be wiser to secure Negro slaves to work it since they could be retained for life, and that antislavery sentiment in the colony in later years reflected the lack of necessity for that form of slavery in the province. The prevalence of small farms and the absence of plantations, plus the early development of commerce and industry, rendered lifelong slavery unnecessary.* Penn, influenced by the new conditions, changed his mind on the issue and, as we have seen, favored manumission, and in 1701 he liberated his own slaves. The colony, consequently, had less Negro slaves than New Jersey and less than half as many as New York. Indentured servants, or white slaves, predominated in the Quaker Province.

### TREATMENT OF THE INDIANS

In certain respects the Quakers were kinder to the Indians than to the Negroes. In 1687 one of the Indians stated that:

> The Strong liquor was first sold us by the Dutch, and they are blind; they had no eyes, they did not see it was for our hurt. The next people that came among us were the Swedes who continued the sale of liquor to us; they were also blind, they had no eyes . . . we knew it to be hurtful to us, but if people will sell it to us, we are so in love with it that we cannot forbear it. When we drink, it makes us mad. . . . Seven score of our people have been killed by reason of drinking it. . . . These people that sell it have no eyes. But now there is a people (Quakers) come to live among us that have eyes; they see it to be for our hurt; they are willing to deny themselves the profit of it for our good. These people have eyes.

* E. R. Turner in that regard makes the interesting and sound illation that the only difference between white and black slavery was in duration of years.

No other group, no other colony, was so friendly with the Indians as the Quakers, and for years Pennsylvania was viewed by the Indians as the home of the "good white men." Penn's letter to the Indians is as memorable as it is singular. With the exception of Roger Williams, no other colonial leader among the English had ever addressed the Indians in such language:

My Friends:

There is a great God and power, that hath made the world, and all things therein, to whom you and I, and all people owe their being, and well-being; and to whom you and I must one day give an account for all that we do in the world.

This great God hath written his law in our hearts, by which we are taught and commanded to love and help, and do good to one another. *Now this great God hath been pleased to make me concerned in your part of the world;* and the King of the country where I live hath given me a great province therein; *but I desire to enjoy it with your love and consent;* that we may always live together, as neighbors and friends; *else what would the great God do to us, who hath made us, not to devour and destroy one another, but to live soberly and kindly together in the world?* now I would have you well observe, that I am very sensible of the unkindness and injustice that have been too much exercised towards you by the people of these parts of the world; who have sought themselves, and to make great advantages by you, rather than to be examples of goodness and patience unto you; which I hear hath been a matter of trouble to you, and caused great grudging and animosities, sometimes to the shedding of blood; which hath made the great God angry. *But I am not such a man;* as is well known in my own country. I have great love and regard towards you; and desire to win and gain your love and friendship, by a kind, just and peaceable life; and the people I send are of the same mind, and shall, in all things, behave themselves accordingly; and, if in anything any shall offend you, or your people, you shall have a full and speedy satisfaction for the same, by an equal number of just men, on both sides; that by no means you may have just occasion of being offended against them.

I shall shortly come to you myself; at which time we may more largely and freely confer and discourse of these matters; in the meantime I have sent my commissioners to treat with you about land, and a firm league of peace; let me desire you to be kind to them, and receive these presents and tokens which I have sent you as a testimony of my good will to you, and my resolution to live justly, peaceably and friendly with you.

I am your loving friend,
William Penn.

After Penn's death, however, that happy relationship ceased. Later governors and representatives of the Penn family treated the Indians with less courtesy and consideration, and by the middle of the eighteenth century open hostility had sprung up between the groups.

### DECLINE OF QUAKER IDEALISM

The Quakers dominated the legislature in Pennsylvania from 1682 to 1756, but their attitudes differed as much as those in other colonies, and the history of Pennsylvania is fraught with those variations. Class divisions among them produced as much dissension as elsewhere. They all agreed only on certain points: pacifism (even there Logan and other Quakers demurred) and the refusal to take oaths or doff their hats. Beyond that they differed in wealth, power, privilege, distinction. The battle between the people and the proprietors continued unabated. Even after the Quakers lost power, the conflict continued, and none other than Benjamin Franklin led the opposition group, which insisted that the Crown take over the colony from the proprietary family.

What ruined the Quakers and the popular cause in Pennsylvania was accretion of wealth and prestige and the development of economic and class distinctions, which today find an unfortunate and ironic culmination in the plutocrat Herbert Hoover. Hoover represents but one of the many Quakers who have become plutocrats in recent generations. Centuries before, however, in the days of George Fox, such types had already begun to acquire ascendancy in Quaker communities. Fox writes about the people of wealth and position who attended his meetings.[29] In other places he comments on the people of quality he met along the eastern shore of Maryland. By this time the early communist tradition of many of the European Quakers was forgotten, and even a man as sincere as George Fox was not averse to the presence of such personages. The truth is, as his *Journal* copiously illustrates, that he was immensely impressed by their attendance. He constantly commented upon the magistrates, judges, wives of councillors, justices of the peace, captains, sheriffs, and other individuals of the "upper-rank of people" and "persons of note" who listened to his words. Unlike the earlier Quakers, Fox was conscious of rank, position, and wealth, and it was this consciousness that ultimately led to the destruction of the idealism to which the original Quakers had given birth.*

Penn himself, as we have observed, was far from guiltless of luxurious living; although a believer in Quaker doctrine, he did not practice the humbler virtues of his sect. He was a rich Quaker and he lived in accordance with his wealth. He preferred the rich Quakers to the poor ones, because the former were sympathetic with his aims, whereas the latter were not. The poor Quakers retained something of the essence of apostolic Christianity; the rich Quakers retained only the form of it. David Lloyd appealed to the poor Quakers, especially those in the rural districts; Penn appealed to the wealthier, who in the main lived in the more urban sections of the colony.

But in the last analysis Penn, with all his defects, was superior to all the other colonial proprietors. It is true that he advocated the prosecution of David Lloyd, urged Logan to "bow him to better manners and gain him, or prosecute to the rigour of the law," and even threatened that he would "have that mischievous man, David Lloyd, brought on his knees . . . let his defenders do and say what they will," but the fact remains that there were no rebellions or revolts in the colony. David Lloyd's fight with Penn never became violent, never acquired the character of internecine warfare, as did the struggles of Bacon, Culpeper, Leisler, Fendall, and Coode. This difference resulted from two factors: the Quakers' refusal to bear arms and Penn's willingness to compromise rather than struggle. In any other colony the conflict between Lloyd and Penn would have terminated in violence; Quakerism alone prevented that catastrophe. The pacifism of the Quakers did not eliminate conflict, but it did discourage military strife.

* This accounts in great part for the fact that the more genuine and less wealthy Quakers forged westward. Today, for instance, two-thirds of the Quakers are to be found west of the Alleghenies. In Indiana and Ohio there are more Quakers at the present time than along the whole Atlantic seaboard.[30]

## III

### INFLUENCE OF THE SWEDES

Pennsylvania, to be sure, was not founded exclusively by Quakers. In fact, the pioneers in the province were Swedes who settled first in the territory now known as Delaware, and then migrated into Pennsylvania. The first church to be established in the colony was Swedish; not many years after its doors were opened in 1646, another Swedish Church was organized. The influence of the Swedes upon colonial life in Pennsylvania was far more decisive than is customarily conceded. Philadelphia's city flag, for example, is the same as the national flag of Sweden—blue and yellow.[31] The Swedes constructed the first houses and founded the first government and the first series of courts in the province. The Swedish settlers, in the main, belonged to the same economic class as the original Quakers and the Germans and Scotch-Irish who came later—the poor but upward-struggling lower middle class—and their economic, social, and moral attitudes were emphatically similar. The same attitudes prevailed among the New England settlers. The great bulk of them lived lives of stern and severe discipline; gaiety was anathema to them. They eschewed on principle the joys and jollities of the wealthier, aristocratic classes. Only those among them who were rich or had begun to acquire riches deviated from such discipline.

The Quakers took over most of what the Swedes had contributed and wove it into their own cultural pattern. They carried on the same moral traditions as the other Dissenter groups, except that they laid stress also upon certain attitudes peculiar to their creed. Their view of marriage, for example, did not differ from that of the Pilgrims or Puritans. Penn himself had declared, "never marry but for love, but see that thou lovest what is lovely." The Quakers, however, were zealous endogamists. Any Quaker marrying a non-Quaker was immediately expelled from the Society.[32] Adultery was viewed with the same abhorrence as in New England, even though the penalties differed. For the first offense of infidelity, the person convicted was to be publicly whipped and sent to prison for one year; for the second offense, the imprisonment was to be for life.

Although parents often sold their children into slavery after they arrived, they were supposed to instruct them in the virtues of the embryonic bourgeois morality of the time. The Quakers exalted the family and the home into an ideal. Penn himself had encouraged education in order that "all scandalous living may be prevented, and that youth may be successively trained up in virtue and useful knowledge and arts." In order to keep children out of mischief and to see that when they grew up they did not become indigents, he insisted that they be taught a trade; idleness among young and old, he was convinced, was the breeder of immorality and crime. To a large extent, Pennsylvania's advanced school system was a product of that conviction.

## IV

### DEVELOPMENT OF NORTHERN COMMERCE

The political and economic struggle in Pennsylvania did not cease after David Lloyd's victories; it merely changed. Like the other Middle Atlantic and the New England colonies, Pennsylvania suffered from the fact that its staples were not what the mother country needed. It could not exchange its commodities for English goods as the Southern countries could with their tobacco, rice, indigo, and cotton crops. What made matters worse was England's refusal to purchase wheat, flour, fish, and livestock from the colonies, because these products threatened to undermine her own agricultural interests. In order to meet that difficulty the colonists had to devise those techniques of exchange that finally established American commercialism upon a sound basis.

It was this very disadvantage which led to the development of that network of commerce in the North which gave it a large part of its superiority over the South. The very fact that the South found it easy to exchange its products for English goods thwarted its commercial advance. It did not have to concern itself, as did the North, with evolving those schemes and stratagems of exchange that are the *sine qua non* of commerce. The New England and Middle Atlantic states needed English things as much as the South, but since the English would not buy what they produced, they learned how to sell them at higher prices to other peoples. This necessity inspired contacts and relationships, cultivated plans and evolutions of enterprise, which ultimately resulted in greater profits for the North than the South was ever able to make from its transactions with the old country.

Boston, Philadelphia, New York, were all outgrowths of such enterprise. They speedily became the emporia of the new world, and it was not long before they rivaled English cities in both size and significance. With the exception of Charleston, the South developed no such cities. It did not need them. Its contacts and exchanges were relatively simple, and the problem of supplying its needs was even simpler.

### PHILADELPHIA: THE LONDON OF THE NEW WORLD

The hub of Pennsylvania's prosperity was Philadelphia, which for a considerable time was superior to New York as a center of seaboard commerce. The name of the city in all likelihood was derived from the Philadelphists' sect in London, although it is possible that the name sprang from other origins. At all events, it was first used by the Philadelphists, whose leader was Jane Leade, with whom Kelpius came into contact when he visited London before he founded his Woman in the Wilderness colony in Pennsylvania.[33] As Philadelphia grew, the character of Pennsylvania altered. The fight for assembly rights, waged by David Lloyd, changed now to a fight against the special claims of the proprietary family. This fight was led by none other than Benjamin Franklin, who made Philadelphia his home.

Penn's descendants lacked his generosity and vision. His sons in particular were of an ungenerous nature, and ruled the colony unwisely and inhumanely. They were shrewd but not sagacious, conniving but not courageous. They succeeded in aggravating the conflict between the colonists and themselves; until 1884 they forced the populace to pay them and their heirs a feudal revenue, the total sum of which was unjustly heavy, amounting to over £150,000.

### THE QUITRENT CONFLICT

In a number of the colonies quitrents provided an impressive part of the income of the various proprietors. In feudal days quitrents were a monetary contribution on the part of the commoner or tenant to the lord in appreciation of which the former was freed of (or quitted of) any further obligations. The English aristocracy, as Andrews has keenly stressed, viewed America as a new source of quitrent profits,[34] and they did their best to fasten this burden upon the populace. The latter, however, waged such a strenuous battle against the burden that it never became a final fixture. The fact that New England had escaped the quitrent burden established a precedent and inspired the other colonies with the belief that they could evade it also if they opposed it with sufficient determination. New England, incidentally, never suffered from the conflicts that arose in the other colonies as by-products of the quitrent issue.*

No proprietor or proprietary group, however, was so successful in collecting quitrents from the colonists as Penn and his family. Before 1713, Dunaway writes, "the regular price of common land was five pounds per hundred acres with one shilling quitrent ... [later] price was raised to ten pounds per hundred acres with two shillings quitrent and continued at this rate until 1732. Then because immigration had increased rapidly the price was advanced to fifteen pounds per hundred acres with a quitrent of a half-penny per acre and remained at this figure for more than thirty years." [36] Quitrents, as we have seen, additions as they were to the purchase price of land, were a feudal appendage. Penn justified their imposition by insisting that they be paid in lieu of taxes. Until the French and Indian War, there were no taxes in Pennsylvania except an excise tax. What happened was that long after Penn had left the colony, long after he was dead, and long after his sons had died, his family descendants continued to collect an accumulative income from quitrents. The colonists struggled constantly to rid themselves of this economic burden. Whenever possible they refused to pay; where that was impossible they tried to pass legislation nullifying quitrents, but, as has been noted, it was not until 1884 that all payment on them ceased.

## THE PENNS' REFUSAL TO BE TAXED

The colonists objected not only to this exploitation but also to the refusal of the Penns to allow their lands to be taxed by the Assembly.

* Bond describes the unsuccessful attempts made to impose quitrents upon Massachusetts first by Edward Randolph, and then later by Andros, and also the vigorous opposition raised against them, especially by Increase Mather.[35]

Upon one occasion, after Braddock's defeat in the French and Indian War, when money was direly needed, William Penn offered to give £5,000 to the government, but only with the understanding that the money was to be viewed as a donation and not as a tax. He would not grant the right of the people to tax the proprietor. Like all feudal proprietors, he viewed that right as inviolate. He had refused to grant money to the Assembly when it had insisted that he pay taxes on his land; he was willing to co-operate but not to be coerced.

The people, however, voiced their sentiments through the Assembly, which, owing to the efforts of David Lloyd, had acquired decisive power; they urged that the Penn lands be taxed like all other lands, and when they ultimately discovered that the proprietary family would not submit to their demand, they insisted that the colony be converted from a proprietary to a royal one. Very soon they translated this opposition into a movement, and within a few years Benjamin Franklin was elected to go to England to present demands to the king. The demands concluded that "royal instructions are not [an] obstacle . . . but some private instructions from our Proprietaries, who in every place of their conduct towards the people of this province for some years past appear to be aiming to subvert the valuable privileges granted us by the charters from King Charles and their worthy father, in consequence of which under Providence this province was settled and is now become a great income to them." [37] Later, in the same letter, the author argued that it was the proprietary party "whose ambitious views seem bent on enslaving us," and thereupon declared that if the colony surrendered to their domination "we can no longer pretend to claim the title of being the freemen of Pennsylvania."

### FRANKLIN'S DEFEAT

Franklin found both the Penns and the Crown unresponsive to his appeal. Both feared the popular threat that he represented.[38] Disappointed and disgusted with the apathy with which his demands were received, Franklin paid a pound to have a letter printed refuting the attacks upon Pennsylvania that had been made at the time in England, and later, as cited before, he sponsored the publication of a book written by an English lawyer, Richard Jackson, called *An Historical Review of the Constitution and Government of Penn-*

*sylvania.* The book stated in unambiguous, declarative language the case of the Pennsylvania Assembly, of which Franklin was the defender and champion.[39] Franklin had been rebuffed by William Pitt, opposed by Charles Yorke, and dismissed as a trouble-maker by a multiplying number of representatives and officials of the government. He was sure, however, that this book would win these people to his side. Instead, it overwhelmed him with a typhoon of abuse. The object of the book was to "support the cause of the Assembly and people of Pennsylvania against the encroachments and arbitrary designs of the Proprietaries."

Despite Franklin's long-suffering patience, impressive logic, and foxy stratagems, he was beaten in the battle. The Privy Council ruled against the Assembly, and Franklin returned home a defeated man. But the Assembly did not cease its fight. After John Penn, who came over in 1763, proved to be as bad a governor as those who had preceded him, the Assembly adjourned, and addressed an immediate appeal to the colonists to decide whether they wanted Pennsylvania to continue as a proprietary colony or to become a royal one. The vote was overwhelmingly in favor of the Crown and against the proprietor. More than 3,000 people voted in favor of Crown sovereignty. The proprietors' group could muster only three hundred signatures in their favor.[40]

## THE FINAL VICTORY

It is altogether likely that eventually the Assembly would have won the conflict; but shortly after the Stamp Act was passed the struggle that ultimately led to the Revolutionary War became so importunate and took on such a grave aspect that everything else was overshadowed. The Assembly became less concerned with whether it was to become a royal colony than with whether there was to be any royal domination at all. Benjamin Franklin, who had been huzzahed at Chester when he set off for England on money subscribed by merchants, now became a new kind of hero. No longer was he fighting against proprietors; he was fighting for a free country, free from the oppressions and tyrannies of proprietors, councils, governors, and kings.

## CHAPTER XVII

# Delaware: The Swedish Utopia

*"This is what I most humbly recommend to your excellency," Governor Rising wrote, "to procure for me a good wife . . . relying for this object upon your excellency with more confidence than any other person in the world."*

DELAWARE, which was the first of the colonies to sign the Constitution, has right to boast, as it does, of being the first state in the United States of America. It was smaller than any other of the thirteen colonies with the exception of Rhode Island. It was founded by Swedes, who called the territory New Sweden, but it was soon swallowed up by William Penn and became part of the colony of Pennsylvania. Only after a prolonged conflict did Delaware, originally known as the "Lower Counties," finally manage to shake loose from Penn's tenacious grip and establish itself as an independent colony. Not until the Revolutionary War, however, was its independent status indisputably recognized.[1]

The "New Sweden Company" was organized in 1637. Half of its backers were Dutch, and the men who headed the group dispatched to America was Peter Minuit, ex-governor of the New Netherlands. This Swedish group, setting sail from Gothenburg in two small but sturdy vessels, the *Key of Kalmar* and the *Bird Griffin*, landed at a place called Paradise Point, which became known as Fort Christina and, ultimately, as the city of Wilmington. Originally William Usselinx, the founder of the Dutch West India Company, sponsored the organization of the Swedish Trading Company. He convinced the Swedish king, Gustavus Adolphus, that Sweden should extend its influence into new worlds. He became the head of the Swedish South Company, and undoubtedly all his plans would have succeeded if the king had not died and the German war consumed the interest of the country.[2]

### THE RISE AND FALL OF THE SWEDES

Peter Minuit carried on where the king left off. Minuit, who became the first governor of New Sweden, had already had experience in a similar capacity in the New Netherlands, and was acquainted with the difficulties that arose with the foundation of a new settlement. Peter Minuit was soon succeeded as governor by Johan Printz, under whose rule, which lasted until 1653, the colony became exclusively Swedish. The Dutch in New Netherlands disliked the presence of the Swedes because they competed in the fur trade and conflicts between them multiplied. There were times when the Dutch and Swedes united against the English, but their union was always temporary and never sufficient to combat English power. Very soon the Dutch seized the upper hand and built Fort Casimir, later to be known as New Castle, which overlooked the Delaware River. The fort was captured by the Swedes, but the one-legged Dutchman Peter Stuyvesant, who had lost his limb in a battle with the Portuguese, recaptured it, drove the Swedes from the river, and robbed them of their power.

The Swedes were of sturdy stock, inured to hardship, accustomed to poverty, and ideally equipped for frontier life. The trouble was there were not enough Swedes to put up a fight when one was necessary. It is doubtful whether there were at most ever more than a few hundred Swedes in the colony. In 1647 Johan Printz reported that there were "altogether a hundred and eighty-three souls" in the settlement.[3] Conditions in Sweden did not encourage emigration, and Sweden did not interest itself seriously in colonial enterprise, as was proved by the six-year period (1647-1653) during which not a single ship was dispatched by the old country to its New Sweden colony.

Governor Printz was a warrior by instinct as well as profession. Weighing over four hundred pounds, he was called by the Indians the "big tub," but he made decisions with athletic expedition. Making war, however, without the means necessary to prosecute it, was futile. He could combat the Dutch, as he did, when they were not numerous and were ill-equipped for aggression, but he could not combat any force that had superior numbers and equipment.

After the defeat the Swedes suffered at the hands of Peter Stuyvesant, they experienced an even worse defeat when the English came over and swallowed up the entire territory. After that their influence was practically extinguished. They did not die, but they were culturally absorbed into the English atmosphere. They clung to their native language, however, for over a century and a half.

The English brought with them new wealth, fresh enterprise, and improved methods. Very soon the Swedes themselves profited from the new regime. At one time the Swedes were crudely though adequately clothed, whereas "since the English came," as Thomas Paschal wrote, "they have gotten fine Cloaths, and are going proud." [4]

### DEMOCRACY: A SWEDISH IDEAL

The Swedes did not find the early Quakers incompatible. Their religion was almost as democratic as that of the Quakers. The majority of their rectors in the old country were democratically elected by their populaces—a right guaranteed to the Swede by his constitution [5]—and they carried that tradition over into the new world. They also took with them a profound belief in freedom, born of the struggles the people had waged in earlier days. The Swedish farmer had acquired a belief in himself and in his rights and privileges, and in his rural assemblies had learned to protect and preserve them. He was without that serf psychology which prevailed among so many of the agrarians in other European nations. He emigrated not because of economic or religious oppression but simply because he believed that he could find greater opportunity in the new world.

"One can earn in America three times the Wages for their Labour that they can in England or Wales," Gabriel Thomas asserted, and added, in proof of the successful life of the Swedes, that "there are no beggars to be seen nor need have any the least Occasion or Temptation to take up that Scandalous Lasy Life." He also comments upon the fact that "Barrenness among Women [is] hardly to be heard of, nor are old Maids to be met with for all commonly Marry before they are Twenty years of Age, and seldom any young Married Woman but hath a Child in her Belly, or one upon her Lap." [6] Gabriel Thomas did not exaggerate. Childbearing in Delaware, especially among the Swedes, who had an excess of women, never lost its popularity in colonial days. The following item is indicative of Delawarian proficiency in the art:

> Died in peace in 1771, at Wilmington, Delaware, a pious, elderly matron, who had been mother of 16 children, all married and comfortable; 68 grandchildren, 166 great-grandchildren, and 4 great-great-

grandchildren, in all 238 living offspring survived her. The generation of the just shall be blessed.[7]

### SWEDISH BATHS

Even William Penn had noted that the Swedes as well as the Dutch "have fine children, and almost every house full." More than that, bathing was one of their great ideals. In addition to ordinary baths they had steam baths and other contrivances to cultivate bathing as an art. One account of the time states that "almost every Swede had a bath house." As a description of these baths, one passage is most interesting:

> Men and women use the bath promiscuously without any concealment of dress or being in the least influenced by any emotions of attachment. . . . All the while they are in this hot bath [they] continue to rub themselves and lash every part of their bodies with switches formed of twigs of the birch tree.[8]

### PROCURING A WIFE

With the Swedes marriage was not only sacred but also imperative. When the Swedish governor Rising (Rysingh) was without a wife, he wrote to the Swedish minister to get him one. "This is what I most humbly recommend to your excellency," Rising wrote, "to procure for me a good wife . . . relying for this object upon your excellency with more confidence than any other person in the world." There was nothing latitudinarian, however, about the Swedes' concept of morality. When an unwed, pregnant woman from Maryland arrived in New Castle on January 16, 1677, she was forced to leave the place at once, because, the officials declared, "no such persons may be here harboured," and insisted that "this place [must] not serve and be counted a shelter for whores."[9]

But large families were not enough to save New Sweden from conquest. Schools were opened by the Swedes, ministers were supported, commerce was encouraged, agriculture was advanced, but a small populace with inadequate ammunition cannot survive against a larger populace with more modern armaments and techniques.

The Swedes made speedy and fast friendships with the Indians, but unlike the Dutch and the English, they did not try to inveigle them to fight in their defense. Governor Printz, it is true, had declared that the Indians were "not to be trusted" and stated that if he "should receive a couple of hundred good soldiers and in addition necessary means and good officers, then with the help of God not a single savage will be allowed to live in this river."[10] The Swedish populace, however, did not share his hostility toward the red man. The ecclesiastic Campanius described a council among the Indians whereat the Indians debated whether they should annihilate the Swedes because the latter lacked colored cloths, shining kettles, and gunpowder. The decision of the Indians was negative, because, they said, treasuring still their previous experience, we "will love the Swedes and the Swedes shall be our good friends."[11]

### BEST BREWERS IN THE LAND

In the meantime the Swedes found the fur trade most prosperous. Governor Printz's report is eloquently illustrative of their success:

> The returns which it has been possible to bring together in a hurry are herewith sent over, namely, whole beavers, 1,300, one-third part beavers 538, half beavers 299, and one-fourth part beavers 5, total, small and large beavers altogether, 2,142 pieces. The tobacco which is now sent over makes all together 20,467 lbs. And how the trade has progressed here in the last year as well as now, since the ship was here, the commissary's account and written relation will fully show.[12]

The colony had planned its economy upon a simple scale. Agriculture, cattle-raising, and trade with the Indians were all the colonists expected to promote. After a time they added brewing to their production, and the beer they made under the supervision of the governor was the best that could be found in the country.

### THE LONG SWEDE

The English, not the Dutch, ultimately quelled the Swedes. The latter did not surrender without protest. Henry Coleman and Marcus Jacobson, who claimed to be the son of the Swedish general Coningsmarke, fought bitterly against English authority. As a matter of fact, they tried to start an insurrection, claiming that Swedish ships were on the way and would be able to strengthen their struggle. Jacobson and Coleman were arrested, and the former, familiarly known as the "Long Swede" or "Long Finn," was taken to New York in irons, tried, convicted, and sent to the Barbados, where he was sold as a slave. Before he was shipped away, he was severely whipped, and branded on the forehead with the letter R and on his breast with an inscription denouncing him as a rebel. All his followers and accomplices were forced to forfeit to the king one-half of their goods, and their other possessions were subject to additional mulcts and fines. The governor had accused Jacobson of going "up and down from one place to another, frequently raising speeches, very seditious and false, tending to the disturbance of his majesty's peace," [13] and in order to prevent any extension or repetition of such insurrection, he urged that such taxes should be imposed upon the people, "as may not give them liberty to entertain any other thoughts than how to discharge them."

### TREATMENT OF JEWS

In order to attract colonists to Delaware which, despite its large families, remained sparsely settled, quitrents were waived for three years for all people who established their habitat in the territory. But even that inducement did not populate the colony. Jews, who had been excluded from so many colonies and treated with such unfairness in others, were invited by the Swedes to come to the settlement and were granted the right to trade along the Delaware. After the Swedes were defeated by the Dutch, the latter, under the rulership of the myopic and tempestuous Peter Stuyvesant, attempted to rescind the right and block the Jews from entrance into the province. The Jews in question, Abraham Lucena, Salvador D'Andrade, and Jacob Cohen, had merely asked that they be allowed "to travel, reside, and trade here as other inhabitants and to enjoy all privileges." [14] If the Swedes had remained in power, the Jews would have had no difficulty in establishing themselves in the colony. The New Netherlands' council, however, opposed their presence, and stated that "for weighty reasons is the request expressed in general terms declined." The fact that the Jews had already embarked with their goods made the Dutch willing to allow them to sell what they could, but immediately thereafter they were instructed to leave the territory. This experience of the Jews was, as we have already indicated, by no means singular.

### CONFLICT BETWEEN PENN AND THE PEOPLE

Fundamentally, the Swedes, English, Finns, Dutch, and Jews who populated the Lower Counties believed in the same lower middle-class philosophy of life. Different though they were in birth and heritage, they were similar in economic aspiration. If they had been allowed to go their own way, no conflicts would have occurred. They objected, just as did the people of Pennsylvania, to proprietary privilege and persecution. Their fight against Penn was a good fight insofar as it was linked with the fight for similar rights in other colonies. Their battle was abetted by Lord Baltimore, who was not interested in helping them but in thwarting Penn, and who, in his covetous desire to defy Penn's claims to the territory, was willing to lend his support to any groups or elements that would undermine Penn's influence and power.[15] Lord Baltimore went so far as to send agents and agitators into Penn's province to provoke trouble, and it was not long before the Lower Counties demanded a separate and independent assembly.

The Delaware territory had been granted originally to the Quaker proprietor by James II, who felt that Penn, as his foster son, deserved it. James, however, had to abdicate in such a hasty, melodramatic fashion that he did not find time to sign the charter, and for years the controversy between the Maryland and the Pennsylvania proprietors continued. It was not until the charter was discovered, six decades later, and adduced in the famous lawsuit between the representatives of the two proprietors, that the conflict was ended.

### ANOTHER PURITAN STRONGHOLD

In moral and criminal matters the Lower Counties were no less severe than the Puritans. Like all Dissenting groups, they made morality a mania. As we have already observed, what is commonly known as Puritanism in this country was not confined to New England but pervaded every colony along the seaboard in colonial times. Throughout the Counties any persons guilty of sodomy, buggery, rape, or robbery were put to death. In the case of Negro slaves, the death penalty was meted out with ruthless expedition, and the owner was refunded by the county treasury two-thirds of the value of the slave executed. Negroes convicted of rape were pilloried, their ears being nailed to the structure and then cropped off close to the head. Negro slaves—not white slaves or white freemen—who were condemned to death for theft could be spared the penalty, "in Mercy to the said owners," if the latter would inflict such corporal punishment upon the culprits "as may be requisite for a Terror to others of their colour."[16] For lesser crimes black slaves were led to a bridge "with their arms extended and tied to a pole across their necks, a cart going before them," and for three successive days were harshly whipped as they passed, and afterwards were put in irons and confined to prison. For blasphemy, whites as well as blacks were pilloried for two hours, branded with the letter B, and given thirty-nine lashes before the eyes of neighbors and friends.*

In brief, men were subjected in the Lower Counties—New Castle, Kent, and Sussex—to laws no less severe and extreme than those in Massachusetts.

Even after the Swedes were vanquished, their simple agrarian economy continued. The English did little to change it. Down until the Revolutionary War Delaware remained a fairly quiet, tepid province, idyllic in spirit but unprogressive in vision. It had little contact with the commercial traffic of the day. It had suffered less than the other colonies in trials and hardships. No pestilences or famines assailed it, and no bitter, vengeful Indian tribes invaded it. Moreover, its land was always extraordinarily fertile and its climate exceptionally felicitous.

Delaware's original conflict had been with William Penn, whose concern for the collection of quitrents had inspired the Delawarians to oppose him and win their independence from Pennsylvania in 1702. That victory won, the conflict which ensued was one familiar to the other colonies—namely, that between the people and the official aristocracy and its scabrous bureaucrats. That conflict during the Revolutionary War acquired a violence which shook the bowels of the colony.

### DIONYSIUS: TYRANT OF DELAWARE

A large part of that conflict revolved about the perplexing and paradoxical character of George Read, who was the only Southern

* Although black slaves were owned in early days on South River, the first official importation of them occurred in 1663 on the ship *Gideon*.[17]

statesman to sign Congress's petition to the king in 1774, to sign the Declaration of Independence, and also to sign the Constitution of the United States. Read had been born in Maryland, but as a child had been brought to Delaware by his father.[18] In time, backed by the wealthy landowners, he became the most important personage in the province, which had been known not only as the "Lower Counties" but later as "Lower Pennsylvania" [19] before it "became called Delaware."

George Read's life is still obscure because of the inadequacy of documents and because of prejudice and partisanship. Certain facts about his life are clear: he was attorney-general for the Lower Counties; he was elected to Congress in 1774; he was a signer of the three historical documents alluded to in the previous paragraph; he was elected a member of the United States Senate, and at the expiration of his term was re-elected to the same office. In addition, he was the author of the first constitution of the state.[20] Later he was made Chief Justice of Delaware, which office he held until his death in 1798.

In many senses, bad as well as good, he can be described as the "father of Delaware." He certainly fathered the laws of the colony in its later days and authored its laws when it first became a state.

But beneath all that were undercurrents of conflict and contradiction. Was George Read a true Revolutionist? or was he really in favor of the king even when he signed the Declaration of Independence?

Dr. James Tilton raised those questions in his arresting pamphlet *Biographical History of Dionysius, Tyrant of Delaware* (1788). George Read's grandson, scarcely an unpartisan commentator, tried to dismiss Tilton's arguments as an expression of ill-will springing out of an unfriendly decision on the part of his grandfather. Read, it seems, relieved Tilton of an office of decided significance.

Who was Dr. Tilton? He was "surgeon-general" of the American army; was praised by Washington for his "meritorious labors"; had been, like Thomas Paine, in favor of the Revolution from the very beginning.[21] He naturally opposed and loathed those political cunctators who hesitated to side with the revolutionaries until the last, and his hostility to George Read sprang originally from his contempt for Read's initial refusal to vote in favor of independence. In addition to his military services, Dr. Tilton had been state treasurer from

1778 to 1781 and a delegate to Congress from 1783 to 1785. In 1786 the Tilton Hospital was named in his honor, and in 1798 the Delaware Medical Society gave him an additional honor. In short, Dr. Tilton, who had served his country faithfully during the Revolutionary War, offering his life upon numerous occasions, and who was known as "a judicious and skilled physician . . . held in great respect both among the laity and among his professional brethren," [22] was hardly the type of man to vociferate or explode without due cause.

The first point at issue was that George Read in the beginning had refused to sign the Declaration of Independence, although later when he saw he had no alternative he did sign it. Read's arguments were familiar at the time; they showed no originality. In Congress many of the revolutionary and patriotic Congressmen described him as "better fitted for the district of St. James than the region of America." Read was above and beyond all a "safe man." He would take no chances. He backed the Revolutionists only when he realized that to continue to back the king would be folly.

That Read was a representative of the ruling class in Delaware requires no verbal proof. The proof was in his actions. He wanted to protect those in power, including himself, and the only reason he eventually signed the Declaration of Independence was that he feared opposition would unseat him. In other words, he was a brilliant man with a pussyfooter's psychology.

## DR. TILTON'S CHARGE

It may be that Dr. Tilton was biased, unfair, and inaccurate in his analysis of the role of Read. Nevertheless, there can be no doubt that Read was a colonial politician who dealt out patronage with a generous hand when he was sure to receive a generous reward for it. The patriots of Delaware, however, refused to tolerate Read's anti-revolutionary attitude, and protests against it spread.[23] In Dover, a justice of the peace, Clark, was pilloried and battered with eggs and other missiles because he supported Read and opposed independence. After he was released, Clark assembled a group of men and decided to march upon Dover, but when he found himself faced by a determined and defiant populace, aided by an imposing infantry, he gave up the fight, disbanded his followers, and returned home.

In Sussex an even more serious insurrection occurred. There the Tories organized themselves in such effective form that Congress, which the reactionaries defied, had to send two battalions and one regiment to subdue them. In the inquiry that followed, it was proved that on the part of the reactionaries there had been wholesale spying and plotting and perfidious correspondence with the British.

### THE CLASS FACTOR

Although part of the conflict between Read and Tilton was personal, underlying it were antagonistic class attitudes. Read was always on the side of the rich, the conservatives; Tilton on that of the less fortunate, democratic, lower middle class which made up in courage for what it lacked in wealth. After the Revolutionary War, that conflict once more assumed major significance—but with a different cast—and a new act in the American drama was begun.

## CHAPTER XVIII

# New Jersey: Colony of Riot and Confusion

*No bishop, no King.*

—JAMES I

*If this be the administering Laws for the protection and preservation of her Majesty's subjects, Then have we been the most mistaken Men in the World and have had the falsest Notion of Things, calling that Cruelty, Oppression and Injustice which are the very direct Opposites, and those things Slavery, Imprisonment and Hardship which are Freedom, Liberty and Ease, and must henceforth take France, Denmark, the Muscovian, Ottoman and Eastern Empires to be the best Models of a gentle and happy Government.*

—The Reply of the House of Representatives of the Province of New Jersey to an Answer Made by His Excellency, Edward Viscount Cornbury, 1707

UNLIKE Maryland and Pennsylvania, each of which had only one proprietor, New Jersey had almost a score. Its history as a proprietary colony was rife with conflict between the proprietors themselves and between the proprietors and the people. Divided into West Jersey and East Jersey, the colony lacked a sense of unity. Its respective rulers conflicted so much with each other that the province could not advance and prosper. At length the proprietors of the two Jerseys surrendered their political authority to the Crown, but retained their economic privileges and claim to the land.[1]

The territory, known then as Nova Caesaria as well as New Jersey—at one time it was said to have been called New Canary [2]—was originally owned by the Duke of York, who, shortly after he acquired it, gave it, in what was either a gesture of generosity or an act of payment, to John Lord Berkeley and Sir George Carteret,* both of whom were also proprietors of Carolina. In 1665 they sent

* The colony derived its final name from George Carteret, who between 1643 and 1651 had ruled over the Isle of Jersey.

over, in the good ship *Philip*, Carteret's cousin, Philip Carteret, to act as governor of the province. In order to attract people to the territory, Colonel Richard Nicolls, the Duke of York's governor, had granted certain privileges of independent government and religious toleration, but had been powerless to permit the election of an assembly. The new proprietors, among their concessions, immediately included the right to elect an Assembly, a right that delighted the populace. All religions were permitted to be practiced save Roman Catholicism.[3]

### THE BATTLE FOR AN ASSEMBLY

The battle for the right to have an assembly endowed with the power to enact laws and enforce their execution was, as we have repeatedly seen, the great conflict of the colonial period. It was the farthest reach of democracy of that day. The New Jersey proprietors took the political bull by the horns when they granted that right without a struggle. A little later, however, after one of the early rebellions, they reneged on the issue. Philip Carteret went to England and returned with a new document: *Declaration of the true interest and Meaning of us the Lords Proprietors and Explanation of these Concessions*. This document robbed the Assembly of its authoritative power and placed that power in the hands of the governor and council. The Assembly refused to accept this new dictum, and Carteret adjourned it against its will. Not until there was a change in proprietors was this situation again altered.

The population of the colony was motley, a mosaic composed of many peoples. The English constituted the main motif and dominated the pattern. And these English were of a most active, vigorous, and decisive type, being scions of the Puritan and Dissenter tradition; they ventured into the Jerseys because it was a new land where they hoped they would be free to worship as they pleased and, if necessary, to persecute those who worshiped differently.

The frontier in America then was vertical as well as horizontal, and many New Englanders, finding life too circumscribed and unprogressive in their communities, moved southward rather than westward in their search for a new habitat. Pursuing the vertical frontier, they landed in New Jersey and New York, and found that their homes, though in a wilderness, were closer to the civilization of that day than those on the horizontal frontier, sweeping westward into mischievous and chartless stretches of space.

New Jersey early became a haven for New Englanders, especially those who were searching for larger profits and greater freedom. In Massachusetts and Connecticut there had been religious disputes of such an acrid variety that many settlers had deserted the New England colonies and invaded the Jerseys. The first settlements founded by the New Englanders were Middletown and Shrewsbury, both of which were havens of refuge as well as prospective centers of commerce. John Bowne, Richard Stout, Edward Wharton, William Reape, all of whom were among the founders of these West Jersey communities, were people who had suffered from theocratic tyranny and ventured upon this second migration to escape it. Among them were Baptists, Anabaptists, Quakers, and other Dissenters who had found life unendurable in Massachusetts. Some of the Quakers among the group had tried living in New York, but during the dark days of Stuyvesant's dictatorship had found themselves as much subject to persecution and arrest there as in New England.

### NEWARK: THE NEW ZION

To Newark and the surrounding territory of East Jersey migrated a different group of New Englanders, who were eager to establish a more thoroughgoing theocracy than existed at that time in Massachusetts. Their fanaticism had strengthened instead of weakened with the years. In Newark they hoped to create a fresh Zion and dedicate themselves anew to its ideals. They attempted to carry on there the same ascetic traditions that had prevailed originally in New England, forbidding every semblance of enjoyment, cerebral as well as sensual, meting out severe punishments for the slightest misdemeanors and the death penalty for a score of what they construed as major crimes.

In other words, East Jersey for a time became impregnated with the same spirit that dominated and vitiated New England. The attempt to combine ecclesiastical and civil government, however, failed, and the dream of those New Englanders who had hoped to establish a theocratic commonwealth was shattered. In the beginning their political organization was far from democratic. Only church members, for example, could hold office and vote. All the old asceticisms of

New England extended their strangulating hold over East Jersey. Calvin's punitive sword threatened the body as well as the spirit of the settlers.[4]

Before long, however, the outlook changed. The town meetinghouse became the focus of social life, and soon it became filled with people who did not share the sacrosanct view of life of these founding zealots. After the inauguration of the Berkeley-Carteret regime, which provided religious freedom for all sects, Quakers and Baptists who formerly had settled mainly in West Jersey now settled in many villages and towns and brought democracy where autocracy had prevailed before. The class distinctions that had been observed in the meetinghouse disappeared after the Dissenter elements succeeded in establishing themselves as members of the community.

Village and town life in New Jersey followed the New England pattern. Everybody knew everyone else; shops and stores were within walking distance; the minister did not have to travel far to visit his parishioners; the magistrate did not have to become an itinerant to try his cases, and artisans did not have to walk far to do their work. Even when the community expanded and farmers began to occupy the outlying lands, the village remained the hub of enterprise. Everyone turned to it; everything flowed from it. It is true that the farther the farmer moved from the village, the less he was able to profit from its advantages, but he seldom lost complete contact with it. Before long, as expansion continued, he would find another village springing up, nearer than the old one from which he derived. Unlike the Southern farmer, he was seldom isolated from some center of social life; he almost always had a village or town nucleus, from which he could secure intangible as well as tangible advantages and assets.

For a number of generations New Englanders continued to percolate down into New Jersey. It was by no means uncommon for New England ministers to be summoned to New Jersey; in fact, many of the leading preachers in the colony were of New England origin.[5] But in time the New England influence weakened, changed, dissolved. Telluric factors made it impossible for it to survive. New elements wore off its sheen, blunted its edges.

## EAST JERSEY VERSUS WEST JERSEY

Although New Jersey is still a single state and was officially considered a single colony, in the seventeenth and early eighteenth centuries it was often viewed as two colonies. The rulership at times was the same, but the natures of the sections were not. East Jersey was largely a New England product; West Jersey was mainly a Quaker province. East Jersey carried on the puritanic traditions of New England, meting out the death penalty for a score of offenses, whereas West Jersey practically eliminated that extreme from its penal procedure. No public executions were ever known to have occurred in either Burlington or Salem.[6] In East Jersey parents could have a child that struck them put to death, whereas among the Quakers of West Jersey no such issue ever arose. The Quakers even indentured their children for brief periods, so that they could learn a trade, and there is no record of any of their children ever assaulting their parents. The East Jerseyites, like the old New Englanders, were severe in their treatment of the populace, whereas the Quakers were gentle almost to a fault. Needless to say, the Quaker communities were far more happy than the Puritan.

Owing to its happy geography, West Jersey soon developed a plantation aristocracy not unlike that which sprang up in the Southern colonies, and the differences between the two Jerseys came to resemble in considerable degree those between the Carolinas. The Quaker influence, however, kept West Jersey from adopting the hedonistic psychology of the South Carolinian plantisocrats. The presence of John Woolman alone was sufficient to confine them to the painfully straight and narrow path. Even after he died of smallpox, his moral influence continued.

## LIFE OF THE SLAVES AND SERVANTS

William Moraley, an indentured servant, has provided us with a vivid picture of the social life at the time. In places he becomes excited about the prospects of the land, and calls it "the best poor Man's Country in the World."[7] He speaks of "Cyder" as being the most popular drink, and notes that in some houses as many as one hundred fifty barrels a year were manufactured. He comments upon the status of the Negroes, whose slavery he deplores:

The Condition of the Negroes are very bad by reason of the severity of the Laws, there being no Laws made in favor of these unhappy Wretches: For the least Trespass they undergo the severest Punishment; but their Masters make them some amends by suffering them to marry, which makes them easier and prevents their running away. . . . The laws against them are so severe that being caught after a running away, they are unmercifully whipped; and if they die under the Discipline their Masters suffer no punishment, there being no Law against murdering them. So if one Man kills another's Slave, he is only obliged to pay his value to the Master besides Damages that may accrue for the loss of him in his Business.

I have often heard them say they did not think God made them Slaves any more than other Men and wondered that Christians, especially Englishmen, should use them so barbarously.

His picture of the life of the indentured slaves is scarcely more heartening:

The Condition of bought Servants is very hard notwithstanding . . . it is expressly stipulated that they shall have at their arrival all the Necessaries specified in (their) Indentures . . . such as Clothes, Meat and Drink; yet when a Complaint is made to a Magistrate against the Master for Non-performance, the Master is generally heard before the Servant, and it is ten to one if he does not get his Licks for his Pains as I have experienced . . . to my cost.

### WITCHCRAFT TRIALS IN EAST JERSEY

Particularly interesting is his description of the witchcraft craze which, in more active and violent form, spread such havoc in Massachusetts. In East Jersey no witches were executed, but they were ducked in the traditional style:

On Mount Holly certain old Women of Melancholick Physogonomy had got the Character of Witches, and being questioned on that account and not able to clear themselves, were obliged to undergo a Ducking in order to prove whether or not they were such. The notion ran if they sunk they were no Witches; but if they swam they were and should be punished as such . . . But this not satisfying one Jonathan Wright, he proposed to weigh them in the scales against the Bible and concluded if they were Witches they would not weigh so heavy as the Bible, but to the surprise of the beholders they weighed down both Prophets and Apostles.

A letter from Charles Gordon toward the close of the seventeenth century confirms certain of Moraley's observations. "No unbyassed and indifferent Person will speak ill of the Land," he wrote, "it is both pleasant and wholesome and industrious people after some few years labour may lead a pleasant, easie life and want for nothing." Contrary to Moraley, he considers the life of the white slaves or indentured servants a relatively happy one. "If Servants knew what a Countrey this is for them and that they may live like little Lairds here," he stated, "I think they would not be so Shey as they are to come."[8] Evidence does not support Charles Gordon's conclusion. The experience of Moraley and that of the vast majority of other indentured servants exemplify in horrible detail the exact opposite.

### STRUGGLE AGAINST FEUDAL PRIVILEGE

The New Englanders who had migrated to East Jersey were not used to feudal authority and found proprietary rule intolerable. They were willing if need be to submit to a king, but not to a proprietor. Moreover, the land grants they had received from Governor Nicolls, the Duke of York's emissary, they discovered were invalid under the rule of Philip Carteret, the representative of the Berkeley-Carteret clique. The battle to retain their rights led to one of the most fiercely waged conflicts in the history of the colony.[9] Meetings were held, speeches made, protests issued, manifestoes published, and plans and plots initiated that were designed to protect their property and overthrow the proprietors. They even invited Captain James Carteret, son of the septuagenarian proprietor, to support their cause. They held an assembly which reaffirmed their rights to the land they had purchased under Governor Nicolls' rules, emancipated them from the necessity of paying quitrents, and strengthened their rights as free individuals and colonists. They arrested various officials, assumed control of the government, and had the assembly legalize all these actions. Their assembly was declared illegal by the proprietors, however, because the governor had not summoned it, and James Carteret was denounced by his father, ruled against by the Crown, and exiled from the colony.

But the struggle did not end there. The Duke of York tried to placate the rebellious colonists by giving them three years' time in which to pay their quitrents, but they threatened further insurrection, and despite official inquiries and suits, the matter never was settled amicably. Down to the time of the Revolutionary War it remained a bitter and burning issue.[10] Some places did reluctantly pay their quitrents, but the majority either paid intermittently or stubbornly refused to pay at all.

It is important to note that the quitrent issue as well as the matter of ownership was at stake in the conflict. The New Englanders were unaccustomed to paying such an anachronistic form of taxation, which seemed unreasonable and unjust in their eyes, and they were determined to resist it. The battle over quitrents continued unabated in all Middle Atlantic and Southern colonies until the Revolutionary War.[11] Quitrents made an issue on which men were willing, if need be, to fight and die.

## TRIAL BY JURY

The struggle against quitrents was part of the same democratic struggle against another of the vestiges of feudal economics. In the "quitrent colonies" the proprietors had the past on their side; the insurgents had the future on theirs. The law, which is always closer akin to the past than to the future, was against the insurgents, but the spirit of the age was for them. Even in the case of trial by jury, the future was on their side.

At one time kings and nobles could arrest a man and keep him in prison to the end of his days if they wished; no trial was needed to establish his guilt. In other cases they themselves or one of their lackeys would judge him in a secret chamber wherein he was defenseless before them. Trial by jury ended that tyranny; it was one of the greatest contributions to progress that the middle class bequeathed to modern civilization. No longer was the individual, merchant or commoner, subject to the arbitrary whims of an aristocrat. If accused of a crime he had to be tried before he could be punished, and tried not by his *superiors* in social and economic rank but by his *peers*.

Modern liberty is founded upon that principle and privilege.

Trial by jury was carried over to the colonies direct from England. No man could be tried in East Jersey except by "a Jury of his Peers," and a child "under ten years of age" was to select the names of the jurors from a hat or other convenience.[12] We have an interesting account by James Nevill, clerk of Salem Court, of how important trial by jury was viewed by the colonists of West Jersey, where the right also existed:

> The fairest flower that now grows in ye garden of Englishmen's liberties is a fair tryall by peers or twelve men of his neighborhood.... It is my opinion that a jury of twelve good and honest men of the neighborhood are as good judges of the equitable sense of the law and the intent and meaning of the law-makers as they are of the letter of the law.

In fighting the proprietors on these grounds, the colonists were preparing the way, however unconsciously, for those greater freedoms that were to become so significant a part of the American heritage.

It is no wonder, therefore, that this period in East Jersey's history is familiarly known as "The Revolution."

## SAMUEL JENINGS: STORMY PETREL OF THE QUAKERS

The battle between the respective proprietors in New Jersey occasioned many difficulties. At times the proprietors divided themselves into two groups, the English group being opposed to the Scotch-Irish and other non-English ones. Beneath it all, to be sure, was the struggle between the proprietors and the people. Nevertheless there were proprietors, especially among the Quakers, who were progressive in outlook and defended the people's interests as well as their own. The best representative of that group was the proprietor Samuel Jenings,* an intrepid and indomitable Quaker who had come to America in 1680.

Jenings had been originally a minister, and he embodied in good

* His name is also spelled "Jennings," but in certain of his original signatures it is "Jenings"—hence my spelling.

measure the ardent faith and fanaticism of his profession.[13] Denounced by his enemies as the "wicked, designing man," he was known to his friends as a generous personality and a noble reformer. As one writer put it, Samuel Jenings "did more than any of his contemporaries in organizing the civil government of West Jersey." [14] He was also praised as a man who "studied peace and the welfare of mankind." [15] *

When the Duke of York in 1680 sold the province to Edward Byllinge, William Penn, Gawen Lawrie, Nicholas Lucas, John Eldridge, and Edmund Warner, and assigned the powers of government to Edward Byllinge, a new conflict ensued. Byllinge, who had originally appointed Jenings as his deputy governor, later decided to remove the latter from his post because he had yielded too readily to popular pressure and given the people privileges of a markedly liberal character. The people of the province resented this undemocratic assumption of authority on the part of Byllinge and voted to keep Jenings in office. Byllinge found himself blocked on all sides. Jenings solidified his position by granting additional privileges to the people, guaranteeing them that no law, act, or statute could be passed without the approval of the Assembly, and limiting his own rights to those determined by the Assembly. The paper that the deputies drew up in defense of their action was taken to England by Jenings and Budd, who were to plead with the king against the despotism of Byllinge.† Unfortunately they never saw the king, who unhesitatingly decided in favor of Byllinge; the latter then appointed John Skene as his representative to replace Jenings. Although the conflict did not cease at that point, Jenings himself withdrew from it, and took up residence in Philadelphia.[18]

Jenings's successor, Governor Thomas Olive, was admitted to office only after the Assembly had approved of him and Byllinge had

* Smith, the well-known historian of New Jersey, described Jenings as "tender, disinterested, and with great opportunities, he left but small estate." [16]

† The declaration of the Assembly in that regard is worthy of quotation: "Be it hereby enacted and resolved by the Proprietors & Freeholders within the Province of West Jersey in free Assembly met, that the matter relating their demand and Vindication of their right to govern against Edward Billing's pretense to the same shall be proceeded in; and first, that a Demand to Edward Billings for his confirmation of what he hath sold, shall first be made. In pursuance whereof the Assembly unanimously nominate, elect and chuse Governor Samuel Jenings and Thomas Budd to negotiate the same affair in England, and commissionate and Impower them for the Transacting the same." [17]

agreed to allow the Assembly to retain its authoritative power. The legislation that Jenings had recommended and endorsed, giving power to the Assembly, guaranteeing trial by jury, providing freedom from unjust taxation, survived. He had labored to protect person and property from the arbitrary power of Byllinge by depriving him of legislative and judiciary power.[19] Although a proprietor himself, Jenings had paved the ground for the recalcitrant and rebellious attitudes that were to emerge and mature in the Revolutionary War, and ultimately find fruition in the democratic concepts of the nineteenth century.

Behind Jenings's fight was more than a man: there was a fundamental belief, a profound conviction, a driving movement. Naturally enough, it was the Quakers, the most democratic of all the Dissenters, who represented that attitude and movement. Their constitution granting those rights and privileges can be truly called a Quaker constitution; in fact, it was the first Quaker constitution of Pennsylvania. West Jersey was primarily a Quaker province, and Quaker convictions and ideals dominated there. The curious part of it is that a large percentage of the Quakers in the province were people who had been previously imprisoned in England for attending Quaker meetings and defending Quaker principles. What the Quakers did in New Jersey marked a milestone in the history of American liberty.* They were as usual in the forefront of the struggle for freedom and independence from superior authority, in politics as well as in religion; and in this struggle, as in a number of others that followed, they fought out in miniature form many of the issues that came to dramatic culmination and transfiguration in the Revolutionary War.

* William Penn (and the eleven other Quakers) who purchased that section of the colony avowed that they did so in order to provide a refuge for the Scotch Presbyterians, also known as the Scotch-Covenanters.[20] However complicated the motivations for the purchase might have been, the fact is that *the Quakers were pledged by principle to aid all oppressed groups and afford refuge for the persecuted.*

## II

### JEREMIAH BASSE—ANTI-PROPRIETARY GOVERNOR

It must not be thought that in these conflicts men's attitudes and desires were always idealistic. The characters of men are often far less inspiring than the movements they lead. In most cases they are more ready to take individual advantage of the immediate opportunities of a situation than to sacrifice themselves to the social idealism of a cause. We always admire those people who have been willing to risk their own lives in behalf of something that means more to a nation, a race, a group, a class, than to themselves as individuals. The whole theory of heroism springs from that source.

Many of the New Jersey leaders were not men of heroic caliber. They were opportunists, not idealists. In a great number of cases it was Quaker philosophy that endowed their individualism with an idealistic cast. History, however, is very often the product of such intellectual miscegenation. Jenings himself was a proprietor, defended the cause of the proprietors, yet at the same time in his various conflicts was more progressive than many of the anti-proprietary leaders. Many of the most progressive platforms, programs, and laws have resulted from "inside deals," political chicaneries, conspiratorial necessities, and not from the self-abnegatory dreams and ideals of noble men.

No better illustration of this can be found than that of Jeremiah Basse, who in East Jersey effected some of the same changes that Jenings had effected in West Jersey. Basse was far from being an idealist, and yet in his struggle against the proprietary interests he introduced reforms of a most progressive nature. East Jersey had always been less advanced than West Jersey; its government was more authoritarian than popular; its constitution originally lacked the democratic and libertarian character of its sister province. Basse had never been noted for progressivism, and, as his later life revealed, he never clung to it when the tides of fortune broke against it. Nevertheless, it was through his early fight that East Jersey acquired many of its most advanced reforms.

Basse assumed the governorship of East Jersey in 1697, superseding Andrew Hamilton, who had been appointed governor by the proprietors in 1693. The English Parliament had passed a law in 1697 requiring all colonial governors to be of English birth. The fact that Hamilton was of Scotch extraction jeopardized his authority. Ten of the proprietors living in England urged the appointment of Basse as Hamilton's successor, but other proprietors refused to accept Basse and continued to support Hamilton. Chaos resulted. Hamilton set sail for England, but the vessel he embarked upon was captured by the French, and all the books and papers he had brought with him as proof of the excellence of his administration were lost or stolen.[21]

### POPULAR LEGISLATION

Opposed by most of the proprietors living in the colony, Basse convoked the Assembly in 1699 and attempted to carry out the orders the English proprietors had given him. The Assembly, however, seizing advantage of the situation, passed laws of a popular and anti-proprietary character. They forbade election of any proprietor's deputy or representative and endowed the individual colonists with rights and privileges almost equal to those possessed by the populace in West Jersey.[22]

In order to retain power, Basse approved of these laws, to the delight of the populace but to the dismay of the proprietors.[23] Thus, by a caprice of circumstance, the people profited from a fight in which they had not been originally involved. The proprietors fought back, defying Basse's power, but the latter had all offenders jailed and subjected the province to terroristic rule. The proprietors responded by hiring hoodlums and gangsters to break into the jails, assault the sheriffs, and free the prisoners.[24] All officers attempting to carry out the orders of the Basse government were threatened, and many of them were attacked and wounded. Both sides were equally willing to resort to violence in their struggle for power. Bedlam prevailed.

Assailed though he was on all sides, Basse might have continued his fight had it not also been for the bitter battle that he also had to carry on with the Governor of New York. The hostility between the two colonies was an old and bitter one which reached its height when Basse approved of the General Assembly's decree, establishing a custom house at Perth Amboy and insisting that all ships heading for East Jersey must stop at Perth Amboy first. Governor Fletcher of New York protested, declaring that Basse was making war upon the Gothamites, and Lord Bellamont, Fletcher's successor, forbade the printing and distribution of circulars announcing the opening of the Perth Amboy port. The conflict was eventually taken to the Crown, which decided in favor of Bellamont instead of Basse. Basse refused to compromise with Bellamont, however; he issued a proclamation denouncing the New York governor, defended the rights of Perth Amboy, and when a vessel arrived at the Jersey port, saw to it that it was loaded with cargo and equipped to leave. The New York governor frustrated Basse's plans by dispatching an armed force to the city and capturing the ship. Although the Court of Admiralty decided against East Jersey on the issue, later, when "the matter was brought before the Court of the King's Bench," the decision was reversed.[25] *

### BASSE VERSUS HAMILTON

Caught in the maëlstrom of these various conflicts, Basse decided that the best thing for him to do was to go to England and settle them once and for all. He left his friend, Andrew Bowne, who was also anti-proprietary in his ideology, in charge of the colony during his absence. The proprietary forces, led by Morris and Willocks, succeeded in having Basse removed from office and Hamilton restored as governor. In a letter written to Jeremiah Basse, it was stated that Morris had declared that he "would Embroil the Country in Blood" in order to maintain Colonel Hamilton as governor.[26] But the people opposed Colonel Hamilton; after all, Basse had approved of those laws, which were essential to their interests. Ham-

* This conflict between New York and New Jersey had many repercussions. The New York governor, Andros, had arrested everyone who opposed his domination in that regard, officials as well as commoners, the powerful as well as the powerless. In 1680 he had arrested Philip Carteret, capturing him in his bed and transporting him as a prisoner to New York, where he forced the latter to refuse to compete with New York until a decision regarding the conflict was reached in London. Later, after James I's abdication, Andros was seized by the people of Boston and imprisoned, in retaliation for his high-handed tactics as viceroy of New England, as well as Governor of New York and New Jersey.

The rise and fall of Andros at this period was determined by the coronation and abdication of James II. James II endowed Andros with authority over New England, New York, and New Jersey. It was the abdication of James II in 1688 that made it possible for the Bostonians to arrest Andros in 1689 and for the New Jersey proprietors to regain their power over their colony.

ilton was forced to dissolve an Assembly, and this resulted in the growth of rebellious sentiment, the increase of political protests and the spread of seditious literature. Social conflagration ensued. Bloodshed occurred in several places, especially in Middletown and Elizabethtown, where the insurgent forces, led by Richard Salter and Samuel Carter, openly defied the Hamilton-Morris regime. Salter and Carter armed themselves and their followers, appeared in full military array, and defied the new authorities to attack them. They assaulted representatives of the proprietors, spat in the faces of judges, disrupted courts, and created such a pandemonium throughout the province that confusion was more confounded. More than that, they imprisoned the governor and thumbed their noses at the proprietors.[27]

### SURRENDER OF JERSEY TO THE CROWN

The result was simple: neither Basse nor Hamilton won. The Crown took over the colony and established peace among the bellicose factions. The proprietors had no choice. They could not maintain order in the province, and they needed a higher authority to achieve it. The Crown supplied that necessity.*

In the meanwhile Basse, whose idealism, as we have said, was far from exemplary, fostered his future by securing a royal patent as secretary of Lord Cornbury, who became the new governor of the territory. Basse, having begun his career as an Anabaptist minister, ended it as a rather mercurial politician. His reputation suffered from his associations with the unhappy Cornbury regime, and was not greatly improved by his connections with the movement led by Daniel Coxe. Violently antagonistic to the proprietors as he had been, he experienced little difficulty, it would seem, in two-facedly establishing an alliance with the next governor Robert Hunter, after the latter had destroyed the last remnants of the anti-proprietary forces in the colony. He was appointed attorney-general by

* Penn strenuously objected to this surrender of the colony to the Crown. In a letter to Logan, Nov. 4, 1703 (Penn-Logan correspondence), he declared that "the surrender was knavishly contrived to betray the people, as I told the people, and . . . I promised the Friends concerned, if they would yield to stop the surrender a few days, I would have got them a better bargain."

Morris, a proprietor himself, believed that surrendering the powers of government to the Crown, with the provisio that the proprietors should still maintain their right to the land, was a victory for the proprietary party.[28]

Hunter, in which capacity he functioned well; later he wrote a history of St. Mary's, which has literary merit as well as documentary value.

### CORNBURY'S DYNASTY

After Lord Cornbury's appointment by the Crown, Basse's role became less conspicuous. Lord Cornbury was the first New York governor who was also the Governor of New Jersey, and until 1738 the two colonies continued to be politically conjoined. The trouble with Cornbury was that he was as unsagacious as he was irascible, and at the same time patently corrupt.* Cornbury satisfied no one. He strove assiduously to strengthen the power of the Crown and weaken that of the Assembly, and this naturally evoked the opposition and hostility of the colonists. He insisted that the Assembly possessed only those rights which Queen Anne was willing to extend to it. This was reactionary doctrine and was bound to create discord.

Besides, Cornbury was disliked by the people for personal as well as political reasons. He suffered from a peculiar perversion—that of desiring to appear in feminine attire. He even had the audacity to appear "on the ramparts of the fort" in such dress.[30] Rev. Thorowgood Moore was so bold as to insist that Lord Cornbury should not be allowed to take communion and should be excommunicated from the church.

Cornbury was instructed by the queen to appoint a council, and among those he included was Samuel Jenings, although the Earl of Nottingham had listed Jenings as "undesirable."[31] Jenings, still the West Jersey Quaker proprietor, by this time had returned to the political fray, and when appointed to the council he refused the honor, preferring to remain in the Assembly, where he would be able to exercise greater influence.[32] † Later, Jenings was chosen

* Not long after his rule began, he was accused of "several misappropriations of public funds," and a law was passed giving the Assembly the right to appoint a "provisional treasurer" to guard the public moneys.[29]

† Samuel Jenings insisted that he be dismissed from the council because he wished to be "chosen into the Assembly, where he knew he could oppose the Queen's service more effectually than he could do in the Councill." Such were the words of Lord Cornbury in his letter of June 7, 1707, to the Lords of Trade.[33] Other reactionaries of the time were equally opposed to Jenings. Samuel Jenings declared "he would no longer serve the Queen as one of her Councill." Colonel Robert Quary, another enemy of Jenings, wrote: "his pretence was that he could not bear the charge of it, but the true reason was that it was not in his

speaker of the Assembly, wherein he fought with determined vigor to defend the interests of the proprietors against those of the Crown. It was Jenings who wrote the letter, or address, to the Crown that resulted in Cornbury's recall.*

## JENINGS'S REPLY TO CORNBURY

Jenings had fought Basse, who in turn had denounced Jenings as "a bigoted Quaker preacher" [35] † and had lent his support to Colonel Andrew Hamilton, whom he strove to establish as governor.[37] Jenings had fought Cornbury, who called him "the most impudent man he ever knew," and had had him removed from office; in addition Jenings had delivered and written some of the most vigorous and volcanic diatribes of the day. In the famous *Reply* to Cornbury, which was made by "the House of Representatives of the Province of New Jersey" in 1707, his hand was conspicuously present. The character of the *Reply* is significant:

If this be the administering Laws for the protection and preservation of her Majesty's Subjects, Then have we been the most mistaken Men in the World and have had the falsest Notion of Things, calling that Cruelty, Oppression and Injustice which are the very direct Opposites; and those things Slavery, Imprisonment and Hardship which are Freedom, Liberty and Ease, and must henceforth take France, Denmark, the

power to doe so much mischief to the Queen's interests as he might do in the Assembly into which he was sure to be chosen." It was in that type of language that Jenings was castigated by his adversaries.

It is true that Jenings did not forget his interests as a proprietor, but neither did he forget his Quaker belief in the freedom and independence of the individual. The Quakers in that respect anticipated Rousseau and Jefferson with their belief in the essential equality of man. Jenings, it is true, did not give up his proprietorship, but neither did Jefferson surrender his wealth when he wrote the Declaration of Independence. More of Jefferson's ideas about equality and justice were derived from the American Dissenters, especially the Quakers, than from French sources, as has usually been contended.

* As speaker of the Assembly, Jenings drew up a *Remonstrance* against Cornbury (May 8, 1707) in which he stated: "It is notoriously known that many considerable sums of money have been raised to procure the Dissolution of the first Assembly . . . (that) this house has great reason to believe the money so gathered was given to Lord Cornbury and did Induce him to Dissolve the then Assembly and put so many mean and mercenary men into Office, by which corrupt Practise Men of the best Estates are severely harassed, Her Majesty's good Subjects in this Province so impoverished, that they are not able to give that Support to Her Majesty's Government as is desired or as they would otherwise be inclined to." Although Jenings's name was signed to the *Remonstrance,* it is not impossible that Lewis Morris actually wrote it, as Cornbury alleged.[34]

† Basse also denounced a great number of his other opponents in similar language.[36]

Muscovian, Ottoman and Eastern Empire to be the best Models of a gentle and happy Government....

Jenings, it is true, was defending the cause of the proprietors against that of the Crown, but the very nature of the conflict led him to identify that cause with the greater cause of freedom. Although it was freedom and protection for the proprietors that he was mainly interested in, he was forced, as a Quaker, to defend freedom as a principle.

Like all Quakers, Jenings loathed the pomp and parade, the ceremony and cant, of Cornbury's regime. He detested its churches with their dim, dull lights, their gaudy robes and theatric ritual; he despised its courts, which lacked the plainness and simplicity of humble places, disdained its attitudes and affectations, deplored its moral and economic corruption.

Jenings's motivations were not unmixed ones. He had his own economic interests at stake, as a proprietor, but at the same time also those of conscience. He might defend the interests of the proprietors against the Crown, but at the same time he never lost sight of the masses as people. The early Quakers were too closely bound to the people to disregard or dismiss them. Other groups could, but not the seventeenth and eighteenth century Quakers. Even Penn with all his selfish concern for the collection of his quitrents was as generous as Roger Williams in his attitudes toward the Indians and the Negroes, and also in his belief in the possibilities of individual and social reform.

### THE QUAKER THREAT

Cornbury knew well whereof he spoke when he declared that the Crown cannot rule in any sovereign sense "as long as the Quakers are admitted to serve in the Assembly."[38] Cornbury made a bold effort, as he himself asserted, to prevent the Quakers from acquiring office in New Jersey—he forbade their appearing in courts as witnesses and refused to allow them to become jurors—but Queen Anne's order not to discriminate against any religious group made it impossible for him to exclude them from all official positions. The result was that the Quakers, everlastingly concerned in those days with the fundamental issue of religious freedom and political independence, became a spiritual thorn in his side, bruising him so badly that when he was recalled to England he was happy at least in the thought that never again would he have to deal with that fierce and forbidding tribe of religious democrats.

When Cornbury originally came into office, the Crown provided that the governor was to hold his position at its pleasure, that the council was to be appointed by it, and that no one could be elected to the General Assembly who did not own a landed estate of at least one thousand acres, or a personal estate of five hundred pounds sterling. The Assembly was to be convened or adjourned at the discretion of the governor, who also possessed the power of veto and control over the courts. The Assembly was to be used as a money-raising instrument and as a protective body for the *status quo*. It was not only to pass laws confirming the property rights of the proprietors but also to assist in the perpetuation of the quitrent "racket." More than that, in order to consolidate power in the hands of the few, it was to enact a law preventing anyone but the proprietors from buying land from the Indians.

In short, the surrender of the Jerseys to the Crown marked a step backward for the populace. But the populace did not accept this defeat without a struggle. When Cornbury convoked the General Assembly in 1703, the new governor found himself faced with far more difficulties than he had anticipated. To begin with, the Assembly balked at the salary the governor requested, and decided to give him far less; in addition, it rewrote most of his resolutions in such a way as to evoke his ire. He prorogued the Assembly and managed by underhanded means to prevent three inimical members from returning to it when he convened it the next year.[39] By this technique he succeeded in getting an Assembly that approved of the salary he desired, but also one that removed all the property restrictions which had been imposed previously upon electors and elected, and permitted all freeholders the right to vote. The board of trade refused to confirm this statute, and in 1705 restored the original property qualifications. Later, in 1708 and 1709, the fourth Assembly reduced the property qualifications to fifty pounds.[40]

### CORNBURY'S RECALL

Cornbury was willing to surrender to the democratic interests on this point in order to win the salary he wanted; once he secured that, nothing else counted. He allied himself with the English proprietors, led by Dockwra and Sonmans, as well as with the populace, in order to gain his ends. The English proprietors hated the controlling majority of proprietors so much that they were willing to make deals with the populace in order to vanquish that majority. Ultimately, though the action was antagonistic to their economic interests, they contributed more than the populace to the overthrow of proprietary government in the Jerseys. In time, however, Cornbury broke completely with the proprietary party and fought it with unremitting fervor. He even agreed to allow the three members he had excluded to return to the next Assembly session. As a matter of fact he was willing to "sell anybody out" for personal gain, and he did. The proprietary party had bribed him first, the anti-proprietary party afterwards.[41] He could be bribed by anyone, but the largest briber won his co-operation. He finally opposed the proprietary forces and backed the anti-proprietary group because the latter was willing to pay more for his support.

In consequence, Cornbury soon found himself without any friends at all; he was attacked not only by the representatives of the people but also by those of the proprietors. Both found their interests jeopardized by his tactics. His defeat was inevitable. The proprietors were as eager to see him removed as the populace. All classes rejoiced when he was recalled and a new governor was appointed.

### LEWIS MORRIS: RENEGADE

Popular causes in colonial days were championed often by persons whose economic interests were far from popular. In proof of that, Lewis Morris, a proprietor, an extraordinary man with contradictory passions and prejudices, is an excellent illustration. Although a wealthy landowner, he allied himself upon more than one occasion with the people's cause. He joined forces with Samuel Jenings, also a proprietor, in opposition to Cornbury, and collaborated with Jenings in the protest that was drawn up by the Assembly and sent to the queen. Later he was appointed chief justice by Robert Hunter, the quick-witted Scotsman who originally had been appointed Governor of Virginia. During Hunter's regime Morris's role was passive and acquiescent. When Cosby was appointed Governor, however, Morris became protestant again and allied himself with James Alexander and William Smith, who had become leaders of the populace. As we have seen, when Peter Zenger was arrested in New York for publishing Morris's articles, the latter immediately got Alexander and Smith to defend Zenger. Very soon the issue developed into a *cause célèbre.* Morris became as ardent a defender of freedom of speech as Alexander and Smith, and Alexander Hamilton, the venerable Philadelphia lawyer, who finally won the case for Zenger.* This was a great advance for a man who in his youth had been a runaway and a rapscallion, and who had spent his formative years in the backlands of Virginia.

Ironically enough, when in 1738 New Jersey achieved political separation from New York and elected him governor, Morris opposed the very principles that formerly he had espoused. He became increasingly conservative in outlook and contumacious in temper. Instead of defending the populace, he attacked it, commenting upon the "insincerity and ignorance among the people," and instead of supporting the Assembly, in which he had so long been a leader, he declared that there was an unfortunate "inclination . . . in the meanest of the people (*who are the majority and whose votes make the Assembly*) to have the sole direction of all the affairs of the government." † (Italics mine.)

Morris continued in office until he died, about which time the colony was plunged once more into a series of "Disorders, Tumults, Riots, Feuds, and Animosities." ‡

* New Jersey in colonial days was not very rich in newspaper production. Its gazette (*New Jersey Gazette*), published originally by Isaac Collins in 1777 (he accepted produce and rags in lieu of money), was discontinued in 1786, and for many years no other paper was published in the state. Although Collins was not a Zenger, it is illuminating to note that in description of the purpose of his paper, he wrote:

"The interests of Religion and Liberty he shall ever think it his peculiar duty to support and at the same time to treat with Contempt the intemperate Effusions of Factious Zealots, whether religious or political, as Enemies of Virtue and the Pests of Civil Order."

† Quotation appearing in Curtis P. Nettels, *The Roots of American Civilization,* pp. 564, 565. This is one of the best oriented and ably recounted histories of American colonial life that has been written. It combines sound research with significant social vision.

‡ Osgood stresses the anti-democratic spirit of the man and minimizes his earlier alliance with the democratic forces.[42]

### THE ORIGIN OF THE LAND RIOTS

This chaos resulted from the sharpening of the conflict between the proprietors and the people. The latter were still determined to avoid the payment of quitrents, and upon a number of occasions violently resisted their collection. The struggle once more harked back to the days of Governor Nicolls, during the Duke of York's regime, when land was bought by many of the settlers direct from the Indians; this land had been claimed by the proprietors when they assumed control of the colony, and they insisted upon the payment of quitrents by all those who lived upon it. The settlers were so strong, however, that the proprietors were afraid to combat them anywhere except in the courts, which they controlled.

The settlers considered their purchases of land from the Indians as incontrovertibly valid. Roger Williams had considered them as such, and they saw no reason to believe that king, queen, or proprietor had any superior claim to them. After all, the Indians had lived on them long before English kings, queens, or proprietors existed. Rev. Daniel Taylor, carrying on the Williams tradition, had written *A Brief Vindication of the Purchasers Against the Proprietors*, defending the Indians and squatters against the proprietors.[43]

The Crown and the proprietors viewed the land as their own, and contended that the settlers had to purchase it from them if the sales were to be legal. But the settlers would not listen to their arguments, and therein resided the conflict that provoked so much confusion and violence in the province. Land riots broke out and spread; the people were up in arms. Whenever the proprietors attempted to take the people's land away from them, the people fought back with increasing vigor.[44] The Crown supported the proprietors in this struggle, but it was as impotent as the latter to quell an opposition that bordered on the verge of revolution. Many of the so-called squatters, as Osgood points out, were "members in good standing of the Presbyterian Churches of Elizabethton, Newark, and towns of the Monmouth purchase... men with substantial properties, as intelligent and socially respectable as were the Anglicans or the proprietors and their supporters."[45]

These free, independent settlers cut down timber, invaded forests, exploited soils, and so violated the property claims of the proprietors. Very soon the latter employed every means at their disposal to evict the squatters from what they considered their territory; writs of ejectment were issued and other legal technicalities were utilized, all in the endeavor to drive the squatters from the lands they had settled. The proprietors even attempted to use military force to effect that end, but the Assembly blocked them there, and it was in the courts that the final conflicts occurred.

### THE BALDWIN EPISODE

But the courts did not intimidate the New Jersey farmers. When Samuel Baldwin, an ambitious rustic, "having been for many years possessed of land lying within Van Gesin's Grant, or Purchase Aforesaid (which the proprietors had surveyed as above) (cut) some logs thereon for his Saw-Mill etc they arrested him to the Supreme Court, put him in Jail, and 30 or 40 writs more (as it was said) to serve on (other) Men for such like Trespasses (as) they called 'em,"[46] the people broke into the jail and freed him. Committees of opposition were created; the spirit of revolt spread abroad in the colony. Convinced that their "Rights, Properties, and Possessions" had been invaded by "the Oppressions and Frauds of the Proprietors," the people were bent upon fighting any further encroachments upon their privilege. Morris pleaded in vain with the Assembly to call out the militia or at least pass the English riot act.[47]

The petition the people drew up was a fundamental challenge to proprietary government. Its importance is borne out most markedly by the reactionary speech delivered in the Assembly by Samuel Nevill, in answer to its demands:

> Then are the Proprietors, Pretenders, and may be stiled the Proprietors so-called, Property carries no Double Face, Sir, it is either Property or not Property, and the Dispute now is, whether the Property in the Soil of this Colony is vested in the Crown of England, or in the Indian Natives. . . . And under such circumstances as ours are, that is a Multitude of People, treading upon the very Heels of Rebellion, if not actually engaged in it . . . as settling upon the Heathen Indians as true owners of the Soil.[48]

Nevill, representing the proprietary cause, attacked the populace because it insisted upon the superiority of its Indian claims over those of the proprietors. Roger Williams, it should be remembered, maintained that the Indian claims were sovereign. After all, the settlers in Nicolls's day had bought their land direct from the Indians and were loath to surrender it to the proprietors, who derived their ownership from the Crown. Conflict was inevitable. Nevill was correct when he insisted that the conflict was "treading upon the very Heels of Rebellion." *

The revolt spread throughout West Jersey, and in places it verged upon revolution; in Elizabethtown, which nurtured a vast part of the insurgent and incendiary sentiment, a pamphlet was published in which it was declared: "No man is naturally entitled to a greater proportion of the earth than another; but tho' it was made for the equal use of all, it may nevertheless be appropriated by every individual." [50]

There was socialist sentiment vibrant in those words—a socialism springing from the frontier, from the land itself, not from the lucubrations and reveries of dreamers and prophets.

The Board of Trade concluded that these land riots, with all their threat and challenge, were as important as Bacon's revolt in Virginia.[51]

It was possible at that time that those revolts might have translated themselves into more dynamic form had it not been for the early threats of the French and Indian War, which gave both forces a common enemy to combat.† The proprietors had called upon the Crown for help, but the settlers were willing to fight the Crown as well as the proprietors, and if the French and Indian War had not intervened, the first battles of the American Revolution might have been fought on Jersey soil.

* George Bancroft, the nineteenth-century historian, and one of the ablest apostles of sweetness and light, described this period with ostrich-like naïveté as one of "comparative tranquility." [49]

† In order to preserve the unity of this volume, I have purposely avoided dealing with the French and Indian War, which will be the starting point of the next volume.

# BOOK IV

# CHAPTER XIX

## The Frontier and the Future

*The whole interest of history lies in the fortunes of the poor . . . the state must consider the poor man, and all voices speak for him. . . . Ours is a country of poor men.*

—RALPH WALDO EMERSON

*The most significant thing about the American frontier is that it lies at the hither edge of free land.*

—FREDERICK JACKSON TURNER

[*Farmers*] *are the true representatives of the great American interest, and are alone to be relied upon for expressing the proper American sentiments.*

—THOMAS JEFFERSON

THE American colonies grew up sandwiched between two frontiers —a frontier of land and a frontier of sea. Those frontiers determined the development and shaped the outlook of the American people. The Indians, who had lived here centuries before, had known only one of those frontiers. The sea was to them not a frontier, but a stopping place; they lacked the craft necessary to explore and exploit it. Their canoes could travel lakes and rivers, negotiate rapids, and survive inland storms, but they could not span the immensity or endure the unpredictable, ungovernable tempers of the sea.

The Europeans who came to the new world had begun to master marine science and had made the sea a viable, if not hospitable, home for enterprise. The sea, for the vast majority of European peoples, those who stayed at home as well as those who emigrated, was the first frontier. There was no land frontier that they could extend, except by war and conquest. The frontier can be just a separating point, a division, and this is what, in nationalistic terms, it has been in Europe.

Norsemen in ancient days had made the sea their frontier, and in their explorations had discovered America and a large part of the unknown world. Various European adventurers had located other parts of the planet, and each part in turn had become a new frontier for the country of the discoverers. This new frontier, in each case, became a new world. It opened up a new horizon for the citizens of the old world, projected for them vistas of hope and dream that they had never shared before.

### FRONTIER FOR THE MULTITUDE

For those unhappy with their lot, whatever the reasons—economic, political or religious—America became for Europeans in the seventeenth century, and has ever since remained, a new frontier for escape and aspiration. Other countries were discovered before America, richer and more profitable lands—India, Cathay, Cipangu—but they were inhabited by large populations, equipped with advanced techniques, dense with expanding enterprise. America, especially North America, was inhabited by an economically backward people, with unadvanced methods and techniques and unexpanding enterprise. Moreover, the land was sparsely settled, with untraveled and uncharted expanses that were not settled at all. Consequently Asia became a frontier for the few, America a frontier for the multitude.

The American frontiers, by land and sea, were providentially felicitous. On the sea there was the mother country, England, as a protector; on land there were alcohol, Christianity, trinkets, and superior arms with which to subdue the natives. The colonists took advantage of them all. Alcohol undermined the morale of the red men, Christianity subdued their spirit, trinkets weakened and won their women, and bullets outshot their arrows. For a considerable time the marine frontier was sufficient. New Englanders then preferred the sea to land as a frontier, because they could make a better living thereby. Later, however, with the introduction of new restrictions, laws, and duties, the profits of the sea became less abundant for the merchants and still less abundant for the rest of the populace.

As profits decreased, opposition to England increased, and emigrations to the West began. If the original settlers had found the near land and sea adequate to their needs, the promise of extending the frontier to the West would have proved less of a lure. When the marine frontier became unable to support the growing population, an extension of the land frontier became a necessity. From that time on, the land became the new compulsive. People are always willing to cling to that which they know if it supplies them with a livelihood; when it no longer does so, they seek new lands that promise fresh opportunity.

For centuries the frontier gave to America a continuous and compelling newness: it was a state of mind as well as a physical reality. People from remote lands who never saw the country were as inspired by it as those who lived in it. In little homes in many parts of the European world—in England, Scotland, Ireland, the Palatinate, Holland, France, Sweden—fathers, mothers, and children, grandfathers, grandmothers, and grandchildren, shared in the American dream. It was a consolation as well as an inspiration, for those who watched others set forth for it, fascinated as by a mirage, always believed that in time they would follow. It was a long journey, but at the end of it, they believed, as at the end of the rainbow, there was the pot of gold waiting for all, regardless of wealth, culture, or station.

### MANKIND IN ITS SHIRT-SLEEVES

No country in the world has provided so much democracy for as many people as America. Greek democracy was not democracy at all except for a privileged minority; European democracy was still in the embryo in the seventeenth century. Even American democracy, as has been shown, was circumscribed in the original colonies. Only on the frontier did those circumscriptions vanish. There, for a considerable time, the class distinctions of Europe did not prevail. The limitations of suffrage imposed upon the settlers in the New England, Middle Atlantic, and Southern colonies did not extend to the Western frontier. The American frontier was indeed a place, as Ralph Waldo Emerson said, where "the human race poured out over the continent to do itself justice; all mankind in its shirt-sleeves; not grimacing like poor men in cities, pretending to be rich, but unmistakably taking off its coat to hard work, when labor is sure to pay."

Although the frontier Emerson wrote about was that of the nineteenth century, his observations were equally true of the eighteenth. Emerson understood the significance of the frontier better than any other writer save Whitman. Both of them knew what the frontier meant as a dream as well as a reality. But Europe also knew, however vicariously. "Blessed are you," Carlyle wrote to Emerson in 1835, "where what jargoning soever there be at Washington, the poor man shoulders his ax, and walks into the Western Woods, sure of a nourishing Earth and an overarching Sky! It is verily the Door of Hope to distracted Europe; which otherwise I should see crumbling down into blackness of darkness."

Whitman sang of the "Western youths" whom he saw "tramping with the foremost," carrying aloft the torch of progress which "the older races . . . beyond the seas" had let fall and go out. The West, which was the frontier, he envisioned as "the great heart and trunk of America." Underlying Thoreau's remark about Whitman, "He is Democracy," was the fact that Whitman was the West, the frontier. Whitman was against the "thin sentiment of parlours, parasols, piano-songs, tinkling rhymes" of Europe, and was in favor of the more vigorous and genuine, if rougher and cruder, jargon of the people. He realized that on the frontier democracy for the first time was being truly born. There was no *fake* about it. This was America—and this was the greatest thing that had happened in the history of man.

### SWEET DEMOCRATIC DESPOTS OF THE WEST

Whitman might hail the "sweet democratic despots of the West," but it was Emerson who put their economic philosophy, with a challenge that rang around the world, into its most simple and effective form. The frontier, he insisted, had given to the new world the "general conviction . . . that every young man of good faculty and good habits can by perseverance attain to an adequate estate; if he have a turn for business, and a quick eye for the opportunities which are always offering for investment, he can come to wealth, and in such good season as to enjoy as well as transmit it." More than that, he saw that beneath all this was the democratic independence of the individual so long as the individual can declare that "here in the clam banks and the beech and chestnut forests I shall take leave to breathe and think freely. If you do not like it, if you molest me, I can cross the brook and plant a new state out of reach of anything but squirrels and wild pigeons."

It was of that social philosophy that the frontier was made. Something was born there that had never before been born in the world. That something was *the individual.* In earlier societies the individual attained significance through station, class, wealth, or religion. In frontier society he achieved it by being himself, absolutely, completely, apodictically himself. A man was a man "for a' that," a man because he lived and breathed and had his being in society and his rights and freedoms as a member of it. This was revolutionary doctrine, and it was practiced on the frontier long before it was realized by philosophers or exalted by politicians. Among the early Pilgrims there had been adumbrations of it, and among other groups there had been suggestions of its significance. But it was not until the frontier became a growing, expanding reality that it became the great revolutionizing force in the Western world.

In every European country divisions between economic classes manifested themselves in social form. The aristocracy felt itself infinitely superior to the middle class, which trafficked in "filthy lucre," and the middle class considered itself indubitably superior to the fourth estate which, as manual and menial workers, eked out its livelihood in the most miserable ways known to man. In all European countries that feeling was shared by everyone, kings as well as commoners, masters as well as menials, superiors as well as inferiors. In America, in the early days, a valiant attempt was made to continue it, and along the Atlantic seaboard it survived. On the frontier, however, it died.

It was on the frontier that America was conceived, that all which America has become was born.

The frontier said something that had not been heard before in the ears of men. It said that the poorest man was as good as the richest, the simplest as good as the wisest. "The rifle and the axe," so the frontier saying ran, "made all men equally tall." [1] It also made them equally democratic. They all uniformly despised distinctions, scorned differentiations of rank and privilege. Illustrative of that attitude are the words of Major Anbury, a captured British officer, who wrote of his own experience on that score:

> An instance of it I saw at Colonel Randolph's at Tuckahoe, where three country peasants, who came upon business, entered the room where the Colonel and his company were sitting, took themselves chairs, drew

near the fire, began spitting, pulling off their country boots all over mud, and then opened their business, which was simply about some continental flour to be ground at the Colonel's mill. When they were gone, some one observed what great liberties they took; he replied it was unavoidable, the spirit of independence was converted into equality, and everyone who bore arms esteemed himself upon a footing with his neighbor, and concluded by saying: "No doubt, each of these men conceives himself, in every respect, my equal." [2]

It was that attitude born of the frontier which inspired the provisions in the American Constitution forbidding the creation of titles of nobility or the assumption on the part of an American of any favors or distinctions of aristocratic origin.

In no other country at the time was the word "aristocrat" so scorned and the word "democrat" so exalted. In the coastal colonies, those with aristocratic aspiration loathed the word "democrat," but in the years that followed democracy and not aristocracy triumphed. What occurred was a historical miracle. For the first time in the history of modern man lowly people did not feel lowly, and privileged people did not feel privileged. The average American—farmer, worker, shopkeeper—was emancipated from the feeling of inferiority and servility from which European lower classes suffered. The American stood on his own feet, had his own job, his own farm, his own shop, and within his own domain he felt as independent as a monarch.

He was a man, an individual, an American.

## II

### THE EARLY FRONTIER

In the eighteenth century the frontier was still in an explorative stage. Trappers had been busy for years, thinning forests and carving trails through the bush; other pathfinders and trail-blazers had constructed forts, built villages, initiated enterprise. As far back as 1690, hunters and traders had penetrated into the Cherokee territories, grown wealthy from profits on furs, and returned, like Marco Polo from his Eastern travels, with graphic and glamorous pictures of the country they had explored.* It was hard to resist the land they described—it glowed with such color and charm and vibrated with such promise. Almost a century later (1767), John Finlay and his followers maneuvered their way into the treacherous Kentucky territory, which was then called by the Indians "the Dark and Bloody Grounds." "The report made by Columbus of his discovery of America," wrote John Bradford, "did not produce greater excitement in the Court of Spain than that made by Finlay did in the people of Carolina."[4] Inspired by Finlay's descriptions of the country, Colonel Daniel Boone set out for it early in 1769. Others described the blue-grass territory with equal enthusiasm. "This whole country," wrote Imlay, "abounds in coal which lies almost upon the surface of the ground. . . . This must become in time the most valuable grazing country in all America."[5] Lord Dorchester commented upon Kentucky's limestone soil, and the fecundity of its "wheat, rye, barley and oats and tobacco" production.[6]

In time bands of settlers took to the frontier, organized communities, created settlements. Merchants followed. For a period the seaboard colonists by divers and devious methods tried to claim possession of the frontier lands, but the pioneers defied them and claimed them themselves. Squatter sovereignty triumphed. By 1745 over twenty thousand German immigrants had plunged into the wilderness,[7] swarming into the Shenandoah and scaling the territory beyond. The Scotch-Irish pushed ahead also, pursuing the rivers, clearing the land, establishing communities.

What was important about the frontier, as Turner himself pointed out, was that it was settled by non-English groups—"fused into a mixed race, English in neither nationality nor characteristics."[8] These groups, products of European conflict, knew little of the civilization that had metabolized along the seaboard. They were similar in class outlook, deriving from the lower middle class of their mother lands, but free in large part from the English influences that had dominated the coastal colonies.† In other words, they started practically from scratch. They did not have royal governors or oppressive proprietors to fear or fight. They were concerned not with who

* This country was later to be known as East Tennessee.[3]

† In this connection see the controversy between Benjamin Stolberg and Louis M. Hacker in *The Nation*, Sept. 13, 1933.

claimed the land—Indian maharajahs or Byzantine emperors terrified them no more than English kings or nobles—but with the land itself. They entered it, claimed it, developed it. It was their own. More than that, they were willing to fight for it, and as fighters they achieved an expertness, an excellence, that was ominous if not invincible. To be respected in Kentucky, for example, a man had to be a quick as well as an accurate shooter, and very often in politics a man had to prove his marksmanship before he could win votes. When Henry Clay, eager to advance his candidacy, decided to defend his position in the Kentucky legislature, he was accosted outside the building by frontiersmen who insisted that he could enter only if he could prove his accuracy as a marksman. He did, and American history was influenced accordingly.[9] Frontiersmen, like everyone else, were interested primarily in the needs of their existence.* A good marksman was an asset to the community; a bad marksman, a liability.

### CRUDENESS OF FRONTIER LIFE

The frontiersmen's manner of life was simple, crude, but seldom dull. Almost every possible occasion was used as a dramatic outlet for emotions; religion became an excitement and ecstasy, childbirth a theatrical event, wedding a spectacle. "A wedding," Theodore Roosevelt wrote, "was always a time of festival. . . . If, as generally happened, there was no church, the groom and his friends, all armed, rode to the house of the bride's father, plenty of whiskey being drunk, and the men racing recklessly along the narrow bridle paths, for there were few roads or wheeled vehicles in the backwoods. At the bride's house the ceremony was performed, and then a huge dinner was eaten; after which the fiddling and dancing began, and were continued all the afternoon, and most of the night as well. A party of girls stole off the bride and put her to bed in the loft above; and a party of young men then performed the like service for the groom. The fun was hearty and coarse, and the toasts always included one to the young couple to wish that they might have many children. The neighbors all joined in chopping and roll-

* James Truslow Adams makes a point, and a very good one, to the effect that the American intellect has been profoundly conditioned by that fact. Without question, as has already been shown, the whole American outlook on life has been influenced by this singular factor in its development—something completely unknown to Europe.

ing the logs for the young couple's future house, then in raising the house itself, and finally in feasting and dancing at the house-warming. . . ." [10]

Roosevelt also describes another frontier custom that was most interesting: "In the wilderness a husband was almost a necessity to a woman: her surroundings made the loss of the protector and provider an appalling calamity; and the widow, no matter how sincere her sorrow, soon remarried—for there were many suitors where women were not overplenty. If in such a case the one thought dead returned, the neighbors and parties interested seem frequently to have held a sort of informal court, and to have decided that the woman should choose either of the two men she wished to be her husband, the other being pledged to submit to the decision and leave the settlement. Evidently no one had the least idea that there was any legal irregularity in such proceedings."

Life on the frontier was so simple that at times it bordered on the barbarous. Ignorance bred superstition, and superstition nurtured disease. Education was scorned as an evil thing conjured by the "wiseacres" of the East. What schools the frontier had were open for only a few months in the year, and the character of the teachers was tested not by what they knew but by how much "moonshine" they could imbibe without becoming tremulous upon their feet.[11] Children's diseases were all traced to worms, and the antidotes included salt, pewter, sulphate of iron, and divers forms of emetics and violent cathartics. Gunshot wounds "were treated with slippery-elm bark, while erysipelas, or St. Anthony's fire, was assuaged by the blood of a black cat." [12]

## FRONTIER HUMOR

The frontier gave birth also to a weird, irresponsible, gargantuan sense of humor in which traders slid along the ridges of the rainbow, Indians sliced up the fringes of the sky, and animals became monsters, centaurs, griffins—anything, even humans—in the transfiguring atmosphere of the hinterland. Frontier humor acquired its strength from exaggeration, the magnification of the impossible and the absurd. It was closer to the slapstick than the humorous. Yet it was more than slapstick; it was slapstick with an element of the epical about it. Constance Rourke has emphasized the "tall tale" aspect of it as embodied in the Davy Crockett, Paul Bunyan, Mike Fink legends.[13] There was a boastful extravagance about it which made it irresistibly childish and naïve. "I'm a ring-tailed screamer," Mike Fink exclaimed with typical frontier braggadocio, "an' I take to fightin' like a babe to its mother." [14]

American humor, in its crude, vigorous, expansive aspects, has derived from this frontier source more than from any other.

## SHIFTING FRONTIERS

The early frontiersmen followed the river courses until they merged into the falls; there they stopped. For decades they hesitated to venture farther. It was not until the eighteenth century that they ascended the Alleghenies and hazarded the deeper interior.[15] From then on the pioneers spread out in a cloverleaf formation across territories hitherto unknown to white men. By this time the frontier had changed from a trader's frontier into a farmer's, just as later it was to become transformed in various places into a rancher's and miner's frontier.

## A PARADISE FOR FUR TRADERS

In the beginning the fur trade was the pioneer's obsession; quick money could be made from it. Unlike the French colonists who befriended the Indians, the English plundered them. They made them economic vassals and utilized the so-called Indian commissioners to defend their misdeeds. The chief of the Messagas attacked the white men, saying that "We are not masters of our own things, and pray that we may have our own furs and go and trade where we can find the best market." [16] But the frontiersmen would not allow them that freedom, and this was one of the main causes of conflict between the red men and the white men. The Indian wars that followed and occupied so large a part of frontier life sprang out of that hostility. The English fed the Indians liquor and made them so drunk that they were willing to part with their furs for almost nothing. "We must think you sell it [alcohol]," one of the Sachems said, "with no other design than to destroy us." [17]

Caught between the French on the one side and the English on the other, the Indian tribes on the frontier, unsubdued by white trickery and turpitude, preferred conflict to capitulation.

Wars were the result. When people fight for the protection and defense of their own land, the battle is always a bitter one—which explains why the frontier wars of the period, especially King Philip's War, were so hard-fought and desperate.

Most of the colonies were so concerned with the frontier and with maintaining commercial contact with the frontier towns that they passed divers laws regulating their economic and political relationships. Massachusetts had its general court define specifically the frontier line, and arranged to dispatch soldiers to each frontier town. In some of the frontier towns the inhabitants were not allowed to move without legal permission. If they did, their lands were seized and they themselves were subject to imprisonment if caught. Virginia became so interested in the frontier as a form of military protection that it encouraged many of its settlers to migrate to the backlands and build outposts there.

### THE NEED FOR SALT

One of the most important factors that retarded the extension of the frontier in early days was the lack of salt in the unexplored territories. Without salt it was impossible to preserve meats or make them tasteful; besides, numerous diseases might develop from lack of salt. The first things the pioneers looked for were fresh salt deposits, or the location of those of the Indians and the discovery of techniques whereby salt could be extracted from other substances. For many years, these early frontiersmen had to send back East every year caravans of wagons to cart the salt to their communities. "A bushel of alum salt," Roosevelt noted, "was worth a good cow and a calf." [18] When salt springs were found in Kentucky and the outlying sections of New York, and the settlers learned how to make salt from brine, the whole frontier movement quickened its pace. The first white person to discover the salt-making process was Mrs. Mary Draper Ingles, who learned it from the Shawnee Indians after being captured by them. When she escaped and returned to her people, she taught them the technique.[19] For a time valiant efforts were made to obtain salt by evaporating sea water. The main salt supply was in southwest Virginia, in a place which came to be named Saltville. Even after the Revolution, various states still felt the need of salt so badly that they offered rewards for the discovery of salt licks, and several of them went on record as willing to help subsidize any concern that engaged in the salt-manufacturing business.[20]

Not much later other salt sources were found. The manufacture of salt became simple, and it was not long before it became a common commodity, cheap as maize. But by that time the frontier had already begun to spread across the continent and had erased the old map and made a new.

### SQUATTER SOVEREIGNTY

The American frontier represented one thing: land. Free land! There were pretentious proprietors who endeavored to claim the land, but the frontiersmen scorned them. The land to them was sacred. It dominated their way of life, their outlook upon society, their relationships with people. Despite the claims of Easterners—which explained part of the hostility of the West to the East—the squatters defied the proprietors, took the land, and challenged them to retake it.[21] What they were talking about was simple. They refused to pay quitrents on land they had secured, developed, protected, defended. It was their land—as much as any land is that which people claim—and they refused to acknowledge any other claims to it.

The battle was over quitrents, which occupied so large a part of the class conflict in the East; it awakened no excitement on the frontier. Following the boy's psychology "havers, keepers," they simply turned up their noses at Eastern proprietors who claimed the land as their own and demanded the payment of quitrents in addition. The frontier was too wide and vast a place for such exploitation, as most of the seaboard investors soon discovered. Quitrents were collected with difficulty in the East, but practically never at all in the West. By the time of the Revolutionary War, they had fallen into desuetude.

The geographic remoteness and isolation of the frontier proved a tremendous advantage in the struggle for democracy in the new world. Along the seaboard, where contacts were close, the old European prejudices prevailed. Class divisions were almost as marked in Massachusetts and South Carolina as they were in England. Proprietors and royal governors dominated the life of the colonies, and the people found it difficult to attain their rights as individuals. On the frontier such difficulties vanished. The people who went there were difficult to reach and hard to subdue. They believed in individual rights and not in property-privilege. When Kentucky drew up its constitution, it did not give suffrage only to those who possessed so much wealth *but to every man in the state regardless of how poor or lowly he might be.*

### FRONTIER PROPRIETORS

The frontier had its proprietors, but they were largely proprietors in name only—not that they would not have liked to have been more. The case of Richard Henderson in that regard is strikingly illustrative. The Transylvania Land Company, organized and headed by him, purchased the vast territory stretching between the Ohio and Columbia Rivers. Led by Daniel Boone, whom Henderson had employed for that purpose, the frontiersmen founded in 1776 the settlement of Boonesborough. Previous to that, in 1774, James Harrod and his followers had founded Harrodsburg, and this group refused to accept the domination of Henderson or Boone. Henderson's attempts to collect quitrents from the Harrodsburg settlers resulted in a fiasco. One assembly was held in 1775, and Henderson discovered to his astonishment and disgust that the frontiersmen were not so docile as the people along the coast line.[22] The struggle evoked bitterness on both sides and was terminated by the Virginia Assembly, which invalidated Henderson's claim to the territory but, in order to pacify him, gave him the land bordered by Kentucky and the Green Rivers.*

* Henderson's company was only one of many. These companies were purely, or rather impurely, speculative enterprises. The one organized by Benjamin Franklin with his associates, which went under the name of Vandalia (whether the name of the company suggested Franklinian candor, or whether it was just an accident, will never be determined) ended in a stillbirth. The Holland land company which bought over five million acres in central and western New York never got beyond the embryonic stage. Robert Morris, "the financier of the Revolution," as he is known to history, purchased one million two hundred thousand acres of land a few years after the Revolution, paying for them a mere eight pence an acre. Later Morris bought even more land and became a company himself. Apropos of all this, it is worth noting that most of what is now the states of Alabama and Mississippi was sold to four land companies for the unimpressive sum of $500,000. In time it was learned that this sale was engineered by state legislators, all but one of whom were members of one of the purchasing land companies.

### THE REBELLION OF THE REGULATORS—AGRARIAN DEMOCRATS

Along the North Carolina frontier, the settlers not only refused to pay quitrents but they organized a rebellion, the echoes of which ring still in the ears of modern Americans—and of all modern men. The rebellion, familiarly known as that of the Regulators, is symbolic. It reveals more about the reaction of the populace to the Revolutionary War than the battles of Lexington and Concord, which have been so exalted and apostrophized by poet and historian through the years. The Regulators represented, in their own individualistic, resistant way, something that was beyond the Revolution, beyond the issues that the merchants and planters who backed the Revolution were concerned with. The Regulators wanted an America that was freed from the men at the top, the proprietors, governors, and other authorities who victimized them; an America that gave to the individual the untrammeled opportunity to start out on his own, regardless of his past, his station, his heritage.

In 1766 the Scotch-Irish frontiersmen had built up the Sandy Creek organization, which challenged the officers then in power and insisted that the people should hold their representatives immediately responsible for all their actions and decisions.* In 1768 another organization was created called "The Mob"; this organization later became known as "The Regulation," and its members were known as the Regulators. Their manifesto is of great historical significance:

> We, the subscribers, do voluntarily agree to form ourselves into an association, to assemble ourselves for conference for regulating public grievances and abuses of power, in the following particulars, with others of a like nature that may occur: (1) We will pay no more taxes until we are satisfied that they are agreeable to law, and applied to the purposes therein mentioned, unless we can not help it, or are forced. (2) We will pay no officer any more fees than the law allows, unless we are obliged to do it, and then to show our dislike and bear open testimony against it. (3) We will attend all our meetings of conferences as often as we conveniently can, etc. (4) We will contribute to collections for defraying necessary expenses attending the work, according to our abilities. (5) In case of

* I am mainly indebted to John S. Bassett for his account of the history of the rebellion.[23]

difference in judgment we will submit to the judgment of the majority of our body.[24]

These words were potentially more revolutionary than those voiced by the Eastern merchants and planters who supported the Revolutionary War.* The latter might raise the cry "no taxation without representation," but they were willing enough, as time was to show, to tax and exploit the hinterland so long as England could not tax them. The hinterland, however, was not deceived by the promises of the East and, when the Revolutionary War broke out, refused to participate in it. The Regulators themselves opposed it, for they well remembered that the seaboard potentates had opposed their cause.

The Regulators were attacked on all sides by ecclesiastics, judges, and the governor of the colony. The militia was summoned to put down the rebellion, but most of the militiamen refused to fight the Regulators, who already represented half the population of the territory. Besides, it was impossible for the officers to be certain that the militiamen who did respond to the summons would fire upon the Regulators if so ordered.

The leaders of the Regulators were William Butler and Hermon Husband, both of whom were men of popular appeal and influence. Like most of the Regulators, Butler was a good fellow, belligerently democratic and diabolically courageous. But he knew little about warfare and less about how to conduct a battle. Hermon Husband, a Marylander by birth, knew even less. He was more of an agitator than a military strategist, and his best activity was in

* It is important to remind the reader here that this book is not concerned with the Revolutionary War in any specific sense; whatever it says about that war is incidental rather than fundamental, because the main concern of the book is with pre-Revolutionary War events.

The American Revolutionary War, contrary to the customary conception, was not waged by the people against the Crown. The people were little interested in it. Their rights were not profoundly involved. Whether the colonies continued to be politically joined with England or separated from it was not particularly important to them. They wanted the simple freedoms of the democratic heritage: nothing more, but nothing less.

At the time of the Revolutionary War, as Professor Farrand has shown, less than eight hundred thousand people were interested in its outcome.[25] The total population of the colonies at that time was approximately two and a half million; this means that two-thirds of the population was unconcerned with the war. The war rid the country of the last remaining remnants of feudal tenure; the properties of both the Crown and individual proprietors were absorbed by the states, which for a time became the new proprietors.

the field of oratory and literature. He was a well-known pamphleteer, and some of his writings attracted the attention of Benjamin Franklin, who corresponded with him for a considerable period. James Hunter, the military leader of the group, was not different from Butler and Husband in outlook. He knew as little about commanding an army as Husband knew about governing a state. When the famous battle between the two forces occurred, Hunter is reported as having refused to assume command of the Regulators, because, as he declared, "*We are all freemen, and everyone must command himself.*"

It is doubtful whether any group in those days was so vigorously democratic as the Regulators. In many ways the Regulators were democratic to a fault, as Hunter's words attested, and as other of their actions revealed.

### ANTAGONISM TOWARD LAWYERS

When Butler and Husband were arrested, the Regulators, distrustful of the courts, wrecked the jail, released the men, and spewed contempt upon the government which had imprisoned them. They would have nothing to do with a government that was dominated by bureaucracy and vitiated by corruption. They hated the power the government had allowed to lawyers, whom they condemned as "those cursed hungry caterpillars that will eat out the very bowels of our commonwealth if they are not pulled down from their nests in a very short time." [26] It was natural for frontiersmen who labored hard to live to scorn lawyers who, in their eyes, lived without labor. Frontier literature is replete with diatribes against lawyers, and eloquent with vicious and scabrous expletives and invectives directed against the legal profession. In the pamphlet from which the preceding quotation was taken, there is an attack upon the clerk of the county who, for one minute's work, robs the poor man of twenty-seven days' labor.

Butler and Husband were finally brought to trial, but the governor had to barricade the courthouse and surround it with soldiers to protect the judges and other officials, so frightened was he of another uprising on the part of the populace. In order to get the soldiers, the governor had to appeal to the preachers to denounce the Regulators, to depict them in sulphurous language as so many limbs of Satan, and in addition he had to furnish libations sufficient to induce the support of those who were not swayed by the exhortations of the clergy. The majority of the militiamen who succumbed to these influences were officers, not privates. As in the case of Franco's rebellion in Spain, it was the officers who defended the cause of reaction and the people who supported the cause of freedom. The officers had everything to gain from the perpetuation of the prevailing regime; the privates had little to gain, if anything.

After a dramatic trial in which bitterness rode in the saddle, Husband was acquitted, but Butler was imprisoned for six months and forced to pay a fine of fifty pounds. In the meanwhile, the Regulators sued the governor for peace, and he in turn, happy to put an end to this costly and calamitous rebellion, granted amnesty to all but thirteen. However, the fight against the oligarchy continued. In 1771 it reached a climax in the fierce battle of Alamance, in which the Regulators lost nine men and the government forces nine, many being wounded on both sides. The Regulators were defeated but their cause was not lost. If they failed to revolutionize the government of North Carolina, the struggle they waged was carried on by the rest of the populace in other colonies, and finally in the states, until all oligarchies were overthrown and political democracy was established in their place.*

### THE REVOLT AGAINST SELWYN

George Selwyn, a large landowner, decided, after having allowed a considerable number of pioneers to settle upon his territory, to force them to pay for their possessions. The frontiersmen had cleared away the ground and built on the land, and felt in no sense obligated to Selwyn, who was an absentee owner. When Selwyn sent surveyors to estimate the value of the land and insisted upon the settlers' paying for the acreage they occupied, the latter not only rejected the demands of the Selwyn representatives but drove them away with missiles and buckshot. In addition, they threatened to kill any sheriff who tried to carry out Selwyn's orders to remove them from his land. When Selwyn tried to combat them, they set upon several of his surveyors and thrashed them near to death.

* The next North Carolinian governor, Martin, successor to Tryon, gave special study to the issue and, as Bassett recounts, contended that the revolt of the Regulators was justified.[27]

There were other frontier revolts of similar character in different colonies, but they were less decisive and significant.

### THE FRONTIER AS A BONANZA

The frontier was not only an alluring compulsion for the poor but also a fascinating gamble for the rich. The poor invested their lives in it, the rich their fortunes. Few men of wealth failed to speculate in Western lands. Beginning with the Ohio Company, which was organized in 1748, the West became coveted by speculators as well as by pioneers. The record of the former includes the names of an overwhelming number of American patriots, the more conspicuous of whom were George Washington, who for a time was almost "land-mad," Benjamin Franklin, Patrick Henry, and Robert Morris. Washington not only bought up frontier territory but even contemplated colonizing it with Germans imported from the Palatinate. He first became interested in Western land as a surveyor and then, later, as a land agent for Lord Fairfax. He invested money in the Mississippi Company as well as in the Ohio Company, and continued to buy up territory even after 1763, when the Crown, concerned with keeping peace with the Indians in order to abet the fur trade, forbade further purchases.[28] Dissatisfied with the results of his transactions because, as he wrote, "they had proved more pregnant of perplexities than profit," Washington sold the larger part of his Western possessions. When he died, however, he still owned over forty thousand acres west of the Alleghenies.[29]

Patrick Henry was an even more avid speculator. "Insatiable in money," as Jefferson described him, he even made private deals with the Indians in his attempt to profit from the land market, and after the Revolutionary War was over he dispatched Joseph Martin into the Holston Valley to buy territory to add to his vast estates.[30] Benjamin Franklin, as we have already noted, was interested in the Vandalia project, which finally proved a futile venture. He had stated that "the great country back of the Appalachian Mountains is one of the finest in North America for the extreme richness and fertility of the land; the healthy temperature of the air, and the mildness of the climate." In London, Franklin labored to get the Crown to grant permission to his friends and others to purchase Western lands that were to constitute Vandalia. He succeeded in engaging the aid of Thomas Walpole, an English banker, and the deal that was finally consummated was known as the Walpole grant. So many rich people were interested in the proposition that there is every reason to believe it would have proved most profitable, and Franklin would have waxed wealthy on it, if the Revolutionary War had not broken out and rendered it void.

### LAND SPECULATION

The wild and frenzied interest in land at the time was not unlike the craze for gold that seized the country in the next century. Land speculation was the easiest way to get rich, and few rich men failed to take advantage of it. Poor men claimed the land by squatting on it, rich men by purchasing it from the Indians. Even pioneers like Daniel Boone, whose name has become a legend, undertook their expeditions in the employ of others. Boone was employed by Judge Henderson; other trail-blazers were backed by different speculators. The owners tried to dislodge the squatters, and the squatters armed themselves to combat the representatives of the owners. In many places actual conflicts occurred. Land was something to fight for in those days, when insurance companies, bankers, building associations, and other dry-rot organizations had not yet engulfed it. *Both the classes and the masses were engaged in its exploitation.* Companies were organized to disseminate "Christianity" among the Western Indians, to further the progress of the Lord in the uncharted territories of the wilderness, and men of the Lord as well as politicians, judges, lawyers and physicians partook in the spoils. Ezra Stiles, a preacher and President of Yale, and in addition the grandfather of Oliver Wendell Holmes, was involved, as also were Governor Walcott of Connecticut and many other officials. Even Peter Jefferson, the father of Thomas Jefferson, was one of the speculators.

The land companies multiplied like guinea pigs. At first there were the Ohio Company and the Mississippi Company; then came the Susquehanna Company, the Illinois and Wabash Companies, the Indiana Company, the Delaware Company, the Grand Ohio Company (afterwards known as Vandalia), and too many others to recount.

All were consumed by the same ambition: the possession and exploitation of land. Speculators encouraged immigrants to settle upon their lands in order to increase their value. Large areas were offered as bait to those who would attempt the wilderness and occupy the new territory. Everything was done to populate the country. New Englanders as well as Southerners combined in this invasion of the frontier in search of better lands and larger profits.

Before the Revolutionary War this speculation in frontier lands was widespread; after the Revolution it became gigantic. Patrick Henry became more involved. John Sevier, who attained fame in the battle of King's Mountain, acquired even vaster territories. Robert Morris, a leading patriot, was one of the most egregious adventurers of them all.

### EARLY AMERICAN IMPERIALISM

In colonial days the first people to forge West were the German and Scotch-Irish groups, but not long after they were followed by the English, who swarmed in multitudes across the amorphous frontier horizon. "I saw with wonder," wrote Horatio Gates Spafford, an eighteenth-century contemporary, "that these people, all Yankees, from Massachusetts, Connecticut, and Vermont, were perfectly undismayed, looking forward in hope" to the New Canaan of the West. In the Mohawk Valley he saw "wagons of New England farmers seeking a more friendly soil in what had been the country of the Iroquois." In time many parts of the West became little more than extensions of New England, settled by the younger generation of the founding fathers. It was an exodus, indeed, and before it was completed cities flung as far across the continent as Portland, Oregon, were born of its energy. New England and Virginia and the Carolinas perpetuated themselves in these distant spots, converted them into communities and developed them into cities, colonies, and eventually states. It was an imperialistic migration into lands which were considered part of the national domain. Certainly it was as imperialistic (if the American Indians could conceive of that term) as the conquest of India by the British was to the nations of India.

New England became so concerned with this emigration of her inhabitants to the Western frontier that she began to print leaflets and publish pamphlets which aimed to dissuade her settlers from the enterprise. Her efforts failed, as we all know today, and the frontier was made into a new part of the continent, so new that it matured into the creative influence of a hemisphere—and, indirectly, of the whole sublunary universe in which we live.

### CROGHAN: SPECULATOR PAR EXCELLENCE

One of the leaders in the westward movement was George Croghan, who was the handyman of the frontier. He knew more about the backlands than any other man of his day. Unlike Daniel Boone, or even such types as Mike Fink and Paul Bunyan, who knew the frontier in specific aspects, he knew it in all. He not only lived in frontier lands, as they did, but in addition he was a trader, an Indian agent, and a land promoter. He knew the country from every point of view: the Indians, the squatters, the speculators. He was admired and loathed, trusted and distrusted, befriended and betrayed. Few men won so many friends and created so many enemies. He stalked across the land like an economic phantom, winning concessions from the Indians, extending the interests of the land companies, and promoting the increase of new settlements. More settlements owed their origin to him, it is probable, than to any other man. His trading posts, interspersed throughout the wilderness, were magnets for trade and settlement. They were radiant centers toward which colonists gravitated.*

An Irishman by birth, Croghan was one of the first of his tribe to seize upon the frontier situation and turn it to his own advantage. He had a frontier Tammany psychology. The colonists despised him because he played with everybody and was willing to sell anybody to anybody else if there was enough profit in it for him. Croghan in turn dismissed the settlers as so much riffraff and rabble. His sympathies were with the top dogs and not the underdogs, and he used his sundry abilities to forward the interests of the former upon every occasion. It was natural, therefore, that he should be employed by the officialdom of Pennsylvania to be an Indian agent and to win the support of the Indians so that the fur business could be increased. In order to achieve that end, Croghan undertook to

* For a more detailed treatment of Croghan's role in frontier activities, see Volwiler's study, cited before, which is a thoroughgoing and excellent account of it as well as of the frontier in general.

dislodge the squatters from those territories where the Indians complained most bitterly of white invasion. He did this not because he was a friend of the Indians, as Roger Williams had been, or Penn, or Priber, but because he and the people he represented were more interested in the fur trade than in the fate of the squatters.

### SQUATTERS VERSUS THE INDIANS

That situation occasioned an interesting contradiction. The Croghans and the property-owning proprietors who exploited the lower classes in the East defended the retreating Indians in the West. They did not defend them out of affection or magnanimity of spirit; their motive was unadulteratedly economic. They wanted the furs that the Indians secured and sold. For that reason they were kinder to the red men than the squatters, who were interested not in furs but in finding an endurable place to live. The Indians, because they resented the occupation of lands which had originally belonged to them, considered the squatters enemies. The Indians, naturally, liked the proprietary people better than the squatters, because the former paid them for their efforts whereas the latter killed them whenever they had a chance. The proprietors had enough land of their own and were not interested at that time in seizing Indian lands; they wanted their furs, nothing more. The squatters, who extended the domain of the white men, wanted the land that the Indians had owned for countless centuries.

The Indians were concerned not with reasons but with results. They did not care why the proprietors were their friends so long as they were and remained such; they were not interested in the unhappy conflicts and oppressions that drove the squatters to the frontier and caused them to crowd upon the skirts of the wilderness. All they knew was that anyone who robbed them of their lands was their enemy, and it was the squatters and not the proprietors at this time who were guilty of that offense.

The whole situation represented a curious contradiction in class relationships. The proprietors and their allies, who were the *big* landowners, found it to their advantage to aid the Indians, the most downtrodden group of all, against the squatters, who were the in-between group that had to fight the proprietors on one side and the Indians on the other in order to survive. In the end the squatters were victorious: the proprietors were vanquished in the Revolutionary War and the Indians were murdered in two centuries. Might triumphed!

It was inevitable, then, that the squatters should detest Croghan, who was the proprietors' *man*. More than that, Croghan actually undertook to drive the squatters from Indian territories so that he could win the friendship of the Indians and make certain deals with them that were profitable to his employers. He was not concerned with the animosity toward himself which he stirred up among the squatters, many of whom fought off his men with shot. The squatters were beaten, and they knew it. Croghan had won—once more. He had a habit of winning in everything he attempted.

Croghan's role, as is apparent, was far from a noble one. But it was most effective. In his way he accelerated frontier expansion. He connived against the squatters, it is true, but at the same time, or certainly not very much later, he devoted his services to the land speculators, who became the friends of the Indians because they were willing to pay for the lands they planned to exploit. Croghan was invaluable as liaison between the speculators and the red men. So successful was he in his multifarious transactions that in 1756 he was made Deputy Superintendent of Indian Affairs.

It was a common tendency to call the squatters vagabonds, rogues, and thieves, and Croghan, who was one of the first to entertain the idea of plunging beyond the Appalachians, minced no phrases in denouncing them as persons who refused to regard the sacred rights of property. The whites had made agreements not to settle the territory west of the mountains; they had even threatened to court-martial men who hunted in those lands. Both speculators and squatters had disregarded the agreement. The movement westward was too strong to quell; the Britishers and the coast-land Americans were opposed to it, but they were powerless to retard it. Governor Dunmore of Virginia bewailed it and, in melancholy spirit, wrote that these wandering frontiersmen "acquire no attachment of place . . . they forever imagine the Lands further off are still better than those upon which they are already settled."

The movement went on.

Croghan showed no opposition to frontiersmen as such; his opposition was to those who "squatted" on the land and refused to pay the owners of it their due. He was the central figure in the settlement of Pittsburgh, which in 1760 had a population of less than one hundred fifty people. His house was the largest in the community and was familiarly known as Croghan Hall, and he was commonly addressed as "Colonel Croghan." He was active in expediting the settlement of other parts of Pennsylvania and, in 1770, declared with heartening gusto that "all this spring and summer the roads have been lined with wagons moving to the Ohio." These were the covered wagons of legend, in which progress the history of a nation was involved.

Settlements increased, counties multiplied, and new colonies were in the process of birth. Croghan phrased it well when he said, "One-half of England is now Land mad and everybody there has their eyes fixed on this country." All this had just that effect. It awakened England to a realization of the importance of its American possessions, and in so doing strengthened its determination to hold the colonies even at the cost of war.

Hindered though the land movement was, for speculators as well as for pioneers, by the intervention of the French and Indian War, it developed with renewed rapidity once that war was over.

It was not long before Croghan had acquired over forty thousand acres of land, and a few years later his possessions amounted to over two hundred fifty thousand acres.

### RELIGION AND THE FRONTIER

Everywhere the frontiersmen ventured they carried their religion with them. On the whole, the Western pioneers were poor people who found life on the seaboard unrewarding, and who plunged into the back country because they hoped to acquire a better livelihood there. They were Dissenters, not Puritans; simple, undemanding men who were not concerned with rank, station, or income. All they wanted was a place to house themselves, earn their daily bread, and protect and perpetuate their families. That was little enough to ask.

Their religion was born in Europe, but it acquired new life on the frontier, where it became the central challenge of the community. In earlier days the individual had thought of himself in connection with a group, as part of a religious whole. At this time, in the new world, he began to think of himself as a separate entity, an isolated force, an individual ego. Preachers were not inspirational because they knew any more than other people, or because they had been blessed by a church, but because they echoed what every individual felt. If the echo was strange, oblique, obscure, it was because other ears had not yet learned to sense its significance and underlying meaning.

Protestantism functioned as the psychological midwife in giving birth to the modern ego. But the American frontier functioned in making that ego real, tangible, translating its energies into realities that European conditions did not cultivate or encourage. It developed hysterical, maniacal expressions on the frontier because the isolation of the territory itself induced such reactions. Not the Puritans but the Dissenters gave form to the democratic religious philosophy that matured in the frontier. In Europe that individualistic philosophy was confined mainly to the middle class, whereas in America the opportunities of the frontier, promising every individual the prospect of advance, became the possession of the entire populace. In brief, by making everyone in America individualistic, the frontier made the entire country adopt the psychology of the middle class.[31]

## THE DEMOCRATIC CHALLENGE

It was in the form of religion that the frontier psychology revealed itself in most conspicuous form on American soil. The religious sects who populated the frontier regions were almost exclusively members of the various Dissenting denominations, particularly Baptists and Methodists. They were evangelical in type and democratic in ecclesiastical conviction. Hating the theocratic dictatorship of the Massachusetts colony, the Baptists had made Rhode Island, which Roger Williams had founded in the name of religious liberty, their first center of occupation. But the Baptists had achieved only limited gains in America prior to the middle of the eighteenth century. Although it was the coming of the Great Revival, centered at first around the figure of Jonathan Edwards, which afforded the Baptist movement its first driving impetus, it was the frontier that gave it its great momentum.[32] The Methodists, who like the Episcopalians were almost wiped out in the East in consequence of their reactionary support of England during the Revolutionary War, also found the frontier the most fertile territory in which to spread their doctrines. In fact, only such doctrines as the evangelical religions espoused could make any headway on the frontier.

What was there about these doctrines that made them win such sweeping support in the West? In the first place, they were doctrines that in the East had represented the extremity of lower middle-class independence of outlook, doctrines that appealed to the poorer elements in the population far more than to the wealthier.[33] The theocracy with its Calvinist tenets had stressed class divisions in church as well as in society; places in church had been determined by economic station; and authority had rested in the hands of the ecclesiastics and not in the hands of the individual members of the congregation. In other words, it was dictatorship and not democracy that had prevailed. With the Baptists and Methodists, the situation was reversed. Appealing to the poorer classes, these evangelical religions were overwhelmingly democratic in their emphasis. They threw their entire stress upon the individual and the right of the individual to salvation. They were not interested in theological differentiations and declarations. It was the inner reaction of the individual that counted, the inner vision of the soul that could perceive God and be saved. Redemption and salvation with these evangelical groups was far more of an emotional than an intellectual experience. There was nothing predestinate about their creeds, nothing Calvinistic; salvation was a matter of individual volition, attainable by all. The only test was individual faith, a faith the individual could establish with his Maker without the intercession of an established clergy. It was emotional conviction and not theological purity in which the frontier was interested. In the frontier churches, therefore, the division between preacher and laymen was practically destroyed.* The qualities necessary to make a preacher revolved less about theological training than about religious emotion and insight. Men could become great preachers without theological study if they were religiously inspired. It was this belief that made it possible for lay preachers to become so instrumental in the spread of individualistic doctrines—and for laymen to feel with their religions an intimacy, an intense, emotional intimacy, that had been impossible with the more theological creeds.

Now it was just these individualistic, democratic emotional aspects

* Timothy Flint observes: "Although I universally heard religion spoken of with 'respect' . . . yet they think much less of the necessity of a minister than the people of the North." [34]

of the Baptists' and Methodists' creeds that made them capture the imagination of the frontiersmen.* To be sure, a considerable part of the frontier was settled by men and women who before they deserted the East were members of one or the other of those congregations, but the vast majority who joined them were converts made in the new territories. Those religions fulfilled a definite need in the virgin environment. They defended the cause of the frontiersman in politics,[35] lent validity to his economic form of existence, and provided an outlet for his emotional life which otherwise, in surroundings as barren as those of the frontier, would have been pent-up and suppressed.

## THE INNER LIGHT

Indeed, the revivalistic type of Christianity created by the frontier,† running riot in every form of emotional extreme and finding its anachronistic repercussion even today in the antics of the Holy Rollers and the obscene theatrics of Billy Sunday, was a phenomenon which perhaps has never been seen elsewhere in the modern world.‡ It represented a form of religiosity in which the individual became a vital participant, and into which he plunged with primitive abandon. It provided him with a sesame to truth. It made him the divine possessor of a wisdom that no one else could rob him of, that no one else could surpass, for it was the wisdom of origins and ends, wisdom that mundane minds, critics, scholars, professors, might attack but could never weaken or destroy. It was the possession of this wisdom, this inner light, that helped to give the frontiersman his impregnable confidence, fortified his faith in himself as an individual, made him unashamed of his ignorance and illiteracy, and strengthened his scorn for the culture and punditry of the East. With this individual inner light to guide him, he could defy the rest of the world, defy reason, learning, science.

* Even the Presbyterians, whose creedal origins were very different from those of the Baptists and Methodists, were forced to adopt the same attitudes and practices in the Western regions.

† "Protestant sects," stated Rusk, summarizing the whole tendency, "succeeded in the pioneer West in inverse ratio to their intellectual attainments and in direct ratio to their emotional appeal."[36]

‡ The only other country in the modern world that provided any parallel was czaristic Russia. Along many stretches of the Russian frontier the peasants were given to spasms of religiosity not unlike those on our frontier. But the element of individualism that saturated frontier religion in America was undeveloped in Russia.

This development of religiosity, of course, did not intensify in the West until the nineteenth century. In the eighteenth century, the frontier territory was still too sparsely settled to encourage the growth of sufficient communities so that the church could implant itself as an institution. In fact, as R. S. Cotterill has observed, in Kentucky in the eighteenth century there was a notable "absence of piety in the land." Less than one-tenth of the population in 1792 were church members.[37] Crevecoeur related in his *Letters from an American Farmer* how, in the absence of a church and pastor, he had gathered the people in his vicinity into an improvised meeting place, and had preached to them himself in his own simple, humble way. On the extreme boundaries of the frontier, boundaries that were being steadily pushed into the interior as the population moved onward, religion did not penetrate at all, save as an individual frontiersman observed it in his hut or in the family homestead. The people carried with them the same ascetic moral attitudes that prevailed in the East, but those attitudes broke down under the triturating influences of the frontier environment.*

After the Revolutionary War, when conditions on the coast became economically unstable, owing in part to the closing of the ports of the British West Indies and to the difficulties in trade that grew up between the new government and France and Spain, the prospect of the West became a compelling lure. From that time on, the Westward migration became a force in the affairs of the nation, attracting hordes of pioneers who were determined to found new communities wherever they ventured. It was those communities, increasing in size as the migration continued, that made it possible for religion to grow and disseminate in the West, and finally to extend itself, through the agency of the lay preacher as well as the established cleric, into the remote places of the frontier.

While many of the pioneers set out to create a "New England of the West," as the Ohio Valley was described, it was really a new America that they founded. The intolerances of the East lost their meaning in an environment in which the possibility of control concentrating itself in the hands of a few was removed. Moreover, the individualistic, democratic tendencies of mind that the new conditions

* William MacDonald describes this process vividly if a bit exaggeratedly in his *Spirit and Influence of the American Frontier*.[38]

of life inevitably bred inspired divergence instead of unity of outlook. Where each individual was prone to think himself an authority, where it was the individual inner light that glowed within him and not the outer guiding light of church or state that determined his convictions, dissent was certain to prevail.* The religious history of the West soon became marked by the rise and fall of various sects, one more fantastic and hysterical than the other, and by the splits and divisions of those sects that survived in the struggle.†

## MULTIPLICATION OF SECTS

With all sects, ranging from the Baptists, Methodists, Presbyterians, Campbellites, and Disciples of Jesus, to the Shakers, Groaners, Muggletonians, Come Outers, New Lights, and Mormons, this spirit of independence flared. In no other civilized country has religious liberty ever raced to such wild and savage extremes. The stamping and screaming preachers who populated the frontier, and who were noted for stripping off their upper garments, leaping out of their pulpits at times, and clapping their hands in frenzy between sentences in their sermons,[41] were even less of a spectacle than their congregations, which often exceeded them in their orgies of enthusiasm. Crooning congregations, moaning congregations, shaking congregations, jumping and howling congregations, rolling and wrestling congregations, were popular throughout the West. Camp meetings tumultuous with men and women swaying to strange macabre rhythms, stripped naked often as they were in their ecstasy,[42] spread far west of the Mississippi. In a camp meeting of Presbyterians and Methodists held at Cain Ridge in August 1801, thousands of people gathered for an extended service, lasting uninterruptedly for

* Indeed, it was in such a soil that the religious traditions of the Dissenters could root themselves with best success.[39]

† Terrified at the individualistic nature of frontier religions, many New England preachers advocated that missionaries be sent into the West in order to introduce "the social and religious principles of New England among them." Already, as a result of such superciliousness, the antagonism of the West to the East was developing into an issue. In reply to the New England clergymen the frontier periodical, *The Western Monthly Magazine*, discharged a sharp rejoinder:

"New England's desolate sons are called upon to go among the desolate population of the West for the purpose of sowing virtue in the minds of an ignorant generation. But they are to come not in a mass to excite an envious feeling—how kind! how philanthropic! to spare us the mortification of witnessing the concentrated brilliancy of a mass of cultivated intellects from the glowing East." [40]

nearly a week. Over 1,000 people swooned as a result of the excitement and frenzy of preaching and singing.[43] No excess was too great for those hysterically minded masses in pursuit of the religious experience.

Religion took on a militancy among these people that shattered almost every evidence of restraint. When emotion moved them, no matter how trivial the cause, sects and even new congregations split themselves asunder and set up new sects and new congregations.* The Presbyterians in Lexington, Kentucky, fought each other over a disagreement on psalmody [45] and split in two as a result. The Society of Friends divided themselves into the orthodox and the Hicksians —the latter following the leadership of Elias Hicks.[46] The Baptists split up into the Regular Baptists, the United Baptists, the Hard-Shell Baptists, the Particular Baptists, the General Baptists, and the Primitive and Free-Will Baptists. Feuds sprang up everywhere without the slightest provocation. Religious debates became a common occurrence. Various sects established periodicals that devoted most of their space to spreading their own propaganda and exposing that of their adversaries. Every means of defense and attack was exploited by those religionists in an attempt to establish their varied and conflicting creeds. David Todd, in a letter to Lyman Draper, told of a Baptist preacher who, persecuted and imprisoned, preached to the people through the jail windows, exhorting them to continue to fight for the cause of the Lord. His words, full-throated and vibrant, and gory with threat, made the jail the most popular place in the settlement. People gathered from miles around, perched on hills and trees, clambered on wagon seats, sprawled on the earth—all spellbound by the prophetic wonder and terror of the speech.

While the majority of those sects were intensely individualistic in psychology, a certain number began with communistic conceptions. In the overwhelming majority, to be sure, the influence of the environment militated against their success and caused them to abandon their ideal. Among the more interesting of such communities was that of the Moravians who settled in Pennsylvania and who established there, as part of their Christocracy, a general economy that was

* "The worshippers split on trifling differences. The more trifling the more pertinaciously they cling to them, and where but a few Sabbaths before all seemed union, you soon find that all is discord." [44]

communistic in character. The Amana Community, which originally settled near Buffalo and later moved to Iowa, has remained in Iowa till the present time.[47] The Harmonists settled north of Pittsburgh; the Separatists of Zoar located themselves farther to the west; the Economists who, under the leadership of Doctor Keil, built their original community in Bethel, Missouri, later moved to Aurora, Oregon. Other similar enterprises were the Cedarvale Community in Kansas and the Bishop Hill Swedish Colony in Illinois. In many ways the most memorable community of all were the Shakers, whose center was near Albany, although parties of them ventured as far north as Maine and as far south as Kentucky. More glamorous and in some ways even more memorable than the Shakers were the Perfectionists of the Oneida Community, who established their communism on sexual as well as economic grounds. The disappearance of all those groups, including the Brotherhood of Perfection and the Brethren of Solidarity, can be attributed in the main to the influence of the environment, which tended to encourage individualistic instead of communal endeavor.

The experience of the Quakers was typical. A radical sect in Europe, they became in America a middle-class group that forsook radicalism as soon as the environment began to yield them wealth and power. The only radical doctrine to which they continued to adhere, and which the Mennonites adhere to also to this day, was that of non-violence, which in no sense conflicted with their economic advance.

### THE MORMON IDEAL

The only group that managed to preserve something of its original co-operative spirit amid the individualistic, competitive environment of America was the Mormons. Instead of organizing their communties in the haphazard, devil-may-care manner that characterized most of the Western communities, they pursued a plan of state capitalism and organized their life about a social instead of an individualistic pivot. Centralized control prevailed from the very beginning. Indeed, part of the opposition of the Mormon settlements grew out of this contradiction between their economic way of life and that of the rest of the frontier. The differences reflected in religion, and even in moral concepts, were active elements also in the conflicts that arose between them and their neighbors.

Far west, Brigham Young decided to irrigate the desert land, believing that the Mormons with their co-operative discipline could achieve it; he knew full well that the typical individualistic farmers of the frontier could never do it. As the colony grew through the arrival of the converts, new sub-colonies were marked out, but they were not planted in a go-as-you-please manner like most other frontier developments. Instead, the officers of the church made the reconnaissance, selected the site, and then told enough of the members of each craft or line of business to make the venture a success.[48]

It was the individualistic, democratic philosophy which the Dissenters bequeathed to this country as a religious heritage, plus the geographic and economic nature of the environment which endowed that heritage with new life, that made America the land of pullulating sects and creeds. In England the Dissenting groups multiplied with less frequency because of the limitations of both population and soil. Moreover, as subordinate groups, they tended to split off with less rapidity in England than in America, where they constituted, especially in the frontier regions, the dominant group in the community. While the frontier in particular abetted that tendency, the nature of the Dissenting tradition kept it alive in the old colonies as well as the new.

The division of the country into states, which ofttimes sought to look upon themselves as sovereign units, tended to multiply differences and prevent any effective national organization of churches. Although the West still has the greater number of denominations, the East is not very far behind—which simply goes to prove that while the frontier was a most important factor in determining the multiplication of sects, the whole individualistic tradition upon which the country was founded was more fundamental and decisive. Indiana with one hundred seven denominations stands first; Michigan is a close second with eighty-seven, Iowa following with eighty-five, Kansas with seventy-seven, and California with seventy-four. But when we turn to the East, the discrepancy is far from marked. Pennsylvania, with seventy-nine denominations possessing less than 10,000 members each, takes precedence over most of the Western states. Even Massachusetts, where originally religion was so unified, has fifty denominations. In Connecticut there are thirty denominations, and in Rhode Island "there is a different sect for every 2,000 church members." [49]

### SUFFRAGE FOR ALL MEN

This democracy in religion voiced itself also in politics. The Dissenter tradition pervaded all frontier life. None of the class divisions that prevailed along the seaboard extended beyond the Alleghenies. Everything was equalitarian. In the East men had to battle for suffrage; in Rhode Island, as late as 1842, Dorr was imprisoned for insisting upon the right of the people to vote regardless of wealth or privilege. On the frontier suffrage was viewed as a natural right to which all men were entitled. Vermont, Kentucky, and Tennessee, the first of the frontier states, granted suffrage to all men. The only requirements were that the individual had to be twenty-one years of age and must have lived in the state for one year before he voted.[50] The first written constitution in the new world was that of the Watauga Association, drafted in 1772.[51] This constitution was remarkable not only because of its date but because it was the first document of this kind drawn up by the people without regard for crown or proprietor.*

### AMERICANIZATION OF A CONTINENT

This was the Americanization of a continent. The coastal colonies had preserved and perpetuated European traditions. The West disembarrassed itself of them and crystallized a new tradition conceived in its own image. In the cabin settlements of the frontier, democratic America was born.

The new world was Europeanized before it was Americanized. The men who settled it—Spaniards, Frenchmen, Englishmen, Germans—were products of European culture. In the beginning they strove to make the new country a copy of the old. But the land itself

* If there were space in this narrative, it would be worth-while to deal with such frontier leaders as James Robertson and John Sevier, both of whom did much to give meaning to the West when it was little more than a shadowy, amorphous fling of space. Through their efforts Watauga became the first self-governing settlement west of the Blue Ridge.[52] Robertson, unlike Boone, was more of a settler than a hunter and a trader, and Sevier, a Huguenot, who followed Robertson into the Kentuckian territory, joined hands in the formation of the Watauga Association, which achieved organization in one of the most unorganized settlements of the day.

—its vastness, its unexplored immensity, its tremendous promise of infinite newness—crushed the European influence.

It was the frontier, then, that Americanized the country. Until the end of the nineteenth century that Americanization continued. Peoples from many nations, talking strange tongues, steeped in quaint, weird traditions, wearing fantastic garb, ventured forth into the wilderness, pursued an unknown horizon, and became something new. That newness was American.

Since the closing of the frontier, toward the end of the nineteenth century, America has been becoming an old world. Today it is being Europeanized. Lacking the elasticities of a yielding frontier, it is developing the same class conflicts that have been conspicuous in European history, and has found it increasingly difficult since the World War to afford employment to many millions of its citizens.

### THE END OF THE AGRARIAN DREAM

As a farmer the American years ago learned that land could not be cultivated without capital, and capital was the one thing he did not possess. It was one thing to own land and quite another to work it. The farmer had to build a house or some other kind of shelter to protect his family; he had to have tools, initial livestock, clothing, and all that multiplying variety of odds and ends requisite to an agrarian existence. To obtain these he eventually had to borrow from capitalists, to get credit from them for what he needed. This made him a debtor, and ever since he has remained in the debtor class.* Many farmers, it is true, escaped this debtor status, but the majority found themselves bound to it through the years.

It was the nature of the farmer's economic existence that made him a victim of this new capitalist economy that had taken possession of the land. He had to sell his produce in a fluctuating market but had to pay his debts in a static one. He could not control the productivity of the soil, which was as regular as sunfall, and this fact left him helpless in the hands of his creditors. The irony was that, the richer his harvest, the poorer he became. He paid his debts in terms of produce, and the only time he could pay them was the harvest season.

* Turner was the first to point this out, but among contemporaries more aware of economic factors than Turner is Louis M. Hacker, who in his significant pamphlet *The Farmer Is Doomed,* has achieved a far sounder analysis of the whole problem.

But since all other farmers paid them at the same time, in accordance with nature's inexorable punctuality, the market, governed by the law of supply and demand, was overburdened with produce and prices fell. But his debts did not fall; they remained fixed. What he owed on his mortgage, or the interest therein, did not change; what he owed the storekeeper for merchandise did not change; in simple, whatever he *owed* remained the same, but what he was paid did not. He was paid in terms of the market (which was lowest when he was paid), but he had to pay others in terms of currency. It was natural, therefore, that the farmer was then and still is in favor of a currency inflated sufficiently to cover the discrepancy between what he is paid and what he has to pay. The merchant bought cheap and sold dear; the farmer sold cheap and bought dear. The merchant gained; the farmer lost. To escape the vicious circle, the latter has always been willing to support any monetary scheme, however fantastic, that promises him a way out.*

The history of the frontier has been that of freemen and freedmen who ventured West in search of freedom, but who in the last fifty years have been subjected to a new form of slavery. By freedom these trail-blazers and pioneers meant improved economic opportunity. It was many generations before they realized their error, but when they did, in the late nineteenth century, the Granger and Populist movements were born, and protest and revolt were on the march.

The frontier is dead as an inspiration for pioneers. It is dead too for the millions of unemployed on relief, and also for those increasing hordes of young men and women with ability and training who find it impossible to get jobs commensurate with their capacity. They see—these moody, mutinous multitudes—no hope of work beyond the Appalachians or Rockies. The country has acquired the same gray outlines from coast to coast. Possibilities, opportunities, aspirations, do not vary greatly from state to state. section to section, ocean to ocean.

* The Douglas scheme of financial reform attempted in Alberta, Canada, is illustrative in our time of how determined the farmer is to escape from his currency morass. In this country the AAA, without venturing into financial reform, is trying to accomplish a not dissimilar task. The farmer's plight is even worse today, when he has to compete against an international market in which prices are controlled by world production and not, as in the case of industry, by national tariffs.

## EPILOGUE

# Democracy: The Way Out

THE history of this country has been the history of democracy. Democracy did not come to us like some divinely given thing, sprung from the head of a god or the loins of a goddess, but as a gradual creation, shaped out of the elusive contours of the past, emerging slowly like a vapor from an ancient cistern, acquiring form as it crystallized into substance. In earlier days, among the Greeks and Romans, it had remained amorphous, unsolidified; with the Americans, it became tangible, concrete, peripheral. Democracy to the Greeks meant democracy for the well-to-do, the select, the elite, the superior. It was not democracy for the commoners, the people of the streets, the humble, the lowly, the ne'er-do-wells, the beggars, the impoverished, the desperate. American democracy begins where Greek democracy ended. It is democracy for the poor as well as the rich, for the unsuccessful as well as the successful. What makes it significant is its inclusiveness. It is democracy for car conductors, plumbers, firemen, prize-fighters, laundrymen, baseball pitchers, shop-girls, boilermakers, ticket-takers, tarts, dodos, palookas, gillies, giants, midgets, magicians—regardless of property, regardless of sex.

In a phrase, it is democracy for everyone!

That democracy was won, as we have seen, only after a long, carking struggle. Democracy is always the result of struggle. It has never been achieved in any other way, and it can never be preserved in any other way. But it is an expanding and not a contracting concept; it cannot stand still, but must change with changing environments, must adapt itself to the new necessities of different eras.

The democracy that America achieved in colonial days was an outgrowth of an agrarian nation, a nation born of the upshoots of the land, the effluvia of the rivers, the generosities of wind and sky. It was the democracy of a simple, agricultural people, whose quarrel was not with the way they made a living but with the way proprietors, governors, and politicians interfered with the way they lived.

They needed political power to combat such interference, to thwart such designs.

For people living under such conditions political democracy was enough. Agrarian democracy is adequate in an agrarian country.

But what happened in the nineteenth century and was completed in the twentieth was that America was transformed from an agrarian into an industrial country. Such a revolutionary change necessitates a radical revaluation and readaptation of the concept of democracy. The political democracy adequate in an agrarian country is not adequate in an industrial country. In an agrarian country the farmers at least have the land and the tools necessary to exploit it; in an industrial country the workers do not own the factories and, what is worse, do not even own the tools of production that they use. The factories and the tools are owned by individuals who command and control the destinies of those who work for them. That condition did not prevail among the American farmers, but it does prevail among the American workers.

Because of that change, democracy is being reborn today; a new umbilicus is being severed, a new parentage realized. Democracy has acquired an economic embodiment, added a new tissue. It is the child of a new age.

In an industrial nation, industrial democracy is a necessity if democracy is to be perpetuated. Industrial democracy means endowing every individual with the right to hold his job, in bad times as well as good, and with the right to vote in terms of his job and not in terms of his residence. It means emancipating the individual from economic bondage—bondage to an employer before whom he is defenseless. It means protecting him against economic disaster and defeat—protecting him not against kings, proprietors, and governors, as in colonial days, but against industrial barons, financial magnates, and political demagogues.

Democracy is always a protection, a protection of the people (*demos*) against those in power who wish to take advantage of them, exploit them. In the colonial period political protection was adequate. Today economic protection is imperative. Industrial democracy can provide that protection.

To achieve industrial democracy is the task that confronts us as a nation. In the colonial period we gave democracy a meaning and significance that it lacked in Europe; in later years we added to that meaning and significance by extending and expanding it, widening its periphery, doubling its diameter.

This was the *awakening of America*—the most significant awakening in the modern world. But to be awakened is not enough. To stay awake is more important.

And to stay awake, America must make its democracy dynamic and not static, progressive and not retrogressive; it must make it a perennially growing, vitalizing, creative force.

# REFERENCES

## CHAPTER I


1. *Cambridge History of India,* III, 16.
2. *Ibid.*, p. 116.
3. *Travels of Ludovico Di Varthema,* Hakluyt Society, pp. 106, 117.
4. Friar Jordanus, *The Wonders of the East* (*Circa* 1330), Hakluyt Society, p. 28.
5. A. Appadorai, *Economic Conditions in Southern India* (1000-1500 A.D.), II, 754-755.
6. W. M. Gibbs, *Spices and How to Know Them,* p. 36.
7. *Ibid.*, p. 81.
8. Donald Culross Peattie, *Cargoes and Harvests,* p. 14.
9. W. H. Moreland, *India at the Death of Akbar,* p. 223.
10. *Ibid.*, p. 225.
11. Sir William Foster, *England's Quest of Eastern Trade* (1933), p. 5.
12. Letter of John Montecorvino (fourteenth century), appearing in *Hakluyt Society Records,* trans. and ed. by Colonel Henry Yule, pp. 212-213.
13. *The Book of Ser Marco Polo,* Yule translation, II, 375, 389.
14. Varthema, *op. cit.*, p. 163.
15. *The Book of Duarte Barbosa* (completed about 1518 A.D.), p. 222.
16. Kunwar Mohammed Ashraf, "Life and Conditions of the People of Hindustan (1200-1550 A.D.)," *Journal of the Asiatic Society of Bengal,* p. 207.
17. *Ibid.*, p. 209.
18. Hon. Mountstuart Elphinstone, *The History of India,* I, 317.
19. *The Travels of Niccolò dei Conti in the East, in the Early Part of the Fifteenth Century,* as related by Poggio Bracciolini, p. 21.
20. "The Travels of Athanasius Nikitin, of Twer," from *India in the Fifteenth Century,* ed. by R. H. Major (Hakluyt Society), p. 19.
21. *Book of Marco Polo,* Book III, Chap. 2, p. 253.
22. Engelbert Kaempfer, *History of Japan,* 1690-1692, p. 167.
23. *Cathay and the Way Thither,* trans. and ed. by Col. Sir Henry Yule, I, 157.
24. J. Allan, *The Cambridge Shorter History of India,* p. 179.
25. A. Appadorai, *Economic Conditions in Southern India* (1936), II, 444.
26. Broadhus Mitchell, *Rise of Cotton Mills in the South* (1921), p. 19.
27. John Capper, *The Three Presidencies of India,* p. 353.
28. Ishwari Prasad, "The Rise and Growth of Khilhi Imperialism," *Journal of Indian History,* pp. 147-178.
29. A. Yusuf Ali, *Medieval India: Social and Economic Conditions,* p. 47.
30. Pramathanath Banerjea, *A Study of Indian Economics* (1911), p. 79.
31. H. H. Dodwell, *India,* p. 2.


## CHAPTER II


1. *Numbers,* 15:35, 36.
2. C. H. Haskins, *The Renaissance of the Twelfth Century,* pp. 280-292.


## CHAPTER III


1. An unpublished study in which the author, M. E. Tracy, proves conclusively that Captain Kidd was far from the fierce, danger-defying man of legend.

2. Miriam Beard, *History of the Business Man.*
3. C. H. Haskins, *The Renaissance of the Twelfth Century.*
4. O. A. Marti, *Economic Cause of the Reformation in England,* p. 113.
5. *Ibid.,* p. 146.

## CHAPTER IV

1. Samuel Rawson Gardiner, *The Puritan Revolution,* p. 132.
2. Sir John Marriott, *The Crisis of English Liberty,* pp. 140-146.
3. John Brown, *The English Puritans,* p. 152.
4. *Ibid.,* p. 152.
5. C. Sydney Carter, "Puritanism, Its History, Spirit and Influence," *London Quarterly Review* (October, 1924).

## CHAPTER V

1. Frances Densmore, *The American Indians and Their Music,* p. 14.
2. Thomas Hariot, *A Briefe and True Report of the New Found Land of Virginia* (1588), p. 3.
3. Robert Briffault, *The Mothers,* I, 316.
4. Margaret Mead, *The Changing Culture of an Indian Tribe* (1932), p. 133.
5. G. N. B. Hewitt, *Status of Iroquois Woman* (Annual Reprint of Smithsonian Institution, 1932).
6. *Ibid.*
7. Alexander Goldenweiser, *Early Civilizations,* p. 73.
8. *Ibid.,* p. 79.
9. *The Iroquois Book of Rites,* ed. Horatio Hale (1883), p. 64.
10. Hewitt, *op. cit.,* p. 104.
11. John Esten Cooke, *Virginia, a History of the People* (1886), p. 31.
12. John R. Swanton, "Social Organization of American Tribes," *American Anthropologist* (N.S., VII, 1905), p. 669.
13. George Bird Grinnell, *By Cheyenne Campfires* (1936), p. xiv.
14. Silas Tertius Rand, *Legends of the Micmacs* (1894), Introduction, p. xxxiii.
15. *Handbook of American Indians North of Mexico,* ed. Frederick Webb Hodge (1910), p. 608.
16. Samuel Hopkins, *Historical Memoirs Relating to the Housatunnuk Indians* (1753), p. 34.
17. Lewis H. Morgan, *Ancient Society,* p. 463.
18. Hutchinson, *History of Massachusetts Bay,* I, 462.
19. Paul B. Sears, *Deserts on the March,* p. 40.
20. Thomas Chalkley, *A Journal of the Life, Labours, Travels, etc.* (Feb. 28, 1749), p. 50.
21. Almon Wheeler Lauber, *Indian Slavery in Colonial Times Within the Present Limits of the United States,* p. 30.
22. *Ibid.,* p. 41.
23. *Ibid.,* p. 115.
24. Alice Morse Earle, *Customs and Fashions in Old New England,* p. 84.
25. Verner W. Crane, *The Southern Frontier (1670-1732),* pp. 112, 113.
26. Josselyn, *An Account of Two Voyages to New England* (London, 1764), p. 138.
27. George Catlin, *North American Indians,* p. 274.
28. *Ibid.,* p. 273.
29. Clark Wissler, *The American Indian,* pp. 149, 173.
30. James Adair, *History of the American Indians* (1775), p. 17.
31. Goldenweiser, *op. cit.,* p. 73.
32. Morgan, *Ancient Society,* p. 462.

33. John Heckewelder, *History, Manners, and Customs of the Indian Nations,* p. 330.
34. H. G. Thwaites, *The Colonies,* p. 239.
35. Winsor, *Life of Columbus,* Chap. xii. Quoted from James Oneal, *The Workers in American History,* p. 22.
36. Alice Morse Earle, *op. cit.,* p. 88.
37. John Lawson, *History of North Carolina* (1714), pp. 256-257.
38. *Colonial Records of North Carolina,* V, 143, 581, 1442.
39. Catlin, *op. cit.,* p. 274.
40. Chalkley, *op. cit.,* p. 50.
41. Lawson, *op. cit.,* p. 6.
42. Catlin, *op. cit.,* p. 272.
43. *Loc. cit.*
44. *Ibid.,* p. 288.
45. James Everett Seaver, *A Narrative of the Life of Mary Jemison, the White Woman of the Genesee,* p. 92.
46. *Ibid.,* p. 50.
47. *Ibid.,* p. 70.
48. Edna Kenton, *The Indians of North America* [from the Jesuit Relations and Allied Documents], pp. 11, 12, 32, 38.
49. Hale, *op. cit.,* pp. 96, 97.
50. Seaver, *op. cit.,* p. 47.
51. Elias Boudinot, *The Star in the West,* p. 138.
52. Heckewelder, *op. cit.,* p. 76.
53. Jasper Danckaerts, *Journal, 1679-1680,* pp. 79, 80.
54. J. P. Kinney, *A Continent Lost—A Civilization Won,* p. 3.
55. *Ibid.,* p. 4.
56. *Ibid.,* p. 5.
57. Edward D. Neill, *History of the Virginia Company of London,* pp. 330-332.
58. Densmore, *op. cit.,* p. 84.
59. Quoted from James Ernst, *Roger Williams,* p. 260.
60. Henry Beston, *American Memory* (1937), p. 238.
61. Mari Sandoz, *Old Jules,* p. 132.
62. *The New York Times,* Aug. 9, 1937.
63. *News-Week,* Aug. 28, 1938, p. 13.
64. John M. Oskison, *Tecumseh and His Times,* p. 4.
65. *Ibid.,* p. 5.
66. Richard F. Scholz, "The Redskin's New Prophet," *The Baltimore Evening Sun,* Mar. 22, 1939, p. 21.

## CHAPTER VI

1. *Bradford's History of Plymouth Plantation* (1606-1646), pp. 30-33.
2. *Ibid.,* pp. 30-33.
3. *Ibid.,* pp. 45-46.
4. *Ibid.,* p. 566.
5. *Ibid.,* p. 65.
6. *Ibid.,* p. 116.
7. *Ibid.,* pp. 142-143.
8. *Ibid.,* pp. 110-112.
9. *Ibid.,* pp. 142-143.
10. George Weber, *Outlines of Universal History* (1859), p. 296.
11. Bradford, *op. cit.,* p. 139.
12. *Ibid.,* pp. 146-147.
13. *Ibid.,* p. 147.

14. *Ibid.*, p. 364.
15. *Ibid.*, p. 364.
16. Arthur Calhoun, *Social History of the American Family*, p. 42.
17. *Boston News-Letter*, No. 40, Jan. 15—Jan. 22, 1704.
18. *Boston News-Letter*, No. 69, Aug. 6—Aug. 13, 1705.
19. Oneal, *op. cit.*, p. 46.
20. *Loc. cit.*
21. Henry Beston, *The Book of Gallant Vagabonds* (1925), p. 145.
22. Thomas Morton, *New English Canaan* (1637), p. 278.
23. Fiske, *The Beginnings of New England* (1889), p. 95.
24. Thomas Morton, *op. cit.*, p. 282.

### CHAPTER VII

1. John Callender, *A Historical Discourse on the Civil and Religious Affairs of the Colony of Rhode Island and Providence Plantations in New England* (Boston, 1739), p. 13.
2. Baylies, *History of New Plymouth*, I, 29. Also Benj. Scott Chamberlain, *The Pilgrim Fathers: Neither Puritan nor Persecutors*, p. 36.
3. Hutchinson, *History of Massachusetts*, I, 497, Appendix III.
4. *John Winthrop's Journal*, pp. 124, 125.
5. Quoted from Sandford Fleming, *Children and Puritanism*, p. 27.
6. Cotton Mather, *Early Piety, Exemplified in the Life and Death of Nathaniel Mather*, p. 31.
7. Neal, *op. cit.*, p. 612.
8. Edward Ward, *Trip to New England* (1699), p. 6.
9. *Ibid.*, p. 6.
10. *Ibid.*, p. 7.
11. Winthrop, *op. cit.*, June 14, 1631.
12. *Ibid.*, Sept. 18, 1634.
13. *Ibid.*, July 25, 1638.
14. *Ibid.*, Nov. 11, 1641.
15. *Ibid.*, p. 112.
16. *Ibid.*, pp. 103-104.
17. Quoted from *An Appeal to the Men of New England*, with Mr. Randolph's paper.
18. A letter from Randolph to the Bishop of ————, May 29, 1682.
19. *Journal*, Jan. 1638.
20. Oneal, *op. cit.*, p. 93.
21. Jasper Danckaerts, *Journal*, July 1680, pp. 266-267.
22. Wright, *Literary Culture in Early New England.*
23. Wm. C. Shillaber, Boston, May 1902. Mr. Shillaber's evidence contains a facsimile of the first sheet printed.
24. *Ibid.*
25. Quoted from Samuel Eliot Morrison, *Builders of the Bay Colony*, p. 37.
26. *Ibid.*, quoted from p. 47.
27. *Ibid.*, p. 39.
28. P. A. Bruce, *Social Life of Virginia in the Seventeenth Century* (1907), p. 102.
29. See the author's *Liberation of American Literature*, chap. iii, "The Southern Pattern."
30. See M. E. Tracy, *How Satan Came to Salem* (unpublished mss.), p. 74.
31. Winfield S. Nevins, *Witchcraft in Salem Village* (1916), p. 24.
32. George Lyman Kittredge, *Witchcraft in Old and New England*, p. 362.
33. *Ibid.*, p. 368.

## CHAPTER VIII

1. Address delivered by Reverend Joseph Allen at the centennnial celebration of the town of Northborough, Mass., Aug. 22, 1866.
2. Neal, *op. cit.*, p. 271.
3. Quoted from R. G. Thwaites, *The Colonies*, p. 145.
4. Alexander Johnston, *Connecticut: A Study of a Commonwealth Democracy* (1896), p. 17.
5. John Callender, *An Historical Discourse on the Civil and Religious Affairs of the Colony of Rhode Island and Providence Plantations in New England, America* (Boston, 1739), p. 16.
6. Major Butler, *Fourth Paper* (1652), p. 17.
7. Roger Williams, *Bloody Tenent of Persecution for Cause of Conscience* (1644), p. 2.
8. *Ibid.*, p. 4.
9. *Ibid.*, p. 19.
10. Cotton Mather, *Magnalia Christi Americana,* Book 7, chap. ii, p. 7.
11. Roger Williams, *op. cit.*, p. 130.
12. *Ibid.*, p. 139.
13. *Ibid.*, p. 5.
14. *Ibid.*, p. 15.
15. Joseph S. Clark, *An Historical Discourse, Preached at Plymouth, Mass., at the Twenty-Fifth Anniversary of the Pilgrim Conference of Churches, May 16, 1855.*
16. Oscar Strauss, *Roger Williams,* p. 107.

## CHAPTER IX

1. Quoted from Lewis H. Berens, *The Digger Movement in the Days of the Commonwealth,* p. 74.
2. Mather's *Magnalia,* Book VII, 24.
3. *Ibid.*, p. 24.
4. Quoted from John Barclay, *Select Anecdotes and Instructive Incidents, Taken from Publications of Several Members of the Society of Friends,* p. 151.
5. John Gough, *A History of the People Called Quakers, from Their First Rise to the Present Time,* p. 76.
6. Sewall, *The History of the Rise, Increase and Progress of the Christian People Called Quakers,* p. 355.
7. *The Quaker Catechism—In Answer to That of the Dissenters* (1703), p. 5.
8. Frazer, *Belief in Immortality and the Worship of the Dead,* II, 51, 146, 214, 319.
9. *Ibid.*, p. 363.
10. Karl Kautsky, *Foundations of Christianity,* p. 413.
11. *Op. cit.*, Book VII, 24.
12. Neal, *op. cit.*, p. 322.
13. Cudworth letter quoted from Neal, *loc. cit.*
14. Gooch, *The History of English Democratic Ideas in the Seventeenth Century,* p. 277.
15. Cotton Mather, *op. cit.*, Book VII, chap. iv, 22.
16. *Ibid.*, p. 23.
17. Neal, *op. cit.*, p. 302.
18. *Ibid.*, p. 304.
19. Mather, *op. cit.*, p. 22.
20. *Ibid.*, p. 22.
21. *Ibid.*, p. 22.
22. *Journal,* pp. 105-107.
23. *Op. cit.*, p. 326.
24. Quoted from Braithwaite, *Second Period of Quakerism,* p. 557.

25. Gooch, *op. cit.*, p. 277.

26. *Ibid.*, p. 275.

27. Neal, *op. cit.*, chap. iv, 21.

28. Josselyn, *An Account of Two Voyages to New England* (1674), p. 185.

29. Charles Evans, *Friends in the Seventeenth Century* (1885), p. 588.

30. Quoted from *Narratives of the Indian Wars*, pp. 277-279.

31. *The Quaker Unmasked*, or *Plain Truth*, Humbly Addressed to the Confederation of all the Freemen of Pennsylvania (1764).

32. Thomas Chalkley, *A Journal of the Life, Labours, Travels*, etc. (Feb. 28, 1749, 1706), p. 50.

33. William Penn, *A Brief Account of the Rise and Progress of the People Called Quakers*, p. 30.

34. Pennsylvania German Society, *op. cit.*, p. 16.

35. *Journal of Political Economy*, XXXII (1924), 372.

36. *Loc. cit.*, p. 360.

37. *Loc. cit.*, p. 482.

38. Jacob John Sessler, *Communal Pietism Among Early American Moravians*, p. 8.

39. Sachse, *The German Sectarians in Pennsylvania*, p. 442.

40. Sessler, *op. cit.*, p. 37.

41. *Ibid.*, p. 85.

42. K. S. Pinson, *Pietism and German Nationalism*, p. 44.

43. Pennsylvania German Society, *op. cit.*, p. 109.

44. Robert Barkley, *The Inner Life of the Religious Societies of the Commonwealth*, p. 78.

45. Pennsylvania German Society, *op. cit.*, p. 91.

46. Hannah Adams, *An Alphabetical Compendium of the Various Sects which have appeared in the World from the Beginning of the Christian Era to the Present Day* (1784), p. 113.

47. Penn, *op. cit.*, pp. 18-19.

48. Hannah Adams, *op. cit.*, p. 63.

49. Oliver, *The Puritan Commonwealth*, p. 194.

50. John Henry Blunt, *Dictionary of Sects*, p. 159.

51. Winthrop, *op. cit.*, p. 64.

52. Fiske, *The Beginnings of New England*, p. 177.

53. *Some Notices of Samuel Gorton, during his residence at Plymouth, Portsmouth, and Providence*, ed. Charles Deane, p. 8.

54. Edward Winslow, *Hypocrisie Unmasked. A True Relation of the Proceedings of the Governor and Company of the Massachusetts against Samuel Gorton* (1646), p. 7.

55. *Ibid.*, p. 7.

56. Samuel Gorton, *Simplicities Defense Against Seven Headed Policy*, p. 46.

57. Winslow, *op. cit.*, p. 5.

58. Gorton, *op. cit.*, p. 80.

59. Quoted from Roger Williams's letter to Winthrop, Providence, Aug. 1, 1640.

60. Lewis G. Janes, *Samuel Gorton: A Forgotten Founder of Our Liberties* (1896), p. 34.

61. *Ibid.*, p. 62.

62. *Colonial Records*, May 19, 1652.

63. Gorton, *Commentary on the Lord's Prayer*, p. 101.

64. Rev. George Armistead Leakin, *Maryland Historical Magazine*, I (1906).

65. Rev. Charles Payson Mallery, *Ancient Families of Bohemia Manor*, p. 341.

66. Bartlett B. James, "First Communist Experiment in America," introduction to *Journal of Jasper Danckaerts*, p. xviv.

67. Bartlett B. James, *The Labadist Colony in Maryland*, p. 16.

68. *Maryland Historical Magazine*, *op. cit.*, p. 342.

69. Samuel Bownas, *Account of Life, Travels, and Christian Experiences* (1705), p. 95.

70. Mallery, *op. cit.*, p. 32.
71. Brother Lamech, *Chronicon Ephratense* (1786), p. 12.
72. Phebe Earle Gibbons, *Pennsylvania Dutch and Other Essays* (1882), p. 143.
73. Sidney George Fisher, *The Making of Pennsylvania* (1896), p. 11.
74. Brother Lamech, *op. cit.*, p. 56.
75. Gibbons, *op. cit.*, p. 140.
76. Brother Lamech, *op. cit.*, p. 88.
77. *Ibid.*, p. 107.
78. *Ibid.*, p. 138.
79. Rev. S. G. Zerfass, *Ephrata Cloister Souvenir Book*, p. 16.

## CHAPTER X

1. Dankers (Danckaerts) and Sluyter Journal: *Journal of a Voyage to New York.* (Long Island Historical Society, ed. 1867), p. 218.
2. Hugh Jones, *The Present State of Virginia* (London, 1724), p. 97.
3. *Ibid.*, p. 48.
4. *American History Told by Contemporaries,* I, "Era of Colonization, 1492-1689," p. 222.
5. Articles, Lawes and Orders for the Colony in Virginia—established by Sir Thomas Gates Knight—24 May, 1610, in *Force's Tracts*, p. 10.
6. P. A. Bruce, *op. cit.*, p. 189.
7. *The Virginia Gazette,* No. 11, 1736.
8. Sir Thomas Gates Knight, *op. cit.*, p. 11.
9. Bruce, *op. cit.*, II, 35.
10. *Ibid.*, II, 36.
11. William Waller Henning, *The Statutes at Large: A Collection of all the Laws of Virginia from the First Session of the Legislature in the Year 1619,* I, 551.
12. *Ibid.*, p. 552.
13. *Ibid.*, II, p. 167.
14. Quoted from Alexander Brown, *The First Republic in America*, pp. 250-251.
15. Philip Alexander Bruce, *History of Virginia*, I, 110.
16. Alexander Brown, *English Politics in Early Virginia History*, pp. 37-38.
17. *Ibid.*, p. 74.
18. *William and Mary College Quarterly Historical Magazine*, IX (July 1900), No. 1, 7.
19. Edward D. Neill, *History of the Virginia Company of London*, p. 139.
20. "Proposals for the Reduction of Bacon, 9. 433," *Virginia Magazine of History and Geography*, I (1894).
21. *Strange News from Virginia, Being a Full and True Account of the Life and Death of Nathanael Bacon, Esquire* (London: 1677; printed for Wm. Harris), p. 2.
22. Mrs. An. Cotton, *An Account of Our Late Troubles in Virginia, Written in 1676* (published from the original manuscript in the Richmond, Va., *Enquirer* of Sept. 12, 1804; Washington: Printed by Peter Force, 1835, p. 101).
23. Thomas Mathew, *The Beginning, Progress and Conclusion of Bacon's Rebellion in Virginia in the Years 1675 and 1676* (July 13, 1705; Washington: Printed by Peter Force, 1835, Appendix, p. 26).
24. John Day Burke, *History of Virginia from its First Settlement to the Present Day* (printed by Dickson and Pescud, 1805), II, 159.
25. *Narrative of the Indian and Civil Wars in Virginia, in the Years 1675 and 1676* (published from the original manuscript, in Vol. I, Series 2, of the *Collections of the Massachusetts Historical Society*), p. 9.
26. *Strange News from Virginia, op. cit.*, p. 8.
27. E. Cook, *The Maryland Muse, Containing the History of Colonel Nathaniel Bacon's Rebellion in Virginia, Done in Hudibrastick Verse, from an Old Ms.* (1731).

28. William Ware, *A Memoir of Nathaniel Bacon*, p. 302; from the *Library of American Biography*, ed. Jared Sparks (1844).

29. Joel Shrew, *Tobacco, Its History, Nature, and Effects* (1876), p. 2.

30. Ralph Linton, "Use of Tobacco Among North American Indians," *Field Museum of Natural History Publications* (1924), p. 8.

31. Paul Avery Warner, *Tobaccoland*, p. 25.

32. George Arents, *Tobacco, Its History*, I, Introd., p. 31.

33. *Ibid.*, I, Introd., p. 97.

34. *A King's Denunciation—The Story of Tobacco* (Young and Ottley, Inc., 1934), pp. 11-12.

35. Hugh Jones, *op. cit.*, p. 48.

36. William E. Dodd, *Struggles for Democracy*, pp. 155-156.

37. Edward D. Neill, *Virginia Carolorum* (1886), p. 145.

38. P. A. Bruce, *Institutional History of Virginia in the Seventeenth Century*, II, 576.

39. *Virginia Magazine of History and Biography*, III (January 1896), No. 3, 226.

40. *Ibid.*, Foreword, p. 25.

41. *Ibid.*, II (1894-1895), pp. 408-409.

42. *The New Republic, LXXXXVIII* (April 12, 1939), 262.

## CHAPTER XI

1. Bradley T. Johnson, *The Foundation of Maryland*, Maryland Historical Society (Baltimore: 1883), p. 65.

2. *Maryland Archives*, XLI, 203.

3. E. Milton Altfeld, *The Jew's Struggle for Religious and Civil Liberty in Maryland* (1924), p. 9.

4. Ernest Lloyd Harris, *Church and State in Maryland Colony* (1894), p. 32.

5. Bozman, *The History of Maryland* (1837), p. 195.

6. Mathew Page Andrews, *History of Maryland*, p. 255.

7. Thomas Bray, D.D., *A Memorial Representing the Present State of Religion on the Continent of North America* (London: 1700), appearing in "Religious Conditions and Quakers," Maryland Historical Society, *Fund Publication No. 27*, p. 169.

8. George Petrie, *Church and State in Early Maryland* (1882), p. 35.

9. *Archives of Maryland*, III (July 23, 1658), p. 352.

10. *A Law of Maryland Concerning Religion* (1690). Copied from photostat in New York Public Library.

11. *Father White's Relation of the Colony of Lord Baron of Baltimore* (1642), from Force's *Historical Tracts*, Vol. IV, No. 12.

12. George Alsop, *A Character of the Province of Maryland* (London: 1666), p. 53.

13. Vertress J. Wycoff, *Tobacco Regulation in Colonial Maryland* (1936), p. 1.

14. Thomas W. Griffith, *Sketches of the Early History of Maryland* (Baltimore: 1821), p. 9.

15. Charles M. Andrews, *The Colonial Period of American History*, II, 297.

16. Letter from the Lord Baltimore to the Earle of Anglesey, quoted from *Proceedings of the Council of Maryland* (1676-1681), p. 281.

17. *Archives of Maryland*, Proceedings of the Council, 1636-1667, July 10, 1656, p. 323.

18. *Ibid.*, p. 408.

19. *Maryland Archives*, V, 312.

20. R. G. Thwaites, *The Colonies, 1492-1750*, p. 86.

21. Danckaerts' *Journal*, p. 136.

22. *Maryland Archives*, Letter from the Chancellor of Maryland to Col. Henry Meese, Merchant in London, Concerning the Late Troubles in Maryland, Dec. 29, 1681.

23. Francis Edgar Sparks, *Causes of the Maryland Revolution of 1689* (1896), p. 86.

24. *Col. Henry Darrall's Narrative* (Dec. 31, 1689), appearing in George L. Davis, *The Day-Star of American Freedom* (1855), p. 97.
25. William Haude Brown, *The Lords Baltimore and the Maryland Palatinate*, p. 123.
26. *Ibid.*, p. 124.
27. *Maryland Archives*, Preface to XX, 421.
28. *Ibid.*, p. 421.
29. Sparks, *op. cit.*, p. 100.
30. John Coode, *The Declarations of the Reasons and Motives for the Present Appearing in Arms of Their Majesties Protestant Subjects in the Province of Maryland* (1689), p. 1.
31. Report of Richard Shepherd, Master of the Ship St. George, Appearing in *Proceedings of the Council of Maryland*, Munday 31, October, 1681.
32. Jeffrey R. Brackett, *The Negro in Maryland* (1889), p. 26.
33. *Virginia (and Maryland) Impartially Examined, and Left to Public View, to Be Considered by All Honest and Judicious Men* (London: 1649), p. 59.
34. *Maryland Archives*, I, 107.
35. *Ibid.*, II, October, 1671.
36. *Ibid.*, p. 475.
37. *Ibid.*, p. 441.
38. *Ibid.*, I, 533. Also see M. W. Jernegan, *The American Colonies* (1929), p. 103.
39. *An Act for the Repeale of a Clause in an Act made the 23rd Day of October, 1640, by Leonard Calvert, Esq.*, p. 97.
40. "An Act for All Servants Comeing into the Province with Indentures, Oct. 1654," *Maryland Archives*, p. 352.
41. Danckaerts, *op. cit.*, p. 111.
42. *Ibid.*, p. 112.
43. *Ibid.*, p. 133.
44. *Maryland Archives*, II, 272.
45. Danckaerts, *op. cit.*, pp. 167-168.
46. *Ibid.*, p. 135.
47. *Maryland Archives*, III, 502.
48. Letter to the Archbishop of Canterbury from John Yea, Minister in Maryland, *Proceedings of the Council of Maryland* (May 25, 1676), p. 130.
49. Bray, *op. cit.*, p. 77.
50. James Truslow Adams, *Provincial Society*, p. 137.
51. *Maryland Archives*, IV, 373.
52. *Ibid.*, p. 445.
53. Eben. Cook, *The Sot-Weed Factor* (London: 1708), pp. 6-7.
54. *Ibid.*, p. 54.
55. *The Lords Baltimore and the Maryland Palatinate*, pp. 201-204.
56. James McSherry, *History of Maryland*, p. 88.
57. Cook, *op. cit.*, p. 21.
58. *Ibid.*, p. 26.

## CHAPTER XII

1. Mary Newton Stanard, *The Story of Virginia's First Century*, p. 159.
2. William Eddis, *Letters from America*, Letter VI, Annapolis, Sept. 20, 1770 (London: 1792).
3. *Loc. cit.*
4. John Fiske, *Old Virginia and Her Neighbors*, II, 178.
5. Alfred M. Histon, *Slavery and Servitude in New Jersey* (Camden: 1903), p. 23.
6. Eugene McCormac, *White Servitude in Maryland*, p. 48.
7. Henry Bradshaw Fearon, *Sketches of America* (London: 1818), pp. 149-150.
8. Eddis, *op. cit.*, p. 77.

9. James Curtis Ballagh, "White Servitude in the Colony of Virginia," *Johns Hopkins Studies in Historical and Political Science,* 13th Series, VI-VII (1895), p. 23.

10. *The Virginia Gazette* (1736), No. 17.

11. Quoted from William E. Dodd, *The Old South,* p. 45.

12. Edward D. Neill, *op. cit.,* pp. 160-162.

13. John Harrower, *Diary* (1773), printed in *The American Historical Review,* VI, 74.

14. *Boston News-Letter,* Monday, June 5, to Monday, June 12, 1704.

15. *Ibid.,* Nov. 6 to Nov. 13.

16. *Ibid.,* Apr. 22 to Apr. 29, No. 106.

17. *Ibid.,* Apr. 26 to May 3, No. 211.

18. *Ibid.,* Dec. 29 to Jan. 5, 1709.

19. *Ibid.,* Jun. 26 to Jul. 3, No. 11.

20. *Ibid.,* August 20 to Aug. 27, No. 71.

21. *Ibid.,* Dec. 6 to Dec. 13, No. 243.

22. *New England Courant,* 1721-1726, No. 74, Dec. 24 to Dec. 31.

23. *German Society of Maryland,* pp. 80-81.

24. Karl Frederick Geiser, *Redemptioners and Indentured Servants of the Colony and Commonwealth of Pennsylvania* (New Haven: 1901), p. 23.

25. *Ibid.,* p. 47.

26. *Ibid.,* p. 48.

27. Alfred M. Histon, *Slavery and Servitude in New Jersey* (Camden: 1903; paper read before the Monmouth County Historical Association, Oct. 30, 1902).

28. Eddis, *op. cit.,* p. 50.

29. G. Mittleberger, *Journey to Pennsylvania, 1750,* trans. C. T. Eden (Philadelphia: 1898), p. 23.

30. *Ibid.,* p. 23.

31. Fearon, *op. cit.,* p. 151.

32. *Colonial Records of Pennsylvania,* I, 79.

33. *Ibid.,* p. 79.

34. *Ibid.,* p. 86.

35. Extract from Bernard Roman's *Concise Natural History of East and West Florida* (New York: 1776), pp. 268-273.

36. Gottlieb Mittleberger, *Journey to Pennsylvania in the Year 1750,* p. 20.

37. Frank Reid Diffenderfer, *The German Immigration into Pennsylvania,* Part II, "The Redemptioners" (Lancaster: 1900), p. 149.

38. Samuel Sewall, *The Selling of Joseph* (Boston: 1700), p. 2.

39. *John Saffin, A Brief and Candid Answer to the Late Printed Sheet entitled "The Selling of Joseph"* (1701), p. 3.

40. Charles A. Beard and Mary R. Beard, *The Rise of American Civilization,* I, 105.

41. John R. Spears, *American Slave Trade,* p. 13.

42. Ulrich B. Phillips, *American Negro Slavery,* p. 374.

43. Noah Webster, *Effects of Slavery on Morals and Industry* (1793), p. 18.

44. *Ibid.,* p. 7.

45. Thomas Day, *Fragment of an Original Letter on the Slavery of the Negroes* (1776), p. 24.

46. Henry Bruce, *Life of General Oglethorpe* (1890), p. 132.

47. Dodd, *The Old South,* p. 51.

48. Mary Newton Stanard, *op. cit.,* p. 158.

49. George Fox, *Gospel Family Order, Being a Short Discourse Concerning the Ordering of Families Both of Whites, Blacks, and Indians* (1676), p. 16.

50. Noah Webster, *op. cit.,* p. 37.

51. James Curtis Ballagh, *A History of Slavery in Virginia,* p. 8.

52. *Ibid.,* p. 9.

53. *The African Trade, the Great Pillar and Support of the British Plantation Trade in America* (Signed: A British Merchant, London, Dec. 11, 1744, written to the king).
54. *American History Told by Contemporaries,* I, 300.
55. John Burke, *op. cit.,* I, 211.
56. *The Case of our Fellow Creatures, the Oppressed Africans, Respectfully Recommended to the Serious Consideration of the Legislature of Great Britain by the People Called Quakers* (London: 1783), p. 8.
57. Absalom Jones and Richard Allen (Negroes), *A Narrative of the Proceedings of the Black People During the Late Awful Calamity in Philadelphia, in the Year 1793,* p. 23.
58. Anthony Benezet, *Notes on the Slave Trade* (1780), p. 2.
59. Herbert Apthekar, "American Negro Slave Revolts," *Science and Society,* I, No. 4, 517.
60. Henry Cabot Lodge, *A Short History of the English Colonies in America* (1881), p. 320.
61. C. L. R. James, *History of Negro Revolt,* p. 23.
62. Quoted from George W. Williams, *History of the Negro Race in America,* p. 88.
63. William Sidney Drewry, *The Southampton Insurrection,* p. 85.
64. *Ibid.,* p. 102.
65. C. L. R. James, *op. cit.,* p. 31.
66. *Ibid.,* p. 31.

## CHAPTER XIII

1. John Lawson, *History of North Carolina* (1714; reprinted Richmond, Va., 1937), p. 176.
2. John Fiske, "Maryland and the Far South in the Colonial Period," *Harper's Magazine,* LXVI (1883), 419.
3. James Oglethorpe, *A New and Accurate Account of the Provinces of South Carolina and Georgia* (London: 1733).
4. William Byrd, *A Journey to the Land of Eden and Other Papers,* p. 82.
5. Hugh Talmadge Lefler, *North Carolina History Told by Contemporaries,* p. 45.
6. Byrd, *op. cit.,* p. 81.
7. *Ibid.,* p. 77.
8. *The Fundamental Constitutions of Carolina* (Mar. 1, 1669), drawn up by John Locke, Clause 97.
9. *Ibid.,* Clause 100.
10. *Treatises of Government,* II, Sec. 87.
11. *Letter on Toleration,* p. 130.
12. Lefler, *op. cit.,* p. 22.
13. *Colonial Records of North Carolina,* III, 331-339.
14. *Carolina Described More Fully Than Heretofore,* Being an Impartial Collection made from the Several Relations of that Place in print since its First Planting (Dublin: 1664), p. 18.
15. Robert Horne, "Description of Caroline" (1666), appearing in *Narratives of Early Carolina, 1650-1708,* ed. Alexander S. Salley, Jr., p. 71.
16. Letter of Edward Bland, *ibid.,* p. 5.
17. Account of Samuel Wilson, *ibid.,* p. 167.
18. *Colonial Records of North Carolina,* 1662 to 1712, collected and edited by Wm. L. Saunders, p. xxxiii.
19. *Ibid.,* p. xxxiv.
20. Lefler, *op. cit.,* p. 23.
21. *State Records of North Carolina,* XXIII, 199.
22. Edward McCrady, *The History of South Carolina Under the Proprietary Government, 1670-1719,* p. 143.

23. Harriet Kershaw Leiding, *Charleston—Historic and Romantic,* p. 25.

24. François-Xavier Martin, *History of North Carolina from the Earliest Period* (New Orleans: 1829), p. 167.

25. Hugh Williamson, *History of North Carolina* (1812), p. 130.

26. *North Carolina Records,* I, 1622-1712 (1886). *Papers—The Case Between Thomas Miller, Collector of his Maj. Customs & Capt. Zachariah Gillam, Culpeper, Durant, Craford and others,* etc., p. 286.

27. *Ibid.,* p. 288.

28. *Ibid.,* p. 289.

29. Charles M. Andrews, *Colonial Period of American History,* IV, 198.

30. The Hon. Mr. Justice Riddell, "From Slave to Governor," *The Dalhousie Review,* IX (Halifax, N. C.), pp. 475-480.

31. Hewatt, *History of South Carolina* (1779), I, 102.

32. George Chalmers, *An Introduction to the History of the Revolt of the Colonies* (1782), I, 265.

33. William J. Rivers, *A Sketch of the History of South Carolina* (1856), p. 157.

34. *Ibid.,* p. 159.

35. David Ramsay, *History of South Carolina From Its First Settlement in 1670 to the Year 1808,* II, 202.

36. Edward Bingham Copeland, *Rice* (1924), introduction, p. x.

37. Duncan Clinch Heyward, *Seed From Madagascar* (1937), p. 7.

38. *Observations Concerning Indigo* (London: Mar. 26, 1746), p. 63. Author unknown.

39. John Ledyard, *Methods for Improving the Manufacture of Indigo* (Mar. 1, 1776), p. 49.

40. *Historical Collections of South Carolina,* compiled by B. R. Carroll (1836), II, 203.

41. Ramsay, *op. cit.,* II, 207.

42. Broadhus Mitchell, *Rise of Cotton Mills in the South* (1921), p. 13.

43. James A. B. Scherer, *Cotton as a World Power* (1916), p. 124.

44. H. Salpeter, "Priber's Colony," *The Freeman,* May 1923.

45. "Extract of a Letter from Frederica, Georgia," *South Carolina Historical and Genealogical Magazine,* X, 58.

46. *Ibid.,* p. 58.

47. "Historical Relation of Facts Delivered by Ludovick Grant, Indian Trader, to the Governor of South Carolina," *Charleston Probate Court Book, 1754-1758,* p. 301, appearing in *South Carolina Historical and Genealogical Magazine,* X, 58.

48. *Annual Register* (London: 1760), p. 22.

49. *U. S. Bureau of American Ethnology* (1897-1898), Part I, 36.

50. Grant, *op. cit.,* p. 60.

51. V. W. Crane, "A Lost Utopia of the First American Frontier," *Sewanee Review,* 1919, p. 48.

52. James Adair, *American Indians,* p. 240. Also Ludovick Grant, *op. cit.,* p. 60.

53. *Journal of Antoine Bonnefoy, 1741-1743,* appearing in *Travels in the American Colonies,* ed. N. D. Mereness, introduction, p. 239.

54. *Annual Register,* 1760, p. 23.

## CHAPTER XIV

1. F. Morton Coulter, *A Short History of Georgia* (1933), p. 74.

2. Thomas Stephens, *A Brief Account of the Causes that have Retarded the Progress of the Colony of Georgia* (London: 1743), p. 3.

3. James Oglethorpe, *A New and Accurate Account of the Provinces of South Carolina and Georgia* (London: 1733), p. 34.

4. *Ibid.,* pp. 21, 33.

5. Rev. William Bacon Stevens, M. D., *A History of Georgia,* p. 58.

6. *A New Voyage to Georgia by a Young Gentleman* (London: 1737), pp. 6, 37.

7. Letter of Thos. Lombe, Jan. 31, 1732, to the Trustees for Establishing the Colony of Georgia, quoted from *Reasons for Establishing the Colony of Georgia with Regard to the Trade of Great Britain* (London: 1733), p. 6.

8. *Ibid.*, p. 10.

9. Stevens, *op. cit.*, p. 69.

10. Charles G. Jones, *The English Colonization of Georgia, 1733-1752*, appearing in Justin Winsor's *Narrative and Critical History of America*, V, chap. vi.

11. Quoted from Walter G. Cooper, *The Story of Georgia*, I, 306.

12. Pat. Tailfer, *A True and Historical Narrative of the Colony of Georgia in America* (Charlestown: 1741), p. 114.

13. *A State of the Province of Georgia, attested upon oath in the Court of Savannah* (Nov. 10, 1740), included in Peter Force's *Tracts Relating to the Colonies in North America* (Washington: 1836), I, 11.

14. Benjamin Martyn, *An Imperial Enquiry into the State and Utility of the Province of Georgia* (London: 1741), p. 9.

15. Whitefield's letter, quoted from Williams, *History of the Negro Race in America*, p. 322.

16. Ralph Betts Flanders, *Plantation Slavery in Georgia* (1933), p. 29.

17. Pat. Tailfer, *op. cit.*, p. 53.

18. *Ibid.*, p. 59.

19. *Journal of Rev. Mr. John Wesley, from His Embarking for Georgia to his Return to London* (1739), p. 12.

20. *A New Voyage to Georgia by a Young Gentleman* (London: 1735), p. 55.

21. *Ibid.*, p. 15.

22. Amos A. Ettinger, *J. E. Oglethorpe*, p. 159.

23. *John Wesley's Diary of His Visit to America*, pub. by *The New Orleans Picayune*, p. 7.

24. Letter of Benjamin Martyn to J. E. Oglethorpe, Oct. 18, 1733.

25. Stevens, *op. cit.*, p. 101.

26. *Ibid.*, p. 102.

## CHAPTER XV

1. *Narratives of New Netherland, 1609-1664*, pub. in *Original Narratives of Early American History*, ed. J. F. Jameson, p. 6.

2. Robert Juet's *Third Voyage of Henry Hudson* (1610), p. 26.

3. Llewelyn Powys, *Henry Hudson*, p. 188.

4. Miriam Beard, *A History of the Business Man* (1938), p. 285.

5. *Ibid.*, p. 285.

6. T. J. Wertenbaker, "The Middle Colonies," *The Founding of American Civilization*, p. 31.

7. M. Beard, *op. cit.*, p. 286.

8. *Landmarks of New York* (the City History Club: 1923), p. 10.

9. Nellis Crouse, "The French in New York," *History of the State of New York*, II, 145.

10. Morgan H. Seacord and William S. Hadaway, *Historical Landmarks of New Rochelle*, p. 6.

11. *Records of the Town of New Rochelle, 1669-1828*, trans. Jeanne A. Forbes, p. xiii.

12. Lucian J. Fosdick, *The French Blood in America* (1906), p. 235.

13. *Colonial History of the State of New York* (Holland Documents), I, 123.

14. *New Netherland Narratives, op. cit.*, p. 393.

15. Douglas Campbell, *Historical Fallacies Regarding Colonial New York* (1879), p. 19.

16. Quotation appearing in Curtis P. Nettels, *The Roots of American Civilization* (1938), p. 201.

17. Robert Greenhalgh Albion, *The Rise of New York Port* (1939), p. 3.

18. *Documentary History of the State of New York,* III, 37.
19. John R. Brodhead, *History of New York State,* II, 564.
20. *A Modest and Impartial Narrative of Several Grievances* (New York: 1690), p. 2.
21. *Loyalty Vindicated* (Boston: 1698), p. 13.
22. *Collections of the New York Historical Society,* compiled by George Bancroft, John Romeyn Brodhead, and George Henry Moore (1868), p. 328.
23. Andrews, *The Colonial Period of American History,* III, 134-137.
24. *Collections of the New York Historical Society, op. cit.,* p. 5.
25. *Ibid.,* p. 6.
26. *Ibid.,* p. 11.
27. *Documentary History of the State of New York,* II, 19.
28. *Ibid.,* III, 25.
29. *Collections of the New York Historical Society, op. cit.,* p. 306.
30. *Ibid.,* p. 318.
31. *Ibid.,* p. 309.
32. *Ibid.,* p. 406.
33. *Journal of Proceedings, New York Courts* (1747), p. 1.
34. *New York State Documents,* VII, 1-50.
35. *Journal of the Proceedings Against the Conspirators at New York, 1741 and 1742,* p. 8.
36. *Ibid.,* p. 193.
37. *New York Court Records, 1747* (preface in *Journal of Proceedings*).
38. Charles F. Heartman, *John Peter Zenger* (1934), p. 13.
39. *Supreme Court of Judicature Records: The Trial of John Peter Zenger of New York, Printer* (1752), p. 5.
40. *Ibid.,* p. 10.
41. *The New York Weekly Journal,* No. 3 (Nov. 19, 1733).
42. *Ibid.,* No. 6 (Dec. 10, 1733).
43. *Ibid.,* No. 9 (Dec. 31, 1733).

## CHAPTER XVI

1. *Records of the Catholic Historical Society of Philadelphia,* I, 81.
2. Wyland F. Dunaway, *History of Pennsylvania* (1935), p. 57.
3. Benjamin Franklin, *Historical Review of the Constitution and Government of Pennsylvania* (London: 1759), reprinted in *Works of Benjamin Franklin,* ed. Jared Sparks (1856), III, 123.
4. Correspondence of Penn and Logan, Letter of Oct. 1, 1702 (Lippincott; 1870 ed.), p. 147.
5. *Ibid.,* Letter of Dec. 20, 1702 (p. 148), and May 5, 1703 (p. 202).
6. I, 120.
7. Albert S. Bolles, *Pennsylvania—Province and State, 1609-1790* (1899), pp. 166-168.
8. Sharpless, *The Quaker Experiment in Government,* p. 124.
9. Sharpless, *Quakerism and Politics,* p. 27.
10. *Ibid.,* Letter of July 29, 1703.
11. *Op. cit.,* p. 72.
12. *History of Proprietary Government in Pennsylvania,* p. 285.
13. *Ibid.,* pp. 296-297.
14. "The Courts of Pennsylvania in the Seventeenth Century," *Pennsylvania Magazine of History and Biography,* V (1881), 180, 189.
15. *Ibid.,* p. 189.
16. *The Quakers in the American Colonies,* p. 484.
17. H. Frank Eshelman, "The Struggle and Rise of Popular Power in Pennsylvania's

First Two Decades, 1682-1701," *Pennsylvania Magazine of History and Biography*, XXXIV, 138.

18. *Ibid.*, p. 141.
19. Lawrence Lewis, Jr., "The Courts of Pennsylvania in the Seventeenth Century," *Pennsylvania Magazine of History and Biography*, V (1881), 167.
20. Quoted in Eshelman, *op. cit.*, p. 157.
21. Letter from David Lloyd to George Whitehead, William Meade, and Thomas Lowrie, Aug. 3, 1704.
22. Penn-Logan correspondence, *op. cit.*, p. 339.
23. Letter of Penn to Logan, Nov. 16, 1704.
24. Quoted from Isaac Sharpless, *Quakerism and Politics* (1905), p. 57.
25. *Ibid.*, p. 127.
26. Arthur Pound, *The Penns of Pennsylvania and England*, p. 239.
27. Sharpless, *Political Leaders of Pennsylvania* (1919), p. 108.
28. Edward Raymond Turner, *Slavery in Pennsylvania* (1911), p. 1.
29. George Fox, *Journal*, p. 448.
30. Mode, Peter G., *Frontier Spirit in American Christianity*, p. 84.
31. Thomas Willing Balch, *The Swedish Beginning of Pennsylvania* (1914), p. 17, reprinted from *Proceedings of the American Antiquarian Society*.
32. Calhoun, *op. cit.*, p. 199.
33. *National Society of Colonial Dames*, I, 7.
34. From introduction by Charles M. Andrews to Beverley W. Bond's *The Quit-Rent System in American Colonies*, p. 18.
35. Bond, *op. cit.*, p. 45.
36. Dunaway, *op. cit.*, p. 241.
37. James Pemberton, Letter to H. Brown, Oct. 15, 1755, quoted in Sharpless, *The Quaker Experiment in Government*, p. 114.
38. Jared Sparks, *Life of Benjamin Franklin* (1856), I, 236.
39. Carl Van Doren, *Benjamin Franklin* (1938), p. 284.
40. Bernard Fay, *Life of Franklin* (1929), p. 307.

## CHAPTER XVII

1. *Pennsylvania Magazine*, LIV, 245.
2. *Narratives of Early Pennsylvania, New Jersey and Delaware, 1630-1707*, pp. 57-64.
3. *Readings in Delaware History* (1934), p. 8.
4. *Ibid.*, p. 19.
5. Nils Herlitz, *Sweden*, p. 12.
6. Gabriel Thomas's Account, 1698, in *Readings in Delaware History*, pp. 20-21.
7. Calhoun, *op. cit.*, p. 192.
8. *Swedish Settlements on the Delaware, 1636-1664*, ed. Amandus Johnson (1911), I, 358.
9. Hazard's *Annals*, p. 448.
10. *Narratives of Early Pennsylvania, New Jersey and Delaware, op. cit.*, pp. 102-104.
11. *Swedish Settlements on the Delaware, op. cit.*, p. 196.
12. *Narratives of Early Pennsylvania, New Jersey and Delaware, op. cit.*, p. 106.
13. Hazard, *op. cit.*, pp. 375-377.
14. *Ibid.*, p. 204.
15. J. Thomas Scharf, *History of Delaware* (1888), I, 124.
16. Minutes of the Provincial Council, *Pennsylvania Colonial Records*, II, 405.
17. Scharf, *op. cit.*, p. 180.
18. William T. Read, *Life and Correspondence of George Read* (1870), p. 2.
19. Article by Hon. Richard S. Rodney, Associate Judge of the Supreme Court of Delaware, in *Pennsylvania Magazine*, LIV, 209.
20. Scharf, *op. cit.*, p. 186b.

21. Henry C. Conrad, *History of the State of Delaware* (1908), p. 116.
22. Scharf, *op. cit.*, II, 1056-1058.
23. James Tilton, *Biographical History of Dionysius Tyrant of Delaware* (1788), p. 9.

## CHAPTER XVIII

1. *A Pocket Commentary of the First Settling of New Jersey by Europeans* (printed by Samuel Parker: 1759), p. 14.
2. Samuel Smith, *History of the Colony of Nova Caesaria or New Jersey* (1765), p. 34.
3. Austin Scott, "The Influence of the Proprietors in Founding the State of New Jersey," *Johns Hopkins University Studies*, 3rd Series, VIII (1885), 22.
4. Francis Bazley Lee, *New Jersey as a Colony and as a State*, p. 187.
5. Thomas J. Wertenbaker, *The Founding of American Civilization* (1938), pp. 168-172.
6. Francis Bazley Lee, *op. cit.*, I, 188.
7. William Moraley, *The Infortunate: The Voyage and Adventures of William Moraley, Written by Himself* (1743; 1884 ed.), p. 3.
8. Letter of Charles Gordon to Andrew Irving, in Edinburgh, March 5, 1685, appearing in *The Model of the Government of the Province of East New Jersey in America*, p. 230.
9. Herbert L. Osgood, *The American Colonies* (1924), I, 382.
10. Sydney G. Fisher, *The Quaker Colonies* (1929), p. 170.
11. Beverley W. Bond, *The Quit-Rent System in American Colonies* (1919), p. 32.
12. *A Brief Account of the Province of East New Jersey in America* (1683), p. 24.
13. Samuel Smith, *op. cit.*, p. 125.
14. Thomas Shourds, *History and Genealogy of Fenwick's Colony*, p. 120.
15. Rufus M. Jones, *The Quakers in the American Colonies* (1911), p. 384.
16. *Ibid.*, p. 384.
17. *Archives of New Jersey*, II, 65.
18. Andrews, *op. cit.*, III, 170.
19. Isaac S. Mulford, *A Civil and Political History of New Jersey* (1851), p. 178.
20. Fisher, *op. cit.*, p. 172.
21. *Calendar State Papers*, XX, 344.
22. William A. Whitehead, *East Jersey Under the Proprietary Government* (New Jersey Historical Society: 1846), p. 140.
23. Tanner, *Province of New Jersey, 1664-1738*, p. 94.
24. William A. Whitehead, *op. cit.* (1846), I, 147.
25. *Ibid.*, p. 145.
26. *New Jersey Archives*, II, 329. Letter written from East Jersie, July 1700.
27. Tanner, *op. cit.*, pp. 95-96.
28. *Ibid.*, p. 603.
29. Winsor, *Narrative and Critical History of America*, V, 195.
30. William A. Whitehead, *Early History of Perth Amboy*, p. 214.
31. *New Jersey Archives*, II, 502.
32. *Ibid.*, III, 234.
33. *Ibid.*, Series 1, III, 224.
34. *Ibid.*, Series I, p. 234.
35. *Calendar of State Papers, Colonial, XX* (1702), No. 928, p. 571.
36. *Ibid.*, p. 572.
37. *Ibid.*, p. 97.
38. *New Jersey Archives*, Series 1, p. 234.
39. Mulford, *op. cit.*, p. 288.
40. Tanner, *op. cit.*, p. 323.
41. *Ibid.*, p. 354.
42. Osgood, *op cit.*, IV, 5.
43. *Ibid.*, p. 29.

44. *Ibid.*, p. 77.
45. *Ibid.*, p. 28.
46. *New Jersey Archives* (Parker), VI, 294.
47. Osgood, *op. cit.*, IV, 30.
48. *New Jersey Archives, op. cit.*, p. 331.
49. George Bancroft, *History of the American Revolution* (1852), I, 160.
50. Quotation appearing in Edward C. Kirkland, *A History of American Economic Life* (1932), p. 27.
51. Osgood, *op. cit.*, IV, 35.

## CHAPTER XIX

1. Quoted in Dixon Wecter, *Saga of American Society* (1937), p. 78.
2. *Ibid.*, p. 79.
3. J. W. M. Brezeale, *Life As It Is* (1842), p. 15.
4. *John Bradford's Historical Notes of Kentucky*, compiled by G. W. Stipp (1827), p. 2.
5. G. Imlay, *A Description of the Western Territory of North America* (1793), p. 34.
6. Observations upon the Colony of Kentucky, Lord Dorchester's Letter to Lord Sydney (collection of Kentucky manuscripts, No. 126, Aug. 27, 1789).
7. James Truslow Adams, *Provincial Society* (1927), p. 183.
8. Frederick J. Turner, *The Frontier in American History* (1920), p. 23.
9. Thomas D. Clark, *The Rampaging Frontier*, p. 31.
10. Theodore Roosevelt, *The Winning of the West*, p. 95.
11. Robert Cotterill, *History of Pioneer Kentucky*, pp. 248, 249.
12. *Ibid.*, p. 247.
13. Constance Rourke, *American Humor*, p. 64.
14. Walter Blair and Franklin J. Meine, *Mike Fink*, p. 31.
15. Frederic J. Paxson, *History of the American Frontier* (1924), p. 6.
16. Quotation appearing in Osgood, *op. cit.*, p. 477.
17. *Ibid.*, p. 478.
18. Roosevelt, *op. cit.*, p. 96.
19. *West Virginia Geological Survey*, III (1937), 5.
20. John Christopher Schwab, *The Confederate States of America* (1901), p. 267.
21. F. J. Turner, *Proceedings of the American Historical Review*, p. 262.
22. Ralph Henry Gabriel, *Lure of the Frontier* (1929), pp. 37-38.
23. John S. Bassett, "The Regulators of North Carolina," *Annual Report, American Historical Association* (1894), p. 163.
24. Quoted in Bassett, *op. cit.*, p. 165.
25. Max Farrand, *The Development of the United States*, p. 45.
26. Quoted from a pamphlet of the time, original quotation appearing in Bassett, *op. cit.*, p. 160.
27. Bassett, *op. cit.*, p. 209.
28. Albert T. Volwiler, *George Croghan and the Westward Movement, 1741-1782* (1926), pp. 293-297.
29. A. M. Sakolski, *The Great American Land Bubble* (1932), p. 12.
30. Thomas Perkins Abernethy, *From Frontier to Plantation in Tennessee* (1932), p. 54.
31. Cf. the author's *Passing of the Gods*, pp. 205-220.
32. William Warren Sweet, *Religion on the American Frontier* (the Baptists) (New York: 1931), p. 18.
33. *Ibid.*, p. 17.
34. Timothy Flint, *Recollections of the Last Ten Years in the Valley of the Mississippi*, p. 76.
35. William Warren Sweet, *op. cit.*, pp. 15, 16.
36. R. L. Rusk, *The Literature of the Middle-Western Frontier*, p. 18.

37. Cotterill, *op. cit.*, p. 241.
38. *The Colonial Society of Massachusetts*, p. 177.
39. Thomas Cuming Hall, *op. cit.*, p. 170.
40. *Western Monthly Magazine*, Dec. 1934, p. 655.
41. Frederick L. Paxson, *History of the American Frontier*, p. 180.
42. Dorothy Anne Dondore, *The Prairie—and the Making of Middle America*, p. 176.
43. R. L. Rusk, *op. cit.*, p. 46.
44. Timothy Flint, *op. cit.*, p. 113.
45. W. H. Venable, *Beginnings of Literary Culture in the Ohio Valley* (Cincinnati: 1891), p. 225.
46. Frederick L. Paxson, *op. cit.*, p. 342.
47. Peter G. Mode, *Frontier Spirit in American Christianity*, p. 95.
48. Frederick L. Paxson, *op. cit.*, p. 346.
49. Mode, *op. cit.*, pp. 81-44.
50. Paxson, *op. cit.*, p. 100.
51. James G. Leyburn, *Frontier Folkways* (1935), p. 187.
52. Ralph Henry Gabriel, *The Lure of the Frontier* (1929), p. 27.

# INDEX

B

D

## E

J

N



O

Q



R

## T



## U



## V



## W

## Y



## Z